# MANAGEMENT ACCOUNTING for COSTING and CONTROL 2nd edition

# MANAGEMENT ACCOUNTING for COSTING and CONTROL 2nd edition

V. A. Fatseas

J. E. Bisman

J. F. Williams

Boston  Burr Ridge, IL  Dubuque, IA  Madison, WI  New York
San Francisco  St. Louis  Bangkok  Bogotá  Caracas  Kuala Lumpur
Lisbon  London  Madrid  Mexico City  Milan  Montreal  New Delhi
Santiago  Seoul  Singapore  Sydney  Taipei  Toronto

## McGraw-Hill Australia
A Division of The McGraw·Hill Companies

Copyright © 2004 McGraw-Hill Australia Pty Limited
Additional owners of copyright are named in on-page credits.

Apart from any fair dealing for the purposes of study, research, criticism or review, as permitted under the *Copyright Act*, no part may be reproduced by any process without written permission. Enquiries should be made to the publisher, marked for the attention of the Director of Editorial, at the address below.

Every effort has been made to trace and acknowledge copyright material. Should any infringement have occurred accidentally the authors and publishers tender their apologies.

**Copying for education purposes**
The *Australian Copyright Act 1968* (the Act) allows a maximum of one chapter or 10% of this book, whichever is greater, to be copied by any educational institution for its educational purposes provided that the educational institution (or body that administers it) has given a remuneration to Copyright Agency Limited (CAL) under the Act.

For details of the CAL licence for educational institutions contact: Copyright Agency Limited, Level 19, 157 Liverpool Street, Sydney, NSW 2000. Telephone: (02) 9394 7600. Facsimile: (02) 9394 7601. E-mail: info@copyright.com.au.

**Copying for other purposes**
Except as permitted under the Act (for example a fair dealing for the purposes of study, research, criticism or review) no part of this book may be reproduced, stored in a retrieval system, or transmitted in any form or by any means without prior written permission. All enquiries should be made to the publisher at the address below.

---

**National Library of Australia Cataloguing-in-Publication Data**

Fatseas, V. A. (Victor Andrew).
    Management accounting for costing and control.

    2nd ed.
    Includes index.
    Tertiary students.
    ISBN 0 07 471433 3.

    1. Managerial accounting - Textbooks. 2. Cost accounting -
    Textbooks. I. Bisman, Jayne. II. Williams, J. F., 1945- .
    III. Title.

658.1511

---

Published in Australia by
**McGraw-Hill Australia Pty Limited**
**Level 2, 82 Waterloo Road, North Ryde NSW 2113 Australia**
Director of Editorial: Michael Tully
Developmental Editor: Madeleine Stedman
Publishing Services Manager: Jo Munnelly
Senior Marketing Manager: Susan Talty
Senior Editor / Project Coordinator: Lee Samaniego
Permissions Editor: Colette Hoeben
Freelance Editor: Catherine Page
Cover Designer: Peter Guo
Printed by Ligare Pty Ltd

# CONTENTS

Preface   x

## PART 1: PRODUCT COSTING SYSTEMS   1

**1 Management Accounting Functions**   2
   Financial Accounting versus Management Accounting   2
   Management Accounting Functions   2
     Product Costing Systems   3
     Control Systems   4
   Summary   4
   References   4
   Appendix: Introduction to the Use of Spreadsheets   5
     Financial Modelling   5
       Financial Modelling Packages   5
       Illustrative Example   6
       Demonstration Exercise for Reader   10

**2 Product Costing: Terms and Cost Flows**   15
   Cost and Cost Driver   15
   Direct and Indirect Costs   15
   Variable and Fixed Costs   15
   Unit Costs   16
   Purposes of Product Costing   17
   Elements of Product Cost   17
   Cost Flows   18
     Retailing   18
     Manufacturing   18
   Manufacturing Statement   20
   Summary   23
   Appendix: Using a Spreadsheet for Manufacturing Statements   24
   Questions and Problems   27

**3 Product Costing: Materials, Labour and Overhead**   32
   Materials   33
     Acquisition of Materials   33
     Storage of Materials   34
     Issue of Materials   34
     Stock Shortages   35
     Pricing Issues   35
     Modern Variations   35
   Labour   36
     Payment of Labour   37
     Distribution of Labour Costs   37
     Overtime   38
     Labour Oncosts   38
   Overhead   39
     Control Procedures   40
     Allocating Overhead to Products or Services   40
       Actual Overhead Allocation Rates   41
       Predetermined Overhead Allocation Rates   41
       Capacity Concepts   43
     Cost Pools, Cost Drivers and Overhead Allocation Rates   44
       A Simple Case: One Allocation Rate   44

|  |  |
|---|---|
| Separate Allocation Rates for Each Department | 45 |
| Two Stage Allocation | 46 |
| Direct Method | 47 |
| Step Method | 48 |
| Reciprocal Services Method | 49 |
| Activity Based Costing | 50 |
| Cost Drivers | 50 |
| Types of Activities | 51 |
| ABC Illustrated | 52 |
| Activity Based Management | 54 |
| Summary | 54 |
| References | 55 |
| Appendix A: Accounting for GST | 56 |
| Appendix B: Using a Spreadsheet for Overhead Allocation | 57 |
| Appendix C: Using Matrix Algebra for Reciprocal Overhead Allocation | 59 |
| Questions and Problems | 61 |

**4  Product Costing Systems: Job Costing and Process Costing** — 78

|  |  |
|---|---|
| Job Costing | 79 |
| Raw Materials Stock Ledger Cards | 81 |
| Job Cost Sheets | 82 |
| General Ledger | 85 |
| Job Cost Summary Sheet | 87 |
| Comparison of Job Costs with Estimates | 87 |
| Processing Costing | 88 |
| Equivalent Units | 88 |
| No Opening Work in Process | 90 |
| Opening Work in Process | 91 |
| Weighted Average Cost Method | 91 |
| FIFO Method | 92 |
| Two Processing Departments | 93 |
| Weighted Average Method | 94 |
| Equivalent Unit Calculations - Are they Necessary? | 95 |
| Summary | 96 |
| Reference | 96 |
| Appendix: Using a Spreadsheet for Process Costing Calculations | 97 |
| Questions and Problems | 99 |
| Job Costing Problems | 99 |
| Process Costing Problems | 113 |

**5  Product Costing Systems: Operation Costing and Joint Costs** — 118

|  |  |
|---|---|
| Operation Costing | 118 |
| Joint Costs | 119 |
| Physical Measures Method | 121 |
| Relative Sales Value Method | 121 |
| Costs Incurred after the Split-off Point | 122 |
| Which Method? | 123 |
| Joint Costs and Decision Making | 123 |
| Accounting for By-Products | 123 |
| By-Products with Negative NRV | 124 |
| Summary | 124 |
| Appendix: Using a Spreadsheet for Joint Cost Allocations | 126 |
| Questions and Problems | 127 |

**6  Product Costing Systems: Standard Costs** — 135

|  |  |
|---|---|
| Setting Standards | 136 |

|   |   |
|---|---|
| Accounting for Materials | 137 |
| Purchase | 137 |
| Issue | 138 |
| Accounting for Labour | 139 |
| Accounting for Overhead | 141 |
| Accounting for Finished Goods and Cost of Goods Sold | 141 |
| Ledger Accounts | 142 |
| Alternative Standard Cost Systems | 143 |
| Summary | 144 |
| Appendix: Using a Spreadsheet to Calculate Standard Cost Variances | 145 |
| Questions and Problems | 147 |

**7 Alternative Product Costing Systems: Variable Costing and JIT Costing** — 160

|   |   |
|---|---|
| Why Variable Costing? | 160 |
| Differences Between Variable and Absorption Costing | 160 |
| Reconciliation of Profit | 163 |
| Variable Costing and Management Accounting | 164 |
| External Reporting | 164 |
| Profit Measurement | 164 |
| Asset valuation | 164 |
| Use of Variable Costing | 164 |
| Just in Time Production | 165 |
| JIT Costing | 166 |
| External Reporting | 168 |
| Summary | 169 |
| References | 170 |
| Questions and Problems | 171 |

**PART 2: ACCOUNTING CONTROL SYSTEMS** — 179

**8 Budgeting and Feedforward Control** — 180

|   |   |
|---|---|
| The Concept of Control | 180 |
| Budgeting and Financial Control | 181 |
| Budgeting as a Technical Process | 181 |
| Steps in Budget Preparation | 183 |
| Computer-based Models and 'What If' Analysis | 190 |
| Budgeting as a Choice Process | 192 |
| Perspectives on Choice | 192 |
| References | 193 |
| Questions and Problems | 194 |

**9 Feedback Control: Flexible Budgets and Standard Cost Variances** — 214

|   |   |
|---|---|
| The Control Process | 214 |
| Personal Control and Motivation | 214 |
| Content Theories of Motivation | 215 |
| Process Theories of Motivation | 215 |
| Expectancy Theory | 215 |
| Goal Setting Theory | 216 |
| Relevance of Theories of Motivation | 216 |
| Budgetary Participation | 216 |
| Social Control | 217 |
| Administrative Controls | 217 |
| Feedback Control | 218 |
| Steps in Preparing a Flexible Budget | 219 |
| Flexible Budget Formula | 220 |

|   |   |   |
|---|---|---|
| | Flexible Budgets and Standard Cost Variances | 220 |
| |    Material Variances | 221 |
| |    Labour Variances | 222 |
| |    Variable Overhead Variances | 223 |
| |    Fixed Overhead Variances | 224 |
| |    Accounting Entries for Overhead Variances | 224 |
| | Variance Investigation | 225 |
| | Summary | 225 |
| | References | 227 |
| | Appendix: Using a Spreadsheet to Calculate Standard Cost Variances | 228 |
| | Questions and Problems | 230 |
| **10** | **Responsibility Accounting and Accounting Controls** | **244** |
| | Organisation Structure | 244 |
| | Responsibility Accounting | 244 |
| |    Responsibility Centres | 245 |
| |    Controllable Performance | 245 |
| |    Assembly Foreman's Report | 246 |
| |    Production Manager | 247 |
| | Decentralised Organisations | 249 |
| |    Functional Structure | 249 |
| |    Divisional Structure | 250 |
| |    Matrix Structure | 250 |
| |    Benefits of Decentralisation | 250 |
| |    Disadvantages of Decentralisation | 251 |
| |    Profit Centres | 251 |
| |    Investment Centres | 251 |
| |    Return on Investment | 252 |
| |    Residual Income | 255 |
| |    Economic Value Added (EVA®) | 256 |
| | Criticisms of Responsibility Accounting | 257 |
| | Summary | 258 |
| | References | 259 |
| | Questions and Problems | 260 |
| **11** | **Performance Measurement: Multiple Measures** | **277** |
| | Important Aspects of Performance Measurement | 277 |
| |    Characteristics of Performance Measures | 277 |
| |       Completeness | 277 |
| |       Objectivity | 278 |
| |       Controllability | 278 |
| |    Source of Discrimination | 278 |
| |    Communication | 278 |
| |    Dysfunctional Behaviour | 278 |
| |       Rigid Bureaucratic Behaviour | 278 |
| |       Strategic Behaviour | 279 |
| |       Invalid Data Reporting | 279 |
| |       Resistance | 279 |
| |    Use of Accounting Controls in Performance Evaluation | 279 |
| |    Role of Standard Costs | 280 |
| | Contemporary Management Practices | 281 |
| |    Business Process Re-engineering | 281 |
| |    Total Quality Management | 282 |
| |    Continuous Improvement | 285 |
| |    Benchmarking | 285 |
| |    Strategic Performance Measurement | 286 |
| |       Quality | 286 |

|  |  |
|---|---|
| Cost of Quality | 287 |
| Time | 288 |
| Productivity | 288 |
| Flexibility | 289 |
| Innovation | 289 |
| Multiple Performance Measures | 290 |
| The Balanced Scorecard | 291 |
| Summary | 291 |
| References | 292 |
| Questions and Problems | 293 |

**Appendix: Key Answers to Problems** — 298

**Index** — 307

# PREFACE

One of the perennial problems in trying to design a subject in management accounting is to decide on the order in which topics will be taught. Although this book covers most of the usual topics taught in a first subject in management accounting - product costing systems, budgeting and control systems - it differs from most other books by attempting to cover material, labour and overhead control and cost flows before covering any specific type of product costing system. From years of teaching experience in this field we know that this approach works, and so we have written this book to support this approach.

Another initiative in this text is to integrate the use of computer spreadsheets into the teaching and learning context. In Chapter 1 there is an introduction to spreadsheets which assumes practically no prior knowledge, except to be able to boot up the computer and load up the appropriate spreadsheet package. In Chapter 2 students are introduced to the use of a spreadsheet to develop a manufacturing statement. Chapter 3 introduces the use of a spreadsheet model to perform overhead allocations from service departments to production departments. In Chapter 4 process costing is performed using a spreadsheet model. Standard cost variance analysis is subject to the use of spreadsheets in Chapters 6 and 9. Budgeting employs the use of spreadsheets in Chapter 8. Most of these applications involve the student in developing a model for which there is some guidance in the Appendix to the relevant chapters. These activities represent real integration of accounting and computer usage.

Wherever possible the student is introduced to the relevant research findings in the management accounting literature to support the discussion.

Many of the ideas in this book have been gathered from other management accounting academics with whom we (collectively) have worked at a number of universities. Many of the questions and problems in this book have been collected over many years and are the product of efforts of many colleagues who have designed them, predominantly as examination questions. Despite the influence and possibly unknown contributions of our colleagues, as in all works of this kind, we take full responsibility for the final product and any errors or omissions therein.

In the appendix appear the key answers to problems so as to encourage students to persist with a problem until the correct answers are obtained.


Vic Fatseas
Jayne Bisman
John Williams

# PART 1

# PRODUCT COSTING SYSTEMS

# Chapter 1

# Management Accounting Functions

## FINANCIAL ACCOUNTING versus MANAGEMENT ACCOUNTING

The term **financial accounting** is usually applied to those activities whose primary aim is the production of regular financial reports on profit earned by, and financial position of, an accounting entity in successive 'accounting periods'. Such reports are based on an historical record of financial transactions. The main users of reports of this kind are parties who are not actively engaged in the management or control of the organisation, such as shareholders, lenders, creditors, government, and the public generally - that is, external users.

**Management accounting** gives predominance to the needs of managers for information - that is, it focuses on internal users. Essentially, management accounting is concerned with providing reports and information to assist managers in planning and controlling routine operations, and in making nonroutine decisions and formulating major plans. A further concern of management accounting, however, is the costing of products and services. Major uses of such cost information are to assess the profitability of products, customers, distribution channels, and so on, as well as satisfying external reporting requirements of profit determination and inventory valuation. Thus there is some overlap between financial and management accounting, and the distinction is somewhat arbitrary because many accounting systems are designed to serve both purposes, managerial information and external reporting, simultaneously.

Management accounting frequently makes use of analysis, particularly cost analysis, outside the framework of the formal double-entry accounting system. Therefore it need not be limited by the conventions and standards which govern external, financial accounting. Indeed, many of the concerns of management relate to future actions, and are analysed using subjective, predicted information rather than objective, historical information.

## MANAGEMENT ACCOUNTING FUNCTIONS

Birkett (1992) identified three factors that influence or drive management accounting work: **compliance**, **control** and **competitive support**.

*Compliance* refers to the need to satisfy external regulations and reporting requirements. Thus accountants have to provide for proper recognition of revenues and expenses, and valuation of assets and liabilities. Management accountants design and operate cost accounting systems which value inventories by attaching costs to products.

*Control* is a term which really means the whole process of planning and control. Management accountants assist in planning by developing comprehensive budgets summarising operational plans, and by assessing the financial consequences of longer term investment projects (ie. capital budgeting). The subsequent control aspects concern the design and operation of systems to provide oversight of the use and conservation of resources in achieving organisational plans. Such systems are concerned primarily with accounting as well as nonfinancial performance measures to evaluate people and activities.

*Competitive support* refers to the provision of financial services to the management team in order to enhance the firm's competitiveness. These financial services add value to the organisation by supporting line and process managers in their decision making, so that the management accountant becomes directly involved in the decision process. This focus on lower level management has come about because of the trend towards flatter, less hierarchical organisation structures and a diminished role for middle management. Line and process managers are now empowered to make and implement business decisions and have to be actively supported in these endeavours.

In addition to supporting line and process managers, the competitive support role involves management accountants in strategic processes. They now give direct support in the development of organisational strategies. Management accountants are involved in processes which enhance customer value or provide customer service. They determine profitability of products, customers and distribution channels, and help in pricing decisions. Management accountants provide direct support for continuous improvement initiatives to enhance value, and to reduce costs, and for benchmarking activities which seek to measure products or services against the best levels of performance either within the organisation or outside it. Direct support is also given in addressing what are termed **key success factors**: **quality** of products or services, **time** reduction in responding to customer requests and demands, and **innovation** in developing new products and services.

Over time the relative emphasis on these three key drivers of management accounting work has shifted. In the past, compliance and control activities accounted for the major part of the management accountant's work. Modern organisations, however, place greater emphasis on the need to provide competitive support. Value-adding activities (competitive support) frequently represent the major aspect of the management accountant's work.

In responding to the needs and demands of modern organisations, management accountants rely on the use of product costing systems and control systems.

## *Product Costing Systems*

The first section of this book deals with product costing. Product costing systems are concerned with a detailed classification, analysis and recording of the cost of resources consumed, with a view to allocating a fair share of all manufacturing or service costs to individual units of 'output'. Such units may be broadly labelled as products. In some organisations all units may be different from each other, eg. repair jobs in a garage, printing jobs in a printing works for different customers, custom-built houses, repairs to washing machines, arranging loans for bank clients. In other businesses the units of output may be identical, standardised units, eg. cakes of soap, cans of beer, litres of petrol, tonnes of fertiliser. More detailed recording is required when every unit is different, while some broad averaging techniques can be appropriate for batches of like units.

Product costing systems are designed for three major purposes:

1. **Compliance**: As a means of determining the cost of goods sold (for profit determination) and the cost of unsold inventories of finished goods and work in process (to be recorded in the statement of financial position).

2. **Control**: As a basis for evaluating performance in productive activities and performance of personnel involved. If the cost per unit this period is the same as, or less than in the previous period, then costs would seem to be well controlled.

3. **Competitive support**: As a guide to price setting and other product-related decisions, eg., continue/discontinue, make/buy. Product cost is very useful as a basis for pricing unique jobs. Alternatively, if the price of a product is determined by the market, then product cost information is useful for decisions about product viability. If a product is shown to cost more than it can fetch in the marketplace it is clear that the organisation should cease producing it unless cost reductions are possible.

This third purpose is extremely important and is sometimes overlooked or downplayed. In an increasingly competitive world environment it is becoming essential that product costing systems be more accurate in assigning to products the costs of resources consumed so that correct strategic decisions are taken with respect to selection of products to be manufactured or services to be provided, and to price setting.

## Control Systems

This is the focus of the second section of the book. Control systems are concerned with planning and controlling operations. Planning is the process of formulating and co-ordinating decisions about different phases of the operations of an organisation so that they do not conflict, but combine in pursuit of organisational goals. Control is the process of ensuring that decisions are implemented efficiently and that their consequences are monitored. Control systems involve adequate communication between different individuals and groups, integration of plans of various sections of the organisation, and evaluation of performance of subunits by comparing actual performance with plans, so that discrepancies are reported. Such performance evaluation enables corrective action to be initiated or original plans to be revised.

The design of control systems poses considerable difficulty because of the need to motivate people to act in the interests of the organisation. In particular, the performance evaluation criteria and reward systems used are critical to the success of the control system. Inappropriate criteria can lead to dysfunctional behaviour and consequent undesirable outcomes.

# SUMMARY

This introductory chapter was concerned with identifying the field of management accounting. Although there is some overlap with financial accounting, management accounting is primarily concerned with providing information to assist managers in running a business. Management accounting work is driven by three factors, compliance, control and competitive support. A large part of this work can be achieved by carefully designing and operating product costing systems and control systems.

## References

Birkett, W.P. (1992), "Finance in the Service of Strategy: Controllership in the Nineties", keynote address, Australian Centre for Management Accounting Development, *Conference '92: Towards Seamless Organisations*, August.

# APPENDIX

# INTRODUCTION TO THE USE OF SPREADSHEETS

## *Financial Modelling*

A model is a simplified representation of reality. There are three main types of models, **iconic**, **analogue** and **symbolic**. An iconic model looks like what it represents, for example a map, scale models of aeroplanes, mountain ranges or human organs. An analogue model resembles or has similar characteristics to the phenomenon being observed, for example a graph of net income by month of the year, or the use of animals as analogues of humans in medical experiments. A symbolic model uses symbols to represent the concepts and relationships of a system. Direct labour cost per hour in a production department might depend simply on the number of employees engaged in production, assuming all are paid at the same rate. Thus the relationship between cost and labour could be shown in a symbolic model by the equation

$$C = rX$$

where **C** is total hourly direct labour cost for the department, **r** is the hourly wage rate and **X** the number of employees. Symbolic models tend to be the most useful for business analysis.

Mathematical modelling of business relationships has always been possible but it was the advent of modern computers that caused rapid developments in the area of financial modelling.

The conventional accounting framework itself is, in a sense, a financial model. Corporate modelling refers to the construction and use of a computer-based model to execute the calculations required to produce results of business activities based on given sets of assumptions and predictions. Financial modelling, a slightly narrower term, refers to the development and use of computer-based models to perform the work involved in producing the financial statements normally generated through the accounting framework.

The overall objective of corporate or financial modelling is to develop a computer-based model that will assist managers to prepare effective plans for the future operations of the organisation modelled. This applies to the cyclical activity of preparing annual budgets, and forecasts covering several years of operation. Such a model should also provide assistance when the advent of unexpected major changes in the business environment results in the need, immediately, to produce modified plans to adapt to the new conditions. Such a model, then, needs to embody the significant features of the organisation itself, but unnecessary complexity should be avoided. For most business activities a considerable amount of detail will be required in the model.

In the operation of such a model manual methods would be slow, expensive and liable to arithmetical errors. More importantly, as the date approaches for final plans to be adopted and promulgated, time simply runs out and many **what if** questions remain unanswered. A computer-based model, however, can dramatically reduce the time required for testing a variety of planning assumptions, and answers to *what if* questions may be obtained promptly. Languages and packages have been designed specifically to enable people with very limited knowledge of data processing techniques to build and run financial models through computers.

## Financial Modelling Packages

There are over 50 systems available in Australia. Most companies with models use commercial packages which enable models to be built faster, more cheaply and with more user-friendly features.

Originally financial modelling packages (eg. Foresight, IFPS, EPS) were designed for mainframe computers. Subsequently, with the increasing popularity of microcomputers, there was a rapid proliferation of **spreadsheet** packages (eg. Supercalc, Multiplan, Lotus 1-2-3, Quattro Pro, Excel); at the same time the designers of mainframe packages tended to produce microcomputer versions also.

*1/Management Accounting Functions*

The mainframe packages tend to be logic-oriented consisting of logic and data files, and the system formulates the matrix. For example, in producing an income statement, each row of the matrix represents income statement items such as Sales, Cost of Goods Sold, Net Income etc. while the columns represent time periods such as months, quarters or years. When using this type of package the system's language is used to define rows and columns and to specify how values are to be determined. The matrix is not consulted while programming a model; the user composes logic statements which are saved and run later. For instance, suppose Sales are expected to increase by 10% (compound) per period from a base figure; the user simply writes a system statement to indicate this and when the program is run the system automatically generates the figures for each of the number of periods specified.

Personal or micro computer spreadsheets use the computer's internal memory as a 2-dimensional matrix or worksheet where the rows and columns generally are used in the same way as in mainframe packages, although it is not essential to do so. This spreadsheet, or part thereof, is displayed on the screen, thus concentrating the user's attention on the reporting aspects of the program and encouraging an improved format. As each command is entered calculations are performed automatically so that the user sees immediately what figures result, thus closely resembling the use of pencil and paper (and calculator). One major difference is apparent, however: each cell of a line has to be separately programmed. Taking the same Sales example as above, the base figure would be entered in the first column of the Sales line; the user then moves to the second column and enters a command to increase the previous cell by 10%. To avoid having to keep repeating this procedure cell by cell along the row a **replication** or **copy** command allows the remaining cells of the row to be programmed. So what was accomplished by a single command in logic-oriented packages takes three commands using spreadsheets.

Most popular spreadsheet packages are fairly similar in operation. Once one masters any one package it is relatively painless to learn to use another.

With the development of personal computers and spreadsheet software suitable for use on these machines, the early accounting computer applications concerned with developing financial models extended to other, less comprehensive applications. For example, spreadsheet models were developed by users to analyse capital budgeting projects, or to calculate product costs. In fact, the applications of spreadsheets are limited only by the user's imagination. In this book we will use spreadsheet models for a variety of tasks, from very simple ones to comprehensive budget and financial models. The important thing to remember is that it is worthwhile building a spreadsheet model for any task which is repetitive, and which involves mathematical calculations.

For beginners, below are explanations of the use of two popular spreadsheets, Lotus 1-2-3 (or its clones) [version 2, a DOS version] and Excel 97 [a Windows 97 version], for building an income statement. This will be followed with a step-by-step demonstration exercise for you to follow in building a model of your own. The reader should focus on the spreadsheet which (s)he intends to use. Readers already competent in the use of spreadsheets may wish to skip this section.

### *Illustrative Example*

Suppose that a 3-year forecast is to be prepared, and that in the year immediately preceding the forecast years:

- Sales revenue was $10 000 and is expected to increase at a rate of 10% per annum (compound).
- Gross Margin was 25% of sales revenue and it is expected that this percentage will continue.
- Other Variable Expenses were 15% of sales revenue and this ratio is expected to remain constant.
- Other Fixed Expenses have been estimated at $200 for the first year of the forecast period and are expected to increase by $40 per annum thereafter.

*Required:*

Forecasts of sales, gross margin, other relevant expenses, net profit, and net profit as a percentage of sales for each of the 3 years.

## A Lotus 1-2-3 Model

| A | | B | C | D | E |
|---|---|---|---|---|---|
| 1 | | | YEAR 1 | YEAR 2 | YEAR 3 |
| 2 | | | | | |
| 3 | Sales | 10000 | +B3*1.1 | +C3*1.1 | +D3*1.1 |
| 4 | Cost of Goods Sold | | 0.75*C3 | 0.75*D3 | 0.75*E3 |
| 5 | | | --------- | --------- | --------- |
| 6 | Gross Margin | | +C3-C4 | +D3-D4 | +E3-E4 |
| 7 | | | --------- | --------- | --------- |
| 8 | Other Variable Exp | | +C3*0.15 | +D3*0.15 | +E3*0.15 |
| 9 | Other Fixed Exp | | 200 | +C9+40 | +D9+40 |
| 10 | | | --------- | --------- | --------- |
| 11 | Total Other Exp | | @SUM(C8..C9) | @SUM(D8..D9) | @SUM(E8..E9) |
| 12 | | | --------- | --------- | --------- |
| 13 | Net Profit | | +C6-C11 | +D6-D11 | +E6-E11 |
| 14 | | | ========= | ========= | ========= |
| 15 | Net Profit % | | +C13/C3*100 | +D13/D3*100 | +E13/E3*100 |
| 16 | | | --------- | --------- | --------- |

The following points should be noted:

- Columns are designated by letters of the alphabet, while rows are numbered sequentially. Any particular cell is referenced by column and row, for example the label **Sales** appears in cell **A3**, and **E6** shows a formula **E3-E4**.

- Column A (which has been widened from the default width) has been used for row names, Column B has been preserved as a **history** column for holding figures to be incremented, and Columns C, D and E contain the three years' forecasts.

- Cell contents are entered by moving the cursor to the appropriate cell and keying in text, a number or a formula which appear on the Data Entry Line at the top of the screen. Then the <Enter> key is pressed, causing the text, number or formula calculation results to appear in the spreadsheet cell where the cursor resides.

- In Row 1 the headings **YEAR 1**, **YEAR 2** and **YEAR 3** were entered in **C1**, **D1** and **E1** respectively.

- Row 3 contains Sales forecasts. In **A3** the label **Sales** was entered. In **B3** the preceding year's sales revenue of **$10000** was entered (without $ sign, comma or spaces). In **C3** the formula B3*1.1 was entered, meaning multiply B3 (ie. 10000) by 1.1. It is necessary, however, to precede the **B** with a plus sign, otherwise the spreadsheet package, acting on the first character entered, interprets the entry as text instead of a formula: **+B3*1.1**. To enter the appropriate formulae for **D3** and **E3** the Copy command was used: **/Copy,C3,D3..E3**

  This means copy the formula in **C3** over the range **D3 to E3**; that is, the same formula (B3*1.1) is copied across the specified range of Row 3 but the B3 is automatically incremented successively to C3 and D3 to give the formulae shown.

- In the Cost of Goods Sold line, Row 4, the Year 1 estimate is calculated. If the gross margin is 25% of sales (see data) then the cost of goods sold must be 75% of sales revenue. The formula in **C4** is **.75*C3** (multiply Sales in C3 by 0.75). This can be entered by simply keying in the formula. In this case, however, the POINT facility was used: with the cursor on **C4**, **.75*** was keyed in, and then the upward arrow key ↑ was pressed, causing the cursor to move up one cell to C3, giving .75*C3, and <Enter> pressed to give the result in **C4**. The Copy command was then used to slot in the formulae for **D4** and **E4**.

- Row 5 is used for a single line to be ruled under Cost of Goods Sold figures. This is accomplished by positioning the cursor on **C5** and entering \- (backslash plus hyphen) which causes a single line to be ruled across cell **C5**. The Copy command is then used to copy it across the remaining cells as required. Note that in early spreadsheet packages a row had to be used to rule lines in this way. In more modern packages extra lines are not needed for ruling lines as you can place a border under figures in the same cells as the figures - see the Excel example below.

- Gross Margin (Row 6) is calculated from the formula **C3-C4** for Year 1. **+C3-C4** can be entered directly, or the POINT facility can be used: Plus sign **+**, use upward arrow ↑ to move cursor to **C3**, press MINUS key **-** , use arrows to move cursor to **C4**, press <Enter>. The formula is then copied across to **D5** and **E5**.

- Row 9 could have been entered as data: 200, 240, 280. It was, however, entered as a formula. The forecast **200** was entered in **C9** and incremented by **40** for subsequent years.

- In row 11 the figures in Rows 8 and 9 were added. A formula of the type **+C8+C9** for cell **C11** would have sufficed, but in this case the SUM function was used: **@SUM(C8..C9)**, that is, sum the values in the specified column range **C8 to C9**. SUM is one of a range of special @ functions available which must be preceded by @.

- Although the above model has the **contents** of the cells displayed (ie. the formulae) when using Lotus 123 the calculations rather than the formulae appear in the cells, unless the user specifies otherwise. Therefore, unlike logic-oriented models, the spreadsheet models provide the user with instant calculation results as each cell is programmed.

- To print hard copies of results the **/Print** command is used, to print whatever is displayed. The **/RFT** (Range,Format,Text) command was used to convert the display to formulae in this case. However, the grid (column letters and row numbers) could not be printed in early versions of Lotus 123 - the above printout has been simply keyed in by word processor.

An Excel Model

|    | A | B | C | D | E |
|----|---|---|---|---|---|
| 1  |   |   | YEAR 1 | YEAR 2 | YEAR 3 |
| 2  |   |   |   |   |   |
| 3  | Sales | 10000 | =B3*1.1 | =C3*1.1 | =D3*1.1 |
| 4  | Cost of Goods Sold |   | =0.75*C3 | =0.75*D3 | =0.75*E3 |
| 5  | Gross Margin |   | =C3-C4 | =D3-D4 | =E3-E4 |
| 6  | Other Variable Exp |   | =C3*0.15 | =D3*0.15 | =E3*0.15 |
| 7  | Other Fixed Exp |   | 200 | =C7+40 | =D7+40 |
| 8  | Total Other Exp |   | =SUM(C6:C7) | =SUM(D6:D7) | =SUM(E6:E7) |
| 9  | Net Profit |   | =C5-C8 | =D5-D8 | =E5-E8 |
| 10 | Net Profit % |   | =C9/C3*100 | =D9/D3*100 | =E9/E3*100 |

The following points should be noted:

- As in Lotus 123 columns are designated by letters of the alphabet, while rows are numbered sequentially. Any particular cell is referenced by column and row, for example the label **Sales** appears in cell **A3**, and **E5** shows a formula **E3-E4**.

- Column A (which has been widened from the default width) has been used for row names, Column B has been preserved as a **history** column for holding figures to be incremented, and Columns C, D and E contain the three years' forecasts.

- Cell contents are entered by moving the cursor to the appropriate cell and keying in text, a number or a formula which appear in the active cell and in the Formula Bar at the top of the screen. Then the <Enter> key is pressed, causing the text, number or formula calculation results to appear in the spreadsheet cell where the cursor resides.

*1/Management Accounting Functions*

- In Row 1 the headings **YEAR 1**, **YEAR 2** and **YEAR 3** were entered in **C1**, **D1** and **E1** respectively.

- Row 3 contains Sales forecasts. In **A3** the label **Sales** was entered. In **B3** the preceding year's sales revenue of **$10000** was entered (without $ sign, comma or spaces). In **C3** the formula **B3\*1.1** was entered, meaning multiply B3 (ie. 10000) by 1.1. It is necessary, however, to precede the **B** with an equals sign =, otherwise the spreadsheet package, acting on the first character entered, interprets the entry as text instead of a formula: **=B3\*1.1**. To enter the appropriate formulae for **D3** and **E3** the Copy command was used. This can be done in at least three ways:
    1. Place the cursor on **C3** and use the command **^C** (control C, ie. hold down the <Ctrl> key while you press the letter C). This causes the cell **C3** to be surrounded by a blinking frame, and copies the contents of **C3** to the Clipboard. Then hold down the <Shift> key and press the right arrow so that the highlight is extended from **C3** across to **E3**. Then **either** press <Enter> **or** use the command **^V** (control V). Either results in a copy of the formula from the Clipboard over the range **D3 to E3**; that is, the same formula (=**B3\*1.1**) is copied across the specified range of Row 3 but the **B3** is automatically incremented successively to **C3** and **D3** to give the formulae shown.
    2. Repeat 1 but instead of using the keyboard commands **^C** and **^V** the mouse can be used to enter the commands **Edit Copy** and **Edit Paste** respectively.
    3. With the mouse, click on cell **C3** with the left button. This puts a frame around **C3**. At the bottom right hand corner of the frame is a little square. Click on this with the left button, hold the button down and drag across cells **D3** and **E3**. Release the mouse button and the formula is copied. This is probably the easiest of the three methods.

- In the Cost of Goods Sold line, Row 4, the Year 1 estimate is calculated. If the gross margin is 25% of sales (see data) then the cost of goods sold must be 75% of sales revenue. The formula in **C4** is **=0.75\*C3** (multiply Sales in **C3** by **0.75**). This can be entered by simply keying in the formula. In this case, however, the POINT facility was used: with the cursor on **C4**, **=0.75\*** was keyed in, and then the upward arrow key ↑ was pressed, causing the cursor to move up one cell to **C3**, giving **=0.75\*C3**, and <Enter> pressed to give the result in **C4**. This was then copied across **D4** and **E4**.

- A line has been ruled under Cost of Goods Sold figures. This is accomplished by positioning the cursor on **C3** and highlighting the cells **C3:E3** (C3 through E3) and placing a border under these cells: highlight **C3:E3** by placing the cursor on **C3** and either <Shift> and <Right arrow> or click and drag to highlight **D3** and **E3** as well. Then click on **Format, Cells, Border, Bottom, OK**, or else use the Border Tool on the Formatting Toolbar and select a single underline.

- Gross Margin (Row 5) is calculated from the formula **=C3-C4** for Year 1. **=C3-C4** can be entered directly, or the POINT facility can be used: Equals sign =, use upward arrow ↑ to move cursor to **C3**, press MINUS key -, use arrows to move cursor to **C4**, press <Enter>. The formula is then copied across to **D5** and **E5**.

- Row 6 should require no explanation.

- Row 7 could have been entered as data: 200, 240, 280. It was, however, entered as a formula. The forecast **200** was entered in **C7** (Year 1) and incremented by **40** for subsequent years.

- In row 8 the figures in Rows 6 and 7 were added. A formula of the type **=C6+C7** for cell **C8** would have sufficed, but in this case the SUM function was used: **=SUM(C6:C7)**, that is, sum the values in the specified column range **C6 to C7**. A shortcut is available by clicking on Σ on the Toolbar.

- Single lines were ruled under Rows 5, 7, 8 and 10 (as for Row 4) and a double line under Row 9 (Format, Cells, Border, Style = double underline, and clicking the preset bottom underline box, OK).

*1/Management Accounting Functions*

- Although the above model has the **contents** of the cells displayed (ie. the formulae) when using Excel the calculations rather than the formulae appear in the cells, unless the user specifies otherwise.

- To print hard copies of results the Print command is used: Click on **File, Print, All, OK**. The command **Tools, Options, View** was used, then click on the button beside **Formulas** to convert the display to formulae.

For the sake of completeness the output for this problem (via Excel) is shown below:

|    | A                 | B     | C      | D      | E      |
|----|-------------------|-------|--------|--------|--------|
| 1  |                   |       | YEAR 1 | YEAR 2 | YEAR 3 |
| 2  |                   |       |        |        |        |
| 3  | Sales             | 10000 | 11000  | 12100  | 13310  |
| 4  | Cost of Goods Sold|       | 8250   | 9075   | 9982.5 |
| 5  | Gross Margin      |       | 2750   | 3025   | 3327.5 |
| 6  | Other Variable Exp|       | 1650   | 1815   | 1996.5 |
| 7  | Other Fixed Exp   |       | 200    | 240    | 280    |
| 8  | Total Other Exp   |       | 1850   | 2055   | 2276.5 |
| 9  | Net Profit        |       | 900    | 970    | 1051   |
| 10 | Net profit %      |       | 8.18   | 8.02   | 7.90   |
| 11 |                   |       |        |        |        |

The presentation of the results can be improved by formatting cells to dollars and using commas etc.

Once a model has been built using any type of financial modelling package it is very easy to modify it to examine the likely effects of changes in assumptions. For example, suppose that the above assumption that Sales Revenue would increase by 10% per year is uncertain. What if Sales only increase by 5%? All one has to do is alter the growth rate in the Sales line and the package will provide the new calculations and their effect throughout the model in seconds. It is this ability to answer **what if** questions so easily which makes financial modelling packages such powerful and useful tools of financial analysis.

When building reasonably complex models it is an advantage to place key data and assumptions, which are likely to be varied in simulation runs, at the beginning of the model. As the model is built growth rates and percentage relationships are modelled by reference to the cell location in the key assumptions area of the model. When an assumption is to be varied all the user has to do is alter the figure in the key assumption area, rather than search for the location(s) of such figure in the body of the model.

One last hint for successful modelling: Never recalculate any number already calculated earlier in a model. If the same number is required again for another calculation, obtain that number by reference to its original location. For example, Sales figures might be subsequently required to calculate debtors' balances or cash receipts. The modeller should reference the original calculation, **not** recalculate it. Failure to do this has often led to subsequent problems when assumptions were varied, with the result that balance sheets failed to balance or other problems occurred.

## Demonstration Exercise for Reader

We wish to produce a spreadsheet worksheet which will provide an estimate of net profit for a firm which sells only one product at a price which yields a Gross Margin/Sales Percentage of 25 per cent. During the coming three months the forecast sales are as follows: Month 1 $60 000; Month 2 $80 000; and Month 3 $120 000. The firm pays its sales staff a commission of 10 per cent of sales revenue and incurs other costs which are all fixed at the rate of $10 000 per month.

A spreadsheet demonstration will follow using Excel 97.

## Excel

The worksheet should take the following form. You must load Excel to start a new file:

|   | A | B | C | D | E |
|---|---|---|---|---|---|
| 1 | [Your name] | | | | |
| 2 | [and other ID normally entered on assignments] | | | | |
| 3 | | | | | |
| 4 | | | | | |
| 5 | | | | | |
| 6 | | Month 1 | Month 2 | Month 3 | Total |
| 7 | Sales | Data | Data | Data | Formula |
| 8 | Cost of Goods Sold | Formula | Formula | Formula | Formula |
| 9 | Gross Margin | Formula | Formula | Formula | Formula |
| 10 | Other Expenses | | | | |
| 11 | Commission | Formula | Formula | Formula | Formula |
| 12 | Other | Data | Formula | Formula | Formula |
| 13 | Total Other Expenses | Formula | Formula | Formula | Formula |
| 14 | Net Profit | Formula | Formula | Formula | Formula |

Note: **F2** can be used to edit the contents of a cell.
**Delete** key to delete current character.
**Backspace** (or ← to right of numbers) to delete previous character.
To back out of an entry before the <Enter> button is pressed, press <**Esc**>.

The following steps are recommended:

(1) *Enter the text entries in A1:A5, B6..E6 (row 6 from column B to E)*

Use the arrow keys to move around the worksheet. At A1:A5 Type [YOUR NAME] then Press <Enter>, and so on for any other ID in A2:A5. Enter the column headings in B6:E6

(2) *Enter the text entries in A7:A14*

To indent A11 and A12 entries, begin entries by pressing space bar.

(3) *Widen Column A*

Column A is too narrow for the text entries. Widen it by placing the cursor on the widest entry in Column A and click on **Format**, **Column**, **AutoFit Selection** which results in the column widening to accommodate this entry. Alternatively, you can click on **Format**, **Column**, **Width** and specify the width in terms of the number of standard font characters.

(4) *Enter data in B7:D7*

Go to B7 and Type **60000** then Press <Right Arrow>, and so on for the other cells.

(5) *Enter formula in E7*

Go to E7 and Type =**SUM(B7:D7)** <Enter>
  Or use POINT:- Go to E7 and type =**SUM(**move cursor TO B7, press **:** and then <Right Arrow> to D7, press **)** and <Enter>. Note that the highlight expands to cover the range B7:D7 after pressing colon and <Right Arrow>.
  Or use AutoSum:- Place cursor on E7 and click on Σ on the toolbar. This suggests the formula =**SUM(B7:D7)** and you then press <Enter>.

(6) *Enter formula in B8:* =**B7*.75** <Enter> or =**.75*B7** <Enter>

*1/Management Accounting Functions*

*Copy this formula into C8:D8*

Go to B8 (if you are not already there).
Press **^C** (for Copy); and then while holding down <Shift> use the <Right Arrow> until highlight expands to D8, then **^V**(for Paste). Or use **Edit Copy** and **Edit Paste.** Or click and drag.

(7) *Go to E7 and copy its formula into E8.*

(8) *Enter formula (for Gross Margin) in B9:* **=B7-B8**

*Copy this formula into C9:E9*

With the cursor still on B9, press **^C** (for Copy); hold down <Shift> and <Right Arrow> until the highlight expands to cover the range to E9, then press **^V** (for Paste). Alternatively, you could highlight B9, click on **Edit**, **Copy**, then extend the highlight B9:E9 (with Shift and Right Arrow or using the mouse) and click on **Edit**, **Paste**.

(9) *Enter formula in B11:* **=B7*0.1**, and then *copy this formula into C11:D12*.

(10) *Go to either E7 or E8 and copy the formula into E11.* Or go to E11 and use **AutoSum**.

(11) *Enter data in B12:* **10000**

(12) *Enter formula in C12*

Go to C12, Press = and <Left Arrow> to point to B12, Press **F4** (an absolute reference), <Enter>.

*Copy this formula into D12.*

(13) *Go to E11 and copy the formula into E12*, or go to E12 and use **AutoSum**.

(13) *Enter formula in B13:*

**=B11+B12** directly, or by pointing: Press = <Up Arrow> to point to B11, press +, then <Up Arrow> to B12, <Enter>.

*Copy this formula into C13:E13*

(15) *Enter formula in B14:* **=B9-B13**, and then *copy this formula into C14:E14*

(16) *Enter underlining in rows 8, 9 12, 13 and 14.*

Go to B8 and highlight B8:E8 either by <Shift> and <Right Arrow> or by using the mouse. Then click on **Format Cells Border** and click on appropriate preset box, **OK**.
Repeat for rows 9, 12 and 13.
For row 14, you click on the appropriate double underline **Style**.

(17) *Change the formatting* to improve the presentation of your worksheet, eg. shift headings in B6:E6 to the right by highlighting them and clicking on **Format, Cells, Alignment, Right, OK**. Or use currency format for numeric values (using **Format, Cells, Number, Currency** and the desired **Format Code, OK**). Alternatively, you can click on **$** on the toolbar for a quick currency format. If your numbers change to a row of ##### (overflow condition) you need to widen the columns because the entries exceed the current column width.

(18) *Save your worksheet* calling it DEMO, eg. click on **File, Save, DEMO**. Then clear your worksheet, **File, Close**. You may then retrieve the saved worksheet from your disk into computer memory, ie. **File, Open, DEMO**.

*1/Management Accounting Functions*

(19) *Try changing some of the figures* and see how the worksheet is recalculated, eg. change the Gross Margin/Sales Percentage to, say, 30 per cent; or try to find that level of monthly sales at which the firm will just cover its costs (the breakeven level of sales). Think about ways in which your worksheet could be made more general (so that changes to variable values can be made more easily).

## Using a Data Table

A Data Table enables you to answer **what if** questions. For example, what would be the profit if the gross margin percent changed from 25% to 20%, or 40% or any other percentage? What would happen to profits if the sales estimates were incorrect? And so on. A simple way to find the answers to such questions is to alter the appropriate entries in the model, and examine the new results. The disadvantage of this approach is that you lose your original results and model as you make alterations, and it is rather tedious when looking at a range of possible estimates for a variable. An alternative solution is to use a data table to observe the sensitivity of an output variable of interest to many variations in an input variable in one calculation and without altering the original model.

Let us construct a data table to examine the sensitivity of Month 1 profit to variations in Month 1 sales estimates, and to find the Month 1 sales revenue at which the firm breaks even (makes neither profit nor loss) in Month 1.

(1) Go to G6 and Type the heading **DATA TABLE** and Press <Enter>

(2) Go to G7 and Type the heading **SALES** and Press <Enter>

(3) Go to H7 and Type the heading **PROFIT** and Press <Enter>

(4) Go to G8 and Type **=B7** (a reference to Month 1 Sales) and Press <Right Arrow>. Similarly, at H8 Type **=B14** (a reference to Month 1 Net Profit) and Press <Enter>.

These cells (G8 and H8) display the current values of the cells to which they refer (Month 1 Sales and Month 1 Net Profit), ie. 60000 and -1000. Underneath these figures, we will use column G to specify a range of values for Sales in which we might be interested, and column H will show (when we run the data table) the Month 1 Net Profit associated with each of these sales figures.

It is now necessary to set up the range of values for monthly sales revenue for which we wish to obtain monthly net profit values. Let us investigate sales revenue figures from $0 to $100 000 in increments of $5000.

(5) Go to G9 and enter **0**. With the cursor still on G9, click on **Edit**, **Fill**, **Series**, **Columns**, **Step Value**. There will be a 1 in the **Step Value** box when you click on it. Enter **5000** (the increment we want, making sure you delete the 1) then <Tab> to **Stop Value** and enter **100000**. Then click on **OK**. The cells G9:G29 are then automatically filled with numbers from 0 to 100000 by increments of 5000. In other words, we wish to find the profit associated with each of these sales figures.

(6) Now to run the data table. Highlight the rectangle consisting of the two columns G and H from G8:H29. Then click on **Data**, **Table**, **Column Input Cell**. Enter **B7** (the Month 1 Sales cell) in the Column Input Cell box, then **OK**. .

In a short time the calculated results are displayed. In G8 and H8 you see the original figures. From row 9 onwards you see the Sales figures in column G and the calculated Net Profit figures for each sales value in column H. You cannot see the exact sales volume at which the firm breaks even, but you can get close to it. If you wanted to find the exact figure you could re-specify the sales figures in column G [using **Edit, Fill, Series, Columns, Step Value**] to cover a smaller range around break even point, between 65000 and 70000, with smaller increments. You might have to repeat this a few times to converge on the answer.

*1/Management Accounting Functions*

In case you want to check your model answers, here is a copy of the model output:

|   | A | B | C | D | E | F | G | H |
|---|---|---|---|---|---|---|---|---|
| 1 | [Your name] | | | | | | | |
| 2 | [and other ID normally entered on assignments] | | | | | | | |
| 3 | | | | | | | | |
| 4 | | | | | | | | |
| 5 | | | | | | | | |
| 6 | | Month 1 | Month 2 | Month 3 | Total | | DATA TABLE | |
| 7 | Sales | $60,000 | $80,000 | $120,000 | $260,000 | | SALES | PROFIT |
| 8 | Cost of Goods Sold | $45,000 | $60,000 | $90,000 | $195,000 | | $60,000 | ($1,000) |
| 9 | Gross Margin | $15,000 | $20,000 | $30,000 | $65,000 | | 0 | -10000 |
| 10 | Other Expenses | | | | | | 5000 | -9250 |
| 11 |   Commission | $6,000 | $8,000 | $12,000 | $26,000 | | 10000 | -8500 |
| 12 |   Other | $10,000 | $10,000 | $10,000 | $30,000 | | 15000 | -7750 |
| 13 | Total Other Expenses | $16,000 | $18,000 | $22,000 | $56,000 | | 20000 | -7000 |
| 14 | Net Profit | ($1,000) | $2,000 | $8,000 | $9,000 | | 25000 | -6250 |
| 15 | | | | | | | 30000 | -5500 |
| 16 | | | | | | | 35000 | -4750 |
| 17 | | | | | | | 40000 | -4000 |
| 18 | | | | | | | 45000 | -3250 |
| 19 | | | | | | | 50000 | -2500 |
| 20 | | | | | | | 55000 | -1750 |
| 21 | | | | | | | 60000 | -1000 |
| 22 | | | | | | | 65000 | -250 |
| 23 | | | | | | | 70000 | 500 |
| 24 | | | | | | | 75000 | 1250 |
| 25 | | | | | | | 80000 | 2000 |
| 26 | | | | | | | 85000 | 2750 |
| 27 | | | | | | | 90000 | 3500 |
| 28 | | | | | | | 95000 | 4250 |
| 29 | | | | | | | 100000 | 5000 |

# Chapter 2

# Product Costing: Terms and Cost Flows

## COST and COST DRIVER

A **cost** represents the value of resources supplied or consumed to achieve a specific objective. The conventional accounting measure of cost is in terms of money outlaid for resources, that is historical or outlay cost.

We talk about the cost of **something**, be it the cost of a product produced, the cost of a service provided, the cost of running a department for a month, the cost of an hour of labour, or the cost of a kilowatt-hour of electricity. The activity or item for which a cost is required is known as a **cost object**.

A **cost driver** is any activity or factor that causes costs to change - that is, it drives cost. Examples of a cost driver are the number of units produced, the number of direct labour hours worked, the number of parts produced, the number of service calls made, the dollar value of sales, and the technical complexity of a project.

## DIRECT and INDIRECT COSTS

Whether a cost is classified as a **direct cost** or an **indirect cost** depends on its relationship to a cost object. The terms **direct cost** and **indirect cost** have no meaning unless the cost object is specified. That is, a cost can be direct to a cost object or indirect to it.

When a cost can be traceable to a cost object it is called a direct cost (with respect to that cost object). For example, if a mechanic puts a new set of spark plugs in your motor car, the cost of those plugs is a direct cost to that job (tuning of your car). The salary of a production supervisor is a direct cost of the production department in which (s)he works. The wages of a washing machine serviceman are a direct cost to the machines that he repairs.

When a cost is not easy or feasible to trace to a cost object it is called an indirect cost of that cost object. For example, the cost of the tools and equipment that the mechanic uses to tune your car is an indirect cost of the job of tuning your car because their cost cannot be directly traced to that job. They are direct costs of running the motor repair business but it is not easy to identify or allocate a fair share of their cost to your particular job. The salary of the production supervisor, while a direct cost of the production department, is an indirect cost of the products produced in that department because we cannot feasibly trace his salary cost to individual units of product.

## VARIABLE and FIXED COSTS

A cost may be classified as **variable** or **fixed**, depending upon how its total varies in response to changes in a cost driver. Some costs, such as direct materials, may vary proportionately with changes in the cost driver. These are known as *variable costs* [see Figure 2-1(a)] and may be represented by an equation such as y = bx, where y = total cost, b = variable cost per unit and x = number of units. For example, a car manufacturer may buy a given battery at $50 for each of its cars; the total cost of batteries is $50 multiplied by the number of cars produced.

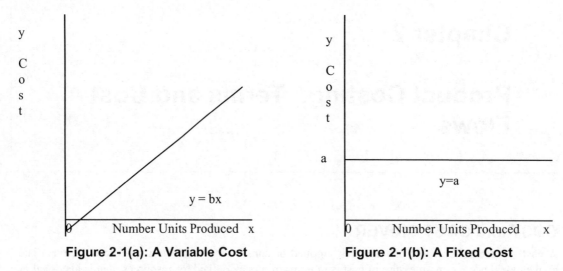

**Figure 2-1(a): A Variable Cost**       **Figure 2-1(b): A Fixed Cost**

Other costs, such as depreciation, rates and executive salaries, may be unaffected in total in a given period by wide changes in cost driver activity. These costs which are constant for a given period, are called **fixed costs** [see Figure 2-1(b)] and may be represented by the equation $y = a$, where a is the y-intercept and represents the cost level regardless of volume.

The classification of a cost item as either fixed or variable depends on whether the cost responds to changes in cost driver activity during a given period. Such changes in cost driver activity are assumed to be moderate ones. Of course, extreme movements in the level of cost driver activity can cause a cost to change from one category to another. For example, if a business ceases all manufacturing, a foreman's salary (normally a fixed cost) may drop to zero (he is made redundant and his services are dispensed with), and hence the foreman's salary becomes a variable cost in response to the cost driver change.

Further, the time period must be specified. Over a period sufficiently long enough (say several years) all costs become variable. For example, a permanent halving of activity level would lead to a reduction in most costs; some managers can be dispensed with, equipment sold and not replaced, and land can be sold or leases terminated. Alternatively, over a period sufficiently short (say half a day) nearly all costs become fixed; for example, all workers have to be paid regardless of activity level because labour cannot be laid off over an extremely short period of time. It is conventional that the time period corresponds to an accounting period such as a month, a quarter or a year, with a year being considered typical.

## UNIT COSTS

Unit costs are averages, found by dividing total cost by some number of units of activity. For example, if 1000 units of Product A are produced for a total cost of $5000, the unit production cost (cost of one unit) is equal to $5000/1000 = $5.

If the costs of producing these 1000 units are all variable, the unit cost of $5 would not change if production were expanded to 1500 units. The total cost would increase to $7500 (1500 x $5), but the unit cost is still $5. Changes in cost driver level of activity affect **total** variable costs but not the variable cost per unit.

On the other hand, if the costs of producing Product A are all fixed costs, the total production costs would not change if production volume altered. However, unit cost would change, because the same total cost would be averaged over a different number of units. For example, if production expanded to 1250 units, the unit cost would decrease to $4 ($5000/1250). Thus, although changes in cost driver activity level do not affect total fixed costs, the **fixed cost per unit** varies with changes in activity level; it varies inversely with activity.

## PURPOSES OF PRODUCT COSTING

Product costing is the process of assigning a fair share of all manufacturing or service costs to individual units of output. As a result of these assignments we make such statements as 'a cake of soap costs 40 cents to manufacture' or 'every cheque account transaction costs our bank $1.80' or to do a wheel alignment costs me $15 when I allow for the costs of labour and equipment'.

We can identify at least four reasons for determining the cost of producing a unit of output:

1. To fulfil external reporting requirements by providing a basis for valuing cost of goods sold for income determination, and for valuing unsold inventories of finished goods and work in process for inclusion in statements of financial position.

2. To assess the efficiency of the production (or service) processes by comparing actual product costs with estimated, or standard costs, with last period's cost (focusing on continuous improvement), or with competitors' costs (benchmarking to match or better world class performance).

3. To provide an input to different decisions, such as:

    (a) setting a price for a product;
    (b) keeping or dropping an existing product;
    (c) pricing products in special situations, e.g., for a special order given excess capacity;
    (d) making or buying components, or finished goods;
    (e) selling as is or processing further.

4. To justify the setting of selling prices which are under the control of price control or price monitoring bodies.

## ELEMENTS OF PRODUCT COST

There are three major cost elements which constitute product cost, **direct materials, direct labour** and **manufacturing overhead**. *Direct materials* refers to the raw materials which are an integral part of the finished good, and traceable to it.[1] For example, in a wooden desk the principal direct material is the timber of which it is made, and its cost is referred to as the direct materials cost. Some materials which might properly be regarded as direct materials are sometimes, in fact, not treated as such. In the wooden desk referred to there might be glue in the joints, but to actually trace the cost of a few dabs of glue to each unit would probably not be cost-effective. Therefore, direct materials are classified as those which are traceable to individual units in an economically feasible manner. Those which it is not economically feasible to trace are treated as **indirect materials**.

*Direct labour* cost comprises the wages of workers who physically participate in the actual production of the product or the provision of the service. That is, it is the cost of the time spent by workers who actually fabricate, machine, assemble, process or otherwise directly participate in the production of a good or the provision of a service. Direct labour does not include the cost of idle time, travelling time (e.g. from one service job to another) or any overtime premium paid, all of which are generally treated as **indirect labour**. Nor does direct labour cost include the cost of foremen, supervisors, materials handlers, cleaners or any other personnel not *directly* engaged in production. These latter costs are also treated as indirect labour.

*Manufacturing overhead* consists of all factory expenses which are not direct material or direct labour costs. It comprises indirect materials, indirect labour and other factory expenses. Indirect materials consist of any materials which are not part of the product (for example, rags used for cleaning, oil for machines) plus those materials which are treated as indirect materials because it is not economically

---

[1] Before material is issued to production it is called *raw material*. After it enters production it is called *direct material*. Often all material costs are entered in a single account labelled *Raw Materials*, issues from which might represent both direct materials and indirect materials (sometimes called *supplies*). Indirect material is a component of manufacturing overhead costs.

feasible to trace them to individual units of product. Indirect labour cost covers all factory labour which is not direct labour. Other overhead costs are items like factory rent, electricity, insurance, depreciation of machinery and maintenance of factory buildings and plant. Manufacturing overhead does not usually include any expenses which are typically regarded as administrative or selling expenses. In some service organisations the term manufacturing overhead is probably not appropriate, but should be called simply, overhead.

A few cost items might be regarded as **direct expense**. This category includes payments such as royalties on each unit produced or on inputs consumed, or payments for subcontract services.

The term **prime cost** is used to describe the sum of direct materials and direct labour (and any direct expense where incurred). **Conversion cost** refers to the sum of direct labour and manufacturing overhead expenses - it is the cost of converting raw materials into a finished product.

Although different goods or services may contain varying proportions of direct materials, direct labour and manufacturing overhead, most products contain all three elements in their production cost. Direct materials cost and direct labour cost are relatively easy to **trace** to individual units of output. The association between manufacturing overhead costs and individual units produced is, however, more tenuous. For example, any link between the incurrence of overhead items such as factory rent or rates, and units produced is quite remote. Therefore overhead costs are usually **allocated** to units of output in a more arbitrary fashion, but with the intention of ensuring that each unit bears a 'fair' share of overhead resources consumed in its production.

## COST FLOWS

### Retailing

A retailer (or merchandiser) buys goods for resale. The cost of goods sold may be determined from the calculation *Opening Inventory + Purchases - Closing Inventory*, as shown in Figure 2-2(a).

| Retailer | Manufacturer |
|---|---|
| Cost of Goods Sold:<br>    Opening Inventory<br>+  Purchases<br>=  Goods Available for Sale<br>-   Closing Inventory<br>=  Cost of Goods Sold | Cost of Goods sold:<br>    Opening Inventory Finished Goods<br>+  Cost of Goods Manufactured<br>=  Goods Available for Sale<br>-   Closing Inventory Finished Goods<br>=  Cost of Goods Sold |

                  Figure 2-2(a)                                          Figure 2-2(b)

Purchases are valued at purchase price plus any inwards freight charges and, in the case of imported goods, such costs as customs duty etc. All other costs of operation are regarded as expenses to be charged against gross profit in calculating net profit. Only the costs identified with the purchase of goods for resale are **product costs**, or **inventoriable costs**, which become expenses (cost of goods sold) at the point of sale. All other costs are **period costs**, charged as expenses in the period in which they are incurred.

### Manufacturing

In a manufacturing business the essential difference is that goods are manufactured, rather than purchased, for resale. Hence to ascertain cost of goods sold we substitute **cost of goods manufactured** for **purchases**, as shown in Figure 2-2(b). It should also be noted that the opening and closing inventories are referred to as inventories of **finished goods**, to distinguish them from other inventories. As depicted in Figure 2-3, in a manufacturing business there are three types of inventory account, **raw materials inventory**, **work-in-process inventory** and **finished goods inventory**. Thus a manufacturer's balance sheet shows three types of inventory under current assets. The Raw Materials account is used to record the cost of materials purchased for use in production. Work-in-Process account shows the cost of partly completed jobs or production. Sometimes it is sub-divided into three separate accounts, materials-in-process, labour-in-process and overhead-in-process. Finished Goods account is used to record the cost of completely manufactured goods on hand.

In contrast to the retailer, the manufacturer includes many costs of operation as product costs. All production costs, including direct materials, direct labour and manufacturing overhead, are treated as product costs which do not become expenses to be matched against revenues until the goods are sold. Only general and administrative expenses and selling and distribution expenses are typically treated as period costs, written off in the period in which they are incurred. Some firms even include administration and selling expenses as overhead expenses forming part of product costs. While such an approach may be appropriate for strategic purposes (e.g., product pricing, or decisions about whether to continue with a product) it is not appropriate for profit measurement and valuation of inventories in financial statements. More than likely accepted inventory valuation practice would necessitate a downward adjustment of *cost* to *realisable market value*.

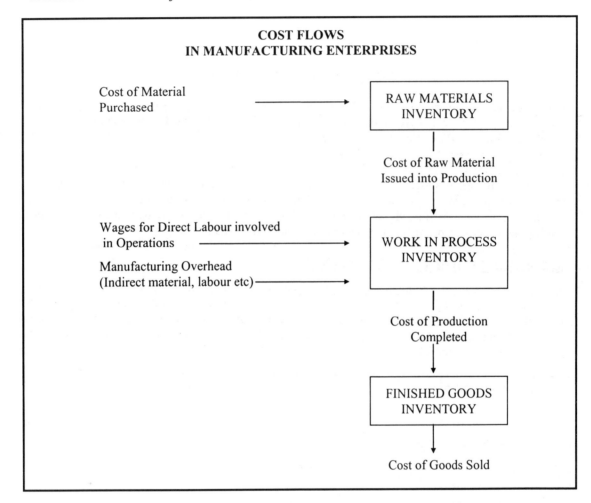

**Figure 2-3**

In Figure 2-4 are shown the flow of manufacturing costs in the general ledger.

## 2/Product Costing: Terms and Cost Flows

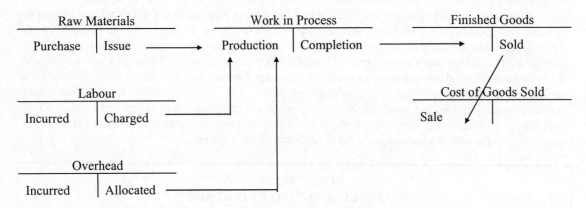

**Figure 2-4: Ledger Cost Flows**

Raw materials and/or components obtained from suppliers are stored (dr asset: Raw Materials Inventory a/c, cr Cash a/c or Accounts Payable a/c). As materials are issued to production their cost is transferred from the Raw Materials a/c to the Work-in-Process a/c in which all production costs are accumulated (dr asset: WIP, cr asset: Raw Materials). Similarly, other resources are consumed (dr expenses: Labour a/c and Overhead a/c, cr Cash a/c, Accounts Payable, etc.) and charged to production (dr asset: WIP, cr expenses: Labour and Overhead). When goods are completed their cost is transferred from the Work-in-Process a/c to the Finished Goods a/c (dr asset: Finished Goods, cr asset: WIP). On sale, the cost of goods sold is transferred from the Finished Goods a/c to the Cost of Goods Sold a/c (dr expense: Cost of Goods Sold, cr asset: Finished Goods).

## MANUFACTURING STATEMENT

The simplest method of determining the cost of goods manufactured, and hence the cost of goods sold, is by means of a manufacturing statement. This is analogous to the physical (or periodic) inventory method for determining cost of goods sold for a retailer. All that is required is a list of expenses incurred during the period plus a valuation of opening and closing inventories (raw materials, work-in-process and finished goods).

---

*Illustrative Example*

On 1 August, 20X0 the Ace Manufacturing Company, which produces a single product, had the following inventory balances:

| | |
|---|---|
| Raw Materials | $ 5 000 |
| Work-in-Process | 10 000 |
| Finished Goods | 20 000 |

During the month of August the following transactions took place:

| | |
|---|---|
| Raw materials purchased | $10 000 |
| Direct labour costs incurred | 20 000 |
| *Other expenses*: | |
| Factory supervision | 12 000 |
| Depreciation plant | 10 000 |
| Electricity and water | 5 000 |

On 31 August, 20X0 the following inventory balances were recorded:

| | |
|---|---|
| Raw Materials | $4 000 |
| Work-in-Process | 11 000 |
| Finished Goods | 18 000 |

*Required*:

Prepare a manufacturing statement for August, 20X0 to determine the cost of goods manufactured. Then determine the cost of goods sold for the month.

### ACE MANUFACTURING COMPANY
*Manufacturing Statement for Month Ended*
*31 August, 20X0*

**Direct Materials**
| | | |
|---|---|---|
| Raw Materials Inventory, 1 Aug 20X0 | $5 000 | |
| Purchases Raw Materials | 10 000 | |
| | 15 000 | |
| Less Raw Materials Inventory, 31 Aug 20X0 | 4 000 | |
| Raw Materials issued to Production | | $11 000 |
| **Direct Labour** | | 20 000 |
| Prime Cost | | 31 000 |
| **Manufacturing Overhead** | | |
| Factory Supervision | 12 000 | |
| Depreciation Plant | 10 000 | |
| Electricity and Water | 5 000 | 27,000 |
| Current Production Costs | | 58 000 |
| Add Work in Process, 1 Aug 20X0 | | 10 000 |
| | | 68 000 |
| Less Work in Process, 31 Aug 20X0 | | 11 000 |
| **Cost of Finished Goods Manufactured** | | $57 000 |

*Statement of Cost of Goods Sold for Month Ended*
*31 August, 20X0*

| | |
|---|---|
| Finished Goods Inventory, 1 Aug 20X0 | $20 000 |
| Add Cost of Goods Manufactured | 57 000 |
| Goods Available for Sale | 77 000 |
| Less Finished Goods Inventory, 31 Aug 20X0 | 18 000 |
| **Cost of Goods Sold** | $59 000 |

The figure identified in the Manufacturing Statement as *prime cost*, $31 000, is only approximate because there were no details provided of the cost components of work in process. Suppose we were given the breakdown of work in process balances as follows:

| | | |
|---|---|---|
| Work in Process, 1 Aug 20X0: | | |
| Materials in Process | $2 000 | |
| Labour in Process | 3 000 | |
| Overhead in Process | 5 000 | |
| | 10 000 | |
| | | |
| Work in Process, 31 Aug 20X0: | | |
| Materials in Process | $3 000 | |
| Labour in Process | 4 000 | |
| Overhead in Process | 4 000 | |
| | 11 000 | |

Then the manufacturing statement would be drawn up as follows:

## ACE MANUFACTURING COMPANY
*Manufacturing Statement for Month Ended*
*31 August, 20X0*

**Direct Materials**

| | | |
|---|---:|---:|
| Raw Materials Inventory, 1 Aug 20X0 | $5 000 | |
| Purchases Raw Materials | 10 000 | |
| | 15 000 | |
| Less Raw Materials Inventory, 31 Aug 20X0 | 4 000 | |
| Raw Materials issued to Production | 11 000 | |
| Add Materials in Process, 1 Aug 20X0 | 2 000 | |
| | 13 000 | |
| Less Materials in Process, 31 Aug 20X0 | 3 000 | |
| Raw Materials in Goods Manufactured | | $10 000 |

**Direct Labour**

| | | |
|---|---:|---:|
| Direct Labour costs incurred | 20 000 | |
| Add Labour in Process, 1 Aug 20X0 | 3 000 | |
| | 23 000 | |
| Less Labour in Process, 31 Aug 20X0 | 4 000 | |
| Direct Labour in Goods Manufactured | | 19 000 |
| **Prime Cost** | | 29 000 |

**Manufacturing Overhead**

| | | |
|---|---:|---:|
| Factory Supervision | 12 000 | |
| Depreciation Plant | 10 000 | |
| Electricity and Water | 5 000 | |
| | 27 000 | |
| Add Overhead in Process, 1 Aug 20X0 | 5 000 | |
| | 32 000 | |
| Less Overhead in Process, 31 Aug 20X0 | 4 000 | |
| Manufacturing Overhead in Goods Manufactured | | 28 000 |
| **Cost of Finished Goods Manufactured** | | $57 000 |

Now we can see that the prime cost (of goods completed during the month) is actually $29 000. If we have this extra detail regarding work-in-process balances we see that the total of each of the major cost elements may be somewhat different from those based on a single summary figure for work in process. The size of the discrepancy depends upon the changes in the balances of Materials in Process, Labour in Process and Overhead in Process between the beginning and end of the period. If there is no change, there is no discrepancy, but the discrepancy grows directly with the size of the change in balances. Note that the setting out of the manufacturing statement is slightly different when we have dissected work-in-process balances. Instead of a single adjustment for the change in work in process at the foot of the statement we have three adjustments, at the end of Direct Materials, Direct Labour and Manufacturing Overhead sections respectively. Of course, the final figure for Cost of Goods Manufactured does not alter, only the relative size of the three cost components.

Since this is a single-product business it would be possible to determine unit product cost by dividing the Cost of Goods Manufactured by the number of units completed. In reality, few firms produce a single product. If Ace Manufacturing Company produced more than one product we would not be able to determine the unit cost of each product from the information contained in a manufacturing statement. This is a major limitation of the manufacturing statement approach to product costing.

## SUMMARY

**Cost** is the value of resources supplied or consumed to achieve a specific objective. A thing being costed is known as the cost object. Costs may be classified as **direct** or **indirect**, and **variable** or **fixed**. **Unit costs** are averages. Variable cost **per unit** does not change with variations in the activity level of a cost driver; fixed cost **per unit** varies **inversely** with changes in cost driver activity level.

**Product costing** is the process of assigning a fair share of all manufacturing or service costs to individual units of output. Direct costs are **traced** to units of product; indirect costs are **allocated** to units of product. Product costs serve four major purposes: financial reporting, assessment of productive efficiency, inputs to decision making, and price justification. There are three major elements of product cost: direct materials, direct labour and (manufacturing) overhead.

In a manufacturing organisation there are three types of inventory account, **raw materials**, **work in process** and **finished goods**. All production costs (direct and indirect) attach to products, are known as **product costs** or **inventoriable costs**, and are not expensed until the goods are sold. All other non-production costs are known as **period costs** and are charged as expenses in the period in which they are incurred. Costs of production are accumulated in the Work-in-Process account(s), transferred to the Finished Goods account on completion, and then to the Cost of Goods Sold account on sale.

A manufacturing statement is the simplest method of determining the cost of completed goods transferred from the Work-in-Process account to the Finished Goods account. Its usefulness for determining unit product costs is limited, however, to the case of a single-product organisation.

*2/Product Costing: Terms and Cost Flows*

# APPENDIX

## Using a Spreadsheet for Manufacturing Statements

Although it is hardly a high-powered use of spreadsheets it is possible to use one for a manufacturing statement. Below is a printout of a spreadsheet model for Illustrative Example 2-1 in this chapter:

|    | A | B | C | D |
|---|---|---|---|---|
| 1 | CHAPTER 2: PRODUCT COSTING - MANUFACTURING STATEMENT | | | |
| 2 | | | | |
| 3 | **DATA** | | | |
| 4 | *Opening Balances for August 20X0* | $ | | |
| 5 | Raw Materials | 5,000 | | |
| 6 | Work-in-Process | 10,000 | | |
| 7 | Finished Goods | 20,000 | | |
| 8 | *Transactions during August 20X0* | | | |
| 9 | Raw materials purchased | 10,000 | | |
| 10 | Direct labour costs incurred | 20,000 | | |
| 11 | Factory supervision | 12,000 | | |
| 12 | Depreciation plant | 10,000 | | |
| 13 | Electricity and water | 5,000 | | |
| 14 | *Closing Balances for August 20X0* | | | |
| 15 | Raw Materials | 4,000 | | |
| 16 | Work-in-Process | 11,000 | | |
| 17 | Finished Goods | 18,000 | | |
| 18 | | | | |
| 19 | **MODEL** | | | |
| 20 | ACE MANUFACTURING COMPANY | | | |
| 21 | Manufacturing Statement for Month Ended | | | |
| 22 | 31 August 20X0 | | | |
| 23 | | | | |
| 24 | **Direct Materials** | $ | $ | |
| 25 | Raw Materials Inventory, 1 Aug 20X0 | 5,000 | | |
| 26 | Purchases Raw Materials | 10,000 | | |
| 27 | | 15,000 | | |
| 28 | *Less* Raw Materials Inventory, 31 Aug 20X0 | 4,000 | | |
| 29 | Raw Materials issued to Production | | 11,000 | |
| 30 | **Direct Labour** | | 20,000 | |
| 31 | **Prime Cost** | | 31,000 | |
| 32 | **Manufacturing Overhead** | | | |
| 33 | Factory supervision | 12,000 | | |
| 34 | Depreciation plant | 10,000 | | |
| 35 | Electricity and water | 5,000 | 27,000 | |
| 36 | *Current Production Costs* | | 58,000 | |
| 37 | *Add* Work in Process, 1 Aug 20X0 | | 10,000 | |
| 38 | | | 68,000 | |
| 39 | *Less* Work in Process, 31 Aug 20X0 | | 11,000 | |
| 40 | **Cost of Goods Manufactured** | | 57,000 | |

Note that the spreadsheet model is divided into two sections, first the data and then the model. It has been set up this way to illustrate how data can be accessed. This is a useful way of setting up models which will be used repeatedly for different sets of data, for then it is simply a matter of changing the data at the top of the model.

## 2/Product Costing: Terms and Cost Flows

A copy of this Excel spreadsheet model showing some of the formulae appears below. Open a new file in your spreadsheet and build this model. Wherever the word FORMULA appears you have to insert the appropriate formula to make the model work.

|    | A | B | C |
|----|---|---|---|
| 1  | CHAPTER 2: PRODUCT COSTING - MANUFA | | |
| 2  | | | |
| 3  | **DATA** | | |
| 4  | *Opening Balances for August 20X0* | $ | |
| 5  | Raw Materials | 5000 | |
| 6  | Work-in-Process | 10000 | |
| 7  | Finished Goods | 20000 | |
| 8  | *Transactions during August 20X0* | | |
| 9  | Raw materials purchased | 10000 | |
| 10 | Direct labour costs incurred | 20000 | |
| 11 | Factory supervision | 12000 | |
| 12 | Depreciation plant | 10000 | |
| 13 | Electricity and water | 5000 | |
| 14 | *Closing Balances for August 20X0* | | |
| 15 | Raw Materials | 4000 | |
| 16 | Work-in-Process | 11000 | |
| 17 | Finished Goods | 18000 | |
| 18 | | | |
| 19 | **MODEL** | | |
| 20 | ACE MANUFACTURIN | | |
| 21 | Manufacturing Statemei | | |
| 22 | 31 August 20X0 | | |
| 23 | | | |
| 24 | **Direct Materials** | $ | $ |
| 25 | Raw Materials Inventory, 1 Aug 20X0 | =B5 | |
| 26 | Purchases Raw Materials | =B9 | |
| 27 | | =SUM(B25:B26) | |
| 28 | *Less* Raw Materials Inventory, 31 Aug 20X0 | FORMULA | |
| 29 | Raw Materials issued to Production | | =B27-B28 |
| 30 | **Direct Labour** | | FORMULA |
| 31 | **Prime Cost** | | FORMULA |
| 32 | **Manufacturing Overhead** | | |
| 33 | Factory supervision | =B11 | |
| 34 | Depreciation plant | FORMULA | |
| 35 | Electricity and water | FORMULA | FORMULA |
| 36 | Current Production Costs | | FORMULA |
| 37 | *Add* Work in Process, 1 Aug 20X0 | | FORMULA |
| 38 | | | FORMULA |
| 39 | *Less* Work in Process, 31 Aug 20X0 | | FORMULA |
| 40 | **Cost of Goods Manufactured** | | FORMULA |

Note that when the formulae are displayed parts of the headings have been chopped off. When you have finished you should get the result on the previous page. Your model should be generalised so that if you change any data the model still works. Of course, if you insert additional transactions in the data fields you will have to amend the model accordingly.

Once your model is correct, add two rows to your model. The first should be labelled **Units produced** and the second **Unit Cost**. Then in column C for the first of these rows insert 1500 (units produced). That is, we will assume the company makes only one product. Underneath, insert a formula to calculate unit cost.

## 2/Product Costing: Terms and Cost Flows

When you have completed this exercise, try changing some of the opening or closing balances (Raw Materials or Work-in-Process or Finished Goods), and see how the Cost of Goods Manufactured and Unit Cost changes.

# QUESTIONS AND PROBLEMS

**2-1** What four purposes of product costing were identified in this chapter?

**2-2** Identify the three major cost elements in the cost of a product or service. Define each.

**2-3** Define **prime cost** and **conversion cost**.

**2-4** What is the major difference in operations between a retailer and a manufacturer? How is this reflected in a **Cost of Goods Sold** statement?

**2-5** What major difference would you expect to find in the balance sheets of retailers and manufacturers?

**2-6** Under what circumstances would prime cost calculated in a manufacturing statement be the same whether Work-in-Process balances were dissected or not?

**2-7** As the chief executive of an organisation manufacturing a wide range of small household electrical appliances, what purposes would you find for the information contained in a single manufacturing statement for your organisation? What other cost information, if any, would be useful, and for what purpose?

**2-8** Which of the following is incorrect?

(a) Direct materials + direct labour = prime cost
(b) Direct labour + manufacturing overhead = conversion cost
(c) Prime cost + conversion cost = cost of goods manufactured
(d) Cost of goods manufactured = direct labour + direct materials + manufacturing overhead
(e) Only one of the above is incorrect

**2-9 Manufacturing statement, work-in-process account**
Use the following information to answer the questions about XYZ Company:

|  | 1/7/X0 $ | 30/6/X1 $ |
|---|---|---|
| *Inventories* |  |  |
| Raw Materials | 1 000 | 950 |
| Work-in-Process | 750 | 1 000 |
| Finished Goods | 500 | 3 000 |
|  |  |  |
| *Costs incurred during year X0/X1* |  |  |
| Purchases of raw materials |  | 4 250 |
| Direct labour costs |  | 4 350 |
| Depreciation - plant and building |  | 450 |
| Insurance – Factory |  | 400 |
| Other factory expenses |  | 750 |

*Required:*

(a) Prepare a manufacturing statement for the period.
(b) Assuming that 1000 units were produced during the period, what was the cost of each unit?
(c) Draw a T-account for Work-in-Process and make the appropriate entries to reflect the year's activities.

## 2-10 Prepare a manufacturing statement

The following is an extract of debit balances ($'000) from the books of Gadgets Ltd as at 30 June, 20X1:

| | |
|---|---:|
| Administrative Expenses | 306 |
| Advertising | 5 189 |
| Bad Debts | 150 |
| Cartage Inwards | 4 063 |
| Depreciation on Plant | 1 257 |
| Discount Expense | 300 |
| Factory Expenses | 1 469 |
| Factory Rent | 924 |
| Machinery Maintenance | 1 529 |
| Materials Purchased | 64 270 |
| Office Rent | 200 |
| Office Salaries | 4 718 |
| Power and Fuel (factory) | 1 919 |
| Printing and Stationery | 880 |
| Raw Materials Inventory, 1 July, 20X0 | 12 000 |
| Wages - Direct | 19 828 |
| Wages - Indirect | 1 221 |
| Work-in-Process, 1 July, 20X0 | 8 444 |

The inventory of raw materials at 30 June, 20X1 was valued at $16 098.
The work in process at 30 June, 20X1 was valued at $9448.

*Required:*

Draft a suitable manufacturing statement to show the cost of goods manufactured for the year.

**2-11 Prepare manufacturing statement and statement of financial performance**

The following information has been obtained from the books of Bradman Manufacturing Co. Ltd at 30 September, 20X7:

| | | | |
|---|---|---|---|
| *Inventories, 30/9/X6:* | | | |
| Finished Goods | | | $250 000 |
| Raw Materials | | | 200 000 |
| Work in Process: | Material | 65 000 | |
| | Labour | 26 000 | |
| | Expense | 15 000 | 106 000 |
| *Inventories, 30/9/X7:* | | | |
| Finished Goods | | | 90 000 |
| Raw Materials | | | 70 000 |
| Work in Process: | Material | 26 000 | |
| | Labour | 12 000 | |
| | Expense | 7 000 | 45 000 |

| *Summary of transactions for year* | |
|---|---|
| Raw material purchases | 1 400 000 |
| Duty and Inward Charges on raw materials | 60 000 |
| Productive labour | 370 000 |
| Manufacturing expense | 190 000 |
| Sales of finished goods | 4 100 000 |
| Advertising | 30 000 |
| Audit Fee | 1 050 |
| Discounts to debtors | 7 200 |
| Discounts from creditors | 5 100 |
| Cartage Outwards | 17 000 |
| Insurance | 12 000 |
| Light and power (Office) | 20 000 |
| General Expenses | 23 000 |
| Rates | 24 000 |
| Salaries (Office) | 360 000 |
| Salaries (Factory) | 490 000 |
| Travellers' Commission | 110 000 |

Adjustments are to be made in respect of the following:

(a) Accrued expenses:
Salaries (Office) $1110, Salaries (Factory) $1700
(b) Insurance paid in advance, $200
(c) Provide for taxation liability for current year, $250 000
(d) Provision for depreciation of factory plant, $18 000
(e) Insurance and rates are to be apportioned three-quarters to the factory and one-quarter to the office.

*Required:*

(a) Prepare a manufacturing statement for the year.
(b) Prepare a statement of financial performance for the year.

## 2/Product Costing: Terms and Cost Flows

**2-12 Incomplete records – reconstruct accounts or manufacturing statement**

An auditor is trying to reconstruct some records for a client whose business premises were gutted by fire. Can you help the auditor by finding the unknown figures?

| | |
|---|---|
| Opening balance Finished Goods | $10 000 |
| Direct materials consumed in production | ? |
| Direct labour incurred | 16 000 |
| Manufacturing overhead | 9 000 |
| Cash paid to trade creditors | 13 000 |
| Sales | 50 000 |
| Opening balance Accounts Receivable | 4 000 |
| Closing balance Accounts Receivable | 6 000 |
| Opening balance Accounts Payable | 2 000 |
| Closing balance Accounts Payable | 4 000 |
| Cost of goods sold | ? |
| Opening balance Work-in-Process | 4 000 |
| Closing balance Work-in-Process | 5 000 |
| Closing balance Finished Goods | ? |
| Opening balance Raw Materials | 2 000 |
| Closing balance Raw Materials | 3 000 |
| Gross margin | 20 000 |

**2-13 Manufacturing statement**

From the Younger Manufacturing Company's adjusted trial balance as at 31 December, 20X1, the following account balances have been obtained:

| | |
|---|---|
| Raw Materials, 1 January, 20X1 | $75 000 |
| Work-in-Process, 1 January, 20X1 | 21 200 |
| Finished Goods, 1 January, 20X1 | 50 000 |
| Purchases | 198 000 |
| Purchases Returns and Allowances | 3 000 |
| Direct Labour | 125 000 |
| Indirect Labour | 40 000 |
| Heat, Light and Power | 35 000 |
| Insurance on Factory | 6 000 |
| Factory and Machine Maintenance | 8 000 |
| Factory Supplies | 6 000 |
| Depreciation  - Factory Building | 9 000 |
|                     - Equipment | 39 000 |
| Rates and Taxes on Factory | 3 600 |

In addition, raw materials costing $187 000 were used, the cost of goods manufactured for the year 20X1 was $440 000, and the cost of goods sold was $430 000.

*Required:*

(a) A statement of cost of goods manufactured for the year 20X1.
(b) Suppose that the equivalent of 200 000 units were produced. What was the unit cost of production?
(c) If production next year is predicted to be 150 000 units, would you expect the unit cost for the direct materials component to be the same next year (given no price changes)? Why?

Would you expect the unit cost for the depreciation components to be the same next year? (Assume depreciation is on a straight line basis.) Why?

### 2-14 Manufacturing statement and statement of financial performance

747 Productions operates an advertising agency. The data below is for the three months ended 31 March 20X1.

| | | |
|---|---:|---:|
| Billings to clients | | $248 000 |
| Commissions paid | | 20 000 |
| Sales salaries | | 30 000 |
| Delivery expenses | | 16 000 |
| Administrative salaries | | 40 000 |
| Materials purchased | | 87 000 |
| Production staff - artists | $16 000 | |
| - lithographers | 18 450 | |
| - printers | 19 240 | |
| - photographers | 17 380 | 71 070 |
| Miscellaneous studio costs | | 6 400 |
| Rent[1] | | 4 800 |
| Depreciation office equipment | | 2 900 |
| Depreciation production equipment | | 3 750 |
| Waxes, emulsions and lacquers | | 1 250 |
| Electric power [1] | | 600 |
| Materials 1.1.X1 | | 12 000 |
| Materials 31.3.X1 | | 11 500 |
| Production-in-process 1.1.X1 | | 37 300 |
| Production-in-process 31.3.X1 | | 29 950 |

[1] Is apportioned in the ratio 3:1 between the studio and the remaining activities.

*Required:*

(a) Classify each of the above items into the following categories:
 (i) revenue
 (ii) product costs
 (iii) period costs

(b) Prepare a manufacturing statement and a statement of financial performance for the three months ending 31 March, 20X1.

# Chapter 3

# Product Costing: Materials, Labour and Overhead

As discussed in Chapter 2, product (or service) costs represent the costs of resources consumed in production, and may be classified into three main cost elements, direct materials, direct labour and (manufacturing) overhead. In this chapter our concern is to understand how a product costing system[1] traces these costs from their incurrence in the production process to arrive at a unit cost for products or services.

Traditional product costing systems accumulate material, labour and overhead costs in a Work-in-Process account. As production is completed the costs of completed units is transferred from the Work-in-Process account to a Finished Goods account, and then to a Cost of Goods Sold account when invoiced to customers. Figure 3-1 illustrates the cost flows. At any time there will be balances in the three inventory accounts (double-outlined boxes) representing unused raw materials, unfinished work in process, and unsold finished goods.

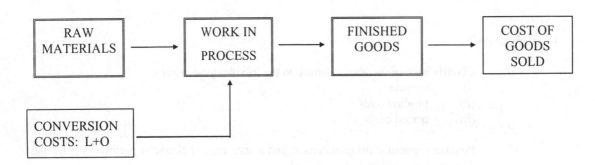

Figure 3-1: Traditional Product Costing System

Modern manufacturing systems may operate in what is termed a **just-in-time** (JIT) production environment where inventories are reduced to a minimum, or completely eliminated. JIT production is a demand-pull system whose objective is to produce a product only when needed, and only in the quantities demanded by customers. Ideally, in a JIT system, raw materials are delivered just in time to be incorporated in production, so that there are no unused raw materials on hand. There are no buffer inventories of work in process at or between each work station because production in a work station takes place only after a signal from a succeeding operation indicates the need to produce. There are no finished goods inventories because production only occurs when units are demanded by customers. In practice, rather than zero inventories, there is a tendency to hold some inventories, albeit at low levels. The JIT production system has resulted in some simplified product costing and recording processes. Many variants are possible, but one approach, known as **backflush costing**,[2] eliminates the inventory accounts, as in Figure 3-2.

---

[1] The term *product costing* is meant to imply the costing of units of manufactured products, or of services provided by a service organisation. Similarly, the term *product* includes services.

[2] See, for example, Foster and Horngren (1987, 1988).

Even backflush costing has a number of variants. A common version employs only one inventory account (Raw and In Process) as follows. Raw materials go directly to Raw-and-In-Process account, with conversion costs (direct labour and overhead) accumulated in a Conversion Cost account. These costs are progressively charged to Cost of Goods Sold account. At any point in time, when needed (e.g. at balance date), those costs contained in the Cost of Goods Sold account representing unsold finished goods can be *backflushed* to a Finished Goods account - that is, the Cost of Goods Sold balance is reduced to reflect the fact that not all output was actually sold during the period. Not everyone favours this approach which has been criticised by at least one group of authors as being nothing more than a "dressed-up version of the periodic system".[3]

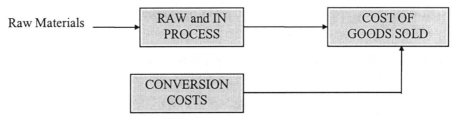

**Figure 3-2: JIT Product Costing System**

A more detailed treatment of JIT costing is found in Chapter 7. In the following descriptions of cost flows the traditional system will be described.

## MATERIALS

A cost accounting system traces the flow of materials through the stages of acquisition, storage and usage. Each of these is discussed in turn.

### *Acquisition of Materials*

As production (or service) departments require materials for particular orders (if producing to customer order) or for production batches (if producing for stock), an authorised departmental officer (e.g., supervisor or foreman) requests materials from the materials department by completing a **materials requisition**. The materials storekeeper will issue such materials from the store. As the inventory of each item of raw material runs low (reaches the reorder point) the storekeeper will prepare a **purchase requisition**, detailing the quantity of material required. Such quantity may be determined by the size of the materials requisition, or as a result of general purchasing policy in relation to that material item (e.g., it is bought in lots of 500 units).

The purchase requisition is forwarded to the purchasing department where a purchasing officer checks that the requisition has been approved by an authorised individual - this check is necessary to prevent employees ordering personal goods on the firm's account. Then the purchasing officer decides on the supplier with whom the order will be placed: either a regular supplier if it is a routine purchase, or as a result of requesting quotations if the purchase is unusual. The purchasing officer then completes a **purchase order** describing such details as material specifications, quantity, cost and date required. It is not uncommon to require that a purchase order should be approved by another authorised person so as to avoid conflicts of interest. Purchasing officers may be placed in a position in which they are tempted to accept gifts for placing orders with certain suppliers who may try to gain company business this way rather than through competitive pricing.

The purchase order is sent to the supplier, with copies to the receiving department and the accounting department. When the supplier delivers the goods the driver asks a receiving department officer to sign a **delivery docket**, acknowledging receipt of the quantities of goods mentioned. This document essentially provides evidence to the supplier that the goods were delivered and not stolen or otherwise disposed of. The receiving department counts and inspects all items received and prepares a **receiving report**, which may be simply their copy of the purchase order suitably annotated. The purpose of the receiving report is to ascertain that all goods ordered were received, and fixes responsibility for the quantity and condition of the goods received onto the receiving personnel.

---

[3]  See Calvasina, Calvasina and Calvasina (1989).

A **supplier's invoice** is sent to the organisation's accounting department for processing and payment. The accounting department should match the receiving report with the purchase order and the invoice before payment, and before recording the transaction: Dr Materials Control (increase in an asset) and Cr Accounts Payable if purchased on credit (increase in a liability) or Cr Bank if purchased for cash (decrease in an asset). A general journal entry would look like this:

| | | |
|---|---|---|
| Materials Control (or Raw Materials) | xxx | |
| Accounts Payable (or Bank) | | xxx |

The sum recorded should include any inward freight charges, etc. which add to the cost of the materials. In Australia the entry would be complicated by the need to account for GST – see Appendix A for an illustration.

The purchasing process described above may have many variants in practice, depending on the size of the organisation, documents used, and the particular control systems in place.

## Storage of Materials

Once the materials have been received it is necessary to protect them and facilitate access by means of adequate storage facilities. Such storage facilities should provide physical protection from the elements, where necessary. Manufacturing organisations have been known to leave raw materials or components exposed to the weather. Frequently this is of no consequence, but sometimes it leads to deterioration, necessitating restoration before use - this is costly, and may eventually reduce the life of the products in which such materials have been used. For example, steel products rust in the weather. In wire making from steel rods, the production process may include treatment of the rods to remove rust. Car companies in Australia have had to clean superficial rust from body panels before priming them with paint.

Adequate storage facilities also help to prevent loss by theft. Thus, some form of security system is desirable. Storage facilities should also provide for ease of subsequent location of individual items when required for production.

In addition to adequate storage facilities, control is also exercised through the use of Stores Ledger Cards which form a subsidiary ledger for the Materials Control account. Typically, a separate card or computer record (see Figure 3-3) is used for each item of material.

Item: _____

| Date | Received | | | Issued | | | Balance | | |
|---|---|---|---|---|---|---|---|---|---|
| | Qty | Unit Cost | Total Cost | Qty | Unit Cost | Total Cost | Qty | Unit Cost | Total Cost |
| | | | | | | | | | |
| | | | | | | | | | |

**Figure 3-3: Stores Ledger Card**

At the same time as an entry is made in the Materials Control account, entries are made in the corresponding stores ledger cards. For example, entries in **Received** column of stores ledger cards should total to debits in Materials Control, while entries in **Issued** column of stores ledger cards should equal credits in Materials Control.

The *quantities* shown in **Balance** column of stores ledger cards should agree with physical balances in the store.

## Issue of Materials

The document authorising the issue of materials is a Materials Requisition, properly authorised by, for example, a production foreman. A company would not want employees requisitioning materials for their own private use, hence the need for proper authorisation. The materials requisition usually shows the department requesting the material, and is the source document for recording the transfer of costs from Materials Control to Work-in-Process (if it is direct material) or to Overhead Control (if it is indirect material, or supplies). If $500 of raw materials were used in production and $50 of indirect material were requisitioned, the entries would be Dr Work-in-Process (increase in asset) and Overhead Control (increase in expense), Cr Materials Control (decrease in asset):

| Work-in-Process | $500 | |
| Overhead Control | $50 | |
| Materials Control (& stores ledger cards) | | $550 |

If excess materials were requisitioned and subsequently returned to the store they would be accompanied by a Return-to-Store Note, and a reversal of the above entry would be made in respect of the cost of materials returned.

## Stock Shortages

If a perpetual inventory system is used for raw materials, a physical stocktake should agree with stores ledger card balances for each item. If such comparisons reveal shortages, e.g. $10 shortage, the material balance must be amended:

| Inventory Shortage | $10 | |
| Materials Control (& stock ledger cards) | | $10 |

## Pricing Issues

As materials are acquired over time there is every chance that, for any particular item, supplies on hand may exceed any single order quantity, or may be a mix of units purchased at different prices (as prices change, usually upwards). Normally good inventory management dictates that the oldest stock should be used first, that is a FIFO (first-in-first-out) flow. This practice minimises problems of deterioration and changes in model or style, etc. It is not necessary, however, for materials to be **costed** on the same basis as the physical flow. Some argue that if the cost of manufacture is to reflect current prices, then a LIFO (last-in-first-out) **assumption** should be adopted. Other possibilities are to price issues at *weighted average cost* or at *standard cost*, or even at current replacement cost.

To illustrate, assume that a television manufacturer has, at 1 August, a supply of capacitors of 100 units purchased at $1 each. On 3 August a further 100 units were purchased, but the unit price had doubled to $2. On 5 August 150 capacitors were requisitioned to production. What cost should be charged to Work-in-Process (and transferred from Materials Control)?

Figure 3-4 shows two possibilities, using the FIFO and LIFO assumptions. Using FIFO it is assumed that the opening balance of 100 units @ $1 ($100) is issued first, and that the other 50 cost $2 each ($100), pricing the issue in total at $200, leaving a balance of 50 units @ $2 ($100). Alternatively, the LIFO approach assumes that the most recently acquired 100 units @ $2 ($200) are issued first and that the other 50 came from the opening balance @ $1 ($50), pricing the issue in total at $250, leaving a balance of 50 units @ $1 ($50).

As can be seen, the FIFO approach has led to cheaper production cost, but values the closing inventory of capacitors at current market price, whereas LIFO involved more current production cost but shows closing inventory at less than current market value. Another approach to changing prices might be to revalue inventory on hand to current replacement cost, and issue at that cost. On revaluation a holding gain would be recognised: debit Materials Control, and credit Holding Gain with the change in current replacement cost.

## Modern Variations

Traditionally organisations carried inventories of raw materials and component parts for a number of reasons:
- to ensure smooth production runs by having materials readily available
- as a safeguard against variability in raw material delivery time
- to take advantage of quantity discounts by buying in bulk
- as a hedge against future price increases

| Item: Capacitors | | | | | | | | | |
|---|---|---|---|---|---|---|---|---|---|
| Date | Received | | | Issued | | | Balance | | |
| | Qty | Unit Cost | Total Cost | Qty | Unit Cost | Total Cost | Qty | Unit Cost | Total Cost |
| Aug 1 | | | | | | | 100 | $1.00 | $100.00 |
| 3 | 100 | $2.00 | $200.00 | | | | 100 | $1.00 | $100.00 |
| | | | | | | | 100 | $2.00 | $200.00 |
| 5 | | FIFO | | 100 | $1.00 | $100.00 | | | |
| | | | | 50 | $2.00 | $100.00 | 50 | $2.00 | $100.00 |
| Or | | LIFO | | 100 | $2.00 | $200.00 | | | |
| | | | | 50 | $1.00 | $50.00 | 50 | $1.00 | $50.00 |

**Figure 3-4: Pricing Issues using FIFO and LIFO**

Modern organisations use JIT principles to achieve the same objectives without the need to carry inventories. They develop linkages with a selected, few suppliers. In order to foster mutual confidence and trust they negotiate long term contracts with these suppliers for the delivery of quality materials, at stipulated prices, and as needed. In technologically sophisticated situations, orders can be placed electronically via computer linkages. Such arrangements alter and simplify ordering and control procedures and reduce the need for large raw material storage facilities and associated labour.

## LABOUR

Accounting for labour is not as straightforward as for materials because of
(a) an obligation on the part of employers to make deductions from gross salaries and wages in respect of PAYG (pay as you go) taxation and other deductions authorised by the employee and agreed to by the employer - e.g., deductions for employee superannuation contributions, hospital insurance, union subscriptions and life insurance premiums; and
(b) the necessity for employers to provide for labour oncosts (sometimes called fringe benefits) in the form of sick leave, annual leave, long service leave, etc.

There are two aspects to recording labour costs:

(1) the recording of payments to employees for time worked, and
(2) the distribution of labour costs among activities.

To begin with, we shall ignore labour oncosts. Assume that the weekly payroll is as follows:

| | | $ |
|---|---|---|
| **Gross Payroll** | | |
| Factory direct labour | | 300 000 |
| Factory indirect labour | | 150 000 |
| Selling labour | | 200 000 |
| Administrative labour | | 100 000 |
| **Total** | | 750 000 |
| **Deductions**: | | |
| PAYG tax | | 200 000 |
| Superannuation | | |
| (employee contributions) | | 40 000 |
| Hospital insurance | | 5 000 |
| Union dues | | 5 000 |
| **Total** | | 250 000 |
| **Cash required** | | 500 000 |

## Payment of Labour

There are two source records on which payments are based. Human Resource records contain details of each employee's rate of pay, while some form of attendance record (e.g. bundy clock card) is evidence of hours actually at work.

The accounting entry to record weekly payments for labour would be:

| | | |
|---|---|---|
| Accrued Payroll (for gross pay) | $ 750 000 | |
| Bank (for net pay) | | $500 000 |
| PAYG Tax | | 200 000 |
| Superannuation Fund | | 40 000 |
| Hospital Insurance Funds | | 5 000 |
| Union | | 5 000 |

At agreed (or legislated) intervals the employer would pass on the deductions withheld from employees' pay to the relevant bodies. If this were done weekly (more likely monthly) the entry would be:

| | | |
|---|---|---|
| PAYG Tax | $200 000 | |
| Superannuation Fund | 40 000 | |
| Hospital Insurance Funds | 5 000 | |
| Union | 5 000 | |
| Bank | | $250 000 |

## Distribution of Labour Costs

At regular intervals, usually monthly, the gross labour costs incurred would be distributed to Work-in-Process (factory direct labour), Overhead Control (factory indirect labour), and to Selling and Administration expense accounts (other labour). While the dissection of labour costs into selling and administration is relatively straightforward, it is a more demanding task to separate factory labour costs into direct and indirect. As well as discriminating between those workers whose labour costs are normally classified as either direct or indirect, it is also necessary to examine direct labour workers' time records to dissect their time into direct and indirect labour categories, and to allocate direct labour time to jobs or processes. The data recorded on labour time records show the time spent on each job or process (direct labour), and any idle time or other time not spent working directly on the production of goods (indirect labour). Since all time should be accounted for and expensed, the total time recorded on time records should be reconcilable with attendance records, and forms the basis for control of labour costs.

Using the data for the weekly payroll in our example, the accounting entry to record the distribution of labour costs would be:

| | | |
|---|---|---|
| Work-in-Process | $300 000 | |
| Overhead Control | 150 000 | |
| Selling Expense | 200 000 | |
| Administration Expense | 100 000 | |
| Accrued Payroll | | $750 000 |

At any particular balance date the balance of Accrued Payroll should be equal to wages earned but unpaid (usually because balance date does not coincide with pay day). Thus at the end of a reporting period it becomes necessary to make a balance day adjustment. Suppose that at year end there are 2 days' labour costs earned but unpaid (i.e., 2/5 of the week's total). Then the required entry would be:

| | | |
|---|---|---|
| Work-in-Process | $120 000 | |
| Overhead Control | 60 000 | |
| Selling Expense | 80 000 | |
| Administration Expense | 40 000 | |
| Accrued Payroll | | $300 000 |

*3/Product Costing: Materials, Labour and Overhead*

## Overtime

Normal work time (usually 35 to 40 hours per week) is paid at normal award rates. Time worked in excess of normal time is called overtime, and is usually paid at overtime rates, e.g., normal time plus 50%, or normal time plus 100% or even more. The percentage loading for overtime is referred to as an overtime premium. It is customary, especially when the overall workload necessitates overtime hours, to debit Work-in-Process with the normal rate of pay for all hours worked, and charge (debit) Overhead Control with the overtime premium paid.

For example, suppose an employee works 50 hours (all direct labour) in one week, consisting of 40 hours at normal time, 4 hours at night at a premium of 50%, and 6 hours at the weekend at a premium of 100%. Assume the normal hourly rate of pay is $10. Then the employee would earn $580 calculated as follows:

```
40 hours @ $10 =   $400
 4 hours @  15 =     60
 6 hours @  20 =    120
    Total      =    580
```

The labour distribution would be:

```
Direct Labour:                    Indirect Labour:
50 hours @ $10 = $500             4 hours @ $ 5 = $20
                                  6 hours @  10 =  60
                         Total overtime premium   80
```

If, however, the overtime hours worked were at the request of a customer who was prepared to pay for overtime work for speedy completion of a particular job, then all $580 would be charged to Work-in-Process as direct labour.

## Labour Oncosts

The gross wages paid to employees when they are **actually working** is not the full cost of employing them. Employers have to meet a number of associated costs including payroll tax, annual leave and loading, sick leave, public holidays, long service leave, workers' compensation insurance and employer's superannuation contributions.

The cost of some of these may be relatively uncertain. For example, long service leave entitlements may accrue only after some prescribed minimum period of service, so that an employee must remain for that period to be eligible. Further, the exact cost of long service leave entitlements may be unpredictable because it will be based on future, unknown wage rates when the leave is taken (or cashed in on termination of employment). The size of labour oncosts may be substantial. Suppose an employee's award rate is $500 per week. Then the actual cost to the employer may be significantly larger. Consider the following:

```
Annual wages paid - 52 weeks @ $500                    $26 000
Annual leave loading - 17.5% x 4 weeks                     350
Total paid to employee                                  26 350
Pro-rated long service leave - 1/15 yrs x 13 wks x $500    433
                                                        26 783
Workers' compensation insurance - say 8% (x $26 783)     2 143
Superannuation contribution - say 9%(26 000+433)         2 379
                                                        31 305
Average annual weeks worked:
    Nominal                                                 52
    Less:  Annual leave              4
           Sick leave                2
           Public holidays           2                       8
                                                            44
Actual cost to employer: $31 305/44 = $711
```

We see that although the notional wage paid is $500 per week, with labour oncosts the actual cost to the employer is $711 per week. Thus labour oncosts, in this example, add about 42% to gross wages.

Ideally, labour oncosts should be provided for continuously as they are accrued, and charged to production at the same time (although of course there is some uncertainty involved, especially in the case of long service leave). Another consideration is whether labour oncosts in respect of direct labour workers should be treated as direct labour or as overhead. Since there is a causal link between the size of labour oncosts and direct labour hours worked, it may be argued that it is appropriate to record oncosts as a direct labour cost:

*As direct labour:*

| | | |
|---|---|---|
| Work-in-Process | $711 | |
| Accrued Payroll | | $500 |
| Provision for Annual Leave (4 wks*$500 + $350)/44 | | 53 |
| Provision for Long Service Leave (433/44) | | 10 |
| Provision for WCI (2143/44) | | 48 |
| Provision for Superannuation contributions (2379/44) | | 54 |
| Provision for Sick Leave (2 wks*500/44) | | 23 |
| Provision for Public Holidays (2 wks*500/44) | | 23 |

An alternative, perhaps less defensible but common approach, is to record them as overhead:

*As overhead:*

| | | |
|---|---|---|
| Work-in-Process | $500 | |
| Overhead Control | 211 | |
| Accrued Payroll | | $500 |
| Provision for Annual Leave | | 53 |
| Provision for Long Service Leave | | 10 |
| Provision for WCI | | 48 |
| Provision for Superannuation contributions | | 54 |
| Provision for Sick Leave | | 23 |
| Provision for Public Holidays | | 23 |

Then, when the employee actually takes up an entitlement, such as annual leave, the entries would be:

| | | |
|---|---|---|
| Provision for Annual Leave | $2 350 | |
| Accrued Payroll | | $2 350 |
| | | |
| Accrued Payroll | $2 350 | |
| Bank | | $2 350 |

The last entry above has ignored the PAYG tax which would be deducted when the employee is paid for annual leave; i.e. the employee would not receive the full $2350.

Some organisations delay recognition of many labour oncosts until they are actually paid, an undesirable practice. Others recognise these expenses when they pay them, but make adjustments at balance date to give recognition to accrued obligations. These days, with computerised payroll packages, there is no excuse for failing to continuously accrue provisions for oncosts.

## OVERHEAD

Overhead comprises all production (or service) costs other than direct materials, direct expense, or direct labour. Overhead has some unique characteristics which differentiate it from direct materials and direct labour, and result in different accounting treatment. First, by definition, overhead consists of those costs which cannot be traced directly to products. Second, total overhead that should be allocated to production during an accounting period may not be known until the end of the period, long after some of the production has been completed and sold. Finally, overhead may fluctuate considerably from month to month because of factors other than production volume.

3/Product Costing: Materials, Labour and Overhead

There are two basic problems to solve with overhead:

(1) how to exercise control over overhead costs; and
(2) how to allocate to products their fair share of overhead costs.

## Control Procedures

In general, overhead costs are controlled through the use of budgets and responsibility centres. Budgets contain estimates of what cost levels should be attained in a period. Each person responsible for controlling the activities of a department or cost centre in an organisation will be held responsible for controlling the costs which (s)he can influence, and for ensuring that actual costs incurred meet budget.

Some overhead costs are uniquely associated with particular cost centres or departments, for example, the cost of setting up machines in a production department. Therefore people in charge of these centres are held responsible for containing these costs within their budgets.

Other overhead costs are common to a number of segments and are more difficult to control because of divided responsibility for their incurrence. For example, the costs incurred by a repairs and maintenance department depend, not only on decisions by the head of that department, but also on the amount of service requested or demanded by other departments, say a production department supervisor.

Employing these ideas, every overhead cost item has to be associated with one or more responsibility centre, so that somebody is charged with the duty of controlling each and every overhead cost item. The costs thus collected in a responsibility centre are known as a **cost pool**, see Figure 3-5.

**Figure 3-5: Overhead Cost Pool**

Some of these responsibility centres are centres (or departments) in which actual production takes place, i.e. they are **production** cost centres (or departments). Others are centres which simply provide support to the production function, and are known as **support service** cost centres (or sometimes simply service departments). For product costing purposes it is necessary to allocate to production all overheads: that portion of those costs associated with production centres and which are identified as overhead, as well as all costs associated with service centres. To achieve this, each of the overhead cost pools in support service centres are first transferred (or allocated) to production cost centre overhead pools. When all overheads are thus gathered in appropriate pools in production cost centres they are then allocated to products which pass through the production centres.

## Allocating Overhead to Products or Services

In order to get a reasonable statement of the cost of each unit produced or of each service provided, it is necessary to allocate all overhead to products on some suitable basis. There is no precise or accurate means of doing so, but every endeavour should be made to allocate overhead in accordance with the relative consumption of overhead services by individual products. The ideal is to establish the cause of the level of overhead costs incurred. There may be one or more causal factors **driving** overhead costs. We refer to these causal factors as **cost drivers**, i.e. the activities which drive such costs. For example, overhead costs may be driven by the number of machine hours worked, and hence the amount of overhead allocated to a unit of product would depend on the number of machine hours consumed in producing one unit of that product.

In the past, fairly simplistic allocation procedures were adopted, using a single allocation base, or very few bases, such as direct labour hours or direct labour cost in labour-intensive production departments, or machine hours in machine-intensive processes. Thus, if a factory worked 100 000 direct labour hours, and wished to allocate $200 000 overhead on the basis of direct labour hours worked, the overhead allocation rate[4] would be $200 000/100 000 DLH = $2 per direct labour hour (DLH). Then, if a unit of product required 3 direct labour hours, the overhead cost allocated to each unit would be 3 x $2 = $6. Such procedures worked well enough when materials and labour made up the greatest proportion of unit product cost and overheads were only a minor portion of product cost. These days, many production processes are machine-intensive, employing robotics and computer-integrated manufacturing methods. Consequently, direct labour is often only a minor proportion of product cost, while overhead costs have increased dramatically. Because overhead costs often represent a much larger, perhaps the largest proportion of total product cost, it is desirable to improve the methods of allocating overhead to products by seeking appropriate cost drivers which better reflect the actual pattern of resource consumption by products.

## **Actual** Overhead Allocation Rates

One way of allocating overhead to production is to wait until the end of a period, say a month, to find out what overhead costs have been incurred, and then allocate these to production. For example, suppose that at the end of the period we find that the **actual** overhead costs incurred were $315 000 in a factory and that the cost driver is direct labour hours; and that 90 000 direct labour hours were worked during the period. Therefore the accounting entry to record the actual overhead would be:

| | | |
|---|---|---|
| Overhead Control | $315 000 | |
| Sundry Accounts | | $315 000 |

The actual overhead allocation rate, which is determined at the end of the period, is calculated from $315 000/90 000 DLH, that is $3.50 per DLH. The appropriate accounting entry to allocate overhead to production would be:

| | | |
|---|---|---|
| Work-in-Process (90 000 DLH @ $3.50) | $315 000 | |
| Overhead Control | | $315 000 |

The problem with using an actual overhead allocation rate is that it is impossible to determine the rate, and hence the unit cost of production, until the end of the period. If the organisation is using *cost plus* pricing it cannot determine the cost of work for customers until the period is finished, and quoting of prices might be difficult. A further problem is that product costs would tend to vary inversely with the level of productive activity, because many overhead costs are fixed costs in the short term; in periods of low activity these fixed costs are spread over a lower number of direct labour or machine hours etc., and units produced in this period experience higher unit fixed overhead costs. Finally, overhead costs can vary seasonally, or even month to month, resulting in fluctuating product costs for identical volumes of production in different months.

## **Predetermined** Overhead Allocation Rates

The solution to the problem of using actual overhead rates is to **predict** the expected rate over a period long enough to avoid short term fluctuations (usually a year), and use this predetermined rate to cost production. Rather than calculate the **actual** allocation rate, what is required is an estimate of overhead and of the cost driver activity level to compute a **predetermined** rate. The predetermined rate is then used to cost production. To illustrate, we continue with the example. Suppose that the normal level of activity for the factory is 100 000 direct labour hours per period, that this is our best estimate of cost driver activity level, and that the budgeted **overhead** costs for the period are:

| | |
|---|---|
| Budgeted fixed overhead | $200 000 |
| Budgeted variable overhead | $1 per DLH |

Thus the total budgeted overhead for the period is:

$200 000 + (100 000 DLH x $1 per DLH) = $300 000.

---

[4] Other terms which are used are **overhead recovery rate** and **overhead application rate**. Thus we speak of overhead being allocated or recovered or applied. The preferred term is **allocated**, so that we say **overhead allocation rate**.

At the beginning of the period a predetermined overhead allocation rate is calculated using predicted overhead costs and predicted cost driver activity level:

$$\text{Predetermined overhead rate} = \frac{\text{Budgeted Overhead}}{\text{Budgeted DLH}}$$

$$= \frac{\$300\,000}{100\,000 \text{ DLH}}$$

$$= \$3 \text{ per DLH.}$$

Overhead would then be allocated to units of product throughout the period, based on their consumption of direct labour hours, at the rate of $3 per DLH. Given that 90 000 DLH were worked, the overhead allocated would be $270 000 (90 000 @ $3), somewhat less than the actual overhead costs incurred, $315 000 (from the previous page).

When we use predetermined overhead rates it is useful to use two accounts, one for actual overhead incurred (Overhead Control), and the other for overhead allocated to production (Overhead Allocated). Using this approach, the accounting entries in total for the period are equivalent to:

| | | |
|---|---|---|
| Overhead Control | $315 000 | |
|     Sundry accounts | | $315 000 |
| (Actual overhead incurred) | | |
| | | |
| Work-in-Process (90 000 DLH @ $3) | $270 000 | |
|     Overhead Allocated | | $270 000 |
| (Overhead allocated to production) | | |

The use of a predetermined rate overcomes the problems of timeliness, and short term fluctuations in product cost, but provides an additional problem of what to do when, at the end of the period, the actual overhead incurred does not match the sum allocated to production via the predetermined rate. In this example, only $270 000 has been allocated to production, while the actual overhead incurred was $315 000, a variance (difference) of $45 000. Thus overhead has been under-allocated by $45 000. This variance has two components: (1) $15 000 because actual overhead of $315 000 exceeded budgeted overhead of $300 000; and (2) $30 000 because the actual DLH were only 90 000 instead of the 100 000 predicted at the normal level: 10 000 hours difference @ $3 per DLH.

Actual overhead has been accumulated on the debit side of the of the Overhead Control account, and the allocated overhead has been accumulated on the credit side of the Overhead Allocated account:

| Overhead Control | | Overhead Allocated | |
|---|---|---|---|
| Sundry a/cs 315 000 | | | WIP 270 000 |

At the end of the period the Overhead Allocated account is closed off by transferring its balance to the Overhead Control account:

| | | |
|---|---|---|
| Overhead Allocated | $270 000 | |
|     Overhead Control | | $270 000 |

| Overhead Control | | Overhead Allocated | |
|---|---|---|---|
| Sundry a/cs 315 000 | O/H Allocated 270 000 | O/H Control <u>270 000</u> | WIP <u>270 000</u> |

The difference between the two sides of the Overhead Control account can then be transferred to a variance account:

| | | |
|---|---|---|
| Overhead Variance | $45 000 | |
| Overhead Control | | $45 000 |

| Overhead Control | Overhead Variance |
|---|---|
| Sundry a/cs 315 000 \| O/H Allocated 270 000<br>\| O/H Variance 45 000 | O/H Control 45 000 \| |

Finally, this variance is usually disposed of. In this case, we have failed to allocate all the actual overhead by $45 000. With the benefit of hindsight, we see that the allocated overhead rate needed to be increased by $0.50 per DLH ($45 000/90 000 DLH). If all units produced were sold, the easiest solution would be to adjust the Cost of Goods Sold account:

| | | |
|---|---|---|
| Cost of Goods Sold | $45 000 | |
| Overhead Variance | | $45 000 |

| Cost of Goods Sold | Overhead Variance |
|---|---|
| O/H Variance 45 000 \| | O/H Control 45 000 \| COGS 45 000 |

Even if all production were not sold, provided the variance is relatively small (say less than 10% of the total overhead incurred), it would still be disposed of by writing off to (adjusting) Cost of Goods Sold. If the variance is relatively large, it may be **prorated** over Work-in-Process, Finished Goods and Cost of Goods Sold, on the grounds that all three accounts have been under-costed. Proration consists of apportioning the variance in proportion to (a) the allocated overhead component of the three accounts (preferred method), or (b) the unadjusted closing balances of the three accounts (suitable when the overhead is a constant proportion of total cost of all production). For example:

| | | |
|---|---|---|
| Work-in-Process | $5 000 | |
| Finished Goods | 10 000 | |
| Cost of Goods Sold | 30 000 | |
| Overhead Variance | | $45 000 |

The fundamental objective in prorating the overhead variance is to obtain a more accurate measure of the costs of work in process, finished goods and cost of goods sold. Nevertheless, proration is usually only undertaken when failure to do so would materially affect inventory valuations; the usual course is to just write off the whole variance to Cost of Goods Sold.

## Capacity Concepts

In our example above, although the budgeted overhead for the period was $300 000, the overhead allocated was only $270 000. The reason that the whole $300 000 was not allocated is that the predicted 100 000 DLH level of activity was not realised. If different denominator levels of cost driver activity are used in calculating a predetermined overhead rate, the resulting rates will differ. We can express the denominator level of activity in terms of a particular measure of capacity. Common measures of capacity are:

**Theoretical capacity** (or maximum capacity) which assumes production occurs 100% of the time, with no allowances for breakdowns, maintenance or idle time; this is clearly unachievable, except perhaps for short periods.

**Practical capacity**, a more realistic level, which deducts from theoretical capacity allowances for unavoidable interruptions, such as maintenance or repair time; it is the maximum level of efficient operations.

**Normal capacity** which represents a long run average operating level over a number of years, e.g. 5 years.

**Expected annual capacity** which is the anticipated level for the coming year.

The use of different capacity measures will result in different predetermined overhead rates because the budgeted **fixed** overhead will be spread over different denominator levels of activity. In developing cost data for product-related decisions (pricing, product mix) it is important that an appropriate capacity measure is used in calculating the overhead rate, and hence product cost.

It may be argued that product costs should include only those costs that are reasonably necessary to manufacture the product. Any costs arising from the existence of excess capacity from over-investment in manufacturing facilities should be excluded. Therefore the appropriate capacity measure is practical capacity. Anything less than practical capacity as a denominator in calculating a predetermined overhead rate would result in allocating to products an excessive share of capacity costs. Organisations which can more closely match their capacity to their requirements and avoid idle capacity costs will have lower product costs, and be able to compete at a lower selling price. Therefore the use of a denominator activity level which is less than the engineered (practical) capacity of a facility will be inappropriate when pricing products in competition with efficient manufacturers.

We now examine in more detail how predetermined overhead rates may be determined.

## Cost Pools, Cost Drivers and Overhead Allocation Rates

### A Simple Case: One Allocation Rate

One of the simplest situations occurs when there is only one production cost centre (or department, or process) through which all products pass. In such a situation, all budgeted overhead costs are collected into one or more cost pools within the production department and predetermined overhead allocation rates are calculated using the appropriate cost drivers. In the extreme, if only a single allocation rate is used, it is simply a matter of transferring all budgeted overhead costs from the various responsibility centres to the production centre, into a single cost pool. A predetermined overhead allocation rate is calculated by dividing the total pool by the estimated cost driver activity level. Then overhead is allocated to production using this rate, which is called a **plant-wide rate** because it is a single rate for the whole plant.

Even when there is more than one production department it may be legitimate, under certain conditions, to use a single, plant-wide rate.

### *Illustrative Example 3-1*

*ABC Manufacturing Company produces two products, A and B, in two production departments, $P_1$ and $P_2$. It is believed that overhead costs are driven by two separate cost drivers, machine hours in $P_1$ and direct labour hours in $P_2$. The number of direct labour hours and machine hours required to process a unit of each product in each department are as follows:*

| Production Department | Product A DLH[1] | Product A MH[2] | Product B DLH | Product B MH |
|---|---|---|---|---|
| $P_1$ | 5 | 1 | 4 | ½ |
| $P_2$ | 2 | ½ | 4 | 1 |
| Total | 7 | 1½ | 8 | 1½ |

1. DLH = Direct Labour Hours    2. MH = Machine Hours

*For the coming year the budgeted overhead is $300 000, and it is expected that 6000 units of product A and 2000 units of product B will be produced.*

For simplicity, it has been decided that direct labour hours will be used as the cost driver for overhead allocation purposes, that expected annual capacity will be used in the denominator, and that a single, plant-wide rate is appropriate.

Thus, budgeted activity level (expected annual capacity) in DLH

$$= 6000 \times 7 \text{ DLH} + 2000 \times 8 \text{ DLH}$$
$$= 58\,000 \text{ DLH}.$$

The predetermined overhead rate $= \dfrac{\text{Budgeted Overhead}}{\text{Budgeted DLH}}$

$= \dfrac{\$300\,000}{58\,000 \text{ DLH}}$

$= \$5.17$ per DLH.

Then the overhead allocated to each product would be:

> Product A: 7 DLH x $5.17 = $36.19
> Product B: 8 DLH x $5.17 = $41.36

## Separate Allocation Rates for Each Department

Suppose that instead of a single cost driver and a single plant-wide rate, a separate allocation rate, reflecting the appropriate cost driver, is used in each department, viz, machine hours in department $P_1$ and direct labour hours in department $P_2$. This approach is sometimes described as the use of **departmental rates** as opposed to a **plant-wide rate**.

The budgeted overhead costs must be gathered into two cost pools, one in each production department. Suppose the $300 000 consists of $210 000 in department $P_1$ and $90 000 in $P_2$. Budgeted cost driver activity levels (expected annual capacity) are 6000 x 1 MH + 2000 x ½ MH = 7000 MH in $P_1$ and 6000 x 2 DLH + 2000 x 4 DLH = 20 000 DLH in $P_2$. The predetermined overhead rates are then calculated as follows:

|  | $P_1$ | $P_2$ |
|---|---|---|
| Budgeted overhead cost (pool): | $210 000 | $90 000 |
| Budgeted cost driver activity level: | 7000 MH | 20 000 DLH |
| Predetermined overhead rates: | $\dfrac{\$210\,000}{7000 \text{ MH}}$ | $\dfrac{\$90\,000}{20\,000 \text{ DLH}}$ |
|  | = $30 / MH | = $4.50 / DLH |

The overhead allocated to each product is then:

> A: 1 MH x $30 + 2 DLH x $4.50 = $30 + $9 = $39
> B: ½ MH x $30 + 4 DLH x $4.50 = $15 + $18 = $33

If we look back at the data in Example 3-1 we note that in $P_2$ the ratio of DLH to MH is the same for each product: 2:½ (=4:1) for Product A and 4:1 for Product B. This tells us that we could have used MH instead of DLH as a cost driver for the $P_2$ cost pool:

Overhead rate $= \dfrac{\$90\,000}{5000 \text{ MH}} = \$18$ per MH

Then the overhead allocated to each product would be calculated:

> A: 1 MH x $30 + ½ MH x $18 = $30 + $9 = $39
> B: ½ MH x $30 + 1 MH x $18 = $15 + $18 = $33

This gives the same product costs as above using DLH as the cost driver in department $P_2$ because the DLH and MH usage is correlated in department $P_2$. Note, however, that although MH is used as the cost driver in each department, it was still necessary to have separate departmental rates. It would not be correct to use a single pool of overhead costs and a plant-wide rate based on MH because this would have under-costed product A and over-costed product B by allocating $37.50 overhead to each product [1½ MH x ($300 000/12 000 MH)]. The reason for this is that the products do not consume machine resources in the same ratio **across** departments: product A consumes MH in the ratio 1:½ across departments $P_1$ and $P_2$ while product B consumes MH in the ratio ½:1. It is clear that A consumes proportionately more machine hours in the expensive department $P_1$ ($210 000) while B consumes proportionately more machine hours in the cheap department $P_2$ ($90 000), and hence A should bear a larger overhead cost. If you wish to check this type of analysis, assume that instead of ½ MH, product B requires 2 MH in $P_1$, and thus the ratio of MH consumption for B is 2:1 across departments, the same ratio as A. Then recalculate separate departmental rates using MH as the cost driver, and compare with a plant-wide rate also using MH as the cost driver. Now they should result in the same answer, because the ratio of MH across departments is the same for both products.

Thus we can establish two basic rules in overhead allocation (when expected annual capacity is used in the denominator):

1. **Within** a given production cost centre it does not matter which of several cost drivers is used to allocate overhead to products **if all products consume these cost drivers in a constant ratio** (that is, cost driver consumption is correlated across products).

    Identification of those cost drivers which are consumed by all products in a constant ratio within a production cost centre allows multiple overhead cost pools (using different cost drivers) to be amalgamated into a single cost pool which is allocated to products using a single allocation base.

2. **Across** production cost centres whose overhead cost pools are driven by the same cost driver, separate cost centre (departmental) rates must be used **unless all products consume the cost driver in a constant ratio in every cost centre**.

    Identification of a cost driver which is consumed by all products in a constant ratio across production cost centres permits the amalgamation of multiple cost centre overhead cost pools into a single cost pool and substitution of a plant-wide rate for separate departmental rates. Such a situation would be a rare event.

## Two Stage Allocation

In Example 3-1 the total budgeted overhead was $300 000. It was further assumed that $210 000 was associated with production department $P_1$ and $90 000 with $P_2$. In fact, the total overhead of $300 000 represents budgeted overhead directly associated with production cost centres plus a share of overhead associated with support services. The allocation of support services costs to production cost centres is the focus of this section. When separate departmental overhead rates are used it is first necessary to allocate support service costs to production cost centres (first stage) before then allocating all overhead to products (second stage).

### *Illustrative Example 3-2*

*Furthering illustrative example 3-1, suppose that there are two support service centres, $S_1$ and $S_2$ providing support to $P_1$ and $P_2$. The total overhead of $300 000 was first associated with these responsibility centres as shown in Table 3-1.*

| Costs | $S_1$ | $S_2$ | $P_1$ | $P_2$ | Total |
|---|---|---|---|---|---|
| Supervision |  |  | 30 000 | 25 000 | $ 55 000 |
| Other indirect labour | 30 000 | 55 000 |  |  | $ 85 000 |
| Depreciation |  |  | 60 000 | 20 000 | $ 80 000 |
| Electricity | 10 000 | 5 000 | 10 000 | 5 000 | $ 30 000 |
| Receiving | 30 000 |  |  |  | $ 30 000 |
| Shipping | 20 000 |  |  |  | $ 20 000 |
| Total | $90 000 | $60 000 | $100 000 | $50 000 | $300 000 |

**Table 3-1: Overhead Costs by Departments**

In order to allocate the support service centre costs of $90 000 in $S_1$ and $60 000 in $S_2$ to production cost centres it is necessary to establish the appropriate cost driver for each service centre's costs, and the relative consumption of each cost driver by each production department. Remember, the cost driver drives the level of costs, and hence relative consumption of a cost driver (e.g., direct labour hours, machine hours etc.) represents a measure of the relative cost incurred.

Suppose that we have converted the consumption of service centre resources to percentages, and thus we can summarise the relative consumption of support services by the matrix expressed in percentages, in Table 3-2. In this conversion process we ignore a service centre's consumption of its own services, and thus zeros are shown at the intersection of $S_1$ row and $S_1$ column, and $S_2$ row and $S_2$ column. To illustrate, suppose the cost driver for $S_1$ was kg of material consumed, the consumption data being 2000 kg by $S_1$, 9500 kg by $S_2$, 31 500 kg by $P_1$ and 9000 kg by $P_2$. Ignoring the 2000 kg consumed by itself, other centres' consumption totals 50 000 kg. Thus $S_2$ consumes 9500/50 000 = 19%, $P_1$ consumes 31 500/50 000 = 63%, and $P_2$ consumes 9000/50 000 = 18%. A similar conversion to percentages was performed for services supplied by $S_2$, using number of employees in each department as the cost driver, 5 employees in $S_1$, 10 in $S_2$, 30 in $P_1$ and 15 in $P_2$, a total of 60 employees. Ignoring the 10 employees in $S_2$ leaves a total of 50 employees. Thus $S_1$ consumes 5/50 = 10% of $S_2$'s service, $P_1$ consumes 30/50 = 60% and $P_2$ consumes 15/50 = 30%.

|  |  | \multicolumn{5}{c}{Service Consumed By:} |
|---|---|---|---|---|---|---|
| Service Supplied By: |  | $S_1$ | $S_2$ | $P_1$ | $P_2$ | Total |
|  | $S_1$ | 0 | 19 | 63 | 18 | 100 |
|  | $S_2$ | 10 | 0 | 60 | 30 | 100 |

**Table 3-2: Percentage Consumption of Support Services**

Reading across the rows indicates how a support service centre's services are supplied to other centres. For example, 10% of $S_2$'s services are supplied to $S_1$, 60% supplied to $P_1$ and 30% supplied to $P_2$. Alternatively, reading down the columns indicates how each cost centre consumes support services. $P_1$ consumes 63% of $S_1$'s services and 60% of $S_2$'s services.

There are at least three conventional methods for allocating support centre costs to production centres, the **direct** method, the **step** method and the **reciprocal services** method. Each is illustrated in turn using manual calculations. Appendix B shows an Excel spreadsheet model to solve this example.

## Direct Method

The direct method is the simplest of the three. It ignores the fact that support services may be consumed by other service centres. It is assumed that only the production centres consume support services, whereas in reality support services are frequently provided to other support service centres as well as to production centres. In Table 3-3 the first line labelled "Overhead costs" shows the overhead cost pools by department as depicted in the bottom row of Table 3-1. In the second row of Table 3-3 we re-allocate $S_1$ costs of $90 000. First, we credit the $S_1$ account with its total cost (credits are in parentheses) and debit the $P_1$ and $P_2$ accounts - that is, we transfer the $90 000 from $S_1$ to $P_1$ and $P_2$. We see from Table 3-2 that $P_1$ consumes 63% of $S_1$'s services and $P_2$ consumes 18% of $S_1$'s services. Hence we allocate 63/(63+18) or 7/9 of $S_1$'s costs to $P_1$ (7/9x90 000=70 000) and 2/9 to $P_2$ (2/9x90 000=20 000). Similarly, in the third row we allocate 60/(60+30) or 6/9 of $S_2$'s costs to $P_1$ (6/9x60 000=40 000) and 3/9 to $P_2$ (3/9x60 000=20 000). Row and column totals are calculated. Note that all the overhead costs have now been pooled in the two production departments.

|  | $S_1$ | $S_2$ | $P_1$ | $P_2$ | TOTAL |
|---|---|---|---|---|---|
| Overhead costs | 90 000 | 60 000 | 100 000 | 50 000 | 300 000 |
| Reallocate $S_1$ | (90 000) | 0 | 70 000 | 20 000 | 0 |
| Reallocate $S_2$ | 0 | (60 000) | 40 000 | 20 000 | 0 |
|  | 0 | 0 | 210 000 | 90 000 | 300 000 |

**Table 3-3: Direct Method of Allocation**

Clearly it was the direct method which was used to allocate the overhead costs of $300 000 to each production cost centre in Illustrative Example 3-1, giving $210 000 in $P_1$ and $90 000 in $P_2$.

We have now completed the first stage of the two stage allocation process by allocating service department costs to production departments. The second stage involves allocating these overhead costs, now accumulated in the production centre cost pools, to the products using separate departmental rates. Using the same cost drivers of MH in $P_1$ and DLH in $P_2$, the overhead rates would be:

$P_1$: $210 000 / 7000 MH = $30 per MH
$P_2$: $ 90 000 / 20 000 DLH = $4.50 per DLH

Then the overhead allocated to each product would be:

A: 1 MH x $30 + 2 DLH x $4.50 = $30 + $9 = $39
B: ½ MH x $30 + 4 DLH x $4.50 = $15 + $18 = $33

These results, of course, are the same as those in Example 3-1.

## Step Method

A major criticism of the direct method of allocation is that it completely ignores any services rendered by one service centre to another. It is not uncommon for service centres to provide service to other service centres. For example, a building maintenance centre would provide service to a materials handling centre, or a staff cafeteria would provide service to repairs and maintenance centre employees.

The step (or step-down) method gives partial recognition to such reciprocal services in a sequence of allocations. The order of allocation determines which service centre interrelationships will be recognised and which will not, so that the outcome is problematic.

The basic approach is to select a service centre to begin with, and to allocate its costs to all other centres (production and service) to which it provides service. On the second round, another service centre's costs (augmented by any costs allocated to it from the first round) are allocated to all other departments **excluding** the previous service centre whose costs have already been distributed. And so the process continues until all service centres' costs have been redistributed. The general rule is that once a service centre's costs have been distributed, no further allocations are made to that centre. All that remains then is to determine the order of allocation of service centre costs.

Various rules have been suggested for determining the sequence of allocations, based either on measures of quantity of service supplied to other service centres, or on the size of the service centres' costs, or both. One such rule which we shall follow is to allocate in order of percentage of service given to other service centres; start with the centre which renders the highest percentage of its total services to other **service** centres, and end with the centre which renders the lowest percentage of its total services to other service centres. If there is a tie at any selection point, then select the centre with the highest level of costs to be distributed.

Following this rule, we have to choose between $S_1$ and $S_2$ to commence the sequence. From Table 3-2 $S_1$ is selected because 19% of its service is provided to $S_2$, whereas only 10% of $S_2$'s service is provided to $S_1$. Hence, from Table 3-2, 19% of $90 000 ($17 100) goes to $S_2$, 63% of $90 000 ($56 700) goes to $P_1$ and 18% of $90 000 ($16 200) goes to $P_2$.

Then $S_2$'s costs of $77 100, the original $60 000 plus the allocation of $17 100 from $S_1$, are allocated. Since $S_1$ has already been allocated we do not further allocate to it. But $P_1$'s 60% plus $P_2$'s 30% do not add to 100%. So we allocate in their proportions: 60/(60+30) or 2/3 to $P_1$ (2/3x77 100 = 51 400) and 1/3 to $P_2$ (1/3x77 100=25 700). The allocations are shown in Table 3-4.

|  | $S_1$ | $S_2$ | $P_1$ | $P_2$ | TOTAL |
|---|---|---|---|---|---|
| Overhead costs | 90 000 | 60 000 | 100 000 | 50 000 | 300 000 |
| Reallocate $S_1$ | (90 000) | 17 100 | 56 700 | 16 200 | 0 |
| Reallocate $S_2$ | 0 | (77 100) | 51 400 | 25 700 | 0 |
|  | 0 | 0 | 208 100 | 91 900 | 300 000 |

**Table 3-4: Step Method of Allocation**

The second stage allocation would be as follows:

$P_1$: $208 100 / 7000 MH = $29.73 per MH (rounded to 2 decimal places)
$P_2$: $ 91 900 / 20 000 DLH = $4.60 per DLH

Then the overhead allocated to each product would be (calculations not rounded but display is):

| |
|---|
| A: 1 MH x $29.73 + 2 DLH x $4.60 = $29.73 + $9.19 = $38.92 |
| B: ½ MH x $29.73 + 4 DLH x $4.60 = $14.86 + $18.38 = $33.24 |

## Reciprocal Services Method

Although the step method gives some recognition to reciprocal services it does not take complete account of them because once a service centre's costs have been distributed no other service centre's costs are distributed to it. A more complete reflection of inter-service centre activity is provided by the reciprocal services method. This technique uses simultaneous equations, or more generally, matrix algebra to solve the allocation problem.

Referring again to Table 3-2, and reading down the first two columns, we see that $S_1$ receives 10% of $S_2$'s service and $S_2$ receives 19% of $S_1$'s service. Hence the costs to be distributed from $S_1$ and $S_2$ to $P_1$ and $P_2$ will be calculated as follows:

$$S_1 = 90\,000 + 0.1S_2$$
$$S_2 = 60\,000 + 0.19S_1$$

Note that $S_1$ and $S_2$ will both total more than the original $90 000 and $60 000 because they will include a share of each other's costs. We have only two equations with two unknowns which can be easily solved by substitution as shown below. Matrix algebra is a more general method for solving for any number of service centres and production centres and is illustrated in Appendix C using Excel.

| | | |
|---|---|---|
| | $S_1 = 90\,000 + 0.1S_2$ | (1) |
| | $S_2 = 60\,000 + 0.19S_1$ | (2) |
| Substitute for $S_2$ in (1): | $S_1 = 90\,000 + 0.1(60\,000 + 0.19S_1)$ | |
| | $= 90\,000 + 6000 + 0.019S_1$ | |
| | $S_1 - 0.019S_1 = 96\,000$ | |
| | $0.981S_1 = 96\,000$ | |
| | $S_1 = 96\,000/0.981$ | |
| | $= 97\,859$ | |
| Substitute into (2): | $S_2 = 60\,000 + 0.19(97\,859)$ | |
| | $= 60\,000 + 18\,593$ | |
| | $= 78\,593$ | |

Note that these costs total more than the original sum (90 000 + 60 000), but this is all right because we simply transfer to $P_1$ and $P_2$ the percentages shown in Table 3-2: 63% of $S_1$'s costs go to $P_1$ (0.63 x 97 859 = 61 651) and 18% go to $P_2$ (0.18 x 97 859=17 615); 60% of $S_2$'s costs go to $P_1$ (0.6 x 78 593 = 47 156) and 30% go to $P_2$ (0.3x78 593=23 578). The allocations are shown in Table 3-5.

| | $S_1$ | $S_2$ | $P_1$ | $P_2$ | TOTAL |
|---|---|---|---|---|---|
| Overhead costs | 90 000 | 60 000 | 100 000 | 50 000 | 300 000 |
| Reallocate $S_1$ | (97 859) | 18 593 | 61 651 | 17 615 | 0 |
| Reallocate $S_2$ | 7 859 | (78 593) | 47 156 | 23 578 | 0 |
| | 0 | 0 | 208 807 | 91 193 | 300 000 |

**Table 3-5: Reciprocal Services Method of Allocation**

The second stage allocation would be as follows:

$P_1$: $208 807 / 7000 MH = $29.84 per MH (rounded to 2 decimal places)
$P_2$: $91 193 / 20 000 DLH = $4.56 per DLH

Then the overhead allocated to each product would be (calculations not rounded but display is):

> A: 1 MH x $29.84 + 2 DLH x $4.56 = $29.84 + $9.12 = $38.96
> B: ½ MH x $29.84 + 4 DLH x $4.56 = $14.92 + $18.24 = $33.16

The final overhead allocated to each production department under the three methods is as follows:

| Method | $P_1$ | $P_2$ |
|---|---|---|
| Direct | $210 000 | $90 000 |
| Step | 208 100 | 91 900 |
| Reciprocal Services | 208 807 | 91 193 |

The overhead cost component of each product under the three methods is:

| Method | A | B |
|---|---|---|
| Direct | $39.00 | $33.00 |
| Step | 38.92 | 33.24 |
| Reciprocal Services | 38.96 | 33.16 |

In this example there is not a large difference from using the three methods, and hence the cost of a unit of each product does not differ markedly whichever method is used. This may frequently be the case, which probably explains why many firms have simply used the direct method. Perhaps a more serious problem than the choice among these three methods is the use of such volume-based cost drivers as MH and DLH for allocating **all** overhead to products when some overheads are definitely activity- or transaction-related rather than volume-related. Activity-based costing (or ABC) has been promulgated because of the distortions which the use of volume-related allocation rates can produce in product costs. Such distortions are especially important when making product-related decisions such as pricing, selecting a product-mix, make or buy a component, continue or discontinue a product, etc.

## *Activity Based Costing*

The basic assumption behind the **traditional** two stage overhead allocation method is that there is no direct link between the support centre activities and the products manufactured. Therefore service centre costs are first allocated to production centres because it is in these centres that products are actually worked on. Consequently, there should be a closer link between production centre activities and products, and the allocation to products of all overheads at this point should be more reliable.

Activity based costing (ABC) rejects this assumption and seeks to identify cost drivers that directly link all activities, service centre activities as well as production centre activities, to the products manufactured. Then the costs of all these activities are assigned to products, via the activity cost drivers, according to each product's relative consumption of these activities. Thus ABC eliminates the step of allocating service centre costs to production centres and assigns them directly to products.

A second feature of ABC concerns the range of activities performed in manufacturing or service processes and the type of cost drivers used in the allocation process. Traditional methods of allocating overhead to products use volume-based cost drivers such as direct labour hours or machine hours. Unfortunately, not all overhead costs are volume-related. Some are driven by transactions or activities.

### Cost Drivers

One of the lessons of ABC is that the use of volume-related cost drivers **alone** can produce misleading product cost information. For example, setup costs incurred in setting up machines for production runs are driven basically by the **number of setups** performed (or the number of setup hours worked) rather than by the volume of production. Often the setup time involved is the same for all products. Once a machine is set up for a production run no further setup cost is incurred whether 10 units or 10 000 units are produced. Hence the setup cost allocated to each unit of product should be much lower in the case of products manufactured in long production runs. High-volume products are often produced in long production runs, requiring only a few setups, while low-volume products are often produced in a number of shorter production runs. If setup costs are allocated to units of production using a measure of total volume (e.g., units of all products produced, machine hours, direct labour hours, etc.) it is almost inevitable that the high-volume products will be allocated a disproportionately larger share of setup costs, and the low-volume products will be allocated a smaller share of setup costs than they are responsible for causing.

To illustrate, in Example 3-1, 6000 units of A and 2000 units of B were to be produced. Suppose that each product is produced in one production run, first product A, and second product B (i.e. two production runs in total). Suppose also that it takes the same setup time and resources for each product, costing $3600 per setup. Using a volume cost driver, such as the number of units produced, the setup cost per unit of product might be calculated as follows:

> Setup costs = 2 setups x $3600 = $7200 to be allocated
> Number of units = 6000 + 2000 = 8000
> Setup cost per unit = $7200/8000 = $0.90 per unit for both A and B.

A more realistic costing process using the number of setups as the cost driver would allocate the setup costs as follows:

> Product A:     1 setup x $3600) = $3600
> Product B:     1 setup x $3600) = $3600
> Setup cost for Product A = $3600/6000 units = $0.60 per unit
> Setup cost for Product B = $3600/2000 units = $1.80 per unit

Thus, using volume based cost drivers, the classic cross-subsidisation problem arises of high-volume products being over-costed and subsidising low-volume products which are under-costed. In the above example, using a simple volume-related cost driver each product was allocated a setup cost of $0.90 per unit. Yet when the setup costs are allocated on the proper basis of relative consumption, the setup overhead cost per unit of the low volume product is actually three times that of the high volume product. This type of situation can lead to incorrect pricing, or other faulty product-related decisions such as dropping profitable products and maintaining unprofitable ones. In a similar manner, a number of other overhead costs may be driven by activities rather than by production volume.

## Types of Activities

In identifying activity cost drivers to be used in allocating overhead costs it is useful to distinguish different categories of production activities. Cooper (1990) has described a four-category classification: unit-level, batch-level, product-level (sustaining), and facility-level activities.

- **Unit-level activities** are performed each time a unit is produced, and hence their activity levels are related to the number of units produced. Therefore their costs may be allocated using volume drivers such as number of units produced, or other cost drivers that relate directly to the number of units produced, such as direct labour hours and machine hours. Examples include supervision of direct labour workers, depreciation and maintenance of machines, electricity consumed by machines, and inspection of every unit for quality.

- **Batch-level activities** are performed each time a batch of units is produced. Their activity levels are related to the number of batches produced, regardless of the number of units in the batches. These costs may be allocated using batch-level cost drivers. Examples of batch-level activities include setups, production scheduling, materials handling, purchase orders, and number of deliveries.

- **Product-level (sustaining) activities** are performed when needed to support the various products produced. Their activity levels tend to vary with the number of products and product lines. These activities are not always performed every time a new batch is produced, and the demand for these activities is independent of production volumes. These costs would be allocated via product-level cost drivers. Examples of product-level activities include engineering actions to maintain product specifications, development and testing of process routines, and development of product testing procedures.

- **Facility-level activities** are performed to support the upkeep of the plant. They are not related to the number of units or batches produced, or to the number of products. Examples include plant management, rent, plant maintenance, landscaping, lighting, security and plant accounting.

3/Product Costing: Materials, Labour and Overhead

Of the four levels of activity, the first three are product-related. For these it is possible to measure the demands placed on them by individual products. The fourth category, facility-level activities, is the most difficult to handle under the ABC philosophy. The problem is that these activities and their costs are common to a variety of products and it is not possible to identify their relative consumption by each product. Therefore it is sometimes recommended that they not be allocated to products but written off as period expenses. Nevertheless, many companies using an ABC system do allocate facility-level costs to products.

## ABC Illustrated

### Illustrative Example 3-3

Refer to the overhead costs shown in Table 3-1. Suppose that $S_1$ is concerned with materials handling and finished goods shipments, while $S_2$ is primarily involved in production scheduling and setups.

*A re-appraisal of these overhead costs and their activity cost drivers reveals the following information:*

In $S_1$: Other indirect labour costs of $30 000 are batch-related, driven by the number of production runs.
Electricity costs of $10 000 are unit-related, driven by the total number of direct labour hours in production departments $P_1$ and $P_2$.
Receiving costs of $30 000 are batch-related, driven by the number of receipts of components and materials. A new, incoming shipment of each component for each product is received at the commencement of each production run.
Shipping costs of $20 000 are batch-related, incurred preparing goods for shipment to customers, and are driven predominantly by the number of outward shipments.

In $S_2$: Other indirect labour costs of $55 000 are batch-related, driven by the number of production setups. Each product requires the same resources for each setup.
Electricity costs of $5000 are unit-related, driven by the number of machine hours in $P_1$.

$P_1, P_2$: All costs are unit-related.
Supervision costs are driven by the number of direct labour hours in each centre and Depreciation costs by the number of machine hours in each centre.
Electricity costs are driven by the number of machine hours in $P_1$ and direct labour hours in $P_2$.

*Other production data are shown in Table 3-6:*

|  | Product A | Product B |
| --- | --- | --- |
| Production | 6000 units in 1 run | 2000 units in 10 runs |
| Material components | 5 per unit | 10 per unit |
| Shipments of finished Goods | 6000 units in 3 shipments | 2000 units in 20 shipments |

**Table 3-6: Production Data**

From Table 3-6 we see that there are 11 production runs in total, 1 for Product A and 10 for Product B. Assuming a JIT purchasing system and a different supplier for each component, there are 105 receipts of material, 5 for Product A (5 receipts x 1 production run) and 100 receipts for Product B (10 receipts x 10 production runs). Similarly there are 23 shipments of finished goods (3 for Product A and 20 for Product B). All this information is summarised in Table 3-7:

*3/Product Costing: Materials, Labour and Overhead*

| Activity | | Total Cost | Cost Driver | Expected Capacity of Cost Driver |
|---|---|---|---|---|
| Supervision | - $P_1$ | $30 000 | Direct labour hours in $P_1$ | 38 000 |
|  | - $P_2$ | $25 000 | Direct labour hours in $P_2$ | 20 000 |
| Other indirect labour | - $S_1$ | $30 000 | Production runs | 11 |
|  | - $S_2$ | $55 000 | Setups | 11 |
| Depreciation | - $P_1$ | $60 000 | Machine hours in $P_1$ | 7 000 |
|  | - $P_2$ | $20 000 | Machine hours in $P_2$ | 5 000 |
| Electricity | - $S_1$ | $10 000 | DLH in ($P_1 + P_2$) | 58 000 |
|  | - $S_2$ | $5 000 | MH in $P_1$ | 7 000 |
|  | - $P_1$ | $10 000 | MH in $P_1$ | 7 000 |
|  | - $P_2$ | $5 000 | DLH in $P_2$ | 20 000 |
| Receiving | - $S_1$ | $30 000 | Receipts of materials | 105 |
| Shipping | - $S_1$ | $20 000 | FG shipments out | 23 |

**Table 3-7: Activity Cost Driver Analysis**

Table 3-8 shows how the overhead costs are allocated to products using ABC, based on the data derived in Table 3-7. The fourth column of Table 3-8 is derived by dividing the figures in the second column (Total Cost) by the figures in the third column (Cost Driver Capacity). For example, in row 3 the rate is $30 000 / 11 runs = $2727.27 per production run. Columns 5 and 6 show the quantity of each cost driver consumed by one unit of each product. For example, in the first row we see the number of DLH consumed in $P_1$ by products A and B (5 DLH and 4 DLH respectively); these figures came from the data in Example 3-1. Column 7 is calculated by multiplying column 5 by column 4 (5 DLH x $0.79/DLH = $3.95).

In row 3, Product A requires only 1 run of 6000 units, so that the *other indirect labour* costs in $S_1$ are spread over 6000 units. Column 7 is obtained by multiplying column 5 by column 4 (1/6000 x $2727.27 = $0.45). Similarly, column 8 is calculated by multiplying column 6 by column 4 (10/2000 x $2727.27 = $13.64); that is, Product B's share of $S_1$ indirect labour is 10/2000 of 1/11 of $30 000, or 10/11 of $30 000 which is then spread over the 2000 units of B produced.

| Overhead Cost Pool | | Total Cost | Cost Driver Capacity | Rate/unit of Cost Driver | Cost Driver Consumption Product A | Cost Driver Consumption Product B | Overhead Allocation per Unit of Product Product A | Overhead Allocation per Unit of Product Product B |
|---|---|---|---|---|---|---|---|---|
| Supervision | - P1 | $30 000 | 38 000 DLH | $0.79 | 5 | 4 | $3.95 | $3.16 |
|  | - P2 | $25 000 | 20 000 DLH | $1.25 | 2 | 4 | $2.50 | $5.00 |
| Other ind. labour | - S1 | $30 000 | 11 runs | $2727.27 | 1/6000 | 10/2000 | $0.45 | $13.64 |
|  | - S2 | $55 000 | 11 setups | $5000.00 | 1/6000 | 10/2000 | $0.83 | $25.00 |
| Depreciation | - P1 | $60 000 | 7000 MH | $8.57 | 1 | 0.5 | $8.57 | $4.29 |
|  | - P2 | $20 000 | 5000 MH | $4.00 | 0.5 | 1 | $2.00 | $4.00 |
| Electricity | - S1 | $10 000 | 58 000 DLH | $0.17 | 7 | 8 | $1.21 | $1.38 |
|  | - S2 | $5 000 | 7000 MH | $0.71 | 1 | 0.5 | $0.71 | $0.36 |
|  | - P1 | $10 000 | 7000 MH | $1.43 | 1 | 0.5 | $1.43 | $0.71 |
|  | - P2 | $5000 | 20 000 DLH | $0.25 | 2 | 4 | $0.50 | $1.00 |
| Receiving | - S1 | $30 000 | 105 receipts | $285.71 | 5/6000 | 100/2000 | $0.24 | $14.29 |
| Shipping | - S1 | $20 000 | 23 shipments | $869.57 | 3/6000 | 20/2000 | $0.43 | $8.70 |
| | Total | $300 000 | | | | | $22.83 | $81.51 |

**Table 3-8: Activity Based Costing Overhead Cost Allocation**

It is apparent from Tables 3-7 and 3-8 that some activity cost pools use the same cost drivers. This means that they can be amalgamated, reducing the number of allocation rates. The two *other indirect labour* cost pools can be amalgamated, as can *electricity* in $S_2$ and $P_1$ with *depreciation* in $P_1$. Three other activity cost pools can be amalgamated because of correlation in the consumption of the cost drivers by each product. In production department P₂ both products consume DLH and MH in the same ratio of 2:1. Thus *supervision* in P₂, *depreciation* in P₂ and *electricity* in P₂ can all be combined using either DLH or MH as the allocation base (we will use MH). Table 3-9 illustrates this simplification.

| Overhead Cost Pool | | Total Cost | Cost Driver Capacity | Rate/unit of Cost Driver | Cost Driver Consumption | Cost Driver Consumption | Overhead Allocation per Unit of Product | Overhead Allocation per Unit of Product |
|---|---|---|---|---|---|---|---|---|
| | | | | | Product A | Product B | Product A | Product B |
| Supervision | - P1 | $30 000 | 38 000 DLH | $0.79 | 5 | 4 | $3.95 | $3.16 |
| Supervn + Elec+Depn | -P2 | $50 000 | 5 000 MH | $10.00 | 0.5 | 1 | $5.00 | $10.00 |
| Other ind. labour | - S1+S2 | $85 000 | 11 runs | $7727.27 | 1/6000 | 10/2000 | $1.29 | $38.64 |
| Depn +Elec | - P1+S2 | $75 000 | 7000 MH | $10.71 | 1 | 0.5 | $10.71 | $5.36 |
| Electricity | - S1 | $10 000 | 58 000 DLH | $0.17 | 7 | 8 | $1.21 | $1.38 |
| Receiving | - S1 | $30 000 | 105 receipts | $285.71 | 5/6000 | 100/2000 | $0.24 | $14.29 |
| Shipping | - S1 | $20 000 | 23 shipments | $869.57 | 3/6000 | 20/2000 | $0.43 | $8.70 |
| | Total | $300 000 | | | | | $22.83 | $81.51 |

**Table 3-9: Simplified ABC**

Let us compare the overhead cost component of each product using activity based costing with the results using traditional costing:

| Method | A | B |
|---|---|---|
| *Traditional costing* | | |
| Direct | $39.00 | $33.00 |
| Step | 38.92 | 33.24 |
| Reciprocal Services | 38.96 | 33.16 |
| *Activity based costing* | 22.83 | 81.51 |

So we see that when we take account of the numerous transactions required for product B compared with the number required for product A, the cost of overhead allocated to the low volume product B soars to $81.51 while the overhead cost of the high volume product A drops to $22.83. Clearly the sole use of volume-based cost drivers and reallocating service centre costs to production centres was severely distorting product costs, and distortions of this magnitude do not seem to be unusual.

## *Activity Based Management*

When managers base decisions on activity based costing information we say that they are engaging in activity based management (ABM). Such decisions can encompass any that use ABC analysis to improve the profitability of the organisation. For example, ABM includes decisions to modify product prices, or product mix, or customer mix, or to change suppliers or alter product design. ABM includes finding ways to perform activities more efficiently, or to eliminate the need to perform them at all (that is, to try to eliminate non-value-added activities - see Chapter 7).

# SUMMARY

This chapter focused on the detailed processes for controlling and recording material, labour and overhead costs. Part of the recording process involves tracing direct costs and allocating indirect costs to individual products or services in order to obtain unit costs. These unit product costs can then be used for financial reporting purposes, determining cost of goods sold and valuing unsold inventories. More importantly, the unit product costs can be used for making product-related decisions: pricing, selecting a product mix, make or buy components, continue or discontinue a product or product line.

A cost accounting system traces the flow of materials through the stages of acquisition, storage and usage. Direct materials costs can usually be readily traced to products.

Accounting for labour involves recording gross wages earned, payments to employees, and authorised deductions withheld. Labour costs are also distributed to activities and products. Direct labour costs can also be traced to products, usually without difficulty.

The control of overhead costs is achieved primarily through the use of budgets and responsibility centres; overhead costs are traced to responsibility centres, which are either service centres or production centres. Allocating overhead to products for product-costing purposes is usually performed by using predetermined overhead allocation rates based on judicious selection of appropriate cost drivers. The determination of these allocation rates under traditional costing involves first reallocating budgeted service centre costs to production centres, and then allocating the pooled budgeted overhead costs to products via predetermined rates.

This traditional method of allocating overheads to products relies on the use of volume-based cost drivers. Activity based costing attempts to more accurately trace overhead to products by recognising that some overhead costs are driven by activities (or transactions) rather than by volume. Further, activity costs are allocated directly to products, eliminating the intermediate step of reallocating all costs to production centres. For product-related decisions it is preferable to use activity-based costing. Any decisions based on ABC information are part of what is called activity based management.

## REFERENCES

Calvasina, R.V., Calvasina, E.J. and Calvasina, G.E. (1989), "Beware the New Accounting Myths", *Management Accounting*, December, 41-45.

Cooper, R. (1987), "The Two-Stage Procedure in Cost Accounting: Part One", *Journal of Cost Management for the Manufacturing Industry*, 1, 2, Summer, 43-51.

Cooper, R. (1987), "The Two-Stage Procedure in Cost Accounting: Part Two", *Journal of Cost Management for the Manufacturing Industry*, 1, 3, Fall, 39-45.

Cooper, R. (1990), "Cost Classification in Unit-Based and Activity-Based Manufacturing Cost Systems", *Journal of Cost Management*, Fall, 4-14.

Foster, G. and Horngren, C.T. (1987), "Cost Accounting and Cost Management Issues", *Management Accounting*, June, 19-25.

Foster, G. and Horngren, C.T. (1988), "Cost Accounting and Cost Management in a JIT Environment", *Journal of Cost Management for the Manufacturing Industry*, Winter, 4-14.

Shank, J.K. and Govindarajan, V. (1988), "The Perils of Cost Allocation Based on Production Volumes", *Accounting Horizons*, December, 71-79.

*3/Product Costing: Materials, Labour and Overhead*

## APPENDIX A

### Accounting for GST

In Australia a Goods and Services Tax (GST) of 10% is levied on the supply of goods and services. Thus a firm pays GST on goods and services purchased, increasing their cost by 10%. The firm collects GST on goods and services sold, increasing the revenue by 10%. It deducts the tax paid on purchases from the tax it charges on sales and pays the balance to the Australian Taxation Office (ATO). Essentially the firm is a collection agency for the ATO.

Generally sales revenue, purchases, expenses and assets are shown net of GST. That is, GST is excluded from the gross figures in the accounts. The GST component is recorded in a GST clearing account, the balance of which appears on the balance sheet normally as a current liability (firm owes GST to the ATO) or possibly as a current asset if the account is in debit.

On the other hand, accounts payable and accounts receivable have the GST included and are recorded in the accounts at the gross amounts. This is because the gross (total) amount of the transaction will be paid or received by the firm.

### *Illustrative Example 3-4*

*On 1 August a manufacturer purchases on credit raw materials costing $1000 plus 10% GST.*

The entries would be:

| | | |
|---|---|---|
| Materials Control | $1 000 | |
| GST Clearing | 100 | |
| Accounts Payable | | $1 100 |

Note that the Materials Control account shows the cost net of GST, while the supplier is owed the gross cost including GST. The manufacturer must pay the GST to the creditor but it will be offset against credits for GST to be collected on sales.

### *Illustrative Example 3-5*

*This is a continuation of Example 3-4. On 5 August the manufacturer sells on credit finished goods which cost $2000 (excluding GST) for $3300 (including GST).*

The entries would be:

| | | |
|---|---|---|
| Cost of Goods Sold | $2 000 | |
| Finished Goods | | $2 000 |
| | | |
| Accounts Receivable | $3 300 | |
| GST Clearing | | 300 |
| Sales | | $3 000 |

Note that the sales revenue is recorded at $3000, net of GST, while the debtor owes the gross sum of $3300 including GST. The GST of 10% can be calculated as 1/11 of the sales revenue: 1/11 of $3300 = $300.

The GST Clearing account now looks like this, with a balance of $200 owing to the ATO; that is, the $300 to be collected from the debtor minus the $100 to be paid to the creditor on the input raw material.

**GST Clearing**

| | | | | |
|---|---|---|---|---|
| Aug-01 Accounts Payable | 100 | Aug-05 Accounts Receivable | | 300 |
| 05 Balance | 200 | | | |
| | 300 | | | 300 |
| | | Aug-05 Balance | | 200 |

56

# APPENDIX B

## Using a Spreadsheet for Overhead Allocation

Below is a printout of a spreadsheet model designed to allocate overhead costs from service centres to production centres. This model shows the numbers for the example in this chapter, but has been generalised to work for any similar problem involving two service centres and two production centres. The formulae for the first two columns of this model are shown on the next page. You should copy these onto a spreadsheet file which you could name OHDALCN2.XLS (in EXCEL, or other appropriate extension in other spreadsheets) and construct the other columns C,D,E,F. You may wish to make use of this model to solve similar problems. You have to change the percentages in the table, rows 6 and 7, columns B:E. Actually, they do not have to be percentages, but can simply be the appropriate numbers associated with the chosen cost driver (direct labour hours, machine hours, number of employees, etc.), and they can add to any number, not necessarily 100. Also, you must change the initial allocations of overhead to each cost centre, row 11 columns B to E.

There is a circular reference in this model but you can overcome that problem by ensuring that there are a number of iterations so that it will converge on the answer. Check that Excel will perform a number of iterations by opening Tools/Options/Calculation and ticking the box beside Iterations – make it 100 iterations if you like. If you cannot overcome the circular reference problem insert a number instead of the formula in the troublesome cell to get it started, and then change the number to the formula.

|    | A | B | C | D | E | F | G |
|----|---|---|---|---|---|---|---|
| 1  |   |   | OVERHEAD COST ALLOCATION - |   |   |   |   |
| 2  |   | SERVICE CENTRE COSTS TO PRODUCTION CENTRES |   |   |   |   |   |
| 3  |   |   |   |   |   |   |   |
| 4  |   | Percentage Consumption of Support Services |   |   |   |   |   |
| 5  |   |   | S1 | S2 | P1 | P2 | TOTAL |
| 6  | S1 | 0 | 19 | 63 | 18 | 100 |   |
| 7  | S2 | 10 | 0 | 60 | 30 | 100 |   |
| 8  |   |   |   |   |   |   |   |
| 9  |   | Overhead Costs Charged to Service and Production Centres |   |   |   |   |   |
| 10 |   | S1 | S2 | P1 | P2 | TOTAL |   |
| 11 |   | 90,000 | 60,000 | 100,000 | 50,000 | 300,000 |   |
| 12 |   |   |   |   |   |   |   |
| 13 |   | DIRECT METHOD OF ALLOCATION |   |   |   |   |   |
| 14 |   | S1 | S2 | P1 | P2 | TOTAL |   |
| 15 | Overhead costs | 90,000 | 60,000 | 100,000 | 50,000 | 300,000 |   |
| 16 | Reallocate S1 | (90,000) | 0 | 70,000 | 20,000 | 0 |   |
| 17 | Reallocate S2 | 0 | (60,000) | 40,000 | 20,000 | 0 |   |
| 18 |   | 0 | 0 | 210,000 | 90,000 | 300,000 |   |
| 19 |   |   |   |   |   |   |   |
| 20 |   | STEP METHOD OF ALLOCATION |   |   |   |   |   |
| 21 |   | S1 | S2 | P1 | P2 | TOTAL |   |
| 22 | Overhead costs | 90,000 | 60,000 | 100,000 | 50,000 | 300,000 |   |
| 23 | Reallocate S1 | (90,000) | 17,100 | 56,700 | 16,200 | 0 |   |
| 24 | Reallocate S2 | 0 | (77,100) | 51,400 | 25,700 | 0 |   |
| 25 |   | 0 | 0 | 208,100 | 91,900 | 300,000 |   |
| 26 |   |   |   |   |   |   |   |
| 27 |   | RECIPROCAL SERVICES METHOD OF ALLOCATION |   |   |   |   |   |
| 28 |   | S1 | S2 | P1 | P2 | TOTAL |   |
| 29 | Overhead costs | 90,000 | 60,000 | 100,000 | 50,000 | 300,000 |   |
| 30 | Reallocate S1 | (97,859) | 18,593 | 61,651 | 17,615 | 0 |   |
| 31 | Reallocate S2 | 7,859 | (78,593) | 47,156 | 23,578 | 0 |   |
| 32 |   | 0 | 0 | 208,807 | 91,193 | 300,000 |   |
| 33 |   |   |   |   |   |   |   |

## 3/Product Costing: Materials, Labour and Overhead

|    | A | B |
|----|---|---|
| 1  |   |   |
| 2  |   | **SERVICE CENTRE COSTS TO PRODUCTION CENTRES** |
| 3  |   |   |
| 4  |   | **Percentage Consumption of Support Services** |
| 5  |   | S1 |
| 6  | S1 | 0 |
| 7  | S2 | 10 |
| 8  |   |   |
| 9  | Overhead Costs Charged to Serv |   |
| 10 |   | S1 |
| 11 |   | 90000 |
| 12 |   |   |
| 13 |   | **DIRECT METHOD OF ALLOCATION** |
| 14 |   | S1 |
| 15 | Overhead costs | =B11 |
| 16 | Reallocate S1 | =-B15 |
| 17 | Reallocate S2 | =B15+B16 |
| 18 |   | =SUM(B15:B17) |
| 19 |   |   |
| 20 |   | **STEP METHOD OF ALLOCATION** |
| 21 |   | S1 |
| 22 | Overhead costs | =B11 |
| 23 | =IF(B23<0,"Reallocate S1","Reallocate S2") | =IF(C6/F6>B7/F7,-B22,IF(AND(C6/F6=B7/F7,B22>C22),-B22,B7/(F7-C7)*-C23)) |
| 24 | =IF(B24<0,"Reallocate S1","Reallocate S2") | =-SUM(B22:B23) |
| 25 |   | =SUM(B22:B24) |
| 26 |   |   |
| 27 |   | **RECIPROCAL SERVICES METHOD OF ALLOCATION** |
| 28 |   | S1 |
| 29 | Overhead costs | =B11 |
| 30 | Reallocate S1 | =-(B29+B7/(F7-C7)*-C31) |
| 31 | Reallocate S2 | =B7/($F7-$C7)*-$C31 |
| 32 |   | =SUM(B29:B31) |
| 33 |   |   |

*3/Product Costing: Materials, Labour and Overhead*

## APPENDIX C

### Using Matrix Algebra for Reciprocal Overhead Allocation

Once there are more than two service centres and two production centres, the simultaneous equation method is not satisfactory. Instead, we can use matrix algebra to solve the problem. On the next page is the output from an Excel model to solve the reciprocal services method for the same problem as in the chapter. Although there are only two service centres and two production centres, this method will work for any number of centres.

Let us reproduce Table 3-2 showing the Percentage Consumption of Support Services:

|  |  | \multicolumn{5}{c}{*Service Consumed By:*} |
|---|---|---|---|---|---|---|
| *Service* |  | $S_1$ | $S_2$ | $P_1$ | $P_2$ | Total |
| *Supplied* | $S_1$ | 0 | 19 | 63 | 18 | 100 |
| *By:* | $S_2$ | 10 | 0 | 60 | 30 | 100 |

Now we insert this data into the Excel spreadsheet (next page) as shown in the range A4:F7 with some minor modifications. First, percentages are shown as decimals or you can enter as decimals and reformat as percentages if you like. Instead of zeros at the intersection of S1 and S2 rows and columns respectively we put in –1 (or –100%). We also include P1 and P2 in the 4x4 matrix, with zeros everywhere except at the intersection of P1 row and column and P2 row and column where we insert the number 1 (or 100%)

In column G, rows 4 to 7 we insert the overhead costs which were initially allocated to S1, S2, P1 and P2, with the total in G8.

We then highlight the range C11:F14 where we are going to place the inverse of the coefficient matrix in C4:F7. Note that the matrix must be a square matrix. With the cursor on the first cell of the highlighted range, ie on C11, enter the formula =**MINVERSE(** and then highlight the coefficient matrix to be inverted, ie C4:F7. That is, we have keyed in the formula =**MINVERSE(C4:F7)**. Then press CTRL-SHIFT-ENTER simultaneously. This results in the inverse coefficients in C11:F14.

Now we multiply the inverse coefficients by the costs to be allocated. In cell C17 we enter =**C11*$G$4**, which produces the result (91,743). Copy this formula across D11:F11. Similarly in row 18 multiply the inverse coefficients from row 12 by theS2 costs of $60,000 in G5. And so on. Finally, sum the columns C17:C20, D17:D20, E17:E20 and F17:F20. Then in G21 sum the costs of P1 and P2, ie E21:F21 to check that the original $300,000 has been properly accounted for.

|   | A | B | C | D | E | F | G |
|---|---|---|---|---|---|---|---|
| 1 | RECIPROCAL SERVICES METHOD OF OVERHEAD ALLOCATION ||||||||
| 2 | | | | | | | |
| 3 | | TO: | S1 | S2 | P1 | P2 | COSTS |
| 4 | FROM | S1 | -1 | 0.19 | 0.63 | 0.18 | $90,000 |
| 5 | | S2 | 0.1 | -1 | 0.6 | 0.3 | 60,000 |
| 6 | | P1 | 0 | 0 | 1 | 0 | 100,000 |
| 7 | | P2 | 0 | 0 | 0 | 1 | 50,000 |
| 8 | | | | | | | $300,000 |
| 9 | | | | | | | |
| 10 | | TO: | S1 | S2 | P1 | P2 | |
| 11 | FROM | S1 | -1.019368 | -0.1936799 | 0.7584098 | 0.2415902 | |
| 12 | | S2 | -0.1019368 | -1.019368 | 0.675841 | 0.324159 | |
| 13 | | P1 | 0 | 0 | 1 | 0 | |
| 14 | | P2 | 0 | 0 | 0 | 1 | |
| 15 | | | | | | | |
| 16 | | TO: | S1 | S2 | P1 | P2 | |
| 17 | FROM | S1 | (91,743) | (17,431) | $68,257 | $21,743 | |
| 18 | | S2 | (6,116) | (61,162) | 40,550 | 19,450 | |
| 19 | | P1 | 0 | 0 | 100,000 | 0 | |
| 20 | | P2 | 0 | 0 | 0 | 50,000 | |
| 21 | | | (97,859) | (78,593) | $208,807 | $91,193 | $300,000 |

You will note that the two negative figures in C21 and D21 represent the service centre costs to be reallocated. Compare these with the figures in Table 3-5 – they should be the same. The final costs in the production centres P1 and P2 are $208,807 and $91,193 (to the nearest dollar), the same result as found in Table 3-5.

This system will work for any size matrix, as long as it is a square matrix.

## QUESTIONS AND PROBLEMS

3-1 Distinguish between a materials requisition and a purchase requisition.

3-2 What is the purpose of
 (a) a purchase order?
 (b) a supplier's invoice?
 (c) a receiving report?

3-3 "If a perpetual inventory system is used for recording movements of raw materials there is no need to conduct a physical stocktake."
Do you agree? Why?

3-4 Recording labour costs involves two interlocking double entries, reflecting the two aspects of labour costs to be accounted for. Explain.

3-5 What are the source documents for
 (a) the distribution of labour costs to direct and indirect labour?
 (b) payment of wages?

3-6 Should overtime payments be treated as direct labour, or as overhead?

3-7 What is meant by
 (a) an overhead cost pool?
 (b) a cost driver?
 (c) a production cost centre?
 (d) a support service cost centre?

3-8 What disadvantages are there in using actual overhead allocation rates for allocating overhead to products or services?

3-9 What relationship exists among product costs, capacity concepts and organisational competitiveness?

3-10 **Within a production cost centre**, when is it desirable to use more than one allocation rate to allocate overhead to products? When is one rate sufficient?

3-11 Under what conditions will a plant-wide overhead allocation rate produce the same product cost as separate departmental rates?

3-12 A product cross-subsidisation problem arises when high-volume products are over-costed and low-volume products are under-costed. Explain how such a situation can arise, and how you might go about correcting it.

3-13 Given the following documents,
 (a) invoice
 (b) materials received form
 (c) materials requisition form
 (d) purchase requisition
 (e) purchase order

The typical sequence in a materials handling system is:
A a,b,c,d,e
B d,e,b,a,c
C c,d,e,b,a
D c,b,a,d,e
E e,a,b,d,c

*3/Product Costing: Materials, Labour and Overhead*

**3-14** **Understanding the entries in the Materials Control account**
The Materials Control account balances were $25 000 on 1 April and $15 000 on 30 April. Raw materials purchased during April were $100 000. (All materials were direct materials).

*Required:*
A journal entry to record the cost of raw materials placed in production during April.

**3-15** **Understanding the entries in the Materials Control account with GST**
The Materials Control account balances were $10 000 on 1 May and $15 000 on 31 May. Raw materials issued to production during May cost $45 000. (All direct materials).

*Required:*
A journal entry to record the cost of raw materials purchased (all on credit) during May, given that a 10% GST is paid on purchases.

**3-16** **Understanding the entries in the Materials Control account**
The Materials Control account balances were $20 000 on 1 June and $10 000 on 30 June. Raw materials purchased during June cost $60 000. Direct materials issued to production during June were $55 000.

*Required:*
A journal entry to record the cost of raw materials issued as indirect materials during June.

**3-17** **Understanding the entries in the Accrued Payroll account**
Salaries and wages payable to factory employees were $7000 on 1 March and $5000 on 31 March. Gross salaries and wages paid during March totalled $23 000. March's direct labour totalled $17 000.

*Required:*
The general journal entry for recording salaries and wages earned by factory employees during March.

**3-18** **Understanding the entries in the Accrued Payroll account**
Salaries and wages payable to factory employees were $10 000 on 1 February and $20 000 on 28 February. February's factory salaries and wages expenses were $40 000 direct labour and $20 000 indirect labour.

*Required:*
The general journal entry for recording salaries and wages paid to factory employees during February.

**3-19** **Journal entry for long service leave**
A correct journal entry to provide for long service leave is:

    A      Provision for Long Service Leave
                  Accrued Payroll

    B      Overhead Control
                  Provision for Long Service Leave

    C      Work-in-Process
                  Accrued Payroll

    D      Provision for Long Service Leave
                  Overhead Allocated

    E      Work-in-Process
                  Overhead Allocated

## 3-20 Payroll: direct and indirect labour

J. Brown worked for 46 hours during the pay week ending Friday April 24. His normal working week consists of 35 hours, of which 31 hours were spent on production while the remaining 4 hours were non-productive idle time. Brown worked 3 hours overtime at a premium of 50% on Monday April 20 because a customer required work finished by Tuesday April 21 even if overtime had to be worked to complete it. Brown worked a further 8 hours overtime on Wednesday April 22 on other production. It is the policy of the company to pay an overtime premium of 100% after the first 3 hours *on any one day*. Brown's normal wage rate is $8 per hour.

*Required:*
(a) Calculate Brown's gross pay for the week.
(b) Indicate the sum to be treated as indirect labour.

## 3-21 Payroll entries

The Inert Company has a gross payroll of $8000 per day. Withholdings for PAYG taxes are $2400 per day. There are no other deductions from employees' earnings. The firm works five days per week, Monday to Friday inclusive. The payroll period covers Thursday to Wednesday inclusive and the payroll for the week is paid on the following Friday.

Gross payroll consists of $4800 direct labour, $1600 indirect factory labour, $1120 selling expenses and $480 general and administrative expenses each day. The following calendar should be used to answer the questions:

### July

| Sun | Mon | Tue | Wed | Thu | Fri | Sat |
|---|---|---|---|---|---|---|
| 1 | 2 | 3 | 4 | 5 | 6 | 7 |
| 8 | 9 | 10 | 11 | 12 | 13 | 14 |
| 15 | 16 | 17 | 18 | 19 | 20 | 21 |
| 22 | 23 | 24 | 25 | 26 | 27 | 28 |
| 29 | 30 | 31 | | | | |

(a) What is the total amount to be credited to Accrued Payroll in respect of July earnings?
(b) If balance day adjustments are performed at the end of each month, what would be the balance in Accrued Payroll account at the close of business on July 31?
(c) Suppose that a single journal entry is made on the last day of each month to record the distribution of total labour costs for the month, but that entries are made each Friday to record payment of wages and withholdings. Also, PAYG taxes withheld are remitted to the Taxation Department at the end of each month.
  (i) Show the weekly journal entry.
  (ii) Construct the necessary ledger accounts to show all entries in respect of labour costs during the month of July.

## 3-22 Reconstruct Work-in-Process account

On 1 September a company's Work-in-Process account had a balance of $10 000. During the month raw materials of $50 000 were placed into production, direct labour costs of $30 000 were incurred, and the balance of the account at 30 September was $12 000. If the cost of completed production for the month had been $110 000, what would have been the entry to record factory overhead allocated?

*3/Product Costing: Materials, Labour and Overhead*

**3-23 Reconstruct Work-in-Process account**

On 1 October a company's Work-in-Process account had a balance of $5000. During the month raw materials of $30 000 were placed into production, direct labour costs of $45 000 were incurred, factory overhead of $50 000 was allocated, and the balance of the account at 31 October was $10 000. What would have been the entry to record the cost of completed production for the month?

**3-24 Allocation of overhead**

In the Rubbery Figures Company, the overhead allocation rate per machine hour was based on budgeted factory overhead of $510 000 and normal capacity of 200 000 machine hours.

Actual factory overhead incurred for the year amounted to $540 000, and actual machine hours worked were 210 000.

What was the amount of under-allocated or over-allocated overhead for the year?

**3-25 Allocation of overhead**

A company's overhead allocation rate per machine hour was based on budgeted factory overhead of $400 000 and practical capacity of 100 000 machine hours.

Actual factory overhead incurred for the year amounted to $390 000, and actual machine hours worked were 98 000.

What was the amount of under-allocated or over-allocated overhead for the year?

**3-26 Working backwards: determining budgeted overhead given the allocation rate**

The overhead allocation rate for a plant is expressed in terms of a rate per direct labour hour, and is based on budgeted factory overhead at normal capacity. Normal capacity is 100 000 direct labour hours per annum. In a given year the actual factory overhead incurred was $330 000, actual direct labour hours worked were 110 000, and overhead over-allocated was $57 200.

What must the budgeted overhead for the year have been?

**3-27 Journal entry to close overhead accounts**

A correct journal entry to close the overhead accounts at the end of the period and to transfer over-allocated overhead is:

A    Overhead Allocated
        Under/Over Allocated Overhead
            Overhead Control

B    Overhead Control
        Overhead Allocated
        Cost of Sales

C    Overhead Allocated
    Work-in-Process
    Cost of Sales
    Finished Goods
        Overhead Control

D    Overhead Allocated
        Overhead Control
        Cost of Sales

E    None of the above

## 3-28 Multiple choice: allocation of overhead
Which of the following statements is false?

A    Once a service department's costs have been re-allocated by the step method no other service department costs are to be charged back to it.

B    The most accurate service department re-allocation method is the direct method.

C    Perfect correlation in the consumption of cost drivers across products can reduce the number of cost pools required and the number of overhead allocation rates necessary.

D    The practical capacity of a manufacturing firm is usually less than the theoretical capacity.

E    The use of direct labour cost as a cost driver produces the same results as the use of direct labour hours in overhead allocation when wage rates are uniform.

## 3-29 Comprehensive question on overhead
The Kensington Company has two departments, Machining and Finishing. Monthly overhead costs are estimated to behave as follows:

| | |
|---|---|
| Machining: | $40 000 + $40 per machine hour |
| Finishing: | $40 per direct labour hour |

The Machining department uses 1000 machine hours and 400 direct labour hours monthly. The Finishing department uses 600 direct labour hours monthly.

*Required:*
(a) A plant-wide overhead rate using direct labour hours as the cost driver.
(b) Departmental overhead rates using direct labour hours as the cost driver in both Machining and Finishing Departments.
(c) Departmental overhead rates using machine hours as the cost driver in the Machining department and direct labour hours as the cost driver in the Finishing department.
(d) An order is received requiring 20 direct labour hours and 20 machine hours in the Machining department and 40 direct labour hours in the Finishing department. Calculate the overhead allocated to this work using each of the three overhead rates determined in parts (a), (b) and (c).
(e) In both (a) and (b) direct labour hours is used as the cost driver. Why, then, doesn't the plantwide rate in (a) give the same overhead cost for the order as the departmental rates in (b)?
(f) Suppose that the order required 30 direct labour hours in the Finishing Department (rather than 40 DLH). What would be the overhead cost for the order using the overhead rates determined in parts (a) and (b) respectively? Why do you get this result?
(g) Departmental overhead rates are calculated in both (b) and (c). Why do they produce different overhead costs for the order?
(h) Suppose that the order required 50 machine hours in the Machining Department (rather than 20 MH). What would be the overhead cost for the order using the overhead rates determined in parts (b) and (c) respectively? Why do you get this result?

## 3-30 Predetermined overhead rate
The Lawson Company uses a predetermined rate based on normal capacity for allocating overhead to production. Normal capacity is 100 000 direct labour hours per annum. The behaviour of overhead costs has been studied and is estimated to be $180 000 of fixed overhead per annum and $4.70 of variable overhead per direct labour hour worked.

During the year ended 30 June, 20X5, production required 120 000 direct labour hours, and total overhead costs incurred were $725 000.

*Required:*
(a) Calculate the predetermined overhead rate correct to two decimal places.
(b) Determine the under-allocated or over-allocated overhead for the year ended 30 June, 20X5.

**3-31  Overhead allocation: rate and allocation to jobs**
Kirk Ltd allocates overhead to individual jobs by the use of predetermined overhead rates using direct labour hours as the cost driver. The following budget estimates were made for the year ending 31 December, 20X9:

| | |
|---|---|
| Fixed manufacturing overhead | $60 000 |
| Variable manufacturing overhead per direct labour hour | $1.50 |
| Direct labour cost | $200 000 |
| Direct labour hours | 40 000 |

*Required:*
(a) What is the predetermined overhead allocation rate for the year?
(b) During the year Job 154 was completed, requiring $200 of direct materials and a direct labour cost of $500. What was the total cost of Job 154?
(c) The total overhead incurred during the year was $140 000, and 42 250 direct labour hours were worked. What was the overhead variance for the year?

**3-32  Allocating service department costs to production departments: direct and step methods**
Kiddypower Ltd produces and sells children's party boxes containing food and gifts. The company has two production departments, Component Preparation and Party Box Assembly, and two service departments, Stores and Materials Handling. The current costs of these departments are:

| | Component Preparation $ | Party Box Assembly $ | Stores $ | Materials Handling $ |
|---|---|---|---|---|
| Direct (to centre) materials & labour | 400 000 | 100 000 | 20 000 | 30 000 |
| Indirect costs | 140 000 | 120 000 | 10 000 | 10 000 |
| Total | 540 000 | 220 000 | 30 000 | 40 000 |

The cost driver for allocating the Stores department's service costs is the number of requisitions from the other departments - Materials Handling 1000, Component Preparation 5000 and Party Box Assembly 4000.

The services of the Materials Handling Department are allocated 20% to Stores, and the remainder evenly between Component Preparation and Party Box Assembly.

(a) Using the direct method to allocate service department costs to production departments, allocated costs to Component Preparation and Party Box Assembly are respectively (to nearest $):

A   $10 556; $ 9 444
B   $36 667; $33 333
C   $31 000; $28 000
D   $15 000; $20 000
E   None of the above

3/Product Costing: Materials, Labour and Overhead

(b) Using the step method to allocate service department costs, and allocating Stores first, the final **total** indirect cost in Party Box Assembly is:

    A    $120 000
    B    $253 500
    C    $125 450
    D    $153 500
    E    $225 450

3-33 **Direct, step and reciprocal methods of overhead allocation**
A firm has two service departments, $S_1$ and $S_2$, and two production departments, $P_1$ and $P_2$. The primary allocation of indirect manufacturing expenses is as follows:

| $S_1$ | $S_2$ | $P_1$ | $P_2$ | Total |
|---|---|---|---|---|
| $9 000 | $8 000 | $20 000 | $33 000 | $70 000 |

The percentage allocation of service centre costs is:

|  | $S_1$ | $S_2$ | $P_1$ | $P_2$ | Total |
|---|---|---|---|---|---|
| $S_1$ | 0 | 20 | 50 | 30 | 100 |
| $S_2$ | 10 | 0 | 45 | 45 | 100 |

Re-allocate the service centre costs to the production departments by
(a) the direct method
(b) the step method
(c) the reciprocal services method.

3-34 **Direct, step and reciprocal methods of overhead allocation**
A firm has two service departments, $S_1$ and $S_2$, and two production departments, $P_1$ and $P_2$. The primary allocation of indirect manufacturing expenses is as follows:

| $S_1$ | $S_2$ | $P_1$ | $P_2$ | Total |
|---|---|---|---|---|
| $20 000 | $10 000 | $40 000 | $50 000 | $120 000 |

The percentage allocation of service centre costs is:

|  | $S_1$ | $S_2$ | $P_1$ | $P_2$ | Total |
|---|---|---|---|---|---|
| $S_1$ | 0 | 15 | 55 | 30 | 100 |
| $S_2$ | 20 | 0 | 40 | 40 | 100 |

Re-allocate the service centre costs to the production departments by
(a) the direct method
(b) the step method
(c) the reciprocal services method.

3-35 **Direct, step and reciprocal methods of overhead allocation: moderately difficult**
Peterson and Company has two production departments (Component Manufacture and Assembly) and two service departments (Staff Cafeteria and Materials Handling). The budgeted costs of these departments are:

|  | Component Manufacture $ | Assembly $ | Cafeteria $ | Materials Handling $ |
|---|---|---|---|---|
| Direct (to centre) material & labour | 300 000 | 200 000 | 4 000 | 12 000 |
| Indirect costs | 140 000 | 120 000 | 2 000 | 4 000 |
|  | 440 000 | 320 000 | 6 000 | 16 000 |

## 3/Product Costing: Materials, Labour and Overhead

The services of the Cafeteria are allocated according to the number of employees in the other departments: Materials Handling has 10 employees, Component Manufacture 30 employees and Assembly 50 employees.

The services of the Materials Handling department are allocated according to the number of budgeted requisitions per period. These are estimated as 20 for the Cafeteria, 40 for Component Manufacture and 40 for Assembly.

*Required:*

Allocate service department costs to the production departments using
(a) the direct method
(b) the step method
(c) the reciprocal services method.

**3-36 Direct, step and reciprocal methods of overhead allocation: moderately difficult**

Charles and Company has two production departments and two service departments. The budgeted costs of these departments are:

|  | $P_1$ $ | $P_2$ $ | $S_1$ $ | $S_2$ $ |
|---|---|---|---|---|
| Direct (to centre) material & labour | 200 000 | 150 000 | 8 000 | 20 000 |
| Indirect costs | 100 000 | 80 000 | 10 000 | 15 000 |
|  | 300 000 | 230 000 | 18 000 | 35 000 |

The services of $S_1$ are allocated according to the number of employees in the other departments: $S_2$ has 20 employees, $P_1$ 30 employees and $P_2$ 30 employees.

The services of $S_2$ are allocated 30% to $S_1$, 20% to $P_1$ and 50% to $P_2$.

*Required:*

Allocate service department costs to the production departments using
(a) the direct method
(b) the step method
(c) the reciprocal services method.

**3-37 Direct, step and reciprocal methods of overhead allocation: 3 service departments**

The Complex Company has five departments in its factory of which $P_1$ and $P_2$ are the only producing departments. The current costs of each department are:

| Service Department | A | $20 000 |
|---|---|---|
|  | B | $40 000 |
|  | C | $20 000 |
| Production Department | $P_1$ | $70 000 |
|  | $P_2$ | $70 000 |

The consumption of services is given in the following table:

|  |  | Service provided to |  |  |  |  |
|---|---|---|---|---|---|---|
|  |  | A | B | C | $P_1$ | $P_2$ |
| Service provided by | A | - | 30% | - | 35% | 35% |
|  | B | 40% | - | - | 40% | 20% |
|  | C | 10% | 10% | - | 50% | 30% |

*3/Product Costing: Materials, Labour and Overhead*

Allocate service department costs to production departments by
(a) the direct method
(b) the step method
(c) the reciprocal services method

**3-38** **Use spreadsheet model to allocate service centre costs**
The Yoohoo Company has 5 departments in its factory, comprising two production departments, $P_1$ and $P_2$, and three service departments, $S_1$, $S_2$ and $S_3$.

The budgeted overhead costs of each department are as follows:

| Service Department | $S_1$ | $ 8 000 |
|---|---|---|
| | $S_2$ | $22 000 |
| | $S_3$ | $10 000 |
| Production Department | $P_1$ | $11 000 |
| | $P_2$ | $24 000 |

The percentage consumption of services is given in the following table:

| | | Service provided to: | | | | |
|---|---|---|---|---|---|---|
| | | $S_1$ | $S_2$ | $S_3$ | $P_1$ | $P_2$ |
| Service | $S_1$ | - | 10% | 10% | 40% | 40% |
| provided | $S_2$ | - | - | 20% | 10% | 70% |
| by | $S_3$ | 10% | 40% | - | 30% | 20% |

Allocate service department costs using
(a) the direct method
(b) the step method, in order of service department cost, largest first
(c) the reciprocal services method.

**3-39** **Journal entry for cost of goods sold**
The Work-in-Process account balance was $100 000 on 1 May and $90 000 on 31 May. During May $50 000 of direct materials were issued to production, employees working directly on production earned $60 000, and overhead allocated for the month was $35 000.

*Required:*
The journal entry to record the cost of production completed during May.

**3-40** **Reconstructing cost accounts**
The following data are available for Producer Ltd for 20X7:

| | Materials Control | Work-in-Process Control | Finished Goods |
|---|---|---|---|
| Opening balances | $ 10 000 | $ 75 000 | $10 000 |
| Purchases | 100 000 | | |
| Direct labour | | 50 000 | |
| Allocated overhead | | 50 000 | |
| Closing balances | 10 000 | 100 000 | 10 000 |

*Required:*
A journal entry to record the cost of goods sold during 20X7.

**3-41** **Reconstructing cost accounts: missing data**
O. Bese, the management accountant for a firm, has been keeping efficient records to date in spite of a low kilojoule diet necessitated by a weight problem. On the morning of 1 September 20X4, however, he went berserk from hunger, and consumed the accounting records. He was overpowered and rushed to hospital. Unfortunately his condition depreciated and he was written off at 4 p.m. An autopsy (with a qualified doctor in attendance) disclosed the following information:

3/Product Costing: Materials, Labour and Overhead

|  |  |
|---|---|
| **Ledger balances:** |  |
| Materials Control 31/8/X4 | $36 000 |
| Work-in-Process 1/8/X4 | 4 000 |
| Finished Goods 1/8/X4 | 40 000 |
| Accounts Payable 1/8/X4 | 20 000 |

An interview with the factory foreman revealed the following additional information:

- Accounts Payable are for direct materials only. The balance on 31 August was $10 000. Payments of $40 000 were made during August.

- A stocktake after O. Bese's autopsy revealed only one unfinished job in the factory. Source documents showed that $2000 (800 hours) of direct labour and $4000 of direct material had been charged to the job.

- The finished goods inventory as at 31 August was $44 000.

- Overhead is allocated by using a predetermined rate that is set at the beginning of each year by forecasting the year's overhead and using forecast direct labour hours as a cost driver. The budget for 20X4 called for a total of 167 539 hours of direct labour and $502 617 of factory overhead.

- Jobs sold during August realised $180 000.

- A total of 18 800 direct labour hours were worked during August. All factory workers receive the same rate of pay.

- Finished jobs are priced at a mark-up of 50% on manufacturing cost.

*Required:*
The balance of Materials Control account at 1/8/X4.

**3-42** **Activity based costing: easy**
The Australian Bank allocates central processing costs to products using average daily account balances as a cost driver.

Two important products are savings accounts and cheque accounts, whose average daily balances are $1000 and $200 respectively. There are 5000 of each type of account. The total monthly cost of operating the central processing unit is $65 000.

(a) How much central processing cost would be allocated to the average savings account and the average cheque account?

(b) A special cost study revealed that three central processing activities explained the level of processing costs: account maintenance, number of deposits, and number of withdrawals (or cheques presented). The cost of these activities is estimated as follows:

|  |  |
|---|---|
| Maintenance | $1.00 per account per month |
| Deposits | $0.50 per deposit |
| Withdrawals | $0.50 per withdrawal (or cheque presented for payment) |

The average number of deposits and withdrawals per account per month are:

|  | Savings a/c | Cheque a/c |
|---|---|---|
| Deposits | 2 | 10 |
| Withdrawals | 2 | 8 |

Based on this activity data, how much central processing cost would be allocated to the average savings account and the average cheque account?

## 3/Product Costing: Materials, Labour and Overhead

**3-43 Multiple cost pools versus single cost pool**

Multiproducts Co. Pty Ltd has four products. Some details follow:

|  | $P_1$ | $P_2$ | $P_3$ | $P_4$ |
|---|---|---|---|---|
| Selling price | $100 | $40 | $60 | $50 |
| Prime cost | $ 45 | $10 | $25 | $15 |
| Direct labour hours/unit | 6 | 1 | 3 | 2 |

Fixed overhead for the factory totals $80 000. A plant-wide overhead rate is used for allocating overhead to products, with direct labour hours as the cost driver.

(a) Assuming that 1000 units of each product are to be produced, calculate the plant-wide overhead rate.
(b) Determine the unit cost of each product.
(c) The company has a rule that any product which earns less than 25% markup on total cost will be dropped. Which products should be dropped?
(d) If any products are dropped no fixed overhead is avoidable, and so all overhead must be allocated to the remaining products. If part (c) indicates that a product should be dropped, re-calculate the overhead rate, total unit cost and markup on the remaining products. Should any products now be dropped? If so, keep repeating this exercise for as long as necessary.
(e) Detailed cost analysis now indicates that the fixed overhead can be separated into four cost pools, each identified with a particular product:

|  | $P_1$ | $P_2$ | $P_3$ | $P_4$ |
|---|---|---|---|---|
| Fixed overhead | $25 000 | $17 500 | $17 500 | 20 000 |

Calculate the fixed overhead rate for each product, calculate the unit cost of each and determine whether any products should be dropped.

Why do your conclusions differ in (e) from in (d)?

**3-44 Activity based costing**

Charles Manufacturing Ltd produces two products, X and Y, and uses activity based costing. The following data summarise activities, overhead cost pools and cost drivers in use:

| Overhead Activity | Overhead Cost | Cost Driver | Cost Driver Consumption by Product X | Consumption by Product Y |
|---|---|---|---|---|
| Machining | $200 000 | Machine Hrs | 20 000 | 20 000 |
| Setups | $ 15 000 | No. Setups | 100 | 50 |
| Receiving | $ 9 000 | No. Receipt | 200 | 400 |
| Packing | $ 60 000 | No. Orders | 800 | 400 |

*Required:*
(a) Assuming that each activity's cost pool is allocated using a separate cost driver, as indicated above, calculate:
  (i) the overhead allocation rate for each overhead cost pool, and
  (ii) the total overhead costs allocated to each product.
(b) Can any overhead cost pools be combined to reduce the number of overhead allocation rates and still produce the same overhead costs for each product? If so, combine them and repeat calculations (a)(i) and (ii).

## 3/Product Costing: Materials, Labour and Overhead

**3-45 Activity based costing**

Toys Ltd manufactures toys and uses an activity based costing system. Activity data, conversion costs and capacity for the month of May were as follows:

| Activity | Cost Driver | Conversion Cost | Actual Capacity |
|---|---|---|---|
| Materials handling | Length of timber | $2200 | 22 000 m |
| Forming & sanding | Direct labour hours | $8000 | 800 DLH |
| Painting | Number of painted toys | $3600 | 12 000 toys |
| Inspection | Number finished toys | $560 | 14 000 toys |
| Packaging | Number finished toys | $2800 | 14 000 toys |

In May two types of toys were produced: Type A and type B. Quantities and data were:

|  | Type A | Type B |
|---|---|---|
| Toys produced | 12 000 | 2000 |
| Direct material cost per toy | $1.20 | $2.00 |
| Metres of timber/toy | 1.5 | 2.0 |
| Direct labour hours/toy | 0.05 | 0.10 |
| Toys painted | 12 000 | none |

How much was the manufacturing cost of each type of toy?

**3-46 Activity based costing**

ABC Company has the following overhead cost pools and cost drivers:

| O/H Cost Pool | Activity Costs | Cost Drivers |
|---|---|---|
| Machine setups | $180 000 | 3000 setup hours |
| Material handling | $120 000 | 60 000 kg material |
| Electricity | $50 000 | 100 000 kilowatt hr |

Two products, A1 and A2 were produced. The following information relates to their production:

|  | Product A1 | Product A2 |
|---|---|---|
| Units produced | 3 000 | 6 000 |
| Direct material cost | $15 000 | $15 000 |
| Direct labour cost | $7 050 | $11 100 |
| Setup hours | 120 | 150 |
| Kg material used | 3 000 | 6 000 |
| Kilowatt hours | 1 500 | 1 800 |

Calculate the total unit cost of each product.

**3-47 Activity based costing versus conventional costing**

Blayney Company's budgeted overhead costs for March were:

| Setups | $90 000 |
| Material handling | 120 000 |
| Inspections (quality) | 30 000 |
| Electricity | 60 000 |

Blayney's cost accounting system allocates overhead costs to products using machine hours as the cost driver. Estimated machine hours for March were 75 000.

The company has recently lost some tenders and the managing director has asked the management accountant to try using an ABC costing system. The following data were collected:

| Activity | Cost Driver | Capacity |
|---|---|---|
| Setups | Number setups | 1 500 |
| Material handling | Material moves | 7 500 |
| Inspections | Number | 4 500 |
| Electricity | KW hours | 30 000 |

The company has received a request to tender to supply 1000 units of one of its products, P6. The following estimates have been prepared for the production of 1000 units of P6:

| Direct material cost | $20 000 |
|---|---|
| Direct labour cost | $50 000 |
| Machine hours | 1 800 |
| Direct labour hours | 2 000 |
| Kilowatt hours electricity | 2 000 |
| Number of material moves | 40 |
| Number of setups | 5 |
| Number of inspections | 20 |

*Required:*
(a) Calculate the estimated cost per unit of P6 under the current costing system.
(b) Calculate the estimated cost per unit of P6 using activity based costing.

**3-48** **Activity based costing versus conventional costing**
Innovative Company manufactures two products, P1 and P2. Overhead costs for the coming year are estimated to be $1 000 000. Unit costs and production data are estimated to be as follows:

|  | P1 | P2 |
|---|---|---|
| Direct material cost | $15.00 | $22.00 |
| Direct labour cost ($6/hr) | $12.00 | $30 |
| Production (units) | 10 000 | 6 000 |

*Required:*
(a) Calculate the total cost per unit for each product if overhead costs are allocated to products on the basis of number of units produced.
(b) Calculate the total cost per unit for each product if overhead costs are allocated to products on the basis of direct labour hours.
(b) Calculate the total cost per unit for each product if an ABC approach is used based on the following additional information.

| Cost Driver | Activity Cost | Cost Driver Units Demanded by P1 | Cost Driver Units Demanded by P2 |
|---|---|---|---|
| Setups | $200 000 | 200 | 800 |
| Purchase orders | $300 000 | 400 | 200 |
| Machine hours | $250 000 | 4 000 | 12 000 |
| Shipments | $250 000 | 400 | 600 |

## 3-49 Activity based costing

Sturt Company Pty Ltd produces two models of petrol lawnmowers, Standard and Deluxe. The following projections have been obtained for 20X4:

|  | 20X4 Estimates | |
|---|---|---|
|  | **Standard** | **Deluxe** |
| Annual sales (units) | 400 000 | 50 000 |
| Selling price | $400 | $600 |
| Prime cost per unit | $160 | $240 |
| Overhead cost per unit* | $150 | $150 |
| Gross Profit per unit | $90 | $210 |

* Using direct labour hours as the cost driver at the rate of $15/DLH

Upon examining the estimates the marketing manager was very impressed with the profitability of the Deluxe mower and suggested that more emphasis should be placed on producing and selling this product. The manufacturing manager objected, arguing that he did not believe the accountants' relative costing of the mowers. The management accountant agreed, saying that the company should install an activity based costing system.

On hearing all the arguments, the general manager asked the management accountant to recalculate the product costs using ABC techniques. The management accountant collected the following projected overhead information for 20X4:

| Overhead Activity | Overhead Cost | Cost Driver | Cost Driver Consumption Standard | Cost Driver Consumption Deluxe |
|---|---|---|---|---|
| Setups | $ 1 000 000 | Number Setups | 100 | 150 |
| Machining | $50 000 000 | Machine Hours | 400 000 | 100 000 |
| Engineering | $10 000 000 | Engineering Hours | 150 000 | 50 000 |
| Packing | $ 6 500 000 | Packing Orders | 200 000 | 50 000 |
|  | $67 500 000 |  |  |  |

*Required:*
(a) Using the 20X4 estimates based on conventional costing, calculate gross profit and gross profit percent in total for each mower product line, and for the company as a whole.
(b) Using the activity based costing data recalculate the unit gross profit for each type of mower and total gross profit for each product line and for the company as a whole.
(c) Write a brief report to the general manager evaluating the suggestion of the marketing manager to switch emphasis to the Deluxe model.
(d) On reflection, the management accountant observed that the four activity-based overhead cost pools could be reduced to three giving three overhead allocation rates without any loss of accuracy.
 (i) Explain which two cost pools can be combined and why.
 (ii) Combine these two pools, select an appropriate cost driver, and recalculate the overhead cost per unit for each mower to verify that you get the same overhead cost as in part (b).

## 3-50 Comprehensive review problem

World Class Sweets produces a standard nut chocolate bar which is packaged in a special wrapper for buyers who order a minimum of 10 000 chocolate bars. The wrapper shows the buyer's name and logo.

World Class Sweets has four separate factory departments, two production centres (chocolate bar production, and packaging) and two support service centres (production scheduling, and stores). Their responsibilities are as follows:

*Support service: Production Scheduling*

This centre is responsible for scheduling materials purchases, chocolate bar production and packaging. Recent discussions with schedulers have revealed that about 30% of their time is spent planning materials purchases for stores, 20% scheduling chocolate bar production and 50% scheduling packaging activities.

*Support service: Stores*

This centre is responsible for the control, receipt, storage and issue of all materials and supplies. Recent discussions with the three storemen have revealed that about 10% of their time is spent issuing materials and supplies for chocolate bar production and 40% issuing materials (including chocolate bars) and supplies for packaging. Receiving, storing and controlling materials consumes the other 50% of their time, 30% for chocolate bar production and 20% for packaging. It is believed that the time spent on receiving, storing and controlling materials is directly related to the number of units processed.

*Production: Chocolate bar production*

This centre is responsible for producing the standard nut chocolate bar into stock.

*Production: Packaging*

This centre is responsible for packaging all work orders in special wrappers according to customer specification. The chocolate bars are taken from stock and fed into specially cushioned hoppers to feed the packaging machines. This centre has 20 technically advanced, high precision packaging machines which are operated by 4 operators including a leading hand supervisor. The functions of the operators are to set up the machines for packaging runs, and to monitor, adjust and restart any machine that is shut down during a packaging run. About one-half of their time is spent in setting up the machines and the rest of their time is spent monitoring the operations of the packaging process. The operators (including the leading hand) work as a team and each may give assistance to the other operators in some circumstances.

**Current cost estimating procedure**

Standard process costing is used to determine product costs in the chocolate bar production centre.

The chocolate bars are transferred in to the packaging centre from the chocolate bar production centre at the standard cost per bar. The packaging wrappers, bearing the customer's endorsement, are bought in from an outside supplier. All other costs in the packaging centre are classed as conversion costs and are allocated to production based on the budgeted cost per 1000 bars. The budgeted packaging centre conversion costs (including allocated support service centre costs) for the year are divided by the budgeted production for the year to determine the budgeted packaging conversion costs per 1000 bars.

The following estimates for the packaging centre have been made for the coming year.

*Packaging output*

It is estimated that 1000 different customer orders will be packaged. For budgeting purposes it is assumed that each order will be for 50 000 bars. Thus 1000 set-ups will be required and 50 000 000 bars will be wrapped. The packaging machines have sufficient capacity to produce this number of bars and it is believed that the 4 operators can cope with the anticipated number of setups.

## 3/Product Costing: Materials, Labour and Overhead

*Budgeted costs and other data*

Production conversion costs:

|  | **Chocolate Bar** | |
|---|---|---|
|  | **Production** | **Packaging** |
| Operator labour | $154 000 | $114 000 |
| Supervision | 46 000 | 46 000 |
| Depreciation | 220 000 | 200 000 |
| Set-up supplies | 10 000 | 20 000 |
| Energy costs | 25 000 | 30 000 |
| Repairs & maintenance costs | 40 000 | 60 000 |
| Occupancy costs (rent, lighting etc.) | 20 000 | 30 000 |
| Allocated support costs | ? | ? |

| Support centre costs: | **Production Schedule** | **Stores** |
|---|---|---|
| Labour | $120 000 | $100 000 |
| Other costs | 30 000 | 20 000 |

### PART A

(1) Allocate the support service centre costs to the production centres. Justify your choice of method and allocation base.

(2) Following the firm's estimating procedure, calculate the budgeted conversion cost for the packaging centre of 1000 bars.

### PART B

Some concern has been expressed about the accuracy of the budgeted conversion costs per 1000 bars for the packaging centre; that the prices being quoted by the firm seem to be out of line with prices quoted by other firms. You have therefore been asked to review existing procedures and prepare a budgeted conversion cost per order using a different procedure.

(1) As part of your review it occurs to you that some of the conversion costs in the packaging department may be related to quite different activities. That is, while some costs are more closely related to process time (proportional to the number of bars packaged), others seem to be related more closely to the number of packaging machine setups.

(a) Classify each of the following conversion costs as being related more closely to (i) process time or (ii) number of set-ups and justify your choices.

(b) Complete a table of the following form, showing the apportionment of packaging department budgeted conversion costs between the two cost pools, namely process time-related costs and setup-related costs:

3/*Product Costing: Materials, Labour and Overhead*

| Cost Items | Process time related costs | Set-up related costs | Total costs |
|---|---|---|---|
| Operator labour costs | | | $114 000 |
| Supervision | | | 46 000 |
| Depreciation | | | 200 000 |
| Setup supplies | | | 20 000 |
| Energy costs | | | 30 000 |
| Repairs & maintenance costs | | | 60 000 |
| Occupancy costs | | | 30 000 |
| Allocated support costs<br> - Production Scheduling<br> - Stores | | | |
| Total | | | |

(c) Having completed the allocation table, calculate:
   (i) the cost per 1000 bars for the total process time-related conversion costs; and
   (ii) the cost per set-up for the setup-related conversion costs.

(2) (a) Calculate the budgeted conversion costs for the packaging centre for customer orders of 20 000 bars and 100 000 bars respectively using:
   (i) the existing allocation procedure; and
   (ii) the revised allocation procedure.

(b) Explain the principal factors which have contributed to the apparent difference in total budgeted conversion costs of the packaging centre for these customer orders.

# Chapter 4

# Product Costing Systems: Job Costing and Process Costing

In Chapter 2 you learned how to prepare a manufacturing statement to summarise the flow of production costs and to calculate the cost of goods manufactured. We concluded that the usefulness of the manufacturing statement approach to product costing is limited to the case where only a single product is produced. In such a situation, unit product cost can be determined by averaging a period's cost of goods manufactured over the number of units produced. Once more than one product is involved, any determination of each product's unit cost would be purely arbitrary.

Even in the case of a single product, to construct a manufacturing statement requires valuations of inventories of work in process. Such valuations should normally be cost-based, necessitating a knowledge of product costs in order to be able to construct such a manufacturing statement in the first place.

In Chapter 3 we examined in detail how material, labour and overhead costs are controlled, and how they are charged to production. In the general ledger, all production costs are collected in the Work-in-Process account (or we could have three separate accounts: Materials-in-Process, Labour-in-Process, Overhead-in-Process). As production is completed, the cost of such completed production is transferred to Finished Goods, and any Work-in-Process balances represent the cost of unfinished work. A basic problem is how to determine the cost of completed production.

The task of costing completed products or services is essentially one of finding a suitable output object to which costs can be traced and attached. Selection of an appropriate output cost object will be influenced significantly by the technology employed in the production process. At the most detailed costing level, the output cost object is a single unit or batch of units, meaning that the resources consumed by each unit or batch can be identified, measured and costed. This can occur when each unit or batch is separately identifiable, is unique, is different from other units or batches of output. Each unit or batch is referred to as a **job**, and the tracing of costs to jobs as **job costing**. Industries that commonly engage in non-repetitive jobbing methods for which job costing is appropriate include construction, furniture, printing, machinery, car repairs, auditing and consulting, hospital cases and research projects.

At the other extreme, the technology employed may be mass/continuous production of standard products or services, through a series of **processes**. In this case the output cost object is a process (or department), and the resources consumed in each process over a period of time are measured and costed, and then averaged over the output of that process. This type of costing system is referred to as **process costing**. Industries that commonly employ process costing methods include chemicals, petroleum, paint, glass, steel, cement, food processing (canneries, flour mills), banking, food preparation, and insurance.

Between these two extremes of job costing and process costing there are found hybrid systems which contain characteristics of both job and process costing. A popular hybrid system is known as **operation costing** which is used where the conversion activities are the same for different products, but the materials used in them differ significantly. For example, some types of clothing have nearly identical labour and overhead inputs but the material differs significantly (eg., wool, silk, cotton, polyester). A typical treatment would be to trace material costs to specific jobs or batches of production (as in job costing), but to calculate conversion costs for the process and average over output (as in process costing).

No matter which costing system is used the detailed recording and tracing of costs to jobs, batches, or processes is performed in subsidiary records, such as job or process cost sheets, which form a subsidiary ledger for the Work-in-Process account in the general ledger. Similarly, more detailed records may support the Finished Goods account; for example, job cost sheets (or cards) can be transferred from the Work-in-Process subsidiary ledger to the Finished Goods subsidiary ledger as jobs are completed.

## JOB COSTING

In a job costing system costs are accumulated by jobs or orders. Because each job or batch receives varying amounts of work, the unit cost per order differs from job to job. Production is performed according to customer specification. Manufacturing is not started until a customer places an order which acts as the production foreman's authority to commence work. The order also acts as the cost accounting department's authority to open a **job cost card** (or **sheet,** or **equivalent computer record**).

The job cost card or job cost sheet typically shows a job number, a brief description of the production order and the number of units required, the commencement and completion dates, and any other relevant information.

Throughout the production period all direct materials are traced to a job via materials requisitions and bills of materials, and recorded on the job card. Similarly, direct labour worked on each job is ascertained from labour time records and recorded on the job card. A share of overhead is allocated to a job using overhead allocation rates[1]; these are usually predetermined rates (see Chapter 3). So overhead is also recorded on the job card which, on completion of the job, shows its total cost. The set of job cards (or sheets) form a subsidiary ledger, which is controlled by the Work-in-Process general ledger account.

### Illustrative Example 4-1

*Southern Cross Tools manufactures machine tools to customer order, and employs a job costing system. The following details are available in respect of operations for March, 20X0:*

**Inventories, 1 March 20X0:**

*Materials*

| | | | |
|---|---|---|---|
| Material A: | 200 units @ $10 | $2000 | |
| Material B: | 450 units @ $8 | 3600 | |
| Indirect materials | | 2000 | $7 600 |

*Work in Process:*

| | Materials | Labour | Overhead | |
|---|---|---|---|---|
| | $ | $ | $ | |
| Job 101 | 3000 | 1000 | 2000 | |
| Job 102 | 2500 | 800 | 1200 | |
| | 5500 | 1800 | 3200 | $10 500 |

*Finished Goods:*
One job, Job 100 — $ 5 000

**Transactions during March 20X0**

1. *Purchases*: Material A: 500 units @ $10.50   $5250
   Material B: 1000 units @ $8.00   $8000

   All purchases were received on 2 March. There were no indirect materials purchased during March.

---

[1] Also called overhead application rates and overhead recovery rates.

4/Product Costing Systems: Job Costing and Process Costing

2. *Material Issues*:

| Date | Requisition # | Job # | Issues (units) | |
|---|---|---|---|---|
| Mar 5 | 254 | 102 | A: 50 | B: 100 |
| 10 | 255 | 103 | A: 400 | B: 200 |
| 20 | 256 | 104 | | B: 600 |

A physical stocktake revealed an inventory of indirect materials at 31 March of $950.

3. *Labour Summary*

| Job # | Amount |
|---|---|
| 101 | $1 500 |
| 102 | 2 000 |
| 103 | 2 500 |
| 104 | 2 750 |
| | 8 750 |
| Indirect labour | 2 750 |
| | $11 500 |

4. Overhead was allocated to jobs at the rate of $80 per machine hour. The number of machine hours used on each job during March was:

| Job | 101 | 15 |
|---|---|---|
| | 102 | 30 |
| | 103 | 25 |
| | 104 | 40 |
| | | 110 |

5. Production completed consisted of Jobs 101, 102 and 103.

6. Overhead incurred (in addition to indirect materials and indirect labour):

| Depreciation | $10 000 |
|---|---|
| Other Cash Expenses | 5 000 |

7. Jobs sold:

| Job | Sales Revenue |
|---|---|
| 100 | $ 6 500 |
| 101 | 10 000 |
| 102 | 12 000 |

8. FIFO is used to charge out materials to jobs.

*Required:*
Show journal entries and general ledger and subsidiary ledger accounts in respect of transactions for March, 20X0.

### 1. *Purchases* (see Item 1)

Total purchases for the month amounted to $13 250 (A: $5250 + B: $8000). The double entry would be:

| Materials Control | $13 250 | |
|---|---|---|
|    Accounts Payable | | $13 250 |

Every entry in a control account, such as in Materials Control, must be supported by entries in subsidiary ledger accounts. These purchases were all direct materials, which must also be recorded in the subsidiary ledger: Raw Materials Stock Ledger Cards [or Stores Ledger Cards]. Note that the two entries in the **Received** column of Material A and Material B stock ledger cards, $5250 and $8000, total to $13 250 as recorded in the general ledger account Materials Control. This company does not maintain subsidiary records for indirect materials and so there is no card for them. Note that where the purchase price differs from the price paid for inventories on hand, the balance column must show the quantities and costs separately – see the March 2 balance for Material A.

### RAW MATERIALS STOCK LEDGER CARDS

#### MATERIAL A

| Date | Received | | | Issued | | | | Balance | | |
|------|----------|--|--|--------|--|--|--|---------|--|--|
| | Qty | Un Cost | Tot Cost | Req # | Qty | Un Cost | Tot Cost | Qty | Un Cost | Tot Cost |
| Mar 1 | | | | | | | | 200 | $10.00 | $2000 |
| 2 | 500 | $10.50 | $5250 | | | | | 200 | $10.00 | $2000 |
| | | | | | | | | 500 | $10.50 | $5250 |
| | | | $5250 | | | | | | | $7250 |

#### MATERIAL B

| Date | Received | | | Issued | | | | Balance | | |
|------|----------|--|--|--------|--|--|--|---------|--|--|
| | Qty | Un Cost | Tot Cost | Req # | Qty | Un Cost | Tot Cost | Qty | Un Cost | Tot Cost |
| Mar 1 | | | | | | | | 450 | $8.00 | $ 3600 |
| 2 | 1000 | $8.00 | $8000 | | | | | 1450 | $8.00 | $11600 |
| | | | $8000 | | | | | | | $11600 |

**2.** *Material Issues (see Item 2 and Item 8)*

The detailed direct material issues are shown in the stock ledger cards, using FIFO, and from these cards we can determine the general ledger entry:

### RAW MATERIALS STOCK LEDGER CARDS

#### MATERIAL A

| Date | Received | | | Issued | | | | Balance | | |
|------|----------|--|--|--------|--|--|--|---------|--|--|
| | Qty | Un Cost | Tot Cost | Req # | Qty | Un Cost | Tot Cost | Qty | Un Cost | Tot Cost |
| Mar 1 | | | | | | | | 200 | $10.00 | $2000 |
| 2 | 500 | $10.50 | $5250 | | | | | 200 | $10.00 | $2000 |
| | | | | | | | | 500 | $10.50 | $5250 |
| 5 | | | | 254 | 50 | $10.00 | $ 500 | 150 | $10.00 | $1500 |
| | | | | | | | | 500 | $10.50 | $5250 |
| 10 | | | | 255 | 150 | $10.00 | $1500 | | | |
| | | | | | 250 | $10.50 | $2625 | 250 | $10.50 | $2625 |
| | | | $5250 | | | | $4625 | | | $2625 |

## MATERIAL B

| Date | Received | | | Issued | | | | Balance | | |
|---|---|---|---|---|---|---|---|---|---|---|
| | Qty | Un Cost | Tot Cost | Req # | Qty | Un Cost | Tot Cost | Qty | Un Cost | Tot Cost |
| Mar 1 | | | | | | | | 450 | $8.00 | $ 3600 |
| 2 | 1000 | $8.00 | $8.00 | | | | | 1450 | $8.00 | $11600 |
| 5 | | | | 254 | 100 | $8.00 | $ 800 | 1350 | $8.00 | $10800 |
| 10 | | | | 255 | 200 | $8.00 | $1600 | 1150 | $8.00 | $9200 |
| 20 | | | | 256 | 600 | $8.00 | $4800 | 550 | $8.00 | $4400 |
| | | | $8000 | | | | $7200 | | | $4400 |

From the two stock cards we see that the total raw material issues were costed at $11 825 ($4625 for Material A + $7200 for Material B). Hence a general journal entry would be:

| Work-in-Process Control | $11 825 | |
|---|---|---|
| Materials Control | | $11 825 |

As well as posting this entry to the general ledger we must also show the details of these direct material issues, which have been debited to Work-in-Process Control, on the individual job cost cards or sheets (subsidiary ledger). From the raw material stock ledger cards above we determine the following details:

Job 102 (Requisition # 254): A: $500 + B: $800 = $1300
Job 103 (Requisition # 255): A: $1500 + $2625 + B: $1600 = $5725
Job 104 (Requisition # 256): B: $4800

The following job cost sheets show the opening balances on 1 March plus the details of the direct material issues recorded in total in the Work-in-Process Control account:

## JOB COST SHEETS

### JOB # 101

| Date | Direct Materials | | Direct Labour | Overhead Allocated | | Total |
|---|---|---|---|---|---|---|
| | Reqn # | $ | $ | Machine Hrs | $ | $ |
| Mar 1 | Balance | 3000 | 1000 | 25 | 2000 | 6000 |

### JOB # 102

| Date | Direct Materials | | Direct Labour | Overhead Allocated | | Total |
|---|---|---|---|---|---|---|
| | Reqn # | $ | $ | Machine Hrs | $ | $ |
| Mar 1 | Balance | 2500 | 800 | 15 | 1200 | 4500 |
| 31 | 254 | 1300 | | | | |

### JOB # 103

| Date | Direct Materials | | Direct Labour | Overhead Allocated | | Total |
|---|---|---|---|---|---|---|
| | Reqn # | $ | $ | Machine Hrs | $ | $ |
| Mar 1 | 255 | 5725 | | | | |

### JOB # 104

| Date | Direct Materials | | Direct Labour | Overhead Allocated | | Total |
|---|---|---|---|---|---|---|
| | Reqn # | $ | $ | Machine Hrs | $ | $ |
| Mar 31 | 256 | 4800 | | | | |

The machine hours of 25 and 15 for Jobs 101 and 102 respectively in the March 1 balance were derived by dividing the overhead allocated of $2000 and $1200 respectively (see Inventories 1 March, 20X0) by $80 (see Item 4 information under Transactions during March).

As there were no purchases of indirect materials during March, the usage of indirect materials must have been equal to the reduction in inventory balances, $2000 - $950 = $1050. The double entry would be:

| | | |
|---|---|---|
| Overhead Control | $1050 | |
| Materials Control | | $1050 |

The credit to Materials Control could alternatively be a credit to Indirect Materials (or Supplies) if a separate account is held for indirect materials.

### 3. Labour *(see item 3)*

From the labour summary we distribute $8750 direct labour cost and $2750 indirect labour as follows:

| | | |
|---|---|---|
| Work-in-Process Control | $8 750 | |
| Overhead Control | 2 750 | |
| Accrued Payroll | | $11 500 |

The debit to Work-in-Process Control is a summary entry, and the individual jobs must show their direct labour cost, which is added to the job cost sheets:

### JOB COST SHEETS

**JOB # 101**

| Date | Direct Materials | | Direct Labour | Overhead Allocated | | Total |
|---|---|---|---|---|---|---|
| | Reqn # | $ | $ | Machine Hrs | $ | $ |
| Mar 1 | Balance | 3000 | 1000 | 25 | 2000 | 6000 |
| Mar 31 | | | **1500** | | | |

**JOB # 102**

| Date | Direct Materials | | Direct Labour | Overhead Allocated | | Total |
|---|---|---|---|---|---|---|
| | Reqn # | $ | $ | Machine Hrs | $ | $ |
| Mar 1 | Balance | 2500 | 800 | 15 | 1200 | 4500 |
| Mar 31 | 254 | 1300 | **2000** | | | |

**JOB # 103**

| Date | Direct Materials | | Direct Labour | Overhead Allocated | | Total |
|---|---|---|---|---|---|---|
| | Reqn # | $ | $ | Machine Hrs | $ | $ |
| Mar 31 | 255 | 5727 | **2500** | | | |

**JOB # 104**

| Date | Direct Materials | | Direct Labour | Overhead Allocated | | Total |
|---|---|---|---|---|---|---|
| | Reqn # | $ | $ | Machine Hrs | $ | $ |
| Mar 31 | 256 | 4800 | **2750** | | | |

### 4. Overhead Allocated *(see Item 4)*

Overhead is allocated to jobs at the rate of $80 per machine hour on the 110 machine hours worked on these jobs, that is a total of $8800:

| Work-in-Process Control | $8800 | |
|---|---|---|
| Overhead Allocated | | $8800 |

The individual jobs must also show the overhead component on the job cost sheets, machine hours used and resulting overhead allocated:

## JOB COST SHEETS

### JOB # 101

| Date | Direct Materials | | Direct Labour | Overhead Allocated | | Total |
|---|---|---|---|---|---|---|
| | Reqn # | $ | $ | Machine Hrs | $ | $ |
| Mar 1 | Balance | 3000 | 1000 | 25 | 2000 | 6000 |
| Mar 31 | | | 1500 | **15** | **1200** | 2700 |
| | Total | 3000 | 2500 | | 3200 | 8700 |

### JOB # 102

| Date | Direct Materials | | Direct Labour | Overhead Allocated | | Total |
|---|---|---|---|---|---|---|
| | Reqn # | $ | $ | Machine Hrs | $ | $ |
| Mar 1 | Balance | 2500 | 800 | 15 | 1200 | 4 500 |
| Mar 31 | 254 | 1300 | 2000 | **30** | **2400** | 5 700 |
| | Total | 3800 | 2800 | | 3600 | 10 200 |

### JOB # 103

| Date | Direct Materials | | Direct Labour | Overhead Allocated | | Total |
|---|---|---|---|---|---|---|
| | Reqn # | $ | $ | Machine Hrs | $ | $ |
| Mar 31 | 255 | 5725 | 2500 | 25 | 2000 | 10 225 |
| | Total | 5725 | 2500 | | 2000 | 10 225 |

### JOB # 104

| Date | Direct Materials | | Direct Labour | Overhead Allocated | | Total |
|---|---|---|---|---|---|---|
| | Reqn # | $ | $ | Machine Hrs | $ | $ |
| Mar 31 | 256 | 4800 | 2750 | **40** | **3200** | 10 750 |
| | | | | | | |

## 5. *Production Completed* (see item 5)

Jobs 101, 102 and 103 were completed, a total cost, from the job cost sheets, of

```
Job 101  $8 700
Job 102  10 200
Job 103  10 225
         29 125
```

The double entry would be:

| Finished Goods Control | $29 125 | |
|---|---|---|
| Work-in-Process Control | | $29 125 |

The job cost sheets for these three jobs could now be removed to become the finished goods subsidiary ledger, while the job cost sheet for the remaining unfinished job, Job 104, represents the closing balance of Work-in-Process, ie. $10 750.

## 6. Overhead Incurred *(see Item 6)*

In addition to the indirect materials and indirect labour, the other actual overhead expenses are Depreciation $10 000 and Other Cash Expenses $5000:

| | | |
|---|---|---|
| Overhead Control | $15 000 | |
|     Accumulated Depreciation | | $10 000 |
|     Bank | | 5 000 |

## 7. Sales *(see Item 7)*

Jobs 100, 101 and 102 were sold, giving rise to the following entries, first to record the cost of sales ($5000+$8700+$10 200) and the second to record the revenue from sales:

| | | |
|---|---|---|
| Cost of Goods Sold | $23 900 | |
|     Finished Goods Control | | $23 900 |
| | | |
| Accounts Receivable | $28 500 | |
|     Sales | | $28 500 |

The closing balance of finished goods is represented by the job cost sheet total for the unsold finished job, Job 103, ie. $10 225.

After these entries were posted to the general ledger it would appear as shown below.

**Southern Cross Tools**
**GENERAL LEDGER**

**Materials Control**

| 20X0 | | | $ | 20X0 | | | $ |
|---|---|---|---|---|---|---|---|
| Mar 1 | Balance | | 7 600 | Mar 31 | Work-in-Process | | 11 825 |
| 31 | Accounts Payable | | 13 250 | | Overhead Control | | 1 050 |
| | | | | | Balance | | 7 975 |
| | | | 20 850 | | | | 20 850 |
| Apr 1 | Balance | | 7 975 | | | | |

**Work-in-Process Control**

| 20X0 | | | $ | 20X0 | | | $ |
|---|---|---|---|---|---|---|---|
| Mar 1 | Balance | | 10 500 | Mar 31 | Finished Goods | | 29 125 |
| 31 | Materials Control | | 11 825 | | | | |
| | Accrued Payroll | | 8 750 | | | | |
| | Overhead Allocated | | 8 800 | | Balance | | 10 750 |
| | | | 39 875 | | | | 39 875 |
| Apr 1 | Balance | | 10 750 | | | | |

**Finished Goods Control**

| 20X0 | | | $ | 20X0 | | | $ |
|---|---|---|---|---|---|---|---|
| Mar 1 | Balance | | 5 000 | Mar 31 | Cost of Goods Sold | | 23 900 |
| 31 | Work-in-Process | | 29 125 | | Balance | | 10 225 |
| | | | 34 125 | | | | 34 225 |
| Apr 1 | Balance | | 10 225 | | | | |

### Overhead Control

| 20X0 | | $ | | | |
|---|---|---|---|---|---|
| Mar 31 | Materials Control | 1 050 | | | |
| | Accrued Payroll | 2 750 | | | |
| | Acc Depreciation | 10 000 | | | |
| | Bank | 5 000 | | | |
| | | 18 800 | | | |

### Accrued Payroll

| | | | 20X0 | | $ |
|---|---|---|---|---|---|
| | | | Mar 31 | Work-in-Process | 8 750 |
| | | | | Overhead Control | 2 750 |
| | | | | | 11 500 |

### Overhead Allocated

| | | | 20X0 | | $ |
|---|---|---|---|---|---|
| | | | Mar 31 | Work-in-Process | 8 800 |

### Cost of Goods Sold

| 20X0 | | $ | | | |
|---|---|---|---|---|---|
| Mar 31 | Finished Goods | 23 900 | | | |

### Sales

| | | | 20X0 | | $ |
|---|---|---|---|---|---|
| | | | Mar 31 | Accounts Receivable | 28 500 |

### Accounts Receivable

| 20X0 | | $ | | | |
|---|---|---|---|---|---|
| Mar 31 | Sales | 28 500 | | | |

### Accounts Payable

| | | | 20X0 | | $ |
|---|---|---|---|---|---|
| | | | Mar 31 | Materials Control | 13 250 |

Note that if GST were to be accounted for both Accounts Receivable and Accounts Payable would be increased by 10% and a GST account would show these taxes. For example:

### Accounts Receivable

| 20X0 | | $ | | | |
|---|---|---|---|---|---|
| Mar 31 | Sales | 28 500 | | | |
| | GST Clearing | 2 850 | | | |
| | | 31 350 | | | |

### Accounts Payable

| | | | 20X0 | | $ |
|---|---|---|---|---|---|
| | | | Mar 31 | Materials Control | 13 250 |
| | | | | GST Clearing | 1 325 |
| | | | | | 14 575 |

*4/Product Costing Systems: Job Costing and Process Costing*

|  |  | GST Clearing |  |  |
|---|---|---|---|---|
| 20X0 |  | | 20X0 | |
| Mar-31 | Accounts Payable | 1 325 | Mar-31 Accounts Receivable | 2 850 |
|  | Balance | 1 525 | | |
|  |  | 2 850 | | 2 850 |
|  |  | | Apr-01 Balance | 1 525 |

You will note that Southern Cross Tools nets off the GST payable on purchases of raw materials ($1325) against that collected on sales ($2850) to leave a balance owing to the ATO of $1525.

## *Job Cost Summary Sheet*

Sometimes it is convenient to summarise the information in the Job cost subsidiary ledger. For example, Southern Cross Tools Job Cost Sheets for March 20X0 could be summarised as shown below.

**Southern Cross Tools: Job Cost Summary Sheet**

|  | Job 101 | Job 102 | Job 103 | Job 104 | Total |
|---|---|---|---|---|---|
| O/Bal | 6,000 | 4,500 | | | 10,500 |
| Mat |  | 1,300 | 5,725 | 4,800 | 11,825 |
| Lab | 1,500 | 2,000 | 2,500 | 2,750 | 8,750 |
| O/Head | 1,200 | 2,400 | 2,000 | 3,200 | 8,800 |
| Total | $8,700 | $10,200 | $10,225 | $10,750 | $39,875 |

| Completed jobs | 101 | 8,700 | |
|---|---|---|---|
|  | 102 | 10,200 | |
|  | 103 | 10,225 | 29,125 |
| Closing WIP | 104 | 10,750 | 10,750 |
| Costs accounted for | | | $39,875 |

## *Comparison of Job Costs with Estimates*

It is often useful to compare the actual costs charged to a job with the estimated cost. Such comparisons provide management with an assessment of production performance, as well as valuable feedback concerning the accuracy of past estimates. Such feedback may provide a guide to the preparation of future job cost estimates for jobs of a similar nature.

# PROCESS COSTING

In a process costing system costs are accumulated and charged to processing departments which add value to the final product. In contrast to job costing, each unit of output is similar, or identical, and such units are produced in large batches or continuously for stock, rather than to specific customer order.

A process cost sheet is used to accumulate the costs incurred in each process (department). Throughout the production period all direct materials are traced to processes, and recorded on the process cost sheets. Conversion costs (direct labour and overhead) are also charged to departments and recorded on the process cost sheets, either **actual** conversion costs, or more commonly **allocated** conversion costs using a predetermined rate. At the end of each period the total costs for a processing department are averaged over the number of units produced.

Often there may be more than one process or department, and production is performed in a sequence of processes. In this case production costs are transferred forward from one process to the next, so that by the end of the last process the units of output bear the costs incurred over all processes. The cost flows in the ledger would appear as shown below:

| WIP – Dept. A | | WIP – Dept. B | | Finished Goods |
|---|---|---|---|---|
| Material, Labour and Overhead Costs | Transfer-out cost of partly completed production | Transfer-in cost of A + Material, Labour and Overhead Costs | Costs of A and B to Finished Goods | Costs of A and B |

## *Equivalent Units*

Process costing would be relatively straightforward if all production which was started during a period were also completed in the same period. For example, if production costs of $1700 were incurred and 1000 units completed, the unit cost would be $1700/1000 = $1.70 per unit.

Complications arise, however, when there are units still in process at the end of a costing period. If, during a month, some units have been completed but others are still in process, how do we average the total costs incurred in the process over the finished and unfinished production? Clearly there should be a higher unit cost attached to each finished unit than to each unfinished unit. The standard solution to this problem is to convert unfinished units to equivalent finished units; eg., 10 units half-complete is treated as equivalent to 5 completed units.

Continuing the previous example, suppose that 1000 units were started, but that only 800 units were completed. The other 200 units still in process were estimated to be 25% complete. We express the 200 incomplete units as 50 equivalent units (0.25 x 200). Thus the total production for the period would be calculated:

$$\begin{aligned}&800 \text{ completed units}\\&\underline{\phantom{0}50} \text{ equivalent (to completed) units}\\&\underline{850} \text{ equivalent units}\end{aligned}$$

Then the production costs of $1700 would be averaged over these equivalent number of units:

$$\text{Cost per equivalent unit} = \frac{\$1700}{850} = \$2 \text{ per unit}$$

Hence the completed units would be costed at $1600 (800 units x $2) and the 200 units of work in process at $100 (50 equivalent units x $2). This is shown on the credit side of Work-in-Process a/c:

## 4/Product Costing Systems: Job Costing and Process Costing

| Work-in-Process | | | |
|---|---|---|---|
| Material, Labour and Overhead | 1700 | Finished Goods | 1600 |
| | | C/Balance | 100 |
| | 1700 | | 1700 |

The above procedure is based on the assumption that production costs are incurred uniformly over time as units proceed from 0% to 100% completion. Although this is usually the case in respect of conversion costs, material costs may be incurred at discrete points in the production process. Obviously some direct material is required to start the process, and when calculating equivalent units, a unit of work in process would be treated as a completed unit for the purpose of allocating such material costs. On the other hand, when charging conversion costs, that same unit of work in process would be treated as incomplete and hence equal to less than one equivalent unit. Additional materials may be added during processing, eg. at the 30% mark, further complicating the calculation of equivalent units.

---

### *Illustrative Example 4-2*

A company starts a batch of 1000 units. Materials are added at the start of the process while conversion costs are incurred uniformly during the processing of the batch. At the end of the period 800 units had been completed, and the closing work in process of 200 units were estimated to be 75% complete. Costs incurred were:

| | | |
|---|---|---|
| | Materials | $2000 |
| | Conversion costs | 3800 |
| | Total costs | $5800 |

*Required:*
Determine the cost of units completed and the cost of work in process at the end of the period.

---

First we calculate the equivalent units, making separate calculations for Materials and Conversion Costs, because of the different timing of the consumption of these resources.

| | Physical Flow | Equivalent Units | |
|---|---|---|---|
| | | **Materials** | **Conversion** |
| Completed units | 800 | 800 | 800 |
| C/Work-in-Process | 200 | 200 | 150 |
| | 1000 | 1000 | 950 |

The column labelled **Physical Flow** reflects the actual number of units regardless of the degree of completion or the costs attached. 800 units were completed, and should be charged accordingly for the full cost of materials and conversion. Hence 800 appears under both the **Materials** and the **Conversion** equivalent units columns. The closing work in process of 200 units should bear the full material cost because materials were added at the start of the process and these units are regarded as complete when apportioning total material costs. Thus the full 200 appears under the **Materials** column. In respect of conversion, the closing work in process is only 75% complete, and thus these 200 units are equivalent to only 200 x 0.75 = 150 completed units - see the **Conversion** column.

Adding the columns, there were 1000 equivalent units over which to spread the material costs, but only 950 equivalent units over which to apportion the conversion costs. Accordingly, the unit product cost is determined:

| | | |
|---|---|---|
| Materials: | $2000/1000 EU = | $2 per unit |
| Conversion: | $3800/950 EU = | $4 per unit |
| Total: | | $6 per unit |

where EU = equivalent units.

Therefore the total production costs incurred, $5800, would be distributed as follows:

4/Product Costing Systems: Job Costing and Process Costing

| | | | | | |
|---|---|---|---|---|---|
| Completed production: | | 800 units x $6 | = | | $4800 |
| Closing WIP: | Materials | 200 EU x $2 | = | $400 | |
| | Conversion | 150 EU x $4 | = | $600 | $1000 |
| | | | | | $5800 |

## No Opening Work in Process

### Illustrative Example 4-3

Identical Products Ltd commences production of a new product on 1 July. Two raw materials, A and B, are used in manufacture: A is added at the beginning of the process and B when processing is 60% complete. Conversion costs are incurred uniformly throughout the processing operation.

During July 1000 units were started, but only 700 were completed. Closing work in process was counted as 300 units, estimated to be 50% complete.

Production costs incurred during July were:

| | | |
|---|---|---|
| Material A | $ 5 000 | |
| Material B | 2 100 | |
| Conversion | 3 400 | |
| | $10 500 | |

The calculations to obtain the allocation of costs between Finished Goods and Closing Work in Process are shown in the following *Production Cost Report*:

**Production Cost Report for Month of July**

| | Physical Flow | Equivalent Units | | |
|---|---|---|---|---|
| | | Mat A | Mat B | Conversion |
| Units in O/WIP | 0 | | | |
| Units started | 1 000 | | | |
| Total units to account for | 1 000 | | | |
| Units completed | 700 | 700 | 700 | 700 |
| Units in C/WIP (50%) | 300 | 300 | 0 | 150 |
| Units accounted for | 1 000 | 1 000 | 700 | 850 |
| Costs to account for: | $10 500 | $5 000 | $2 100 | $3 400 |
| Costs per equivalent unit: | $5 + $3 + $4 = $12 | $5000/1000 = $5 | $2100/700 = $3 | $3400/850 = $4 |
| Distribution of Costs: | | | | |
| Closing WIP | | 300*$5 | 0*$3 | 150*$4 |
| | $ 2 100 | $1 500 | $0 | $600 |
| Finished Goods | $ 8 400 | (700*$12) | | |
| Total costs accounted for | $10 500 | | | |

Note that the equivalent units for C/WIP, in column Mat B, are 0 because these units are only 50% complete whereas Material B is not added until the 60% completion point. Hence no Material B cost has been incurred for C/WIP. Also, note that the total cost per equivalent unit, $12, is obtained by adding the calculated $5, $3 and $4 for Mat A, Mat B and Conversion respectively, and <u>NOT</u> by dividing the total cost of $10 500 by 1000 units. (The latter might be obvious, but many students make this error.) The Work-in-Process account would appear as follows:

## 4/Product Costing Systems: Job Costing and Process Costing

|  | Work-in-Process |  |  |
|---|---|---|---|
| Material A | 5 000 | Finished Goods | 8 400 |
| Material B | 2 100 |  |  |
| Labour & Overhead | 3 400 | Balance | 2 100 |
|  | 10 500 |  | 10 500 |
| Balance | 2 100 |  |  |

### *Opening Work in Process*

> Continuing Illustrative Example 4-3, in the second month, August, a further 1500 units were started. 1400 units were completed (the 300 in process from July, plus 1100 of the 1500 started in August), and closing work in process was counted as 400 units estimated to be 70% complete.
>
> Costs incurred during August were:
>
> | | Material A | $7 500 |
> |---|---|---|
> | | Material B | 6 300 |
> | | Conversion | 6 426 |
> | | | 20 226 |

There is now an additional problem. Because of rising prices, as from 1 August Material B has increased from $3 per unit of product to $3.50, and Conversion costs have increased from $4 per unit of product to $4.20. Consequently the partly completed production in opening work in process is carried forward from July valued at the old prices, while the current month's resources are priced at the new level. It becomes necessary, therefore, to choose between at least two assumptions in separating the costs of production (debits to WIP) between finished goods and closing work in process.

Option 1 is to use the **Weighted Average Cost** method in which the costs attached to O/WIP are simply added to the current month's costs, and the total is averaged over the equivalent units. A solution employing this method is shown below.

**Identical Products Ltd**
**Production Cost Report for Month of August - WEIGHTED AVERAGE COST METHOD**

|  | Physical Flow | Equivalent Units |  |  |
|---|---|---|---|---|
|  |  | Mat A | Mat B | Conversion |
| Units in O/WIP (50%) | 300 |  |  |  |
| Units started | 1500 |  |  |  |
| Total units to account for | 1800 |  |  |  |
| Units completed | 1400 | 1400 | 1400 | 1400 |
| Units in C/WIP (70%) | 400 | 400 | 400 | 280 |
| Units accounted for | 1800 | 1800 | 1800 | 1680 |
| Costs to account for: |  |  |  |  |
|   In Opening WIP | $ 2 100 | $1500 | $ 0 | $ 600 |
|   Current month | $20 226 | $7500 | $6300 | $6426 |
| Total | $22 326 | $9000 | $6300 | $7026 |
| Cost per equivalent unit: | $5+$3.5+$4.18 = $12.68 | $9000/1800 = $5.00 | $6300/1800 = $3.50 | $7026/1680 = $4.18 |
| Distribution of costs: |  | 400*$5 = $2000 | 400*$3.50 = $1400 | 280*$4.18 = $1171 |
| Closing WIP | $ 4 571 |  |  |  |
| Finished Goods | $17 755 | (1400*$12.68) |  |  |
| Total costs accounted for | $22 326 |  |  |  |

Note that the cost per equivalent unit for conversion is $4.18, neither July's $4 nor August's $4.20. In fact, $4.18 is a weighted average which can be verified as follows:

| | |
|---|---|
| Total EU of output in August | 1680 |
| Less EU of output in O/WIP | 150 |
| EU of work done during August | 1530 |

Of the 1680 equivalent units of output, 1530 were costed at $4.20 for conversion, and 150 at $4. The weighted average is thus calculated:

| | |
|---|---|
| 1530/1680 x $4.20 = | $3.82 |
| 150/1680 x $4.00 = | 0.36 |
| | $4.18 |

In the production cost report it will be noticed that under *Costs to account for* there appear two components: costs incurred last month in respect of O/WIP and the current month's costs.

Option 2 is to use the **FIFO** method, which separately traces the costs to complete the opening work in process which bears a mixture of last period's costs and current costs, and then costs the current period's production at current rates.

### Identical Products Ltd
### Production Cost Report for Month of August - FIFO METHOD

| | Physical Flow | Equivalent Units Mat A | Mat B | Conversion |
|---|---|---|---|---|
| Units in O/WIP | 300 | | | |
| Units started | 1500 | | | |
| Total units to account for | 1800 | | | |
| Units completed ex O/WIP | 300 | 0 | 300 | 150 |
| Units started & completed | 1100 | 1100 | 1100 | 1100 |
| Units in C/WIP (70%) | 400 | 400 | 400 | 280 |
| Work done this month | 1800 | 1500 | 1800 | 1530 |
| Costs to account for: | | | | |
| In Opening WIP | $ 2 100 | $1500 | $ 0 | $ 600 |
| Current month | $20 226 | $7500 | $6300 | $6426 |
| Total | $22 326 | $9000 | $6300 | $7026 |
| Cost per equivalent unit for work done this month: | $5+$3.5+$4.2 = $12.70 | $7500/1500 = $5.00 | $6300/1800 = $3.50 | $6426/1530 = $4.20 |
| Distribution of costs: | | 400*$5.00 | 400*$3.50 | 280*$4.20 |
| Closing WIP | $4 576 | = $2000 | = $1400 | = $1176 |
| Finished Goods | | | | |
| - Cost of O/WIP (from above) | $2 100 | $1500 | $ 0 | $ 600 |
| | | 0*$5.00 | 300*$3.50 | 150*$4.20 |
| - Cost to complete O/WIP | $1 680 | = 0 | = $1050 | = $630 |
| | | 1100*$5.00 | 1100*$3.50 | 1100*$4.20 |
| - Started and completed | $13 970 | = $5500 | = $3850 | = $ 4620 |
| | $17 750 | $7000 | $4900 | $5850 |
| Total costs accounted for | $22 326 | | | |

In calculating equivalent units, the units to complete O/WIP are 0 for Material A because it is added at the beginning of the process and so the opening work in process already has Material A cost included. The EU to complete O/WIP are 300 for Material B because none of Material B has been added prior to this month, and the whole 300 units are to be charged for Material B. The EU to complete O/WIP are 150 for Conversion because 50% of the work is still to be done this month.

The *Cost per equivalent unit* calculation is performed for work done this month by dividing current month's costs by *Work done this month*: $7500/1500 for Mat A, $6300/1800 for Mat B and $6426/1530 for Conversion.

When distributing costs, the cost of Finished Goods consists of three components: the costs already incurred in the previous month for O/WIP, the current month's costs incurred to complete that O/WIP (cost per EU times EU completed ex O/WIP), and the current month's costs incurred in starting and completing the remaining finished units. Closing work in process has been costed at current month's prices.

An alternative method for presenting FIFO calculations is shown below. Two major differences are apparent. First, the method of calculating the work done this period is different. In the solution above we calculated *Work done this month* by tracking the completion of opening WIP, adding units started and completed during the month, and then adding closing WIP (work started this month but not completed). The solution below starts with the weighted average approach of adding units completed and units in closing work in process, representing the total output for the month. Then we deduct equivalent units in opening work in process to get work done this month. Both approaches give the same result.

Second, the distribution of costs is simplified here. We have calculated the cost of closing WIP using the current month's costs. Then the cost of finished goods (which has been starred) is simply found by deducting the cost of closing WIP from the total costs incurred.

### A Simplified Approach to FIFO Calculations

|  | Physical Flow | Equiv units Mat A | Mat B | Conversion |
|---|---|---|---|---|
| Units in O/WIP (50%) | 300 |  |  |  |
| Units started | 1,500 |  |  |  |
| Total units to account for | 1,800 |  |  |  |
| Units completed | 1,400 | 1,400 | 1,400 | 1,400 |
| Units in C/WIP (70%) | 400 | 400 | 400 | 280 |
| Units accounted for | 1,800 | 1,800 | 1,800 | 1,680 |
| Less Units in O/WIP | 300 | 300 | 0 | 150 |
| Work done this month | 1,500 | 1,500 | 1,800 | 1,530 |
| Costs to account for: |  |  |  |  |
| In Opening WIP | $2,100 | $1,500 | $0 | $600 |
| Current month | $20,226 | $7,500 | $6,300 | $6,426 |
| Total | $22,326 | $9,000 | $6,300 | $7,026 |
| Cost per equivalent unit for work done this month | $5+$3.5+$4.2 = $12.70 | $7,500/1,500 = $5.00 | $6,300/1,800 = $3.50 | $6,426/1,530 = $4.20 |
| Distribution of costs |  | 400*$5.00= | 400*$3.50= | 280*$4.20= |
| Closing WIP | $4,576 | $2,000 | $1,400 | $1,176 |
| Finished Goods* [TC-C/WIP] | $17,750 | $7,000 | $4,900 | $5,850 |
| Total costs accounted for | $22,326 | $9,000 | $6,300 | $7,026 |

If we compare the weighted average cost method with the FIFO method for this example we find that there is very little difference in the results. This is because the conversion cost difference was the only influence in August.

## *Two Processing Departments*

When sequential processing is required in the production process it is necessary to trace the flow of costs between processes. As work is completed in the first process, the cost of such work is transferred from **Work in Process - Process 1** account to **Work in Process - Process 2** account, rather than to **Finished Goods** account. Costs transferred from a prior process (Work in Process - Process 1) are called **Transferred-in** costs in **Work in Process - Process 2**. The presence of such transferred-in costs requires an additional column when calculating equivalent units. In principle, the equivalent units calculation for transferred-in costs is exactly the same as if another material were added at the beginning of the receiving process. Of course, it is not possible to calculate product costs in Process 2 before they have been calculated for Process 1.

## 4/Product Costing Systems: Job Costing and Process Costing

### Illustrative Example 4-4

Complex Processing Company produces a single product in two sequential processes, Process 1 and Process 2. A single raw material is added at the beginning of Process 1 and further material is added in Process 2 when units are 45% complete. Conversion costs are incurred uniformly throughout both processes. Details for September follow:

| Physical Flows | Process 1 | Process 2 |
|---|---|---|
| O/WIP (units) | 500 (30%) | 200 (40%) |
| Started in September | 2000 | ? |
| Completed and transferred | 2100 | ? |
| C/WIP (units) | 400 (60%) | 500 (50%) |

Costs
O/WIP:
|  |  |  |  |  |
|---|---|---|---|---|
|  |  |  | Transfer-in | $3 000 |
|  | Material | $2 000 | Material | $ 0 |
|  | Conversion | $1 500 | Conversion | $ 600 |
| Current: | Material | $9 360 | Material | $10 250 |
|  | Conversion | $23 400 | Conversion | $16 400 |

*Using the weighted average cost method prepare production cost reports for each process for September to determine the necessary distribution of costs, and construct the Work-in-Process account for each process.*

### Complex Processing Company
### PROCESS 1 - Production Cost Report
### for Month of September - WEIGHTED AVERAGE COST METHOD

|  | Physical Flow | Equivalent Units Material | Equivalent Units Conversion |
|---|---|---|---|
| Units in O/WIP (30%) | 500 |  |  |
| Units started | 2,000 |  |  |
| Total units to account for | 2,500 |  |  |
| Units transferred to P2 | 2,100 | 2,100 | 2,100 |
| Units in C/WIP (60%) | 400 | 400 | 240 |
| Units accounted for | 2,500 | 2,500 | 2,340 |
| Costs to account for: |  |  |  |
|   In Opening WIP | $3,500 | $2,000 | $1,500 |
|   Current month | $32,760 | $9,360 | $23,400 |
| Total | $36,260 | $11,360 | $24,900 |
| Cost per equivalent unit | $15.19 | $4.54 | $10.64 |
| Distribution of costs: |  |  |  |
|   Closing WIP | $4,371 | $1,818 | $2,554 |
|   Transferred to Process 2 | $31,889 | $9,542 | $22,346 |
| Total costs accounted for | $36,260 |  |  |

The cost of the transfer to Process 2 is calculated as $31 889 and will be entered in the Process 2 Production Cost Report.

**Complex Processing Company**
**PROCESS 2 - Production Cost Report**
**for Month of September - WEIGHTED AVERAGE COST METHOD**

|  | Physical Flow | Transfer-in | Material | Conversion |
|---|---|---|---|---|
|  |  | *Equivalent Units* |  |  |
| Units in O/WIP (40%) | 200 |  |  |  |
| Units transferred in from P1 | 2,100 |  |  |  |
| Total units to account for | 2,300 |  |  |  |
| Units completed | 1,800 | 1,800 | 1,800 | 1,800 |
| Units in C/WIP (50%) | 500 | 500 | 500 | 250 |
| Units accounted for | 2,300 | 2,300 | 2,300 | 2,050 |
| Costs to account for: |  |  |  |  |
|   In Opening WIP | $3,600 | $3,000 | $0 | $600 |
|   Current month | $58,539 | $31,889 | $10,250 | $16,400 |
| Total | $62,139 | $34,889 | $10,250 | $17,000 |
| Cost per equivalent unit | $27.92 | $15.17 | $4.46 | $8.29 |
| Distribution of costs: |  |  |  |  |
|   Closing WIP | $11,886 | $7,584 | $2,228 | $2,073 |
|   Finished Goods | $50,253 | $27,304 | $8,022 | $14,927 |
| Total costs accounted for | $62,139 |  |  |  |

The work-in-process accounts would appear thus:

**WIP – Process 1**

| O/Balance | 3 500 | WIP - Process 2 | 31 889 |
|---|---|---|---|
| Material | 9 360 |  |  |
| Labour & O/head | 23 400 | C/Balance | 4 371 |
|  | 36 260 |  | 36 260 |

**WIP – Process 2**

| O/Balance | 3 600 | Finished Goods | 50 253 |
|---|---|---|---|
| WIP - Process 1 | 31,889 |  |  |
| Material | 10 250 |  |  |
| Labour & O/head | 16 400 | C/Balance | 11 886 |
|  | 62 139 |  | 62 139 |

Note in the Process 2 report, units are not **started**, but **transferred in** from Process 1. There is an additional column, **Transfer-in**, under **Equivalent Units**. Transfer in costs are also traced, in addition to Material and Conversion costs. The current month's transfer-in costs of $31 889 came from the calculation in the Process 1 report: *Transferred to Process 2*.

## *Equivalent Unit Calculations - Are they Necessary?*

As you will have observed, the need to calculate equivalent units can make process costing rather complex. Moreover, it is necessary to estimate the closing work in process at the end of each period in terms of both quantity and percentage stage of completion. If there were no work in process at the end of each period the need to calculate equivalent units would disappear, greatly simplifying product costing. Alternatively, if work in process does exist in significant quantities, but is constant in quantity and degree of completion from period to period, it can be ignored by simply averaging current period costs over the number of units completed. Although this approach would provide satisfactory product costs, there remains the problem of valuing work in process inventories for financial reporting purposes.

Skinner (1978) reports that often work in process is quite constant and negligible, and tends to be ignored in costing:

> ... process times are typically measured in minutes rather than hours (although the throughput time in some processes can be as high as three hours). In these circumstances, it is only to be expected that the incomplete work within a process will always be constant and will usually be negligible.

## SUMMARY

The costing of completed products or services requires the identification of a suitable output object to which costs can be traced. A significant influence on the selection of a cost object is the type of technology employed in the production process.

Where each unit or batch of units tends to be unique it is referred to as a job and we usually trace production costs to each job by way of a job costing system. If the technology is one of mass/continuous production of standard products or services we trace production costs to processes and average such costs over the throughput in what we call a process costing system. There may be many hybrid systems between the two extremes of detailed tracing of costs under job costing and broad averaging of costs under process costing, hybrid systems which employ features of both.

Job costing involves tracing costs to each job, and this is achieved by using separate job cards or sheets for accumulating the costs of each job. The total costs of all job cards should equal the costs debited to the Work-in-Process account.

Process costing charges costs to processes or departments and such accumulated costs are averaged over the units passing through the process. Where there is more than one process, costs incurred in one process are transferred to the subsequent process and added to any further costs incurred in cumulative fashion.

The presence of work in process at the end of a period complicates the averaging process, which is then achieved by converting incomplete units to an equivalent number of completed units. It may be questioned whether equivalent unit calculations are really necessary, or are performed in practice.

Because of changing prices it becomes necessary to make an assumption about cost flows in process costing, leading to two common methods: weighted average cost and FIFO.

**REFERENCE**

R.C. Skinner, "Process Costing", *Abacus*, December 1978, 160-170.

*4/Product Costing Systems: Job Costing and Process Costing*

# APPENDIX

## Using a Spreadsheet for Process Costing Calculations

Process costing calculations can be simplified by preparing a spreadsheet to execute the necessary arithmetical manipulations. If you can set up a spreadsheet which is generalised, any problem can be done rapidly. You would require two different spreadsheets, one for weighted average cost method and one for FIFO cost method. Below is a spreadsheet model to solve weighed average problems. It has the data for Illustrative Example 4-3 for August, but will solve any problem by changing the data cells:

|    | A | B | C | D | E | F |
|----|---|---|---|---|---|---|
| 1  | PROCESS COSTING SPREADSHEET 1: WEIGHTED AVERAGE METHOD | | | | | |
| 2  | ENTER PROCESS DETAILS IN COLUMN C | | | | | |
| 3  | - % Completion Material 1 added | | 0% | | | |
| 4  | - % Completion Material 2 added | | 60% | | | |
| 5  | - Conversion costs assumed incurred uniformly | | | | | |
| 6  | | | | | | |
| 7  | ENTER PRODUCTION DETAILS IN COLUMN C | | | | | |
| 8  | - Units in Opening WIP | | 300 | | | |
| 9  | - Units started | | 1,500 | | | |
| 10 | - Units completed | | 1,400 | | | |
| 11 | - Units in Closing WIP | | 400 | | | |
| 12 | - % Completion of O/WIP | | 50% | | | |
| 13 | - % Completion of C/WIP | | 70% | | | |
| 14 | | | | | | |
| 15 | FLOW OF PRODUCTION | | | | | |
| 16 | | PHYSICAL | | | EQUIVALENT UNITS | |
| 17 | | FLOW | %AGE | MAT 1 | MAT 2 | CONVERSION |
| 18 | Units in O/WIP | 300 | 50% | | | |
| 19 | Units started | 1,500 | | | | |
| 20 | Total units to account for | 1,800 | | | | |
| 21 | | | | | | |
| 22 | Units completed | 1,400 | | 1,400 | 1,400 | 1,400 |
| 23 | Units in C/WIP | 400 | 70% | 400 | 400 | 280 |
| 24 | Units accounted for | 1,800 | | 1,800 | 1,800 | 1,680 |
| 25 | | | | | | |
| 26 | COST FLOWS | TOTAL | MAT 1 | MAT 2 | CONVN | |
| 27 | Costs to account for: | | | | | |
| 28 | In Opening WIP | $2,100 | $1,500 | $0 | $600 | |
| 29 | Current period | $20,226 | $7,500 | $6,300 | $6,426 | |
| 30 | Total | $22,326 | $9,000 | $6,300 | $7,026 | |
| 31 | | | | | | |
| 32 | Cost per equivalent unit | $12.68 | $5.00 | $3.50 | $4.18 | |
| 33 | | | | | | |
| 34 | Distribution of costs: | | | | | |
| 35 | Closing WIP | $4,571 | $2,000 | $1,400 | $1,171 | |
| 36 | Finished Goods | $17,755 | $7,000 | $4,900 | $5,855 | |
| 37 | Total costs accounted for | $22,326 | $9,000 | $6,300 | $7,026 | |

You will see that it has been set up for two raw materials and conversion. For problems with only one raw material enter zeros whenever detail is sought about the second material. If a problem has a Transfer-in cost from a previous process you could substitute Material A column as a Transfer-in column. The formulae are shown on the next page.

## 4/Product Costing Systems: Job Costing and Process Costing

| | A | B | C | D | E | F |
|---|---|---|---|---|---|---|
| 1 | PROCESS COSTING SPI | | | | | |
| 2 | ENTER PROCESS DETA | | | | | |
| 3 | - % Completion Material 1 | | 0 | | | |
| 4 | - % Completion Material 2 | | 0.6 | | | |
| 5 | - Conversion costs assum | | | | | |
| 6 | | | | | | |
| 7 | ENTER PRODUCTION DI | | | | | |
| 8 | - Units in Opening WIP | | 300 | | | |
| 9 | - Units started | | 1500 | | | |
| 10 | - Units completed | | 1400 | | | |
| 11 | - Units in Closing WIP | | =C8+C9-C10 | | | |
| 12 | - % Completion of O/WIP | | 0.5 | | | |
| 13 | - % Completion of C/WIP | | 0.7 | | | |
| 14 | | | | | | |
| 15 | FLOW OF PRODUCTION | | | | | |
| 16 | | PHYSICAL | | | EQUIVALENT UNIT | |
| 17 | | FLOW | %AGE | MAT 1 | MAT 2 | CONVERSION |
| 18 | Units in O/WIP | =C8 | =C12 | | | |
| 19 | Units started | =C9 | | | | |
| 20 | Total units to account for | =SUM(B18:B19) | | | | |
| 21 | | | | | | |
| 22 | Units completed | =C10 | | =$B22 | =$B22 | =$B22 |
| 23 | Units in C/WIP | =C11 | =C13 | =IF(C23<C3,0,B23) | =IF(C23<C4,0,B23) | =B23*C23 |
| 24 | Units accounted for | =SUM(B22:B23) | | =SUM(D22:D23) | =SUM(E22:E23) | =SUM(F22:F23) |
| 25 | | | | | | |
| 26 | COST FLOWS | TOTAL | MAT 1 | MAT 2 | CONVN | |
| 27 | Costs to account for: | | | | | |
| 28 | In Opening WIP | =SUM(C28:E28) | 1500 | 0 | 600 | |
| 29 | Current period | =SUM(C29:E29) | 7500 | 6300 | 6426 | |
| 30 | Total | =SUM(C30:E30) | =SUM(C28:C29) | =SUM(D28:D29) | =SUM(E28:E29) | |
| 31 | | | | | | |
| 32 | Cost per equivalent unit | =SUM(C32:E32) | =C30/D24 | =D30/E24 | =E30/F24 | |
| 33 | | | | | | |
| 34 | Distribution of costs: | | | | | |
| 35 | Closing WIP | =SUM(C35:E35) | =C32*D23 | =D32*E23 | =E32*F23 | |
| 36 | Finished Goods | =SUM(C36:E36) | =C32*D22 | =D32*E22 | =E32*F22 | |
| 37 | Total costs accounted for | =SUM(C37:E37) | =SUM(C35:C36) | =SUM(D35:D36) | =SUM(E35:E36) | |

You should be able to build another model to perform the calculations for FIFO.

## QUESTIONS AND PROBLEMS

**4-1** What is the difference between job costing and process costing systems?

**4-2** Name three industries that use

(a) job costing, and
(b) process costing.

### JOB COSTING PROBLEMS: 4-3 to 4-20

**4-3** **Overhead allocation rate and allocation to job**
Sturt Ltd allocates overhead to individual jobs by the use of predetermined overhead rates on a direct labour hour basis. The following budget estimates were made for the year ending 31/12/X9:

| | |
|---|---|
| Fixed manufacturing overhead | $60 000 |
| Variable manufacturing overhead per direct labour hour | $1.50 |
| Direct labour cost | $200 000 |
| Direct labour hours | 40 000 |

During the year the following details were recorded for Job 154:

| | |
|---|---|
| Direct material issued | $200 |
| Direct labour cost | $500 |

All workers are paid at the same rate and actual labour costs equal budgeted costs.

*Required:*
(a) What was the predetermined overhead allocation rate for the year?
(b) What was the total cost of Job 154?
(c) The total overhead incurred for the year amounted to $140 000 and actual direct labour hours worked were 42 250. What was the overhead variance?

**4-4** **Work-in-Process account, overhead variance write-off**
Jobbing Pty Ltd uses a job costing system. The records for July, 20X8 reveal the following:

(a) Direct Materials issued to production cost $96 000.
(b) Direct Labour analysis: 13 000 hours worked for $78 000.
(c) Overhead is allocated at the rate of $4 per direct labour hour.
(d) Total overhead incurred for the month was $54 000.
(e) Production orders that cost $200 000 were completed during the month.
(f) Production orders that cost $190 000 were shipped out and invoiced to customers during the month at a mark-up of 20 per cent on cost.
(g) Work in Process at the beginning of the month was $20 000.
(h) Overhead variances are written off to Cost of Goods Sold.

*Required:*
(a) Reconstruct the Work-in-Process account to determine its balance at 31/7/X8.
(b) Calculate the gross profit for July.

## 4/Product Costing Systems: Job Costing and Process Costing

**4-5  Work-in-Process account, overhead variance write-off**

Made-to-Order Pty Ltd uses a job costing system. The records for March, 20X4 reveal the following:

(a) Direct Materials issued to production cost $100 000.
(b) Direct Labour analysis: 10 000 hours worked for $120 000.
(c) Overhead is allocated at the rate of $6 per direct labour hour.
(d) Total overhead incurred for the month was $55 000.
(e) Production orders that cost $200 000 were completed during the month.
(f) Production orders that cost $150 000 were shipped out and invoiced to customers during the month at a mark-up of 25 per cent on cost.
(g) Work in Process at the beginning of the month was $30 000.
(h) Overhead variances are written off to Cost of Goods Sold.

*Required:*
(a) Reconstruct the Work-in-Process account to determine its balance at 31/3/X4.
(b) Calculate the gross profit for March.


**4-6  Job cost summary sheet (subsidiary ledger)**

Spock Manufacturing Company uses a job costing system. On 1 October, 20X1 Work-in-Process account had a balance of $8600, made up as follows:

| Job No. | Materials | Labour | Overhead | Total |
|---|---|---|---|---|
| 501 | 2480 | 960 | 1060 | 4500 |
| 502 | 2920 | 600 | 580 | 4100 |
|  | 5400 | 1560 | 1640 | 8600 |

At the same date Finished Goods had a balance of $12 000 representing the cost of Job No. 500.

During October material and labour costs, and labour hours were:

| Job No. | Materials Cost $ | Labour Cost $ | Labour Hours |
|---|---|---|---|
| 501 | 400 | 2 240 | 800 |
| 502 | 800 | 3 600 | 1 200 |
| 503 | 6 000 | 1 920 | 600 |
| 504 | 8 000 | 2 480 | 800 |
| 505 | 12 000 | 580 | 200 |
|  | 27 200 | 10 820 | 3 600 |

Overhead is allocated to jobs on a labour hour basis. In a normal month the factory is expected to operate at a volume of 4000 labour hours and factory overhead is expected to be $12 000.

During the month jobs 501, 502 and 504 were completed and transferred to finished goods.

*Required:*
Prepare a Job Cost Sheet summary for the month of October, 20X1, and determine the cost of jobs completed during October as well as the closing balance of the Work-in-Process account at the end of the month.


**4-7  Job cost summary sheet (subsidiary ledger)**

Elizabeth Manufacturing Company uses a job costing system. On 1 July, 20X1 Work-in-Process account had a balance of $14 300, made up as follows:

## 4/Product Costing Systems: Job Costing and Process Costing

| Job No. | Materials | Labour | Overhead | Total |
|---|---|---|---|---|
| 101 | 5000 | 2000 | 1500 | 8 500 |
| 102 | 4000 | 1000 | 800 | 5 800 |
|  | 9000 | 3000 | 2300 | 14 300 |

At the same date Finished Goods had a balance of $10 000 representing the cost of Job No. 100.

During July material and labour costs, and machine hours were:

| Job No. | Materials Cost $ | Labour Cost $ | Machine Hours |
|---|---|---|---|
| 101 | 500 | 2 400 | 1 000 |
| 102 | 1 000 | 4 000 | 1 300 |
| 103 | 6 000 | 2 000 | 800 |
| 104 | 7 000 | 3 000 | 1 200 |
| 105 | 9 000 | 3 000 | 500 |
|  | 23 500 | 14 400 | 4 800 |

Overhead is allocated to jobs on a machine hour basis. In a normal month the factory is expected to operate at a volume of 5000 machine hours and factory overhead is expected to be $20 000.

During the month jobs 101, 103 and 104 were completed and transferred to finished goods.

*Required:*
Prepare a Job Cost Sheet summary for the month of July, 20X1, and determine the cost of jobs completed during July as well as the closing balance of the Work-in-Process account at the end of the month.

4-8   **Reconstruct accounts in general ledger – incomplete information**
Examine the following partially completed T-accounts and additional information for Dinihan Company for April:

```
        Materials Control                          Work in Process
O/Bal        4,000                         O/Bal       8,000
A/cs Payable 16,000 | C/Bal    12,000
                                           Accrd Pay  12,000

        Finished Goods                             Cost of Goods Sold
O/Bal       12,000
            24,000 | C/Bal     16,000

        Overhead Control                           Overhead Allocated
Sundry a/cs  7,000
```

The direct labour wage rate was $20 per hour.
Overhead is allocated at 75% of direct material cost.
During the month sales revenue was $40 000 and selling and administrative costs were $7000.

*Required:*
(a) What was the cost of direct materials issued to production during April?
(b) How much overhead was allocated to products during April?
(c) What was the cost of goods completed during April?
(d) What was the balance of Work-in-Process account at 30 April?
(e) What was the overhead variance during April?
(f) What was the operating profit for April?

## 4/Product Costing Systems: Job Costing and Process Costing

**4-9  Reconstruct WIP account**

Bright Printing Company uses a job costing system. The following entries were made in the Work-in-Process account for the month of September:

| | |
|---|---|
| Opening balance | $8 000 |
| Direct materials issued | 40 000 |
| Direct labour used | 30 000 |
| Overhead allocated | 21 000 |
| Production completed | 90 000 |

Overhead is allocated as a percentage of direct labour cost. There is one job still in process at the end of September, Job 100 which has been charged $2000 for direct labour.

*Required:*
What is the cost of direct materials charged to Job 100 so far?


**4-10  Reconstruct accounts in general ledger – incomplete information**

Given the following incomplete information, reconstruct T-accounts to determine the balance of the Raw Materials account on 1/8/X8:

| | |
|---|---|
| Balance Work-in-Process, 1/8/X8 | $14 000 |
| Balance Finished Goods, 1/8/X8 | $45 000 |

There was one unfinished job on 31/8/X8 bearing $7000 (1000 hours) of direct labour and $9000 of raw materials.

| | |
|---|---|
| Balance Raw Materials, 31/8/X8 | $32 000 |
| Balance Finished Goods, 31/8/X8 | $55 000 |

Overhead is allocated on the basis of 200% of direct labour cost.
Jobs sold during the month realised $770 000.
A total of 20 000 direct labour hours were worked during August. All factory workers received the same rate of pay as for July.
Finished jobs are sold at a mark-up of 40% on manufacturing cost.
Materials purchased during the August cost $135 000.


**4-11  Cost flows in a service organisation**

In February AWP auditors worked 500 hours for Client A and 1,500 hours for Client B. The total number of hours worked were 2000. AWP bills clients at the rate of $150 per hour.

Labour cost for the audit staff is $75 per hour. Overhead is allocated to clients at the rate of $15 per hour. Actual overhead costs for February were $28 000. AWP incurred $100 000 in marketing and administration costs in February.

*Required:*
(a) Show the general ledger entries for labour and overhead costs in T-accounts.
(b) Prepare a statement of financial performance for AWP for February.


**4-12  Job costing in a service company**

Jarratt Associates conduct market research. The company operates a normal job costing system. Cost elements are *direct expenses* (to the jobs), *professional salary expenses* and *overhead costs*. A predetermined rate is used to allocate overhead on the basis of professional hours worked on each job.

The overhead rate for 20X2 was computed from the following budgeted data:

| Budgeted variable overhead | $5 per professional hour |
|---|---|
| Budgeted fixed overhead | $1 000 000 |
| Budgeted professional hours | 250 000 |

A summary of 20X2 results is as follows:

|  | Jobs Finished And Billed | Unfinished Jobs |
|---|---|---|
| Direct expenses | $800 000 | $200 000 |
| Professional salary cost | $4 000 000 | $500 000 |
| Professional hours worked | 200 000 | 25 000 |

Total sales were $9 000 000, selling and administration costs $1 500 000 and total actual overhead was $2 030 000.

*Required:*
(a) Calculate the predetermined overhead rate for 20X2.
(b) Prepare a statement of financial performance for 20X2 with any overhead variance shown as an adjustment to cost of goods sold.

**4-13 Basic job costing entries**

Burk Company operates a job costing system. The following **debit** account balances appeared in the general ledger on 1 September:

| Raw Materials and Supplies | $32 000 |
|---|---|
| Work in Process | 19 000 |
| Finished Goods | 17 500 |
| Overhead Variance | 2 000 |

**Particulars of work in process and completed jobs were:**

| *In process* | *Material* | *Labour* | *Overhead* | *Total* |
|---|---|---|---|---|
| Job 121 | 7 700 | 4 000 | 2 800 | 14 500 |
| Job 122 | 4 500 | 0 | 0 | 4 500 |
|  | 12 200 | 4 000 | 2 800 | 19 000 |
| *Complete* |  |  |  |  |
| Job 119 |  |  |  | 7 700 |
| Job 120 |  |  |  | 9 800 |
|  |  |  |  | 17 500 |

**The following information relates to the month of September:**

| Raw materials and supplies purchased |  |  | $26 660 |
|---|---|---|---|
| Raw materials and supplies issued to jobs: |  |  |  |
| Job 123 |  | $14 000 |  |
| Job 124 |  | 17 500 |  |
| Supplies for general use |  | 1 500 | 33 000 |
| Raw materials and supplies inventory, 30 September (physical check) |  |  | 24 000 |

Payroll distribution:
Direct labour on jobs:

|  |  |  |
|---|---|---|
| 121 | 1 200 |  |
| 122 | 2 900 |  |
| 123 | 5 400 |  |
| 124 | 9 600 |  |
| Indirect labour | 2 000 | 21 100 |

Factory overhead (excluding indirect labour and supplies)  13 200

Jobs invoiced at cost  57 220

Factory overhead is allocated to jobs using a predetermined rate based on direct labour cost.

Job 124 is still in process at 30 September. All other jobs are completed. Job 122, although completed, has not been invoiced.

*Required:*
(a) Complete a job cost summary sheet for September, and show a summary of jobs completed and jobs still in process.
(b) Prepare general ledger T-accounts to record the opening balances and September transactions.

**4-14  Job cost summary sheet (subsidiary ledger) and general ledger accounts**
Klingon Ltd manufactures hi-fi cabinets to customer specifications. A normal job costing system is used. The following information relates to the month of January:

**Extracts from Trial Balance, 1 January:**

| | |
|---|---|
| Raw Materials and Supplies Control | $20 500 |
| Work-in-Process | 50 000 |
| Finished Goods not invoiced | 6 500 |
| | $77 000 |

**Details of work in process obtained from job record cards:**

| Job # | Materials $ | Labour $ | Overhead $ | Total $ |
|---|---|---|---|---|
| 005 | 5000 | 5000 | 6000 | 16 000 |
| 006 | 6500 | 3500 | 4000 | 14 000 |
| 007 | 7000 | 6000 | 7000 | 20 000 |

**Orders issued during January:** Jobs 008, 009.

**Summary of materials issued:**

| Job No. | $ |
|---|---|
| 006 | 1100 |
| 007 | 700 |
| 008 | 4400 |
| 009 | 7800 |
| Supplies | 1000 |

**Labour Analysis and Summary:**

|  | Job No. | Hours | Cost ($) |
|---|---|---|---|
| Direct labour | 006 | 500 | 1200 |
|  | 007 | 850 | 2100 |
|  | 008 | 1250 | 3000 |
|  | 009 | 1500 | 3700 |
| Indirect labour | - | - | 350 |

**Other Information:**

| | |
|---|---|
| Electricity charges for month | $ 700 |
| Depreciation on Plant | 4 000 |
| Factory Rent | 10 000 |

Factory overhead to be allocated to jobs at the rate of $4 per direct labour hour.

Jobs 006 and 007 were finished during the month.

*Required:*

Record the above information in the appropriate ledger accounts and job cost ledger, and determine:
(a) the cost of jobs completed during January;
(b) the closing balance of the Work-in-Process account at the end of January;
(c) the overhead variance for January.

**4-15 Comprehensive job cost records**

The Wild Side Company modifies production motorcycles for superbike racing to customer order. It operates a job costing system. The following information is available for the month of May 20X0:

| **General ledger balances 1/5/X0:** | **$** |
|---|---|
| Direct Materials Control | 50 000 |
| Manufacturing Supplies Control | 10 000 |
| Work-in-Process Control | 29 500 |
| Finished Goods Control (Job #063) | 24 000 |

**Details of work in process from job cards at 1/5/X0 were as follows:**

| Job # | $ Materials | $ Labour | $ Overhead | $ Total |
|---|---|---|---|---|
| 064 | 8000 | 2000 | 4000 | 14 000 |
| 065 | 3000 | 1000 | 2000 | 6 000 |
| 066 | 5000 | 1500 | 3000 | 9 500 |

All these jobs had been started in April.

**Direct Materials issued during May 20X0 were:**

| Job # | $ |
|---|---|
| 065 | 3 000 |
| 066 | 2 000 |
| 067 | 12 000 |
| 068 | 2 000 |

**Supplies issued during May 20X0:** $8000

**Labour Analysis for May 20X0 showed:**
Direct Labour:

| Job # | Hours |
|---|---|
| 064 | 40 |
| 065 | 30 |
| 066 | 100 |
| 067 | 120 |
| 068 | 100 |

Indirect Labour cost: $3000

During the month the direct labour rate was $30 per hour. Factory overhead is allocated on the basis of direct labour dollars. The factory overhead rate is established in January each year.

Jobs 064 and 065 were completed during May and transferred to Finished Goods. No Direct materials or Supplies were purchased during May. Job 063 was sold on 3/5/X0 for $32 000 and Job 064 was sold on 29/5/X0 for $20 000.

**Other information relating to May:**

| | |
|---|---|
| Depreciation charges | $10 000 (4/5 relates to factory operations) |
| Electricity | $1 000 (all relates to factory operations) |
| Factory Rent | $2 000 |

*Required:*

Prepare a statement showing the gross profit for May 20X0, after writing off the overhead variance to Cost of Goods Sold. Show all supporting calculations and/or reconstructions of accounts.

**4-16 Comprehensive job cost records**

Charisma Company operates a small printing works and uses a job costing system. The data below are for the month of July, 20X8.

1. **Balances 1/7/X8:**

| Job No. | Materials | Labour |
|---|---|---|
| 3 | $15 000 | $13 500 |
| 4 | 7 000 | 9 000 |
| 5 | 30 000 | 18 000 |

| | |
|---|---|
| Finished goods inventory (Job 2) | $81 000 |
| Overhead in process | 27 000 |
| Direct materials inventory | 48 000 |
| Indirect materials inventory | 5 000 |

2. **Purchases during July, 20X8:**

| | |
|---|---|
| Direct material | $80 000 |

3. **Sundry factory expenses incurred in July:** $27 000

4. **Labour Analysis for July:**

| | |
|---|---|
| Job 3 | $ 6 750 |
| Job 4 | 27 000 |
| Job 5 | 2 700 |
| Job 6 | 9 000 |
| Indirect labour | $3 000 |

5. **Materials Issued to Production in July:**

| | |
|---|---|
| Job 3 | $22 500 |
| Job 4 | 40 000 |
| Job 5 | 8 000 |
| Job 6 | 17 500 |

Indirect materials $2 800

**Additional Information:**

Jobs 3 and 4 were completed during July. Jobs 2 and 4 were sold during July for $90 000 and $120 000 respectively, as per negotiated contracts.

Overhead is allocated to jobs using direct labour dollars as the cost driver.

A stocktake at 31/7/X8 revealed a shortage in the inventory of direct materials of $2500. An adjustment was subsequently made in the Direct Materials Control account to reflect the stocktake (actual) figure.

Company policy is to transfer under-allocated or over-allocated overhead directly to the Cost of Goods Sold account.

*Required:*

Prepare general ledger T-accounts to record the above information, and show any other records or calculations necessary to determine the following:
(a) The cost of Job 4 as at 1/7/X8.
(b) The balance of Direct Materials Control account as at 31/7/X8.
(c) The gross profit/loss on the sale of Job 4.
(d) The cost of goods sold for July.

**4-17** **Multiple choice – job cost records**

Custom Fabrications produces specialised stands for Hi Fi equipment. Each stand is unique and the firm uses a job costing system. Overhead is allocated to jobs at the rate of $2 per direct labour dollar. The following data relate to the month of September, 20X1:

**Balances 1/9/X1:**
| | |
|---|---|
| Raw Materials | $6 000 (Timber $4000, Paint $1500, Factory Supplies $500) |
| Materials-in-Process | $3 000 (Job 100 $2000, Job 101 $1000) |
| Labour-in-Process | $5 000 (Job 100 $3000, Job 101 $2000) |
| Overhead-in-Process | $10 000 |

**Creditors' invoices received during month:**
| | |
|---|---|
| Purchase of Paint | $1200 |
| Purchase of Timber | $2300 |
| Sundry Factory Expenses | $8900 (excluding any materials) |

**Raw Materials issued during month:**
| | |
|---|---|
| Job 100 | $1000 |
| Job 101 | $1300 |
| Job 102 | $1800 |
| Factory Supplies | $ 300 |

**Labour Analysis for month:**
| | |
|---|---|
| Job 100 | $ 900 |
| Job 101 | $1700 |
| Job 102 | $3100 |
| Indirect Labour | $ 650 |

During the month Jobs 100 and 101 were completed. Job 100 was sold for $18 400.

### 4/Product Costing Systems: Job Costing and Process Costing

*Required:*

(a) The balance of Overhead-in-Process in Job 100 at 1 September was:
(A) $7800 (B) $3000 (C) $6000 (D) $1500 (E) None of the above

(b) Direct labour cost charged to jobs during the month was:
(A) $6350 (B) $11 700 (C) $12 350 (D) $5700 (E) None of the above

(c) What was the balance of the Raw Materials account at the end of September?
(A) $5100 (B) $2100 (C) $9500 (D) $5400 (E) None of the above

(d) What was the overhead variance for the month?
(A) $1850 (B) $2700 (C) $11 400 (D) $1550 (E) None of the above

(e) What was the balance of Materials-in-Process at the end of September?
(A) $1800 (B) $7100 (C) $5300 (D) $3000 (E) None of the above

(f) What was the cost of Job 101?
(A) $11 100 (B) $13 400 (C) $7400 (D) $12 200 (E) None of the above

(g) What was the balance of Finished Goods account at the end of September?
(A) $13 200 (B) $6200 (C) $24 500 (D) $14 700 (E) None of the above

(h) What was the gross profit on Job 100?
(A) $6900 (B) $18 400 (C) $4100 (D) $3700 (E) None of the above

(i) What was the cost so far of Job 102?
(A) $11 100 (B) $13 400 (C) $24 500 (D) $4900 (E) None of the above

**4-18 Comprehensive job cost records**

Neataline manufactures aluminium frame sliding doors to customers' specifications. The firm uses a job costing system. The following information relates to the month of July, 20X5:

**General ledger trial balance as at 1 July, 20X5:**

|  | Dr $ | Cr $ |
|---|---|---|
| Bank |  | 1 200 |
| Direct Materials Control | 2 200 |  |
| Manufacturing Supplies Control | 900 |  |
| Work-in-Process Control | 15 500 |  |
| Finished Goods Control | 3 600 |  |
| Owners' Equity |  | 21 000 |
|  | 22 200 | 22 200 |

**Details of work in process at 1 July, 20X5, as obtained from the job cost cards:**

| Job No. | Direct Materials $ | Direct Labour $ | Allocated Overhead $ |
|---|---|---|---|
| 141 | 2000 | 1500 | 1000 |
| 142 | 1600 | 1400 | 1200 |
| 143 | 3000 | 2100 | 1700 |

**Details of finished goods at 1 July, 20X5:** Job 140, $3600

**Jobs commenced during July:** Jobs 144 and 145

## Labour analysis and details of materials issued during July:

| Job No. | Labour Hours | Labour Cost $ | Materials Cost $ |
|---|---|---|---|
| 141 | 200 | 600 | 600 |
| 142 | 150 | 450 | 500 |
| 143 | 130 | 390 | 400 |
| 144 | 190 | 570 | 1000 |
| 145 | 250 | 750 | 700 |
| Supplies | | | 1100 |
| Indirect labour | 400 | 800 | |

## During July the following transactions took place:

| | |
|---|---|
| Direct materials purchased (cash) | $3900 |
| Manufacturing supplies purchased (cash) | 900 |
| Direct and indirect wages paid | 3560 |
| Overhead expense incurred and paid | 4000 |

Overhead is allocated to jobs at the rate of $4 per direct labour hour.

The following completed jobs were sold to customers for cash during July:

| Job No. | Sales Revenue $ |
|---|---|
| 140 | 4 200 |
| 141 | 5 000 |
| 142 | 7 200 |
| 143 | 10 600 |
| | 27 000 |

At 31 July Job No. 144 had been completed but not yet invoiced to the customer, and Job No. 145 was incomplete.

*Required:*
(a) Prepare the job cost ledger for the month of July.
(b) Prepare the general ledger for the month of July.
(c) Determine the following for the month of July:
  (i) the cost of jobs completed, and the cost of jobs sold;
  (ii) the gross margin on each job sold during July.
(d) Prepare a trial balance as at 31 July, 20X5.
(e) Determine the amount of under-allocated or over-allocated overhead for July and comment on the possible reasons for this.

**4-19 Troubleshooting unreliable job costing records**
Joyce Timber Company manufactures to customer order. The company's net profit for the year ended 30 June 20X4 is shown below:

### Statement of Financial Performance for Year Ended 30 June 20X4

| | | | |
|---|---|---:|---:|
| Sales | | | $2,420,000 |
| Less: Cost of goods sold | | | |
| Materials | | | |
| Inventory, 1/7/03 | $100,000 | | |
| Purchases | 1,125,000 | | |
| | 1,225,000 | | |
| Less Inventory, 30/6/04 | 125,000 | $1,100,000 | |
| Labour | | | |
| Wages paid to factory workers | | 675,000 | |
| Factory Overhead | | | |
| Rent | 125,000 | | |
| Power | 30,000 | | |
| Supplies | 22,500 | | |
| Supervision | 200,000 | | |
| Depreciation | 50,000 | 427,500 | |
| Sub-Contractors' charges | | 125,000 | |
| | | 2,327,500 | |
| Add Work in process, 1/7/03 | | 215,000 | |
| | | 2,542,500 | |
| Less Work in process, 30/6/04 | | 255,000 | 2,287,500 |
| **Gross Profit** | | | 132,500 |
| Less Non-factory expenses | | | 100,000 |
| **Net Profit** | | | $32,500 |

The owner/manager, Jim Joyce, intended to expand the business over the next two years but is now reluctant to do so because of the low profits for the year ended 30 June, 20X4. He asks you to examine the system used to calculate the cost of jobs on which prices charged to customers are based. You investigate and obtain the following information.

- Computer job records are set up for all orders received. Costs of jobs are entered by the data entry assistant. Information for recording costs comes from estimates of material usage supplied by the supervisor, labour time reports prepared by individual workers, and invoices for sub-contactors' charges.
- The factory operates 5 days per week for 52 weeks of the year, that is, 261 days per year. There has been no change in the number of workers employed over the year. All employees receive the same rate of pay and work an 8-hour day 5 days per week. One hour of each day is spent on cleaning, maintenance and handling raw materials delivered to the factory. Each employee receives on full pay a total of 29 days per year for annual leave, public holidays and sick leave.
- Jobs are charged out to customers by adding 25% to direct material costs, 100% to direct labour costs, and including sub-contactors' costs without markup.

You also obtain the following summary of charges to customers for the year:

| | |
|---|---:|
| Materials (at cost plus 25%) | $1 210 000 |
| Labour (at ordinary wage rate plus 100%) | 1 100 000 |
| Sub-contactors' costs | 110 000 |
| Total sales | $2 420 000 |

Details of work in process were also taken from job records:

| | 1/7/03 | 30/6/04 |
|---|---:|---:|
| | $ | $ |
| Material | 50 000 | 150 000 |
| Labour | 150 000 | 100 000 |
| Sub-contact charges | 15 000 | 5 000 |
| | 215 000 | 255 000 |

*Required:*
(a) Based on the figures in the statement of financial performance and the work in process records, calculate for the year the net profit that should have resulted on the basis of the margins added to materials and labour.
(b) Identify and explain what you consider to be the reasons for the difference between your answer to (a) and the net profit of $32 500 shown in the statement of financial performance.
(c) Describe ways in which the existing system of costing and pricing could be improved.

4-20 **Job costing: auto electrical work**
A.C. Generator Pty Ltd specialises in reconditioning motor car alternators. The company provides a same day service, as far as possible, to service stations. A.C. Generator sends a truck around to service stations in the morning to pick up alternators for repairs, and the same truck delivers the reconditioned alternators early in the afternoon. They also accept alternators brought in during the day, by service stations or others (provided the alternator has been removed from the car).

The reconditioning process may be either a minor or major overhaul. A minor overhaul consists of replacing the rectifier, the diodes and the built-in voltage regulator. A major overhaul involves the above, plus rewiring of the coils.

Current material costs to A.C. Generator for one alternator are:

| | |
|---|---|
| 1 rectifier | $21.00 |
| 2 diodes | 15.00 |
| 1 voltage regulator | 18.00 |
| Wiring for coils | 30.00 |

Direct labour costs average $18.00 per hour. It takes one hour to perform a minor overhaul and two hours for a major one. Overhead is based on a predetermined rate of $12 per direct labour hour.

The company charges $126 for a minor overhaul and $216 for a major one.

At the beginning of the week A.C. Generator had the following raw material inventories (all purchased at current prices and paid for) and work-in-process inventories:

| |
|---|
| 50 rectifiers |
| 100 diodes |
| 20 voltage regulators |
| Wiring sufficient for 30 alternators |

10 alternators not completed the previous working day.
5 were minor and 5 were major overhauls. Rectifiers and diodes had been replaced, taking half an hour for each alternator.

During the week a further 200 alternators were accepted, 50 being major overhauls. All but 6 were completed, these having had only the rectifier replaced, a quarter of an hour of labour. All six were minor overhauls.

Material purchases and expenses for the week consisted of:

| Purchases on credit: |
| --- |
| 200 rectifiers |
| 400 diodes |
| 250 voltage regulators |
| Wiring sufficient for 60 alternators |

| Other expenses: | |
| --- | --- |
| Wages for seven auto-electricians | $5040 |
| Wages for driver | 480 |
| Workshop rent | 900 |
| Lease of truck | 200 |
| Petrol etc. for truck | 150 |
| Depreciation of equipment | 500 |
| Other expenses | 300 |

All wages, rent and other expenses were paid in cash.

When there are no alternators to work on, general workshop maintenance duties are performed. The working week is 40 hours. The driver works in the office when not driving (20 hours per week in the office). The truck expenses are treated as overhead.

All work completed during the week was paid for.

The owner-manager performs general managerial duties and draws $1500 per week in salary.

*Required:*

(a) Prepare general ledger entries and a subsidiary ledger for materials to record the week's operations.

(Note: You may care to use the proforma worksheet provided on the next page to assist your calculations.)

(b) Prepare a statement to calculate net profit for the week.

PRO-FORMA WORKSHEET FOR A.C. GENERATOR PTY LTD

|  |  | Rectifiers || Diodes || Volt Regs || Wiring || Labour || Overhead || Total ||
|---|---|---|---|---|---|---|---|---|---|---|---|---|---|---|
|  |  | No | $ | No | $ | No | $ | Alts | $ | Hrs | $ | Hrs | $ | $ | $ |
| O/WIP | Minor |||||||||||||||
|  | Major |||||||||||||||
| To complete O/WIP | Minor |||||||||||||||
|  | Major |||||||||||||||
| New work completed | Minor |||||||||||||||
|  | Major |||||||||||||||
| C/WIP | Minor |||||||||||||||
|  | Major |||||||||||||||
| Completed jobs ||||||||||||||||
| Material issues ||||||||||||||||
| Direct Labour ||||||||||||||||
| Overhead allocated ||||||||||||||||

## PROCESS COSTING PROBLEMS: 4-21 to 4-31

**4-21  Calculating equivalent units**

The following information for June is available for a department in which process costing is used:

| Opening work in process: | 3 000 units | 20% complete as to material |
|---|---|---|
|  |  | 15% complete as to conversion |
| Closing work in process | ? | 10% complete as to material |
|  |  | 30% complete as to conversion |
| Started in June | 15 000 units |  |
| Completed in June | 13 000 units |  |

*Required:*
(a) Calculate the equivalent units of output (i.e. units completed + closing WIP as for weighted average method) for material and conversion in June.
(b) Calculate the equivalent units of work done in June (as for FIFO method) for material and conversion.

**4-22  Calculating equivalent units**

Department A has a process costing system. Materials are added at the beginning of the process and conversion costs are incurred uniformly throughout the process. There is no spoilage in the process. The following additional information for September is available:

Opening work in process:  5 000 units 20% complete
Closing work in process   3 000 units 50% complete
Started in September    10 000 units

*Required*
(a) Calculate the equivalent units of output (i.e. units completed + closing WIP as for weighted average method) for material and conversion in September.
(b) Calculate the equivalent units of work done in September (as for FIFO method) for material and conversion.

**4-23  Calculating equivalent units**

Department B employs a process costing system. Material 1 is added at the beginning of the process while Material 2 is added when the process is 50% complete. Conversion costs are incurred uniformly throughout the process. There is no spoilage in the process. The following additional information for March is available:

> Opening work in process:  4 000 units 40% complete
> Closing work in process    5 000units 30% complete
> Started in March           20 000 units
> Completed in March         19 000 units

*Required*
(a) Calculate the equivalent units of output (i.e. units completed + closing WIP as for weighted average method) for both materials and conversion in March.
(b) Calculate the equivalent units of work done in March (as for FIFO method) for both materials and conversion.

**4-24  Process costing: weighted average cost, no opening work in process**

The following information relates to a production department for September:

| | |
|---|---|
| Units in Work in Process, 1 September | 0 |
| Units started during September | 40 000 |
| Units transferred to next department | 30 000 |

Costs incurred during September:

| | |
|---|---|
| Material X | $300 000 |
| Material Y | 90 000 |
| Direct Labour | 60 000 |
| Overhead | 120 000 |

Material X is introduced at the start of the process while Material Y is added when the product reaches the 75% stage of completion. Conversion costs are added uniformly throughout the process. Ending work in process is 60% complete. The company uses the weighted average cost method for product costing purposes.

*Required:*

Determine:
(a) the average unit cost for Material X in ending work in process;
(b) the total average unit cost for the month of September;
(c) the cost of goods manufactured and transferred out in September;
(d) the ending balance of Work-in-Process account for this process.

**4-25  Weighted average cost: opening and closing WIP, and WIP ledger account**

Paris Paints Company produces a single lacquer paint which passes through two production departments. The following information concerns the first of those production departments.

Direct materials are added at the beginning of the production process and conversion costs are incurred uniformly throughout the process. Total conversion costs are computed as direct labour costs, plus 50% of direct labour costs for the allocation of overhead costs.

The following information is available for May:

**Opening work in process:**
| | |
|---|---|
| Number of units | 3 000 |
| Degree of completion | 40% |
| Material costs | $5 000 |
| Conversion costs | $7 200 |

**May production:**
| | |
|---|---|
| Units started | 30 000 |
| Units completed and transferred to Process 2 | 32 000 |
| Current material costs | $65 000 |
| Current direct labour costs | $40 000 |

**Closing work in process:**
| | |
|---|---|
| Degree of completion | 80% |

The company uses weighted average costing. There is no spoilage or wastage in the production process.

*Required*
(a) Prepare a Production Cost Report for May, showing the allocation of costs to closing work in process and to production transferred to the next department.
(b) Prepare the work-in-process T-account for the first production department for May.

**4-26 Weighted average cost: transfer in, opening and closing work in process**
Boral Ltd uses a weighted average process costing system. For the month of September the following data relate to Department 2:

- 50 000 units were brought in from Department 1 with a cost of $204 000.
- Added materials of $128 000 were used in Department 2 in September, and conversion costs were $154 000.
- All finished product in Department 2 is transferred to Department 3. During September 45 000 units were transferred to Department 3.
- Ending work in process at 30 September in Department 2 consisted of 10 000 units 60% complete.
- Work in process in Department 2 at 1 September consisted of 5000 units 40% complete with $19 000 of Department 1 cost and $6000 of conversion cost added in Department 2.
- Material in Department 2 is added at the halfway point.

*Required:*

Prepare a production cost report for Department 2 for September to calculate the cost of units transferred to Department 3 and the cost of ending work in process.

**4-27 Intermediate process: weighted average cost and FIFO methods**
Given the following information for an intermediate process, determine the cost of goods transferred out using:

(a) the weighted average cost method; and
(b) the FIFO cost method.

4/Product Costing Systems: Job Costing and Process Costing

      Units in beginning work in process (40% complete)  1200
      Units transferred into process  2400
      Units in ending work in process (50% complete)   800

Beginning work-in-process costs:
  Transferred-in costs      $12 000
  Conversion costs        $ 8 000
Current costs:
  Transferred-in           $16 800
  Conversion              $14 400

No materials are added in this process.

**4-28  Weighted average cost and FIFO methods**
The following information relates to the operation of a processing department:

Opening Inventory:
    55 000 units                   30% complete
    Material cost                 $40 000
    Conversion cost            $207 500

Closing Inventory:
    90 000 units 1/3 complete

Units completed 300 000 units

All materials are added at the start of the process, conversion costs are added uniformly throughout the process.

Current costs:
  Materials                    $   203 750
  Conversion                 $1 277 500

*Required:*
Calculate the cost of goods transferred out using
(a)  the weighted average cost method
(b)  FIFO.

**4-29  Weighted average cost and FIFO methods**
The Pymble Processing Company manufactures a single product which passes through two departments, A and B.

All work is commenced in Department A, from which all output is transferred to Department B where additional materials are added when processing is 40% complete.

In Department B labour and overhead costs are treated as being incurred uniformly throughout the process. Overhead is allocated on the basis of 120% of direct labour cost.

For Department B the following information relating to the month of April, 20X0 is available:

Work in process, 1 April: 5000 units, 80% complete. Costs of this work in process include:

    Department A costs                  $16 600
    Department B materials             $ 4 900
    Department B direct labour        $ 8 000

During April 150 000 units were completed and transferred to finished goods inventory. Units transferred in from Department A were charged to Department B at $3 per unit. Department B's costs in April were materials added $145 100 and direct labour $298 000.

On 30 April 10 000 units were in process in Department B and these were estimated to be 30% complete.

*Required:*
For Department B calculate for the month of April the cost of work completed and the cost of work in process as at 30 April, 20X0, using
(a) the weighted average cost method, and
(b) FIFO.

**4-30 Weighted average cost and FIFO methods**

Chemical Processing Ltd produces a pesticide which is used in the extermination of lice in poultry farms. The production process consists of a number of discrete operations: *mixing*, *cooling* and *packaging*. The mixing operation uses a special purpose vat which is highly efficient and results in no waste.

During March, 20X3 100 000 litres of product were completed in the mixing process and transferred to the cooling process. Production and cost records provided the following additional information for the mixing process for the month of March:

Work in process on 1 March totalled 30 000 litres which were 30% complete with respect to material content (costed at $15 000) and 70% complete with respect to conversion effort (costed at $5000). At 31 March work in process was estimated at 40 000 litres, 40% complete as to material and 80% complete as to conversion. Costs incurred during March were $217 000 for materials and $61 000 for conversion.

*Required:*

Calculate the cost of the 100 000 litres transferred to cooling during March and the cost of closing work in process at the end of March, using
(a) the weighted average cost method
(b) the FIFO cost method.

**4-31 Two processing departments: weighted average cost method**

Jones Company produces a product which passes through two processes. Material enters at the beginning of Process 1, and further material is added when Process 2 is 40% complete. Conversion costs are incurred uniformly throughout the duration of both processes. Details for the month of May, 20X5 are:

| Physical Flows | Process 1 | Process 2 |
|---|---|---|
| O/WIP (units) | 1 000 (40%) | 500 (60%) |
| Started in May | 10 000 | ? |
| Completed in Process | 9 000 | ? |
| C/WIP (units) | ? (50%) | 750 (30%) |

| Cost Flows | | | | |
|---|---|---|---|---|
| O/WIP | | | Trf-in | $ 7 500 |
| | Mat. | $5 000 | Mat. | $ 2 500 |
| | Conv. | $4 000 | Conv. | $ 5 000 |
| Current: | Mat. | $60 000 | Mat. | $57 750 |
| | Conv. | $100 000 | Conv. | $69 400 |

*Required:*
Using the weighted average cost method, determine the cost of finished goods completed during May, and the cost of closing work in process in both processing departments as at 31 May, 20X5.

# Chapter 5

# Product Costing Systems: Operation Costing and Joint Costs

## OPERATION COSTING

In the previous chapter we considered two distinct costing systems. A job costing system traces a significant proportion of production costs to individual units or batches, and then tries to average those costs which cannot be identified with such units or batches, over all production. At the other extreme, a process costing system, *all* costs of production for a period are averaged over all production.

Operation costing is a hybrid costing system which reflects characteristics of both job and process costing. Some products, for example men's suits, are processed in batches which pass through one or more standard operations, eg., pattern making, grading, cutting, sewing. Although each batch may vary with respect to the quality or type of cloth used, each unit from any batch consumes an identical amount of an operation's transformation resources. In such situations, conversion costs can be handled as in process costing, by accumulating them for each operation (or process or department) and averaging over all production passing through that operation during the period. Actually, just as in process costing, conversion costs may be allocated using a predetermined rate (we sometimes call this **normal** costing), rather than waiting till the end of the period to allocate the actual conversion costs (called **actual** costing). Direct material, however, would be traced to each batch, as in job costing.

In other cases, some operations may vary for different batches: for example, some batches of suits might be machine sewn, others hand sewn. Or some products might be made from the same material but involve different processing: for example, in manufacturing pine tables, some may be finished in 'the raw', while others may be fine sanded and have clear lacquer sprayed on them resulting in higher conversion costs.

In all these cases there would be features of both job and process costing, and the costing system is sometimes referred to as **operation costing**.

### Illustrative Example 5-1

*Sports Equipment Pty Ltd produces two different grades of baseball bat, known as the Standard and the Deluxe. Both types go through exactly the same production process, but are made from different quality timbers; the Standard uses a cheap timber while the Deluxe uses a very high quality timber with special, desirable properties.*

*Details for the month of August, 20X8 are as follows:*
  **Costs**

|  |  |
|---|---|
| Timber issued to production: | |
| for Standard bat | $30 000 |
| for Deluxe bat | 35 000 |
| Conversion costs | 56 400 |
| | 121 400 |

## 5/Product Costing Systems: Operation Costing and Joint Costs

| Production | Standard | Deluxe |
|---|---|---|
| Opening Work in Process | 0 | 0 |
| Bats completed | 1000 | 500 |
| Closing Work in Process: | | |
|     Standard 60% complete | 500 | |
|     Deluxe 40% complete | | 200 |

*All material is added at the beginning of the operations.*

*Required:* Determine the cost of finished bats and the closing balance of work in process.

Since all timber is added at the beginning of the process, the direct material cost can be calculated as follows:

> Standard: $30 000/1500 = $20
> Deluxe: $35 000/700 = $50

If conversion cost is incurred uniformly throughout the operations, conversion cost per unit can be calculated as follows:

|  | Completed Units | Closing WIP Units | Percent | Equiv Units | Total Equiv Units |
|---|---|---|---|---|---|
| Standard | 1000 | 500 | 60 | 300 | 1300 |
| Deluxe | 500 | 200 | 40 | 80 | 580 |
|  | 1500 | 700 |  | 380 | 1880 |

Conversion cost = $56,400
Conversion cost per equivalent unit: $56,400/1880 = $30

Total cost per finished unit:
    Standard: Material $20 + Conversion $30 = $50
    Deluxe: Material $50 + Conversion $30 = $80

**Finished goods**
    Standard    1000 x $50    $50 000
    Deluxe    500 x $80    40 000    $90 000
**Closing WIP**
    Standard    500 x $20 + 300 EU x $30    $19 000
        200 x $50 + 80 EU x $30    12 400    $31 400
        $121 400

If products pass through a number of operations in which one unit at a time is processed, the idea of estimating the percentage completion of closing work in process becomes a meaningless exercise. For each operation a unit has been processed or it hasn't, so that conversion costs for each operation are averaged over the units which have been processed in that operation, whether they are finished goods or unfinished work in process still to enter later operations.

## JOINT COSTS

In the costing systems examined so far we have been concerned with production processes in which several material inputs are combined into one or more products, eg., a motor vehicle manufacturing plant. Such processes are sometimes called **synthetic** processes. By contrast, some manufacturing processes convert a single raw material into many products. For example, an oil refinery converts crude oil into a number of products such as lubricating oil, diesel fuel, petrol, aviation fuel etc; a pig is converted into pork chops, legs of pork, bacon, ham etc; a log of timber is converted into different timber products; milk is converted into cream, skim milk, butter etc. These processes which result in the conversion of one raw material into several products are called **analytic** processes.

The different products which are derived from the single raw material are referred to as **joint products** which emerge, after some joint processing, at what is called the **split-off point**. The process is illustrated in Figure 5-1.

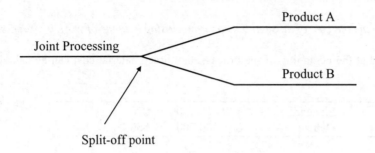

**Figure 5-1: Joint Products**

These joint products may be saleable at split-off, or one or more of the joint products may be further processed to produce saleable products.

The cost of the original raw material plus the cost of processing prior to the split-off point are called **joint costs**.

An analytic process poses difficult problems for product costing because it is not possible to attribute joint costs to individual products in a non-arbitrary fashion. If a butcher buys a beef carcass for $200 and carves it up into a number of different cuts - rump steak, sirloin steak, bladebone steak, silverside etc. - there is no unequivocal method of tracing the original $200 plus carving costs to the different cuts of meat. Any distribution of costs must be purely arbitrary.

Despite the problem of tracing costs to joint products it is necessary to cost them to determine cost of goods sold for a period and to assign values to unsold inventories at balance date. So the accountant resorts to an arbitrary allocation procedure for assigning joint costs, incurred up to the split-off point, to the emerging joint products.

The usual bases for allocating joint costs to products are:

(1) Some physical measure of output: units, weight, volume; or
(2) Ability to bear the charge, eg., relative sales value.

## Illustrative Example 5-2

*A chicken processor buys batches of live chickens which are then killed, dressed and cut into four saleable products: breast fillets, thighs, drumsticks and wings. The remnants are treated as valueless waste.*

*A single batch of input consists of 1000 chickens which are purchased for $3 each ($3000 for the batch). Additional joint processing costs to the split-off point are $1000, making joint costs of $4000 in total.*

*The output yield consists of 1000 breast fillets weighing 400 kg, 2000 thighs weighing 250 kg, 2000 drumsticks weighing 250 kg and 2000 wings weighing 100 kg. The situation may be represented thus:*

# 5/Product Costing Systems: Operation Costing and Joint Costs

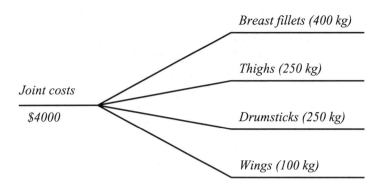

*The selling prices of these products are:*

| | |
|---|---|
| breast fillets | $10.00 per kg |
| thighs | $5.00 per kg |
| drumsticks | $5.00 per kg |
| wings | $2.50 per kg |

*Required:*    *The cost per kg of each of the joint products.*

## Physical Measures Method

Under the physical measures method the joint costs are apportioned among the joint products on the basis of their relative proportions at the split-off point, using a common physical measure of output such as units, weight or volume. In this case the joint costs of $4000 would be apportioned as follows:

| Product | Output (kg) | Joint Costs Apportioned | | Cost Per kg |
|---|---|---|---|---|
| Breast fillets | 400 | 400/1000x$4000= | $1600 | $4.00 |
| Thighs | 250 | 250/1000x$4000= | 1000 | $4.00 |
| Drumsticks | 250 | 250/1000x$4000= | 1000 | $4.00 |
| Wings | 100 | 100/1000x$4000= | 400 | $4.00 |
| | 1000 | | $4000 | |

The cost per kg for each product shown in the last column is derived by dividing the apportioned joint cost by the output in kg shown in column 2; eg., for breast fillets, $1600/400 kg = $4/kg. As you can see, this method produces the same cost of $4 per kilogram for each of the joint products, even though they have different sales values. The respective profit margins are $6 per kg (breast fillets), $1 per kg (thighs and drumsticks) and a loss of $1.50 per kg (wings). Of course, the allocation of the joint costs is arbitrary, so that no decisions (such as drop a product, or price setting) should be based on such information.

## Relative Sales Value Method

The physical measures method takes no account of the ability of the various products to bear their share of allocated joint costs. That is, it gives no weighting to their relative sales values. The relative sales value method, however, apportions the joint costs in direct proportion to the sales value of the products at the split-off point. Accordingly, based on the data in example 5-2, the joint costs would be apportioned as follows:

## 5/Product Costing Systems: Operation Costing and Joint Costs

| Product | Output (kg) | Price per kg | Sales Value | Joint Costs Apportioned | | Costs per kg |
|---|---|---|---|---|---|---|
| Breast fillets | 400 | $10.00 | $4000 | 4000/6750x$4000= | $2370 | $5.93 |
| Thighs | 250 | $5.00 | 1250 | 1250/6750x$4000= | 741 | $2.96 |
| Drumsticks | 250 | $5.00 | 1250 | 1250/6750x$4000= | 741 | $2.96 |
| Wings | 100 | $2.50 | 250 | 250/6750x$4000= | 148 | $1.48 |
| | 1000 | | $6750 | | $4000 | |

The sales values in column 4 are obtained by multiplying the output column by the price/kg column. The joint costs are apportioned to the individual products at the rate of $0.592593 per $1 of sales value. The resulting allocation produces a constant percentage gross margin for each product:

| Product | Selling Price | Cost per kg | Margin per kg | % Margin |
|---|---|---|---|---|
| Breast fillets | $10.00 | $5.93 | $4.07 | 40.74 |
| Thighs | $5.00 | $2.96 | $2.04 | 40.74 |
| Drumsticks | $5.00 | $2.96 | $2.04 | 40.74 |
| Wings | $2.50 | $1.48 | $1.02 | 40.74 |

## Costs Incurred after the Split-off Point

In some processes joint products at the split-off point may not be saleable products, but may require further processing to render them so. Alternatively, they could be processed beyond split-off to form a different, more valuable product. Where such further processing occurs, the cost of a product consists of any further processing costs (referred to as **separable costs**) plus a share of joint costs apportioned to it. In the case where no sales value at the split-off point is available (because the product is not saleable) the net realisable value (NRV) at the split-off point is used. The NRV is calculated as the final sales value less any separable costs. This method is sometimes called the net realisable value method, rather than the relative sales value method.

### Illustrative Example 5-3

*Assume the same data as in example 5-2, except that the product Drumsticks is not saleable without further processing in which the lower part of the leg-bone is chopped off and the skin removed to create the product Lovely Legs. This further processing results in a reduction in output from 250 kg to 200 kg per 1000 chickens. The separable costs of this further processing are $100 per 2000 legs, and Lovely Legs are sold for $8 per kg.*

The allocation of joint costs using the NRV method would be as follows:

| Product | Output (kg) | Price per kg | Sales Value | Separable Costs | NRV | Joint Costs Apportioned | | Joint Cost per kg | Add Separable Costs | Total Unit Cost |
|---|---|---|---|---|---|---|---|---|---|---|
| Breast fillets | 400 | $10.00 | $4000 | | $4000 | 4000/7000x$4000= | $2286 | $5.71 | | $5.71 |
| Thighs | 250 | $5.00 | 1250 | | 1250 | 1250/7000x$4000= | 714 | $2.86 | | $2.86 |
| Lovely Legs | 200 | $8.00 | 1600 | $100 | 1500 | 1500/7000x$4000= | 857 | $4.29 | $0.50 | $4.79 |
| Wings | 100 | $2.50 | 250 | | 250 | 250/7000x$4000= | 143 | $1.43 | | $1.43 |
| | 950 | | $7100 | $100 | $7000 | | $4000 | | | |

The above method treats the separable costs as a reduction in sales value in order to apportion the joint costs, and effectively attributes no earning power to these separable costs. Note that after calculating the joint cost per kg it is necessary to add the separable cost of 50c ($100/200 kg) to obtain the total cost of $4.79 per kg for Lovely Legs.

### *Which Method?*

Both the physical measures method and the relative sales value method are arbitrary but do at least yield product costs for income determination and inventory valuation. As we have seen, the former method results in all products bearing the same cost, while the latter attributes a higher product cost to a higher priced product.

The classical case of joint costs occurs in oil refineries, and has resulted in extensive debate at various inquiries concerned with controlling the price of petrol in Australia. Various tribunals and price setting or control bodies have had to endure endless arguments from oil companies and their adversaries as to what the cost of producing the petrol is, so that a fair return can be added as a mark-up to determine wholesale prices. In the end, of course, there is no satisfactory answer to this problem. Any allocation procedure for apportioning the joint costs is arbitrary, and so there is no 'true' cost that can be established.

### *Joint Costs and Decision Making*

As mentioned earlier, joint cost allocations should not be used as a basis for managerial decision making. A common decision faced by manufacturers of joint products is whether to sell a product at split-off or process further. For example, cuts of pork may be sold as fresh meat or further processed by smoking and curing.

When confronted with a decision as to whether to sell a joint product or process further, the golden rule is to ignore all allocations of joint processing costs. The analysis should simply compare the incremental revenue with the incremental costs of further processing.

For example, referring back to example 5-3, assume that Drumsticks could be sold at split-off for $5 per kg, or when further processed into Lovely Legs for $8 per kg. Should they be processed into Lovely legs? The correct analysis is:

| | | |
|---|---|---|
| Incremental revenue: | (200 kg x $8) - (250 kg x $5) = | $350 |
| Incremental cost: | | 100 |
| Incremental operating profit | | $250 |

Thus it is profitable to process into Lovely Legs, because there is an increase in profits of $250 per 1000 chickens processed.

## ACCOUNTING FOR BY-PRODUCTS

Sometimes products which emerge from joint processing have a relatively low (or insignificant) sales value compared with the sales values of the main joint products, and are referred to as **by-products**. There are many methods of accounting for by-products. However, since by-products are defined to be of relatively minor value, there should not be a significant difference in the results obtained from the various approaches.

Four major methods are found, as summarised in the matrix in Figure 5-2.

From the columns you can see that if a by-product is recognised at the time of production, there must be a closing inventory valuation. The inventory valuation will depend upon the stage of processing of the by-product inventory: if it has not been processed beyond split-off it will be valued at NRV, otherwise at NRV plus separable costs of the further processing. If, however, a by-product is not recognised until the time of sale, no value is attached to unsold inventory.

| By-products Appear in Profit and Loss Statement as | By-products are Recognised at Time of | |
|---|---|---|
| | Production | Sale |
| Reduction in Cost | 1. By-product NRV deducted from joint costs allocated.<br>2. By-product inventory valued at NRV. | 1. By-product NRV deducted from joint costs allocated.<br>2. No value attached to by-product inventory. |
| Separate Revenue | 1. By-product NRV treated as revenue or income.<br>2. By-product inventory valued at NRV. | 1. By-product NRV treated as revenue or income.<br>2. No value attached to by-product inventory. |

**Figure 5-2: Accounting Treatment for By-products**

Focusing on the rows, by-products' net realisable values appear in the profit and loss statement either as a reduction in the cost of the major products or as a separate revenue or other income item.

Referring back to example 5-2, suppose that Wings are treated as a by-product, and that during a period a single batch of 1000 chickens was processed, and all sold except for 10 kg of breast fillets and 10 kg of wings. Statements of financial Performance under the four methods would appear as shown in figure 5-3.

### By-products with Negative NRV

Sometimes a by-product may have a negative net realisable value; that is it costs money to legally dispose of the by-product which has no other use. In this case the by-product disposal cost can be added to the joint processing costs to be allocated to the joint products. This is in effect the same result as deducting the by-product NRV from the joint costs: subtracting a negative NRV from the joint processing costs produces the same result as adding the disposal cost to the joint costs.

## SUMMARY

In this chapter we looked at a hybrid costing system known as operation costing, and the problem of how to cost joint products which emerge from analytic processes.

Operation costing employs features of both job and process costing for batch production in which different materials are used for different batches but all batches undergo the same conversion process. Direct material costs are usually traced to each batch, but conversion costs are averaged over all production which passes through an operation during a period.

For joint products, the joint material and conversion costs incurred prior to split-off are allocated to the joint products in an arbitrary manner. Joint costs are usually allocated on the basis of either some physical measure of output or else the relative sales value of products at the split-off point.

Management decisions should not be based on cost data derived from joint cost allocations. In the typical **sell or process further** decision one should compare incremental revenues (beyond split-off) with incremental (separable) costs. If incremental revenues exceed incremental costs, process further.

When a joint product is of minor value it is often treated as a by-product. Various methods are used to account for by-products, and four are demonstrated in this chapter.

*5/Product Costing Systems: Operation Costing and Joint Costs*

| By-products recognised at | Production | Production | Sale | Sale |
|---|---|---|---|---|
| Appear in P & L Statement as | Cost Reduction | Revenue Item | Cost Reduction | Revenue Item |
| Sales:<br>  Breast fillets (390 kg x $10)<br>  Thighs (250 kg x $5)<br>  Legs (250 kg x $5)<br>  By-product: Wings (90 kg x $2.50) | $3,900.00<br>$1,250.00<br>$1,250.00<br>- | $3,900.00<br>$1,250.00<br>$1,250.00<br>$225.00 | $3,900.00<br>$1,250.00<br>$1,250.00<br>- | $3,900.00<br>$1,250.00<br>$1,250.00<br>$225.00 |
|  | $6,400.00 | $6,625.00 | $6,400.00 | $6,625.00 |
| Cost of Goods Sold:<br>  Joint costs<br>  Less By-product NRV | $4,000.00<br>$225.00 | $4,000.00<br>- | $4,000.00<br>$225.00 | $4,000.00<br>- |
|  | $3,775.00 | $4,000.00 | $3,775.00 | $4,000.00 |
| Less C/Inventory:<br>  Breast fillets *<br>  By-product: Wings (10kg x $2.50) | $57.69<br>$25.00 | $59.26<br>$25.00 | $57.69<br>- | $59.26<br>- |
| Cost of Goods Sold | $3,692.31 | $3,915.74 | $3,717.31 | $3,940.74 |
| GROSS PROFIT | $2,707.69 | $2,709.26 | $2,682.69 | $2,684.26 |

\*
**Cost reduction:** Joint costs are reduced to $3750 [$4000 - (100kg*$2.50)]
These are then allocated to the major products as follows:

| Product | Output (kg) | Price per kg | NRV | Joint Costs Apportioned |  | Cost per kg |
|---|---|---|---|---|---|---|
| Breast fillets | 400 | $10.00 | $4000 | 4000/6500x$3750= | $2308 | $5.77 |
| Thighs | 250 | $5.00 | 1250 | 1250/6500x$3750= | $721 | $2.88 |
| Legs | 250 | $5.00 | 1250 | 1250/6500x$3750= | $721 | $2.88 |
|  | 900 |  | $6500 |  | $3750 |  |

Thus the closing inventory of breast fillets = 10 kg x $5.77 approx.
= $57.69

**Revenue Item:** Closing inventory = 10 kg x $5.93 approx. (from example 5-2)
= $59.26

**Figure 5-3: Accounting for By-products**

*5/Product Costing Systems: Operation Costing and Joint Costs*

## APPENDIX

### Using a Spreadsheet for Joint Cost Allocations

Spreadsheet models to apportion joint costs are easy to build and ensure the accuracy of results. Such models were used for the illustrative examples in this chapter. You should be able to build such models yourself without any help.

Try building two models:

(1)  A model for the physical measures method.

(2)  A second model for the relative sales method. Make allowance for the existence of separable costs. If there are none, those columns can be left blank, and the model should still work.

**Hint:** Have particular problems to solve to guide you when you build your models. Build generalised formulae to sum columns, add or subtract them, and calculate allocated cost per unit. Then only minimal changes need be made for solving other problems.

## QUESTIONS AND PROBLEMS

**5-1** Why is operation costing called a hybrid costing system?

**5-2** Provide examples of three industries which are likely to use operation costing.

**5-3** In operation costing, how are conversion costs typically allocated to product? Explain for the case where products pass through two sequential operations.

**5-4** In operation costing are products costed using actual conversion costs incurred or is a predetermined conversion rate used? Explain.

**5-5** Is it possible to have an activity-based operation costing system? Explain.

**5-6** What are joint products?

**5-7** Distinguish between **joint** costs and **separable** costs.

**5-8** Give three examples of industries in which joint costs are present. List some of the joint products found in each.

**5-9** What is the difference between a **joint product** and a **by-product**?

**5-10** Distinguish between sales value at split-off and net realisable value at split-off. Which of the two should be used under the relative sales value method when apportioning joint costs? When would the other be used, if ever?

**5-11 Operation costing**
Sulu Ltd manufactures two types of warp drives, standard and deluxe. The only difference between the two products is the quality of the materials used; the deluxe uses higher quality materials. Data for the month of October were:

|  | Standard | Deluxe |
| --- | --- | --- |
| Units completed | 100 | 80 |
| Closing WIP | 20* | 40+ |
| Current period material costs | $2400 | $3300 |

\* complete as to material, 50% as to conversion
\+ complete as to material, 75% as to conversion

Labour and overhead costs for the month were $3300. There were no opening inventories.

*Required:*

(a) What was the unit cost of each warp drive?
(b) Calculate the cost of units finished during the month and the closing work in process.

**5-12 Operation costing**
Ace Sports Ltd manufactures composite tennis racquets to fill work orders for specific customers. There are four operations involved in making the racquets: frame construction, painting, stringing and grip fitting. Although the racquets supplied to fill different orders look quite different, in fact they all use the same frame, but are painted in different colours and designs. Painting time is the same for each type of racquet, and they all require the same quality and quantity of paint. The stringing operation is the same for all racquets except for different string quality. All racquets within one work order have the same strings. The same quality grips are used on all racquets, although the colours differ.

## 5/Product Costing Systems: Operation Costing and Joint Costs

In January Ace Sports recommenced operations after having closed down in December for the Christmas break and annual vacations. No inventories of racquets, either finished or in process, were held at the beginning of January. During January four work orders were received and started; all racquets within each order were identical:

| Order No. | | |
|---|---|---|
| 101 | 500 racquets |
| 102 | 750 racquets |
| 103 | 450 racquets |
| 104 | 300 racquets |

Only order number 104 was incomplete at the end of January. Of the 300 racquets in the order, all frames were made but only 250 were painted, 150 strung and 100 gripped.

Costs during January were:

*Materials*
| | | | |
|---|---|---|---|
| Frames | | | $40 000 |
| Paint | | | 2 925 |
| Grips | | | 3 600 |
| Strings: Order | #101 | $2 500 | |
| | #102 | 7 500 | |
| | #103 | 9 000 | |
| | #104 | 1 500 | 20 500 |
| | | | 67 025 |

*Conversion*
| | | |
|---|---|---|
| Framing | $20 000 | |
| Painting | 8 775 | |
| Stringing | 9 250 | |
| Gripping | 3 600 | 41 625 |
| | | 108 650 |

*Required:*
Calculate the cost of goods completed during January (by Work Order), and the cost of ending work in process showing material and conversion components. Actual rather than predetermined conversion costs are allocated to products.

**5-13  Operation costing**

Tim Tricks Ltd manufactures two styles of whoopee cushions – loud and quiet. Unit conversion costs for loud and quiet cushions are identical but loud cushions require twice the quantity of material used for quiet cushions. Materials are all added at the start of production. Conversion costs are incurred uniformly throughout the process. At the end of March work in process consisted of 45 loud cushions (one-third complete) and 50 quiet cushions (half-complete). The company uses a standard cost system and standards are the same in March and April.

During April the following units were completed:

| April – Units completed: | Loud whoopee cushions | 100 |
|---|---|---|
| | Quiet whoopee cushions | 150 |

| Standard costs incurred in April were: | Materials | $2310 |
|---|---|---|
| | Conversion costs | $1800 |

There was no closing work in process at the end of April.

*Required:*
The cost of goods completed during April by type of cushion.

## 5-14 Operation costing: multiple choice

Bibis Blankets Ltd manufactures single and double bed blankets of identical quality. An operations costing system is used by the company.

Unit conversion costs for single and double bed blankets are identical but twice the quantity of material is required to make double bed blankets compared with the single bed variety. Materials are all added at the start of production. Conversion costs are incurred uniformly throughout the process of production.

At the end of June work in process consisted of 30 single bed blankets (two-thirds completed) and 50 double bed blankets (half completed). During July 100 single bed and 150 double bed blankets were completed. There was no closing work in process at the end of July.

The company uses a standard cost system and standards were the same in June and July. Standard costs incurred in July were Materials $5400 and Conversion Costs $3075.

*Required:*
(a) The unit cost of a single bed blanket is (to the nearest cent):

A  $20.61
B  $35.00
C  $55.00
D  $46.77
E  $25.19

(b) The total cost of double bed blankets completed in July was (to the nearest cent):

A  $11 000.00
B  $7015.50
C  $5875.00
D  $8250.00
E  $4005.21

## 5-15 Operation costing: multiple choice

Anyway Products uses three operations in sequence to manufacture an assortment of cleaning agents. In each operation the same procedures, time and costs are used to perform that operation for a given quantity, regardless of the type of cleaning agent being produced.

During May a batch of materials for 1400 litres of Type A was put through the first operation. This was followed in turn by separate batches of materials for 500 litres of Type B and 1600 litres of Type C. All the materials for a batch are introduced at the beginning of that batch. The costs shown below were incurred in May for the first operation:

|  |  |  |
|---|---|---|
| Direct labour |  | $30 600 |
| Factory overhead |  | $14 802 |
| Materials: | Type A | $19 180 |
|  | Type B | $9 000 |
|  | Type C | $14 000 |

All production started in May was completed during the month and transferred to the next operation except for 350 litres of Type C which were 40% complete as to conversion costs. There was no work in process at the beginning of May.

*Required:*
(a) The cost per litre for Type A in May was

    A  $13.70
    B  $27.50
    C  $26.67
    D  $26.62
    E  none of the above

(b) The total cost of production transferred from the first operation during May was

    A  $87 582.00
    B  $82 785.50
    C  $87 825.50
    D  $82 587.50
    E  none of the above

**5-16**   **Joint cost allocation: NRV method**
The Hampton Company produces two chemical products, Mixon and Dixon, as a result of a joint production process. In October 438 000 litres of Mixon were produced and sold for $8 per litre. Also during October 262 000 litres of Dixon were produced. Dixon is not saleable at the split-off point and required further processing costing $60 000. All production of Dixon was then sold for $10 per litre. Joint costs of $700 000 were incurred for October production.

*Required:*
Using the net realisable value at split-off method, calculate the joint costs allocated to Mixon and Dixon.

**5-17**   **Joint cost allocation**
AB Company operates a simple process to produce two separate products from a single basic material. The two products, A and B, are separated simultaneously at a single split-off point. Product A is ready for sale at split-off, while product B is processed further before being sold.

A sells for $3200 per tonne and B for $1600 per tonne. During the year 300 tonnes of A and 200 tonnes of B were produced. Total joint manufacturing costs for the year were $840 000. An additional $80 000 was incurred in processing B from split-off point into saleable form

*Required:*
Using the net realisable value method calculate the allocation of joint costs to A and B respectively.

**5-18**   **Joint product: sell or process further**
200 units of a joint product can be sold at split-off for $0.80 per unit or can be processed further and then sold for $1.20 per unit. Separable costs would total $30 if the product is further processed. The joint costs allocated to the product total $150.

*Required:*
Should the joint product be processed further? What would be the incremental gain or loss from doing so?

## 5-19 Joint cost allocation: physical units and relative sales value methods

Casablanca Ltd produces two joint products, both of which are saleable at the split-off point. There were no opening inventories at 1 April, 20X0. Production and financial details for April 20X0 are as follows:

|  | Product XA1 | Product XA2 |
|---|---|---|
| Production (litres) | 54 000 | 36 000 |
| Sales (litres) | 37 800 | 36 000 |
| Closing inventory (litres) | 16 200 | 0 |
| Selling price per litre | $2 | $6 |

Total joint processing costs for April were $200 000.

*Required:*
Prepare a gross profit statement for each product and in total for April 20X0, using (a) the physical units method, and (b) the relative sales value method to allocate joint costs.

## 5-20 Joint cost allocation: additional processing beyond split-off point

Funbox Ltd produces three joint products, all of which require additional processing beyond the split-off point. There were no opening inventories at 1 April 20X8. Production and financial details for April are as follows:

|  | Product 100 | Product 101 | Product 102 |
|---|---|---|---|
| Production in litres | 18 000 | 12 000 | 10 000 |
| Sales (litres) | 14 000 | 12 000 | 8 000 |
| Closing inventory (litres) | 4 000 | 0 | 2 000 |
| Selling price per litre | $2 | $4 | $10 |
| Costs of additional processing | $9 000 | $9 600 | $15 000 |

Total joint processing costs for April were $60 000. Joint costs are allocated using the net realisable value method. The closing inventories have been through all processing and are ready for sale.

*Required:*
(a) Calculate the gross profit by products for the month of April.
(b) Product 101 can be further processed into Product 103 for an additional $3 per litre, and would sell for $6 per litre. Should Funbox produce Product 103, and what would be the effect on April's net profit of doing so?

## 5-21 Joint cost allocation: additional processing beyond split-off point

In a certain production process 100 000 kg of a single raw material were processed at a cost of $250 000. At split-off two intermediate products, A and B emerged, weighed as 60 000 kg of A and 40 000 kg of B. A was processed further at a cost of $45 000 to produce C, and B was processed further at a cost of $25 000 to produce D. C sold for $4.50 per kg.

(a) If A was allocated $187 500 of the joint production costs under the net realisable value method, what was the selling price of D?
(b) Suppose the firm receives an offer to buy all of product A for $2 per kg at the split-off point. Would the firm be better off selling A or processing further to produce C? By how much?

## 5/Product Costing Systems: Operation Costing and Joint Costs

**5-22 Joint cost allocation: additional processing beyond split-off point**

ABC Company produces three joint products: A, B and C. The material is added at the beginning of the process. At the end of Process 1, the split-off point, the three intermediate products enter three separate further processes. Product A enters Process 2, Product B enters Process 3 and Product C enters Process 4. None of the products can be sold unless the subsequent processing is carried out.

The following information relates to the month of June:

(i) Direct material issued to Process 1, $26 000.

(ii) Conversion costs incurred:

|  | Labour | Overhead |
|---|---|---|
| Process 1 | $10 000 | $14 000 |
| Process 2 | 3 000 | 2 000 |
| Process 3 | 1 000 | 1 000 |
| Process 4 | 600 | 400 |

(iii) There was no work in process at the beginning or end of the month, and no finished goods inventories at the beginning of the month.

(iv) Details of production and sales:

|  | Product |  |  |
|---|---|---|---|
|  | A | B | C |
| Tonnes produced | 500 | 400 | 100 |
| Tonnes ordered | 600 | 600 | 200 |
| Tonnes delivered | 400 | 350 | 50 |
| Selling price/tonne | $110 | $80 | $210 |

All delivery costs are met by customers.

*Required:*
(a) A statement showing the allocation of joint costs to products A, B and C using (i) a physical measures method, and (ii) the relative sales value method.
(b) Suppose that C's price falls to $7 per tonne. It costs $5 per tonne to dump material at the tip. Should Product C be dumped at the split-off point or processed further?

**5-23 Joint cost allocation: additional processing beyond split-off point**

Dissolvo Ltd produces two solvents which it sells to firms in the paint industry. Both solvents arise from a single processing operation from which the two products jointly emerge. Solvent XA384 is then processed through Operation 1 while the other, Solvent XB541 is processed through Operation 2.

During April the company processed 100 000 litres of material input to production, yielding 80 000 litres of XA384 and 20 000 litres of XB541. There was no opening or closing work in process.

Details of processing costs for April were as follows:

|  | Joint Processing | Operation 1 | Operation 2 |
|---|---|---|---|
| Materials | $20 000 |  |  |
| Direct labour | 35 000 | $30 000 | $25 0͡͠ |
| Overhead - Fixed | 15 000 | 10 000 | 14 000 |
|        - Variable | 20 000 | 40 000 | 25 000 |

The fixed overhead costs are largely an allocation of plant fixed costs, allocated between the joint processing operation and operations 1 and 2, and are expected to remain unchanged in total irrespective of any volume changes in the various processing operations.

During April the current selling prices for the products were $1.80 per litre for XA384 and $6.00 per litre for XB541. 70 000 litres of XA384 and 15 000 litres of XB541 were sold at these prices during April.

There were no finished goods inventories at the beginning of April, and there was no loss or spoilage during the month.

*Required:*
Using the relative sales value method,
(a) calculate the cost of closing inventories of XA384 and XB541.
(b) calculate the profit earned by each product during April.

**5-24    Joint cost allocation with by-product**
The Dubbo Rubbo Liniment Company manufactures liniment. Three processes are involved.

Process 1 in which all chemicals etc. are added incurs costs of $124 000 for an output of 17 600 kg. Of this, 1600 kg is a sludge which is generally sold to road builders. The remaining 16 000 kg receives further processing. Of this 16 000 kg, 9000 kg goes on to Process 2 to become 9000 kg of A-grade liniment for an extra cost of $72 000. The A-grade liniment sells for $28 per kg. The other 7000 kg goes to Process 3 to become 7000 kg of B-grade liniment for an extra cost of $48 000. B-grade sells at $24 per kg. Sludge sells at $3.50 per kg, but costs $1 per kg to package safely.

*Required:*
(a) Assuming no opening or closing inventory is held, calculate the gross profit for the major products, using
   (i) the physical units approach to allocate joint costs.
   (ii) the net realisable value approach to allocate joint costs.
(b) Explain the reasons for your treatment of the by-product revenue. Describe one other way in which the by-product could have been dealt with and how this would have affected your answers to (a).

**5-25    Joint and by-products: multiple choice**
Mighty Miners Ltd crushes and refines a mineral ore into three products, silver lead and zinc.

During the year Department 1 processed, at a cost of $420 000, 500 000 kg of ore yielding:
        20 000 kg of silver
        100 000 kg of lead
        60 000 kg of zinc
        320 000 kg of waste rubble which was dumped

Department 2 further refined the silver at a cost of $100 000.

Department 3 further refined the zinc at a cost of $160 000.

Average selling prices of finished products were:   Silver  $20 per kg
                                                            Lead    $1 per kg
                                                            Zinc    $6 per kg

*Required:*
(a) Using the net realisable value method for allocating joint costs, the joint costs allocated to zinc would be:

A  $66 977
B  $140 000
C  $175 814
D  $198 947
E  none of the above

(b) Assume that the waste rubble can be sold as road fill for 20 cents per kg net of selling costs, that it is treated as a by-product, and that its net realisable value is credited against the joint processing costs. What is the total cost per kg (to the nearest cent) of silver?

A  $8.90
B  $9.49
C  $10.50
D  $13.90
E  $14.49

# Chapter 6

# Product Costing Systems: Standard Costs

In the preceding chapters on product costing we have seen that there are three major cost elements in product costs: direct materials, direct labour and overhead. We observed in Chapter 3 that the **actual** direct material and direct labour costs incurred are traced to products and processes. With overhead, however, we noted that it was preferable for various reasons to allocate overhead to products using **pre-determined** rates, rather than wait till the end of a period and allocate actual overhead incurred.

It was but a small step, historically, to query why pre-determined rates should not also be used for direct material and direct labour costs. Such a system would serve a number of purposes. It would simplify the clerical effort involved in product costing because products would simply be costed at the pre-determined, **standard** rate, rather than trying to trace actual costs to each job or process. This would obviate the need to adopt a cost flow assumption such as FIFO or LIFO in calculating cost of goods sold and inventory balances (materials, work in process, finished goods). Further, the use of standard costs facilitates the preparation of budgets, quotations, and pricing policies generally.

Importantly, a standard cost system would also serve other purposes such as motivation of employees (to achieve standard) and as a benchmark for evaluating performance. It would provide a basis for assessing cost efficiency whereby actual costs for a period could be compared with the standard costs that should have been incurred. This, it was argued, would be superior to simply comparing this period's costs with, for example, last period's because last period may have been a period of poor performance and any improvement was not necessarily a great achievement.[1] It would still be necessary to accumulate actual costs during a period, but less detailed tracing would be required. A comparison of actual costs with standard costs would generate variances (differences between actual costs and standard costs) and these variances would facilitate management control of costs.

Thus the notion of standard costs was born. Standard costs are pre-determined costs, which are average costs that should be attained under efficient operating conditions. They result from a determination of physical input standards (e.g., quantity of material or number of direct labour hours required per unit of output) which are priced using standard prices:

> Standard cost = standard quantity of inputs x standard price/unit of input.

This idea of a standard is not confined to manufactured products, but is equally applicable to services (e.g., standard time to repair a car, process a cheque or clean a hotel room). Under a comprehensive standard cost system all inventory accounts and cost of goods sold are maintained or costed in terms of standard cost.

A standard cost system is not an additional cost system. Standard costs may be used in conjunction with any of the costing systems so far examined, although the notion of a *standard* requires a repetitive process in order to be able to establish standards of performance. Thus process costing is a natural application (i.e., standard process costing), more so than job costing where jobs tend to be unique, and hence there are few 'standard' tasks.

---

[1] Note, however, that in modern organisations this argument is no longer regarded as valid. Modern firms focus on continuous improvement initiatives and do compare this period's performance with last period's to see if there has been any improvement.

Setting standard costs requires an assessment of how best to accomplish the tasks involved, and how much each task should cost. The determination of standard costs involves establishing physical standards in terms of resources required. In this process standards may be set at various levels of difficulty. Two common levels are:

**Ideal standards** are based on ideal or maximum performance levels. An ideal (or theoretical or perfection or maximum efficiency) level of performance may be attainable for short periods, but normally will result in unfavourable variances; actual costs will exceed standard costs. When setting ideal standards no allowance is made for waste or spoilage, machine breakdowns or unavoidable idle time. Such standards have not been widely used in the past because they are unattainable and thought to be demoralising for those trying to achieve them. Given recent management trends, however, to eliminate waste and improve quality and efficiency, ideal standards may well be embraced as being consistent with modern management policies.

**Currently attainable standards** are based on high, but attainable levels of performance, making reasonable allowances for fatigue, maintenance, idle time, machine breakdowns and normal spoilage. Just how tight such standards should be is somewhat controversial, and will be discussed in a later chapter.

## *Setting Standards*

When an organisation decides to adopt a standard cost system it must perform a detailed analysis of the entire production process. As with the application of any new technique, often the very act of ascertaining the required information produces substantial savings when attention is focused so closely on activities. Standards are established for materials, labour and overhead.

**Material quantity standards** may be derived from analysis of past records to determine average usage in the case of established products. For new products, industrial and methods engineering studies may be used. Product specifications are drawn up, and from these are prepared bills of materials listing the quantities of each type of material required.

**Labour time standards** are frequently based on time and motion studies. It is necessary to standardise conditions of work so that for each product the number and sequence of operations is standardised. Then the time required for each operation is measured. This is not always an easy task because of the potential human industrial problems associated with setting standards against which performance will be judged. There is a natural tendency by employees to try and build in slack so that future performance will look good or so that the work effort required will not be onerous.

The procedure for establishing pre-determined overhead rates has already been described in Chapter 3.

Before standards are finally decided upon, test runs are usually made. When finalised, the details of the standard cost for each product are recorded on a standard cost specification sheet.

---

### *Illustrative Example 6-1*

*Unique Processing Ltd manufactures a single product whose standard cost specification is as follows:*

| | | |
|---|---|---|
| Direct material: | 2 kg @ $5 per kg | $10 |
| Direct labour: | 1 hr @ $12 per hr | 12 |
| Overhead: | $10 per direct labour hr | 10 |
| | Total standard cost per unit | $32 |

*Normal capacity is 100 000 direct labour hours and total overhead has been budgeted at $1 000 000, resulting in a standard overhead allocation rate of $10 per standard direct labour hour.*

*All inventories (raw materials, work in process and finished goods) are valued at standard cost. Inventories at 1 January 20X1 were:*

|   |   |   |   |
|---|---|---|---|
| Direct materials | Nil | | |
| Supplies | | | $250 000 |
| Work-in-Process | 500 units | 50% complete | $10 500 |
| Finished Goods | 200 units | | $6 400 |

*Direct materials are added at the beginning of the process while conversion costs are incurred uniformly throughout the processing operation.*

*Details of production and transactions for the year are as follows:*

(1) During the year 68 000 units of product were completed and transferred to finished goods. At the end of the year the closing work in process was counted as 2500 units estimated to be 50% complete.

(2) Direct material: 150 000 kg were purchased @ $5.20 per kg, $780 000. 141 000 kg were issued to production.

(3) Gross factory payroll for the year was:
   Direct labour: 68 000 hr @ $12.50 per hr   $850 000
   Indirect labour: 25 000 hr                 $250 000

(4) Overhead (in addition to indirect labour):
   Supplies issued              $200 000
   Factory expenses (all on credit)  $100 000
   Depreciation of plant        $150 000

(5) Sales during the year: 65 000 units sold.

A standard cost system records the standard costs of the standard inputs allowed for the actual production. For example, the standard direct material cost recorded during a period is calculated on the basis of the standard quantity of material that **should** have been used, not the quantity actually used. In order to calculate the standard quantity of material that should have been used it is necessary (with process costing) to determine the equivalent units of work done during the year:

| UNIQUE PROCESSING LTD: Calculation of Work Done during 20X1 ||||
|---|---|---|---|
| FLOW OF PRODUCTION | PHYSICAL FLOW | EQUIVALENT UNITS ||
| | | Material | Conversion |
| Units completed | 68 000 | 68 000 | 68 000 |
| Closing WIP (50%) | 2 500 | 2 500 | 1 250 |
| | 70 500 | 70 500 | 69 250 |
| Less Opening WIP (50%) | 500 | 500 | 250 |
| Work done this period (units) | 70 000 | 70 000 | 69 000 |

## Accounting for Materials

### Purchase

For the Raw Materials inventory account to be maintained at standard cost (actual quantity purchased x **standard price**) it is necessary to extract, at the time of purchase, any variance caused by a difference between actual price paid and standard price, i.e., the material price variance. Naturally the actual

## 6/Product Costing Systems: Standard Costs

expense incurred (actual quantity purchased x *actual price*) must be credited to the supplier's account (and trade creditors control, or accounts payable account).

The material price variance (MPV) is calculated as:

>Actual Quantity **purchased** x (Actual Price - Standard Price),
>i.e., MPV = AQp(AP-SP)

where   AQp = actual quantity purchased
        AP  = actual price per unit
        SP  = standard price per unit

If the actual price is greater than the standard price (AP > SP), and hence the MPV is positive, we say that the variance is unfavourable (UF), and it is **debited** to a Materials Price Variance account. Alternatively, if the MPV is negative (AP < SP), the variance is favourable (F), and it is **credited** to the Materials Price Variance account.

For example 6-1, the variance is calculated as follows:

| |
|---|
| MPV = AQp(AP-SP)<br>= 150 000 kg($5.20 - $5.00)<br>= $30 000 UF     (Unfavourable because AP > SP) |

Alternatively, if the formula is expanded we work in terms of totals. This is useful for providing the data for the accounting entries:

| |
|---|
| MPV = (AQp x AP) - (AQp x SP)<br>= (150 000 x $5.20) - (150 000 x $5.00)<br>= $780 000 - $750 000<br>= $30 000 UF |

The journal entry to record the purchase would be:

| | | |
|---|---|---|
| Materials Control | $750 000 | |
| Materials Price Variance | 30 000 | |
| Accounts Payable | | $780 000 |

Note the result is that the direct material is carried in the inventory account at standard cost, while the full amount owing is credited to the creditor's account.

## Issue

Since the Raw Materials inventory account is maintained at standard cost, any issues of materials are automatically credited to the account at the standard price. If the Work-in-Process account is to be maintained at standard cost, it must be debited with the standard quantity of material that should have been used (i.e., the quantity allowed for the output achieved). At the same time, the raw materials inventory account balance must represent the actual quantity on hand, and so that account must be credited with the actual quantity used (issued). Any difference between the actual quantity used and the standard quantity allowed for the production achieved leads to what is called a material usage variance (also known as material quantity or material efficiency variance).

The material usage variance (MUV) is calculated as:

>(Actual Quantity used - Standard Quantity allowed) x Standard Price,
>i.e., MUV = (AQu-SQa)SP

where   AQu = actual quantity used, i.e. issued from the store
        SQa = standard quantity allowed for the output achieved

Again, positive variances (AQu > SQa) are unfavourable (debits to Materials Usage Variance account), while negative variances (AQu < SQa) are favourable (credits).

Referring to example 6-1, the standard quantity of material allowed is calculated by reference to both the equivalent units of work done (for material) and the standard unit quantity shown in the standard cost specification. Thus 70 000 EU of work done in respect of material, at a standard allowed of 2 kg per unit, gives the standard quantity allowed of 140 000 kg. Then the variance can be calculated:

> MUV = (AQu-SQa)SP
> = (141 000 kg - 140 000 kg) x $5
> = $5000 UF    (Unfavourable because AQu > SQa)

Alternatively, an expansion of the formula gives:

> MUV = (AQu x SP) - (SQa x SP)
> = (141 000 kg x $5) - (140 000 kg x $5)
> = $705 000 - $700 000
> = $5000 UF

The appropriate journal entry to record the issue and usage of materials is:

| | | |
|---|---|---|
| Work-in-Process Control | $700 000 | |
| Materials Usage Variance | 5 000 | |
| Materials Control | | $705 000 |

Note that although the actual usage exceeded the standard usage, the Work-in-Process account is only debited with the standard quantity of material allowed for the output achieved, whereas the Materials account is reduced by the full quantity issued.

## *Accounting for Labour*

To maintain the Work-in-Process account at standard, it must be debited with the standard direct labour cost: standard DLH allowed for output achieved @ standard hourly rate for direct labour.

Referring to example 6-1, the standard number of DLH allowed is calculated as the product of the equivalent units of work done (conversion) and the standard number of DLH per unit in the standard cost specification:

> 69 000 EU x 1 DLH = 69 000 standard DLH

Thus the standard direct labour cost to be debited to Work-in-Process is 69 000 x $12 = $828 000. However, the actual direct labour cost for the year was $850 000, a difference of $22 000. This total variance of $22 000 can be attributed to two causes: (1) a difference between the actual and standard direct labour rates per hour (labour rate or price variance), and (2) a difference between the actual DLH worked and the standard DLH allowed for the given production (labour efficiency or usage variance).

The labour rate variance (LRV) is calculated as:

> Actual Hours worked x (Actual hourly Rate - Standard hourly Rate),
> i.e. LRV = AH(AR-SR)

> where  AH = actual hours worked
> AR = actual hourly rate of pay
> SR = standard hourly rate of pay

Again positive variances (AR > SR) are unfavourable (debits to Labour Rate Variance account) and negative variances (AR < SR) are favourable (credits).

## 6/Product Costing Systems: Standard Costs

In example 6-1 the labour rate variance is:

> LRV = AH(AR−SR)
> = 68 000 DLH($12.50 − $12.00)
> = $34 000 UF   (Unfavourable because AR > SR)

Alternatively,

> LRV = (AH x AR) − (AH x SR)
> = (68 000 x $12.50) − (68 000 x $12.00)
> = $850 000 − $816 000
> = $34 000 UF

The labour efficiency variance (LEV) is calculated as:

(Actual DLH − Standard DLH allowed) x Standard hourly Rate
ie., LEV = (AH−SHa)SR

where   SHa = standard hours allowed for the output produced

Positive variances (AH > SHa) are unfavourable (debits to Labour Efficiency Variance account) and negative variances (AH < SHa) are favourable (credits).

For example 6-1, the labour efficiency variance is:

> LEV = (AH−SHa)SR
> = (68 000 DLH − 69 000 DLH) x $12
> = −$12 000   (Favourable − it is negative, AH < SH)
> or $12 000 F

Alternatively,

> LEV = (AH x SR) − (SHa x SR)
> = (68 000 x $12) − (69 000 x $12)
> = $816 000 − $828 000
> = −$12 000
> or $12 000 F

Thus the total net direct labour variance is the algebraic sum of the rate and efficiency variances: $34 000 UF + $12 000 F = $22 000 UF, as previously calculated.

The appropriate journal entry to record the direct labour obligation and the direct labour standard cost is:

| | | |
|---|---|---|
| Work-in-Process Control | $828 000 | |
| Labour Rate Variance | $34 000 | |
| Labour Efficiency Variance | | $12 000 |
| Accrued Payroll | | $850 000 |

Note that the Work-in-Process account is only debited with the standard hours allowed for the output achieved (priced at the standard rate) whereas the Accrued Payroll account is credited with the actual direct labour gross earnings.

## Accounting for Overhead

The use of pre-determined overhead allocation (or application or recovery) rates has been illustrated previously in Chapter 3. Under a standard cost system the same procedure is used, except that overhead is allocated to Work-in-Process on the basis of **standard hours allowed** for the output achieved, instead of on the basis of **actual hours incurred**.

Continuing with example 6-1, actual overhead costs are (as usual) debited to the Overhead Control account:

| | | |
|---|---|---|
| Overhead Control | $700 000 | |
|     Accrued Payroll (indirect labour) | | $250 000 |
|     Supplies | | $200 000 |
|     Accounts Payable (factory expenses) | | $100 000 |
|     Accumulated Depreciation | | $150 000 |
| (for indirect labour, indirect material, factory expenses on credit, and depreciation of plant) | | |

Overhead is allocated to Work-in-Process at the pre-determined rate of $10 per standard DLH (see standard cost specification). The standard DLH allowed for the output achieved has already been calculated as 69 000 in the section above on labour. Therefore the overhead to be allocated is calculated as 69 000 standard DLH x $10 per standard DLH, that is, $690 000. The appropriate entry is:

| | | |
|---|---|---|
| Work-in-Process | $690 000 | |
|     Overhead Allocated | | $690 000 |

Thus overhead has been under-allocated by $10 000. Actual overhead of $700 000 less allocated overhead of $690 000 gives a total overhead variance of $10 000 UF. This $10 000 variance may be further analysed, as will be demonstrated in a later chapter. For the present, only the total variance will be extracted and recorded:

| | | |
|---|---|---|
| Overhead Allocated | $690 000 | |
| Overhead Variance | $10 000 | |
|     Overhead Control | | $700 000 |

## Accounting for Finished Goods and Cost of Goods Sold

As has been shown above, all debits to the Work-in-Process account are in terms of standard cost. Similarly, transfers from Work-in-Process to Finished Goods account are valued at the standard cost per unit. The total value is calculated as 68 000 units completed x the standard cost per unit of $32, that is $2 176 000. The required entry is:

| | | |
|---|---|---|
| Finished Goods Control | $2 176 000 | |
|     Work-in-Process Control | | $2 176 000 |

This should leave the standard cost of closing work in process as the balance in the Work-in-Process account, consisting of:

| | | |
|---|---|---|
| Material: | 2500 units @ $10 | $25 000 |
| Labour: | 2500 units 50% complete @ $12 | 15 000 |
| Overhead: | 2500 units 50% complete @ $10 | 12 500 |
| | | $52 500 |

The transfer from Finished Goods to Cost of Goods Sold is also at standard: 65 000 units @ $32, a total of $2 080 000. The entry is:

## 6/Product Costing Systems: Standard Costs

| Cost of Goods Sold | $2 080 000 | |
|---|---|---|
| Finished Goods | | $2 080 000 |

This should leave the standard cost of closing finished goods as the balance in the Finished Goods account and may be confirmed as:

3200 units @ $32          $102 400

## Ledger Accounts

The relevant ledger accounts appear as follows:

### GENERAL LEDGER OF UNIQUE PROCESSING LTD

**Materials Control**

| Accounts Payable | $750 000 | Work-in-Process | $700 000 |
|---|---|---|---|
| | | Materials Usage Variance | 5 000 |
| | | Balance c/d | 45 000 |
| | $750 000 | | $750 000 |
| Balance b/d | $45 000 | | |

**Supplies**

| Balance b/d | $250 000 | Overhead Control | $200 000 |
|---|---|---|---|
| | | Balance c/d | 50 000 |
| | $250 000 | | $250 000 |
| Balance b/d | $50 000 | | |

**Work-in-Process Control**

| Balance b/d | $10 500 | Finished Goods | $2 176 000 |
|---|---|---|---|
| Materials Control | 700 000 | Balance c/d | 52 500 |
| Accrued Payroll | 828 000 | | |
| Overhead Allocated | 690 000 | | |
| | $2 228 500 | | $2 228 500 |
| Balance b/d | $52 500 | | |

**Finished Goods Control**

| Balance b/d | $6 400 | Cost of Goods Sold | $2 080 000 |
|---|---|---|---|
| Work-in-Process | 2 176 000 | Balance c/d | 102 400 |
| | $2 182 400 | | $2 182 400 |
| Balance b/d | $102 400 | | |

**Cost of Goods Sold**

| Finished Goods | $2 080 000 | | |
|---|---|---|---|

### Accrued Payroll

| | | | |
|---|---|---|---|
| Labour Efficiency Variance | $12 000 | Work-in-Process | $828 000 |
| Bank | 1 100 000 | Labour Rate Variance | 34 000 |
| | | Overhead Control | 250 000 |
| | $1 112 000 | | $1 112 000 |

### Overhead Control

| | | | |
|---|---|---|---|
| Accrued Payroll | $250 000 | Overhead Allocated | $690 000 |
| Supplies | 200 000 | Overhead Variance | 10 000 |
| Accounts Payable | 100 000 | | |
| Accumulated Depn | 150 000 | | |
| | $700 000 | | $700 000 |

### Overhead Allocated

| | | | |
|---|---|---|---|
| Overhead Control | $690 000 | Work-in-Process | $690 000 |

### Materials Price Variance

| | |
|---|---|
| Accounts Payable | $30 000 |

### Materials Usage Variance

| | |
|---|---|
| Materials Control | $5 000 |

### Labour Rate Variance

| | |
|---|---|
| Accrued Payroll | $34 000 |

### Labour Efficiency Variance

| | | | |
|---|---|---|---|
| | | Accrued Payroll | $12 000 |

### Overhead Variance

| | |
|---|---|
| Overhead Control | $10 000 |

### Accounts Payable

| | | | |
|---|---|---|---|
| | | Materials Control | $750 000 |
| | | Materials Price Variance | 30 000 |
| | | Overhead Control | 100 000 |
| | | | $880 000 |

## *Alternative Standard Cost Systems*

The system illustrated in this chapter maintains inventory accounts in terms of standard costs, and extracts variances at the earliest opportunity. Some systems may recognise variances at different points of time. For example, actual quantities of material and labour at standard prices may be debited to Work-in-Process, and the usage or efficiency variances extracted from that account at the end of the period. Other systems may record actual cost flows in the ledger and maintain standards as memorandum records outside the double entry system, so that variance analysis is not formally incorporated in the ledger. Readers should be aware that such variations exist, and that in practice many variations may be expected.

An unpublished survey (P.E. Angus-Leppan and V.A. Fatseas, 1983) of the top 600 companies (by market capitalisation) listed on the Sydney Stock Exchange found that of the approximately 40% of companies which responded, about 38% reported that they used standard costs. The methods used to determine physical standards were:

| | |
|---|---|
| time and motion studies | 41 companies |
| methods time measurement | 36 companies |
| engineering studies | 47 companies |
| sample runs | 36 companies |
| estimates based on historical studies | 78 companies |

Clearly there is some double counting, meaning that some companies used more than one method.

Price standards were reported to be based on current or expected market prices and were revised

| | |
|---|---|
| monthly | by 8 companies |
| quarterly | by 12 companies |
| half yearly | by 22 companies |
| yearly | by 27 companies |
| on an ongoing basis | by 25 companies. |

## SUMMARY

Product costing systems such as job and process costing systems may record standard costs as well as actual costs in the ledger. Standard costs are carefully pre-determined costs that should be attained under efficient operating conditions. As well as facilitating the distribution of costs between finished goods and work in process, standard costs serve other purposes such as motivation, performance evaluation, planning and budgeting, and pricing.

When employing a standard cost system it is still necessary to record actual costs incurred. A comparison of actual with standard costs produces variances which can be analysed to provide explanations for the differences between the two sets of costs.

*6/Product Costing Systems: Standard Costs*

# APPENDIX

## Using a Spreadsheet to Calculate Standard Cost Variances

It is possible to design a spreadsheet model to calculate standard cost variances. Below is such a model to calculate the variances for Illustrative Example 6-1. The formulas are on the next page.

|    | A | B | C | D | E | F | G | H |
|----|---|---|---|---|---|---|---|---|
| 1  |   | STANDARD COST VARIANCE ANALYSIS |   |   |   |   |   |   |
| 2  |   |   |   |   |   |   |   |   |
| 3  | DATA |   |   |   |   |   |   |   |
| 4  | *MATERIALS* |   |   |   | *LABOUR* |   |   |   |
| 5  | AQp | 150,000 |   |   | AH | 68,000 |   |   |
| 6  | AP | $5.20 |   |   | AR | $12.50 |   |   |
| 7  | SP | $5.00 |   |   | SR | $12.00 |   |   |
| 8  | AQu | 141,000 |   |   |   |   |   |   |
| 9  | SQ/unit | 2.00 |   |   | SH/unit | 1.00 |   |   |
| 10 | Work Done | 70,000 |   |   | Work Done | 69,000 |   |   |
| 11 |   |   |   |   |   |   |   |   |
| 12 | *OVERHEAD* |   |   |   |   |   |   |   |
| 13 | Actual | $700,000 |   |   |   |   |   |   |
| 14 | OH Rate | $10.00 |   |   |   |   |   |   |
| 15 | Work Done | 69,000 |   |   |   |   |   |   |
| 16 |   |   |   |   |   |   |   |   |
| 17 |   |   |   |   |   |   |   |   |
| 18 |   |   |   |   |   |   |   |   |
| 19 | MATERIALS PURCHASES |   |   |   | MATERIALS USAGE |   |   |   |
| 20 | AQp | 150,000 |   |   | AQu | 141,000 |   |   |
| 21 | AP | $5.20 | $780,000.00 |   | SP | $5.00 | $705,000.00 |   |
| 22 |   |   |   |   |   |   |   |   |
| 23 | AQp | 150,000 |   |   | SQa | 140,000 |   |   |
| 24 | SP | $5.00 | $750,000.00 |   | SP | $5.00 | $700,000.00 |   |
| 25 | PRICE VARIANCE |   | $30,000.00 | UF | USAGE VARIANCE |   | $5,000.00 | UF |
| 26 |   |   |   |   |   |   |   |   |
| 27 | LABOUR RATE |   |   |   | LABOUR EFFICIENCY |   |   |   |
| 28 | AH | 68,000 |   |   | AH | 68,000 |   |   |
| 29 | AR | $12.50 | $850,000.00 |   | SR | $12.00 | $816,000.00 |   |
| 30 |   |   |   |   |   |   |   |   |
| 31 | AH | 68,000 |   |   | SHa | 69,000 |   |   |
| 32 | SR | $12.00 | $816,000.00 |   | SR | $12.00 | $828,000.00 |   |
| 33 | RATE VARIANCE |   | $34,000.00 | UF | EFFICIENCY VARIANCE |   | ($12,000) | F |
| 34 |   |   |   |   |   |   |   |   |
| 35 | OVERHEAD |   |   |   |   |   |   |   |
| 36 | ACTUAL OH |   | $700,000.00 |   |   |   |   |   |
| 37 | ALLOCATED OH: |   |   |   |   |   |   |   |
| 38 | RATE | $10.00 |   |   |   |   |   |   |
| 39 | SHa | 69,000 | $690,000.00 |   |   |   |   |   |
| 40 | TOTAL VARIANCE |   | $10,000.00 | UF |   |   |   |   |

145

## 6/Product Costing Systems: Standard Costs

|   | A | B | C | D | E | F | G | H |
|---|---|---|---|---|---|---|---|---|
| 1 |   | STAND/ |   |   |   |   |   |   |
| 2 |   |   |   |   |   |   |   |   |
| 3 | DATA |   |   |   |   |   |   |   |
| 4 | *MATERIALS* |   |   |   | *LABOUR* |   |   |   |
| 5 | AQp | 150000 |   |   | AH | 68000 |   |   |
| 6 | AP | 5.2 |   |   | AR | 12.5 |   |   |
| 7 | SP | 5 |   |   | SR | 12 |   |   |
| 8 | AQu | 141000 |   |   |   |   |   |   |
| 9 | SQ/unit | 2 |   |   | SH/unit | 1 |   |   |
| 10 | Work Done | 70000 |   |   | Work Done | 69000 |   |   |
| 11 |   |   |   |   |   |   |   |   |
| 12 | *OVERHEAD* |   |   |   |   |   |   |   |
| 13 | Actual | 700000 |   |   |   |   |   |   |
| 14 | OH Rate | 10 |   |   |   |   |   |   |
| 15 | Work Done | 69000 |   |   |   |   |   |   |
| 16 |   |   |   |   |   |   |   |   |
| 17 |   |   |   |   |   |   |   |   |
| 18 |   |   |   |   |   |   |   |   |
| 19 | MATERIALS PURCH |   |   |   | MATERIALS USAGE |   |   |   |
| 20 | AQp | =B5 |   |   | AQu | =B8 |   |   |
| 21 | AP | =B6 | =B20*B21 |   | SP | =B7 | =F20*F21 |   |
| 22 |   |   |   |   |   |   |   |   |
| 23 | AQp | =B5 |   |   | SQa | =B9*B10 |   |   |
| 24 | SP | =B7 | =B23*B24 |   | SP | =B7 | =F23*F24 |   |
| 25 | PRICE VARIANCE |   | =C21-C24 | =IF(C25=0,"",IF(C25>0,"UF","F")) | USAGE VARIANCE |   | =G21-G24 | =IF(G25=0,"",IF(G25>0,"UF","F")) |
| 26 |   |   |   |   |   |   |   |   |
| 27 | LABOUR RATE |   |   |   | LABOUR EFFICIENCY |   |   |   |
| 28 | AH | =F5 |   |   | AH | =F5 |   |   |
| 29 | AR | =F6 | =B28*B29 |   | SR | =F7 | =F28*F29 |   |
| 30 |   |   |   |   |   |   |   |   |
| 31 | AH | =B28 |   |   | SHa | =F9*F10 |   |   |
| 32 | SR | =F7 | =B31*B32 |   | SR | =F7 | =F31*F32 |   |
| 33 | RATE VARIANCE |   | =C29-C32 | =IF(C33=0,"",IF(C33>0,"UF","F")) | EFFICIENCY VARIANCE |   | =G29-G32 | =IF(G33=0,"",IF(G33>0,"UF","F")) |
| 34 |   |   |   |   |   |   |   |   |
| 35 | OVERHEAD |   |   |   |   |   |   |   |
| 36 | ACTUAL OH |   | =B13 |   |   |   |   |   |
| 37 | ALLOCATED OH: |   |   |   |   |   |   |   |
| 38 | RATE | =B14 |   |   |   |   |   |   |
| 39 | SHa | =B15 | =B38*B39 |   |   |   |   |   |
| 40 | TOTAL VARIANCE |   | =C36-C39 | =IF(C40=0,"",IF(C40>0,"UF","F")) |   |   |   |   |

# QUESTIONS AND PROBLEMS

**6-1** What are standard costs? How are they set?

**6-2** How are physical standards set for materials and labour?

**6-3** In a standard cost system, how do you determine the amount to debit to Work-in-Process in respect of:
(a) material?
(b) labour?
(c) overhead?

**6-4** Why is the material price variance extracted at the time of purchase of materials?

**6-5** Explain the difference in the calculation of overhead allocated under a normal cost system and a standard cost system.

**6-6** Why is it necessary to record actual production costs in the ledger when using a standard cost system?

**6-7** **Calculating standard cost per unit**
The production manager of Sturt Ltd has estimated that 1000 kg of raw material will be required for a total budgeted cost of $10 000 for a batch of 500 units. It takes a skilled tradesman 15 minutes to convert 1 kg of raw material. The standard charge out rate for skilled labour is $20.00 per hour. Overhead is to be allocated to this batch at the rate of $30 per direct labour hour.

*Required:*
(a) What is the standard cost per unit?
(b) If the batch will be sold at a mark-up of 50% on production cost, what is the gross profit which will be realised on the batch?

**6-8** **Calculating standard cost per unit**
The production manager of Winchester Ltd has estimated that 500 kg of deluxe raw material will be purchased for a total budgeted cost of $500 000 for a special batch of 1000 designer-label executive model widgets. It takes a skilled tradesman 1 hour 20 minutes to convert 1 kg of deluxe raw material. Total overhead to be allocated to this batch is estimated to be $325 000. The standard charge out rate for skilled labour is $8.50 per hour. What is the standard cost per unit?

**6-9** **Raw materials inventory account: value recorded for purchases**
When material price variances are recognised in the accounts at the time of purchase, the book value of raw materials inventory is recorded as:

A  actual quantity at actual price
B  standard quantity at standard price
C  actual quantity at standard price
D  standard quantity at actual price
E  none of the above

**6-10** **Materials price variance: calculation and journal entry**
Your manager insists on the early monitoring of variances for control purposes. You have just purchased 200 000 kg of raw materials for $510 000. 65 000 kg of these materials have been issued to production at a standard cost of $2.60 per kg. Calculate the materials price variance and give the journal entry to record the purchase.

**6-11 Materials usage variance: calculation and journal entry**

During the month 1000 units of product were produced. The standard quantity of direct materials per unit is 10 kg at a standard price of $5 per kg. Actual material issued to production comprised 10 020 kg which were purchased for $4.80 per kg.

*Required:*
(a) Calculate the direct materials usage variance for the month.
(b) Provide a general journal entry to record the issue.

**6-12 Direct material variances**

The cost accountant of Bathurst Glass reported the following information for Department 1:

| | |
|---|---|
| Direct material purchases (at actual prices) | $61 500 |
| Standard cost of material purchased | $60 000 |
| Standard cost of material issued | $52 000 |
| Standard direct material cost per unit of product | $4.00 |
| Actual production | 12 500 units |

*Required:*
Calculate direct material price and usage variances for Department 1.

**6-13 Material price and usage variances**

Standard specifications for a job are 1 litre of paint for every 20 m$^2$ painted, at $15 per litre. The job involved 10 000 m$^2$. Five hundred and fifty litres of paint were purchased and used at a total cost of $7975.

*Required:*
Calculate direct material price and usage variances.

**6-14 Direct labour variances: calculation and journal entry**

The direct labour standard for a product is 2 hours per unit at a standard rate of $15 per hour. Last month 10 000 units were produced, requiring 19 800 direct labour hours at $15.50 per hour.

*Required:*
(a) The direct labour rate and efficiency variances.
(c) A compound journal entry to record the actual direct labour expense, the charge to Work-in-Process and the variances.

**6-15 Direct labour variances**

Regional Airlines Ltd employs one person to handle reservations on its airlines. The standard time allowed to make a reservation is 5 minutes, and the standard direct labour wage for this work is $24 per hour.

During a given period the actual direct labour cost was $144 500, 6000 direct labour hours were worked, and 73 000 reservations were made.

*Required:*
(a) Calculate the labour rate and efficiency variances.
(b) Record this information in a general journal entry.

**6-16  Direct labour variances: calculation and journal entry**

In the Kensington Company standard labour costs are set at $11.20 per hour and standard hours allowed for actual production were 31 250. The total actual labour cost was 96% of the total standard labour cost, whilst the standard labour rate was 25% higher than the actual hourly rate.

*Required:*
(a) The labour rate and efficiency variances.
(b) The journal entry to record the above information.


**6-17  Material and labour variances (straightforward)**

Boralco Company manufactures aluminium beer cans. A unit of production is 10 dozen cans. The following standards apply.

|  | Per Unit (10 dozen) |
|---|---|
| Direct materials: 3 kg @ $1/kg | $3 |
| Direct labour: ¼ hr @ $20 | 5 |

During the month 40 000 units were produced, 130 000 kilograms of material were purchased at $1.02 per kg and 124 000 kg of material were used. Direct labour costs were $215 000 for 10 500 hours worked.

*Required:*
(a) Calculate the materials price and usage variances and direct labour rate and efficiency variances, indicating whether they are favourable or unfavourable.
(b) Prepare journal entries to record the material purchases on credit, the usage of direct materials, and the direct labour liability and usage.
(c) Set up T-accounts and post the journal entries to the general ledger.


**6-18  Material and labour variances**

Virgo Corporation has established the following standards for a unit of one of its products:

|  | Standard Quantity | Standard Price |
|---|---|---|
| Direct materials | 10 kg | $1.50/kg |
| Direct labour | ¼ hr | $10/hour |

During April Virgo purchased 250 000 kg of direct material at a total cost of $362 500. The total wages for April were $68 000, 80 per cent of which were for direct labour. Virgo produced 20 000 units using 202 000 kg of direct material and 5100 direct labour hours.

*Required:*
Calculate direct material price and usage variances and direct labour rate and efficiency variances.


**6-19  Material and labour variances: missing data**

DEF Company provides the following information:

**Direct materials**

| | |
|---|---|
| Standard price | $20 per kg |
| Quantity purchased and used | 500 kg |
| Standard quantity allowed for production | 510 kg |
| Material price variance | $1000 Favourable |

## 6/Product Costing Systems: Standard Costs

**Direct labour**

| | |
|---|---|
| Standard rate | $15.00 per hour |
| Actual rate | $15.20 per hour |
| Standard hours allowed for production | 2000 |
| Direct labour efficiency variance | $495 Unfavourable |

*Required:*
(a) Calculate the actual purchase price per kg for direct materials.
(b) How many direct labour hours were worked and what was the direct labour rate variance?

**6-20 Material and labour variances: calculation and journal entries (moderately difficult)**

Romulan Ltd has set up the following standards for material and labour:

| | PER UNIT |
|---|---|
| Materials: 10 kg @ $6 | $60 |
| Direct labour: 1 hr @ $20 | 20 |

During a month 19 500 units were produced, 197 000 kg of material were used and 20 100 hours of labour were worked. 220 000 kg of materials were purchased for $1 364 000.

*Required:*
(a) Calculate the materials price variance (on purchase) and materials usage variance.
(b) If the total direct labour variance was $1950 unfavourable, what was the actual direct labour rate per hour?
(c) Journal entries to record these facts.

**6-21 Direct labour variances given: work backwards to wage rate**

The Stretch Jeans Company manufactures one product. Its standard cost system assigns indirect costs on the basis of standard direct labour hours. At denominator activity, the standard cost per pair of jeans is as follows:

| | |
|---|---|
| Direct materials: 3 metres @ $5 | $15.00 |
| Direct labour: 0.4 hour @ $20 | 8.00 |
| Indirect costs: 0.4 hour @ $10 | 4.00 |
| | $27.00 |

For the month of April 20X4 the performance report included the following:

| | |
|---|---|
| Direct labour incurred at actual rate | $77 900 |
| Standard direct labour allocated | 72 000 |
| Total direct labour variance | 5 900 |
| Direct labour rate variance | 1 900 UF |
| Direct labour efficiency variance | 4 000 UF |

The following journal entry was made to allocate overhead to Work-in-Process:

| | | |
|---|---|---|
| Work-in-Process | $36 000 | |
| Overhead Allocated | | $36 000 |

*Required:* What was the actual wage rate per hour during April?

**6-22  Standard process costing: calculate standard prime cost and actual labour cost**

Pacific Company uses a standard process costing system, whereby all entries in the Work-in-Process account are recorded at standard cost. A single product is manufactured in one process. The records for September, 20X7 reveal:

Opening Work-in-Process 5000 units (100% complete as to direct materials, 80% complete as to conversion).
40 000 units were started in September and 37 000 units completed.
Closing Work-in-Process was 100% complete as to direct materials and 50% complete as to conversion.

Total debits for September in the Work-in-Process account came to $166 500. Overhead allocated was $55 500. Direct materials charged to production were $37 000.

*Required:*
(a) Calculate the standard prime cost per unit in September.
(b) During September there was an unfavourable direct labour rate variance of $8000, and an unfavourable direct labour efficiency variance of $5000. If the standard direct labour cost per equivalent unit was $2.00, the actual cost of total direct labour used in September must have been:
(A) $71 000, (B) $74 000, (C) $77 000, (D) $85 000, (E) none of these.


**6-23  Standard cost variance analysis: materials, labour and overhead**

Beerok Ltd manufactures jogging shoes and maintains a standard cost accounting system. The following standard costs have been developed for its Marathon Special model:

| | |
|---|---|
| Direct materials (1 kilogram) | $16.00 |
| Direct labour (3 hours) | 24.00 |
| Overhead (DLH basis) | 7.20 |
| | $47.20 |

Production and cost information for July, 20X8 was:

| | |
|---|---|
| Actual direct materials purchased | 1043 kilograms |
| Actual direct materials issued | 880 kilograms |
| Actual output | 900 pairs |
| Actual cost of materials purchased | $15 288 |
| Actual direct labour rate | $8.25 per hour |
| Actual direct labour hours | 2650 |
| Actual overhead costs | $6300 |

*Required:*
Calculate the following standard cost variances for July and provide general journal entries to record the cost flows for July.

(a) materials price
(b) materials usage
(c) direct labour rate
(d) direct labour efficiency
(e) total overhead

## 6/Product Costing Systems: Standard Costs

**6-24** **Standard process costing: equivalent units, standard cost variances, journal entries**

XYZ Company manufactures a single product, Bonzo. The standard cost specification sheet shows the following standards for one unit of Bonzo:

| | |
|---|---|
| 5 kg of material X @ $8/kg | $40 |
| 2 hr direct labour @ $12/hr | 24 |
| Overhead: $6/direct labour hour | 12 |
| Standard cost for 1 unit | $76 |

Material X is added at the commencement of the manufacturing process, while conversion costs are incurred uniformly throughout the process.

Work in process on 1 June, 20X2 consisted of 900 units of Bonzo, two-thirds complete. During June 9900 units were completed. Work in process at 30 June comprised 1000 units 80% complete.

Actual costs incurred in June were:
    60 000 kg of Material X were purchased @ $8.20 per kg.
    51 000 kg of Material X were used.
    19 800 direct labour hours were worked at an average wage rate of $12.40 per hour.
    Actual overhead incurred was $122 000.

*Required:*
(a) Calculate the equivalent units of Bonzo produced in June.
(b) Using your calculations in (a) calculate all standard cost variances that you can from the given data.
(c) Provide journal entries to record these June transactions.

**6-25** **Standard process costing: equivalent units and variances**

Fruit Juices Ltd operates a standard process cost system and manufactures a certain product from two raw materials, A and B, which pass through a single process. Standard costs per finished litre of this product are as follows:

| | |
|---|---|
| Material A, 500 ml @ $5 per litre | $2.50 |
| Material B, 500 ml @ $4 per litre | 2.00 |
| Direct labour, 20 min @ $12 per hr | 4.00 |
| Overhead, $18 per standard DLH | 6.00 |
| Standard cost per litre | $14.50 |

Production details for the month of October are as follows:

| | |
|---|---|
| Opening Work-in-Process, litres (20% complete) | 1 000 |
| Litres started during October | 10 000 |
| Litres completed during October | 9 000 |
| Closing Work-in-Process, litres (40% complete) | 2 000 |

Materials A and B are both added at the start of the process, and conversion costs are allocated uniformly throughout.

Actual costs incurred during October were:

| | |
|---|---|
| Material A, 5500 litres @ $5.20 | $28 600 |
| Material B, 5250 litres @ $3.80 | 19 950 |
| Direct labour, 3360 hr @ $12.50 | 42 000 |
| Overhead costs incurred | 64 000 |

*Required:*
(a) Express the production for October in terms of equivalent units for Material A, Material B and Conversion.
(b) Calculate the total value, at standard cost, of completed production and closing work in process.
(c) Calculate for the month:
  (i) materials price variance for each material and in total.
  (ii) materials usage variance for each material and in total.
  (iii) labour rate variance.
  (iv) labour efficiency variance.
  (v) total overhead variance.

**6-26 Standard process costing: calculating variances**

Tongues Ltd produces a beverage called *OP Jungle Juice*. The ingredients consist of two secret compounds which are manufactured by a subsidiary company. A standard cost system is employed and inventories are maintained at standard cost values. The standard cost specification sheet for the production of a 4-litre bottle of the beverage includes the following information:

| Material: | | |
|---|---|---|
| 1 litre of X @ $1 | $1.00 | |
| 3 litres of Y @ $3 | 9.00 | $10.00 |
| Direct labour: 1 hour @ $10 | | $10.00 |
| Overhead: 1 hour @ $6 | | $6.00 |

Factory operating records for the year disclose the following data:

| Finished output of 4-litre bottles | | 50 000 |
|---|---|---|
| Purchases: | 64 000 litres of X @ $1.10 | |
| | 202 000 litres of Y @ $3.00 | |
| Material usage: | 60 000 litres of X | |
| | 156 000 litres of Y | |
| Direct labour: | 52 000 hours @ $10.50 | |
| Overhead incurred | | $350 000 |

Work-in-Process inventories:
At beginning of year: 20 000 litres 100% complete as to material and 80% complete as to conversion.
At end of year: 24 000 litres 100% complete as to material and two-thirds complete as to conversion.

*Required:*
Calculate all variances that you can.

**6-27 Comprehensive standard job costing: ledger accounts (challenging)**

The Shady Manufacturing Company produces venetian blinds for domestic use. The company manufactures to customer order, only after a representative has measured a customer's windows, quoted a firm price and received a written authority from the customer to proceed.

Shady operates a job costing system and employs standard costs for product costing and cost control. For practical purposes they classify blinds into four approximate widths (1800 mm, 1500 mm, 1200 mm and 900 mm) on which they base their standard costs.

6/*Product Costing Systems: Standard Costs*

The standard costs of these blinds are:

|  | *1800mm* | *1500mm* | *1200mm* | *900mm* |
|---|---|---|---|---|
| Direct material | $30 | $24 | $20 | $16 |
| Direct labour | 24 | 24 | 16 | 16 |
| Overhead | 30 | 30 | 20 | 20 |
|  | $84 | $78 | $56 | $52 |

The standard direct labour rate is $8 per hour and standard direct labour hours are used as the base for overhead application.

Inventories at 1 November, 20X8 at standard cost were:

| Raw Materials | $1000 |
|---|---|
| Work-in-Process | 906 |
| Finished Goods | 336 |

Particulars of work in process and jobs completed were:

*In Process:* Job 102 (ten 1800 mm blinds) and Job 103 (five 1500 mm blinds) were both complete as to material, but 60% complete as to conversion cost.

*Complete:* Job 101 (six 1200 mm blinds).

The following information relates to the week ended 7 November, 20X8:

*Orders Received and Started*

|  | *Number of Blinds* | | | |
|---|---|---|---|---|
|  | *1800mm* | *1500mm* | *1200mm* | *900mm* |
| Job 104 | 6 | 4 | - | 2 |
| 105 | 5 | 3 | 6 | - |
| 106 | 2 | - | - | - |
| 107 | - | 3 | - | - |
| 108 | 2 | 3 | 2 | 2 |
| 109 | 4 | 3 | 2 | 1 |
| 110 | 1 | 2 | 2 | 5 |
|  | 20 | 18 | 12 | 10 |

All jobs except Job 110 were sold. Job 110 was complete as to material only.

Raw materials purchased cost $2100, but their standard cost was $2000.
Raw materials usage was found to be $40 more than standard.

Labour wage rates were at standard, but labour used was one-half an hour less than standard.

Gross wages bill incurred $1680.

Provision was made for annual leave for employees, $400.
Other indirect labour costs were $460.
PAYG tax withheld was $400.

There were no other authorised deductions.

*Required:*

(a) Prepare general ledger accounts to record the above information and state:
   (i) the cost of finished goods transferred
   (ii) the closing balance of Raw Materials account.
(b) What features of this company's operations suggest that the present product costing system is appropriate?
(c) If the company were to install new production equipment which would result in all blinds (irrespective of width) requiring 2.5 direct labour hours and an overhead rate of $12 per direct labour hour, what type of cost system would you recommend for the company's manufacturing operations? Why?

**6-28  Standard process costing: building a spreadsheet model (comprehensive)**

At the end of this problem is a spreadsheet template to assist you in preparing a solution to the following problem:

Garden Products Ltd manufactures a variety of products made of plastic and aluminium components. During winter all production capacity is devoted to the manufacture of lawn sprinklers for the following spring and summer seasons. Other products are manufactured during the remainder of the year. Because of the variety of products manufactured, factory capacity is measured in terms of direct labour hours.

Garden Products uses a standard process costing system. The standard cost of the lawn sprinkler currently produced for 20X0 can be calculated from the following data:

| | |
|---|---|
| Direct materials: | |
| Aluminium | 2.0 kg @ $5.00 per kg |
| Plastic | 1.0 kg @ $3.00 per kg |
| Direct labour | 0.2 hr @ $25.00 per hr |
| Overhead: | |
| Variable | 0.2 hr @ $10.00 per hr |
| Fixed | 0.2 hr @ $5.00 per hr |

Overhead allocation rates are calculated using 15 000 direct labour hours per annum as the denominator volume.

Aluminium is introduced at the start of the process, while plastic is introduced when the product is 30% complete. Conversion costs are incurred uniformly throughout the process.

Production details for July, 20X0 are as follows:

At the beginning of July work in process comprised 500 units estimated to be 20% complete. During July 8500 units were started and 8000 units were completed. Closing work in process was estimated to be 70% complete.

During July the following materials were issued to the production department:

| | |
|---|---|
| Aluminium | 19 000 kg |
| Plastic: | |
| Regular grade | 5 000 kg |
| Low grade | 4 500 kg |

## 6/Product Costing Systems: Standard Costs

In addition, the following labour and overhead costs were incurred:

| Direct labour: | |
| --- | --- |
| Ordinary time | 1750 hr for $46 375 |
| Overtime at ordinary rate | 200 hr for $5 300 |
| Overtime premium | 200 hr for $2 650 |
| | |
| Overhead: | |
| Variable | $15 000 |
| Fixed | $10 000 |

The overhead costs above do not include direct labour overtime premium cost. The company classifies this premium as overhead.

Material price variances are extracted at the time the supplier's invoice is processed. All materials are carried in inventory at standard prices. Material purchases for July were:

| Aluminium | 16 000 kg for $86 400 |
| --- | --- |
| Plastic: | |
| Regular grade | 3 000 kg for $9 600 |
| Low grade* | 6 000 kg for $15 000 |

\* Because of shortages of plastic, the company was forced to purchase lower grade plastic than called for in the standards. Consequently there was an increase in the quantity of material used and the work (including overtime) required to satisfy inspection standards and meet production schedules.

*Required:*
(a) Examine the worksheet template. You will see that it contains three parts:
Part 1: Calculation of equivalent units
Part 2: Calculation of standard cost of production
Part 3: Calculation of standard cost variances

Enter data and build appropriate formulae to complete Part 1 which results in the calculation of equivalent units for work done during the month. Print the results, and formulae.

Now assume that plastic is introduced when the process is 10% complete. Change the DATA entry in cell C6 and print the results. If you need to change any other entry to get the correct results your model is not general enough and should be modified. It is important that no matter what data is entered the model still works correctly. On completion the original data should be saved.

(b) Now complete Part 2. Enter the data for the standard allowances (columns B and C) and construct the formulae as directed. Make sure that the Cost of O/WIP + Cost of work Done this Month = Cost of units completed + Cost of C/WIP. Save your work. Print the results and the formulae.

Explain why Standard Cost of O/WIP + Standard Cost of work Done this Month must equal Standard Cost of Units Completed + Standard Cost of C/WIP.

(c) (i) Complete Part 3. Enter the data regarding costs and quantities of input factors and construct formulae to calculate unit prices as directed. Construct formulae to calculate the variances indicated. You may require @IF formulae. No negative numbers are allowed. Each column (FAVOURABLE and UNFAVOURABLE) should show either a positive value or blank (or zero) for each of the 9 variances. Save and print.

(ii) Assume that instead of starting 8500 units during July the company actually started 10 000 units, although only 8000 units were completed. Change the data in cell C11 and print the results of your whole model. Some of the variances should change in amount and/or sign. Your formulae should have passed this test - if not you should modify them.

Explain clearly and completely why some variances changed in amount and/or sign and some did not. Be specific.

(d) It has been suggested that in practice, equivalent units of opening and closing work in process are often ignored. Refer to the original data used in Part 1 and change the work in process units to zeros. Print the results of your whole model. Some of your variances may now differ from those calculated in Part (c)(i).

Explain clearly why some variances differ from those calculated in Part (c)(i) and some do not. Under what circumstances may the exclusion of work in process in a standard process costing situation be justified?

(e) Refer to the solution to Part (c)(i). Comment on the cost performance as revealed in the schedule of variances.

## 6/Product Costing Systems: Standard Costs

|    | A | B | C | D | E | F |
|---|---|---|---|---|---|---|
| 1 | **STANDARD PROCESS COSTING SPREADSHEET** | | | | | |
| 2 | | | | | | |
| 3 | PART 1 | | DATA AND EQUIVALENT UNIT CALCULATIONS | | | |
| 4 | ENTER PROCESS DETAILS IN COLUMN C | | | | | |
| 5 | - % Completion at which Aluminium is added | | DATA | | | |
| 6 | - % Completion at which Plastic is added | | DATA | | | |
| 7 | - Conversion costs assumed incurred uniformly | | | | | |
| 8 | | | | | | |
| 9 | ENTER PRODUCTION DETAILS IN COLUMN C | | | | | |
| 10 | - Units in Opening WIP | | DATA | | | |
| 11 | - Units started | | DATA | | | |
| 12 | - Units completed | | DATA | | | |
| 13 | - Units in Closing WIP | | FORMULA | | | |
| 14 | - % Completion of O/WIP | | DATA | | | |
| 15 | - % Completion of C/WIP | | DATA | | | |
| 16 | | | | | | |
| 17 | FLOW OF PRODUCTION | PHYSICAL | | | EQUIVALENT UNITS | |
| 18 | | FLOW | %AGE | ALUMINIUM | PLASTIC | CONVERSION |
| 19 | Units in O/WIP | FORMULA | FORMULA | | | |
| 20 | Units started | FORMULA | | | | |
| 21 | Total units to account for | FORMULA | | | | |
| 22 | *Units completed* | | | | | |
| 23 | From O/WIP (EU to complete) | FORMULA | | FORMULA | FORMULA | FORMULA |
| 24 | Started & completed this period | FORMULA | | FORMULA | FORMULA | FORMULA |
| 25 | *Closing WIP (EU completed)* | FORMULA | FORMULA | FORMULA | FORMULA | FORMULA |
| 26 | Units accounted for......................... | FORMULA | | | | |
| 27 | Equivalent units of work done this period........................... | | | FORMULA | FORMULA | FORMULA |
| 28 | | | | | | |
| 29 | PART 2 | | CALCULATION OF STANDARD COST OF PRODUCTION | | | |
| 30 | STANDARD ALLOWANCES for 1 SPRINKLER | **Phys Qty** | **Std Rate** | **Std Cost** | | |
| 31 | Direct Materials | | | | | |
| 32 | Aluminium | DATA | DATA | FORMULA | | |
| 33 | Plastic | DATA | DATA | FORMULA | | |
| 34 | Direct Labour | DATA | DATA | FORMULA | | |
| 35 | Overhead | | | | | |
| 36 | Variable | DATA | DATA | FORMULA | | |
| 37 | Fixed | DATA | DATA | FORMULA | | |
| 38 | | | | FORMULA | | |
| 39 | | | | | | |
| 40 | DETAILS OF STANDARD COST OF PRODUCTION | **Aluminium** | **Plastic** | **Conv Cost** | **Total Cost** | |
| 41 | Standard Cost of Opening WIP | FORMULA | FORMULA | FORMULA | FORMULA | |
| 42 | Standard Cost of Work Done this Month | FORMULA | FORMULA | FORMULA | FORMULA | |
| 43 | | FORMULA | FORMULA | FORMULA | FORMULA | |
| 44 | Standard Cost of Units Completed this Month | FORMULA | FORMULA | FORMULA | FORMULA | |
| 45 | Standard Cost of Closing WIP | FORMULA | FORMULA | FORMULA | FORMULA | |
| 46 | | FORMULA | FORMULA | FORMULA | FORMULA | |
| 47 | | | | | | |
| 48 | PART 3 | | CALCULATION OF STANDARD COST VARIANCES | | | |
| 49 | INPUT FACTORS | **Actual** | | | | |
| 50 | Direct Materials | | | | | |
| 51 | Aluminium | | | | | |
| 52 | Quantity Purchased - kg | DATA | | | | |
| 53 | Sum Paid | DATA | | | | |
| 54 | Price per kg | FORMULA | | | | |
| 55 | Quantity Issued - kg | DATA | | | | |
| 56 | Plastic | | | | | |
| 57 | Regular Grade | | | | | |
| 58 | Quantity Purchased - kg | DATA | | | | |
| 59 | Sum Paid | DATA | | | | |
| 60 | Price per kg | FORMULA | | | | |
| 61 | Quantity Issued - kg | DATA | | | | |
| 62 | Low Grade | | | | | |
| 63 | Quantity Purchased - kg | DATA | | | | |
| 64 | Sum Paid | DATA | | | | |
| 65 | Price per kg | FORMULA | | | | |
| 66 | Quantity Issued - kg | DATA | | | | |
| 67 | Direct Labour | | | | | |
| 68 | Hours Worked | DATA | | | | |
| 69 | Sum Paid | DATA | | | | |
| 70 | Rate Paid per hr | FORMULA | | | | |
| 71 | Overhead Incurred | | | | | |
| 72 | Variable (Includes Overtime Premium) | DATA | | | | |
| 73 | Fixed | DATA | | | | |
| 74 | | | | | | |

*(continued next page)*

*6/Product Costing Systems: Standard Costs*

|    | A | B | C | D | E | F |
|----|---|---|---|---|---|---|
| 75 | DETAILS OF VARIANCES | Favourable | Unfavourable | | | |
| 76 | Materials Price Variances | | | | | |
| 77 | Aluminium | FORMULA | FORMULA | | | |
| 78 | Plastic - Regular | FORMULA | FORMULA | | | |
| 79 | Plastic - Low Grade | FORMULA | FORMULA | | | |
| 80 | Materials Usage Variances | | | | | |
| 81 | Aluminium | FORMULA | FORMULA | | | |
| 82 | Plastic | FORMULA | FORMULA | | | |
| 83 | Direct Labour Rate Variance | FORMULA | FORMULA | | | |
| 84 | Direct Labour Efficiency Variance | FORMULA | FORMULA | | | |
| 85 | Overhead Variances | | | | | |
| 86 | Variable | FORMULA | FORMULA | | | |
| 87 | Fixed | FORMULA | FORMULA | | | |
| 88 | | FORMULA | FORMULA | | | |
| 89 | | | | | | |

# Chapter 7

# Alternative Product Costing Systems: Variable Costing and JIT Costing

In previous chapters we have seen how product costs (material, labour and overhead) are traced or allocated to products using job, process or operation costing. We also have observed that these costs may be either actual costs or standard costs. All the systems illustrated have been examples of what is called **absorption costing**. In a manufacturing environment this means that **all** factory costs have been charged to products, that is they were treated as **product costs**. Or, to put it another way, the products have **absorbed** all factory costs.

## WHY VARIABLE COSTING?

A criticism of absorption costing is that a change in sales revenue does not always reflect a similar change in profit. In an early article, "What Did We Earn Last Month?" (Harris, 1936) a controller had been questioned by his company president as to why profits were down $20 000 on the previous month although sales were up by over $100 000. In order to respond to this very reasonable question, Harris devised an alternative system of cost accounting to show profits as a function of sales. The system was referred to as **direct costing**, although the term **variable costing** is more appropriate. Ever since this time 'direct' costing has been a controversial issue which has attracted a great deal of attention in the accounting literature.

## DIFFERENCES BETWEEN VARIABLE AND ABSORPTION COSTING

The major distinguishing feature of variable costing is that only **variable** production costs are charged to products: direct materials, direct labour and **variable** overhead (direct materials and direct labour typically being regarded as variable costs). Fixed production costs, i.e. **fixed** overhead, is treated as a **period cost** and written off as a lump sum in the period in which it is incurred. It is this treatment of fixed overhead which accounts for the difference in profit that can result from the use of variable and absorption costing methods.

A second distinguishing feature of variable costing is a somewhat different method of calculating profit and presenting statements of financial performance, Figure 7-1.

| ABSORPTION COSTING | | VARIABLE COSTING | | |
|---|---|---|---|---|
| Sales | XXX | Sales | | XXX |
| Less Cost of Sales | XX | Less Variable Costs: | | |
| Gross Profit | XX |   Manufacturing | XX | |
| Less Selling & Administration Expenses | X |   Selling & Admin | XX | XX |
| Net Profit | X | Variable Profit (or Contribution Margin) | | XX |
| | | Less Fixed Costs: | | |
| | |   Manufacturing | X | |
| | |   Selling & Admin | X | XX |
| | | Net Profit | | X |

**Figure 7-1: Absorption versus Variable Costing**

Under absorption costing, the primary cost classification is manufacturing/non-manufacturing. All manufacturing costs are assigned to the product while non-manufacturing costs are written off in the period in which they are incurred.

Variable costing focuses on the behaviour of costs with respect to volume. Costs are treated as fixed or variable with respect to production volume (in the case of manufacturing costs) or sales volume (in the case of selling, distribution and administration costs). Thus it is necessary to identify cost behaviour, preferably in the accounts, although not necessarily. A knowledge of such cost behaviour would permit the preparation of variable costing profit and loss statements without formal separation of fixed and variable costs in the accounts.

Profit under variable costing is determined by deducting all variable costs (manufacturing and selling and administration) from sales revenue to give variable profit (or contribution margin, meaning contribution to fixed costs and profits). From variable profit is deducted all fixed costs (manufacturing and selling and administration) to give net profit.

As will be illustrated, the net profit under the two systems is only the same when the units sold equal the units produced (i.e., no change in inventories).

## *Illustrative Example 7-1*

*A company commenced operations on 1 July, 20X4 making a single product which sold for $50 per unit. Units of product produced and sold during the quarter ended 30 September, 20X4 were as shown below:*

|  | *July* | *August* | *September* |
| --- | --- | --- | --- |
| *Opening inventory* | *0* | *50* | *20* |
| *Units produced* | *150* | *100* | *90* |
| *Available for sale* | *150* | *150* | *110* |
| *Units sold* | *100* | *130* | *90* |
| *Closing inventory* | *50* | *20* | *20* |

*Fixed overhead was expected to average $1000 per month for an expected production level of 100 units per month. Thus, for absorption costing purposes, the predetermined fixed overhead rate was $1000/100 = $10 per unit; any monthly fixed overhead variance was to be written off to Cost of Goods Sold. Under variable costing fixed overhead is not allocated to product so that there can be no fixed overhead variance.*

*Variable overhead was expected to be $5 per unit. Direct materials were expected to cost $10 per unit and direct labour to cost $5 per unit.*

*Thus absorption cost per unit was expected to be $30 ($10+$5+$5+$10) for direct materials, direct labour, variable overhead and fixed overhead respectively), while variable cost per unit was expected to be $20 ($10+$5+$5) for direct materials, direct labour and variable overhead. All actual variable costs per unit turned out to be the same as estimated.*

*Actual revenues and costs for the quarter were as follows:*

|  | *July* | *August* | *September* |
| --- | --- | --- | --- |
| *Sales revenue* | *$5000* | *$6500* | *$4500* |
| *Production costs:* |  |  |  |
| *Direct materials* | *1500* | *1000* | *900* |
| *Direct labour* | *750* | *500* | *450* |
| *Variable overhead* | *750* | *500* | *450* |
| *Fixed overhead* | *1000* | *1000* | *1000* |
| *Selling & Admin Expenses:* |  |  |  |
| *Fixed* | *500* | *500* | *500* |
| *Variable* | *500* | *650* | *450* |

## 7/Variable Costing and JIT Costing

*Required:*
Prepare statements of financial performance for each month assuming:
(a)  a normal absorption costing system; and
(b)  a variable costing system.

The solution follows:

### ABSORPTION COSTING

|  | July $ | July $ | August $ | August $ | September $ | September $ |
|---|---|---|---|---|---|---|
| Sales |  | 5000 |  | 6500 |  | 4500 |
| Less Cost of Sales: |  |  |  |  |  |  |
|   O/Inventory [0,50,20 @ $30] | 0 |  | 1500 |  | 600 |  |
|   Cost of Goods Manufactured [$30 ea] | 4500 |  | 3000 |  | 2700 |  |
|  | 4500 |  | 4500 |  | 3300 |  |
|   Less C/Inventory [50,20,20 @ $30] | 1500 |  | 600 |  | 600 |  |
| Cost of Goods Sold (Normal) | 3000 |  | 3900 |  | 2700 |  |
| Add(Less) Under(Over)-Allocated Fixed Overhead [(50),0,10 @ $10] | (500) |  | 0 |  | 100 |  |
| Adjusted Cost of Goods Sold |  | 2500 |  | 3900 |  | 2800 |
| Gross Profit |  | 2500 |  | 2600 |  | 1700 |
| Less Selling & Admin Expenses: |  |  |  |  |  |  |
|   Variable | 500 |  | 650 |  | 450 |  |
|   Fixed | 500 |  | 500 |  | 500 |  |
|  |  | 1000 |  | 1150 |  | 950 |
| Net Profit |  | 1500 |  | 1450 |  | 750 |

### VARIABLE COSTING

|  | July $ | July $ | August $ | August $ | September $ | September $ |
|---|---|---|---|---|---|---|
| Sales |  | 5000 |  | 6500 |  | 4500 |
| Less Variable Costs: |  |  |  |  |  |  |
|   O/Inventory [0,50,20 @ $20] | 0 |  | 1000 |  | 400 |  |
|   Cost of Goods Manufactured [$20 ea] | 3000 |  | 2000 |  | 1800 |  |
|  | 3000 |  | 3000 |  | 2200 |  |
|   Less C/Inventory [50,20,20 @ $20] | 1000 |  | 400 |  | 400 |  |
| Variable Manufacturing COGS | 2000 |  | 2600 |  | 1800 |  |
|   Variable Selling $ Admin Expenses | 500 |  | 650 |  | 450 |  |
| Total Variable Costs |  | 2500 |  | 3250 |  | 2250 |
| Variable Profit (Contribution Margin) |  | 2500 |  | 3250 |  | 2250 |
| Less Fixed Costs: |  |  |  |  |  |  |
|   Fixed Overhead | 1000 |  | 1000 |  | 1000 |  |
|   Selling & Administration | 500 |  | 500 |  | 500 |  |
|  |  | 1500 |  | 1500 |  | 1500 |
| Net Profit |  | 1000 |  | 1750 |  | 750 |

## RECONCILIATION OF PROFIT

The difference between absorption costing profit and variable costing profit can be attributed to the fact that when sales units do not equal production units the amount of fixed overhead expensed against revenue differs.

Under variable costing the fixed overhead expensed in any period is equal to the fixed overhead incurred during that period. Under absorption costing, however, the amount of fixed overhead expensed depends upon the number of units of product sold.

As you will recall, under absorption costing product costs (direct materials, direct labour and overhead) are attached to the units of product produced, and remain an asset (inventory) until the units are sold, at which point these product costs are expensed. If in any period more units are sold than are produced, the total fixed overhead expensed would exceed the sum incurred: the number of units **sold** x fixed overhead per unit would exceed the number of units **produced** x fixed overhead per unit. Accordingly, absorption costing profit would be lower than variable costing profit because more fixed overhead would be expensed in Cost of Goods Sold under absorption costing than expensed as a period cost under variable costing. Absorption costing profit would be lower by a sum equal to the decrease in finished goods (units) inventory multiplied by the fixed overhead per unit.

In example 7-1, sales exceed production in August (130 units sold, 100 units produced) leading to a decrease in finished goods inventory of 30 units (opening inventory 50, closing inventory 20). Therefore absorption costing profit should be lower than variable costing profit by 30 units x $10 = $300. As we see, this is verified: absorption costing profit of $1450 is lower than variable costing profit of $1750 by $300.

Conversely, in any period in which fewer units are sold than are produced, the total fixed overhead expensed under absorption costing would be less than the sum incurred because part of the period's fixed overhead expense would be inventoried. Then absorption costing profit would be higher than variable costing profit because less fixed overhead would be expensed in Cost of Goods Sold under absorption costing than would be written off as a period expense under variable costing. Absorption costing profit would be higher by a sum equal to the increase in finished goods inventory multiplied by the fixed overhead per unit. In example 7-1, sales are less than production in July (100 units sold, 150 units produced) leading to an increase in finished goods inventory of 50 units (opening inventory 0, closing inventory 50). Therefore absorption costing profit should be higher than variable costing profit by a sum equal to 50 units x $10 = $500. We see that this is the case: absorption costing profit of $1500 is higher than variable costing profit of $1000 by $500.

It will be noted that in September when units sold equalled units produced (no change in finished goods inventory) the profit of $750 is the same under both methods.

Summing up, we can posit two rules:

1. When there is a **decrease** in inventory, absorption costing profit is **lower** than variable costing profit.

2. When there is an **increase** in inventory, absorption costing profit is **higher** than variable costing profit.

and the difference can be shown to be equal to the change in finished goods inventory multiplied by the fixed overhead rate per unit. Of course, such a reconciliation requires that the fixed overhead rate used to cost the opening inventory is the same as the rate in the current period, and that any under-allocated or over-allocated fixed overhead (called a volume variance) is written off in the period. Should either of these conditions not hold, the reconciliation of profit under the two methods becomes more complex.

## VARIABLE COSTING AND MANAGEMENT ACCOUNTING

A number of management accounting techniques are dependent on the ability to identify fixed cost/variable cost behaviour patterns. Such techniques include cost control, budgeting and product mix decisions. Historically, in order to provide such cost information, special studies were undertaken, independently of and outside the formal accounting system. Because of the ongoing nature of cost control and the recurrent need to make short-run operating decisions, attempts were made to integrate fixed/variable cost information into the accounting system. These attempts resulted in the development of variable costing systems.

Opponents of variable costing have been particularly concerned about the exclusion of fixed overhead from product cost because, they claim, it results in undervaluing finished goods inventory and understates the importance of fixed costs in pricing decisions. They argue that it is possible to distinguish between fixed and variable costs in the accounts, thus facilitating management accounting needs, without necessarily charging production and inventory with variable costs only.

It may well be argued that in modern manufacturing settings the adoption of sophisticated production technology has dramatically increased the fixed overhead costs associated with such equipment and correspondingly reduced labour and associated costs. Consequently, it could be claimed that the exclusion of fixed overhead produces inventory costs which are grossly misleading, and thus variable costing should be buried. In any event, the controversy is probably a non-event these days; with the development of computerised data processing methods it is possible, and may be worthwhile, to store sufficiently disaggregated data in the organisation's data base so that the user can access either absorption or variable costing data as required.

## EXTERNAL REPORTING

Although it is generally agreed that variable costing is useful for internal management purposes, at the external financial reporting level the debate about variable costing has assumed a more theoretical nature, involving issues of profit measurement and asset definition and valuation.

### *Profit Measurement*

A fundamental question is whether fixed manufacturing costs are product costs or period costs. Supporters of variable costing argue for the latter, claiming that fixed manufacturing costs represent the costs of providing the necessary operating capacity for a period, and that the benefit has expired at the end of the period, irrespective of the level of operations during that period.

Supporters of absorption costing argue from a matching concept viewpoint. They maintain that all manufacturing costs are product costs, and that the costs of providing capacity are as much the costs of the product as direct materials, labour and variable overhead costs; the product generates revenue, and all expired production costs should be matched against that revenue in the period of sale.

### *Asset Valuation*

An asset may be defined as something which provides future economic benefits, that is, it has service potential. Supporters of variable costing propose a **cost obviation** concept: that only those costs which can be avoided in the future by producing inventory now should be treated as product costs (and hence an asset); that fixed overhead cannot be obviated in the next period by producing additional units in the current period, and therefore the current period's fixed overhead does not provide any future benefit, and thus should be written off against revenue in the current period.

Supporters of absorption costing propose an alternative view that the service potential of an asset is its capacity to contribute revenue in the future: any costs which contribute to the realisation of revenue in the future should be included as inventory costs; fixed overhead costs are equally essential to production as variable costs, and should be treated as costs of the product (i.e., as an asset).

## USE OF VARIABLE COSTING

In the past variable costing has been used by some firms, and was allowable under accounting standards. However, the current Australian Accounting Standard AAS 2 "Inventories" includes all overheads, both fixed and variable, in determining cost (para. 6):

> *Production overheads that relate to bringing inventories to their present location and condition must be systematically allocated in determining the cost of inventories...(para 6.1). The costs of conversion that are fixed production overheads ...are allocated to each item of inventory on the basis of normal operating capacity of the production facilities...(para 6.1.2)*

For taxation purposes, the absorption costing method is required to be used in valuing trading stock. The question as to what is the cost price of manufactured goods was considered by the Victorian Supreme Court in Philip Morris Ltd v. F.C. of T. (1979 ATC 4352). The Court upheld the Commissioner's view that absorption costing was the correct method and that direct costing was a departure from the concept of 'cost' in section 31.

## JUST IN TIME PRODUCTION

In traditional manufacturing there are many activities carried out which do not directly add value to a product; these activities have been called **non-value-added** activities. Despite the fact that such activities add no value to products (especially in the eyes of the customer), the costs of these activities (non-value-added costs) are still included as part of product cost. McIlhattan (1987) has described the total manufacturing time (or throughput time) as consisting of several steps:

o **process time**, which is the amount of time that a product is actually being worked on. We can also call this **value-added time**.
o **inspection time**, which is the time spent assuring high quality products or reworking the product to an acceptable quality level.
o **move time**, which is the time spent moving the product from one location to another.
o **queue time**, which is the time spent waiting, for processing or moving or inspecting etc.
o **storage time**, which is the time spent in stock before shipment.

Of these five steps, only process time adds value to the product. All the other activities add cost but no value to the product, and are called non-value-added activities. If non-value-added time can be eliminated, throughput time is minimised and the resultant efficient production process should minimise product costs. In many organisations actual process time may be less than 10% of throughput time, so that there are large potential gains in efficiency to be achieved, and the proportion of process time to throughput time represents an important performance measure.

The manufacturers' solution to the problem of non-value-added activities has been an attempt to move to a just-in-time (JIT) production system. JIT production implies that any production will take place only in response to demand for the final product. As orders are placed for products they are produced in response to this demand - it is a demand pull system. Instead of producing for stock and thus holding inventories of finished goods, production is completed just in time for sale. Similarly, raw materials are received just in time to enter the production process rather than be stored in a storeroom. Instead of producing large batches in long production runs, the emphasis is on small batches.

The primary aim of JIT production is to eliminate as far as possible, all non-value-added activities. JIT systems pursue the goals of zero inventories, zero defects, flexibility in production, and zero interruptions to production: set-up times for production runs are reduced; production runs are smaller to ensure that products move continuously through the process to eliminate queue time and interruptions; product quality is improved to eliminate defects and the associated costs of scrap, rework, inspection and returns; worker involvement is sought to motivate them for continuous improvements; cellular production techniques are adopted to produce a product or major component from start to finish in one 'cell' ('a factory within a factory') to reduce travel distances and in-process inventory between machines or work stations.

A feature of JIT production is a shift, from the traditional notion of holding three sets of inventories (raw materials, work in process and finished goods) as buffers against variations in supply and demand and uneven work flows at different work stations, to holding small or even zero inventories. Inventories are simply thought of as waste. They occupy space, tie up money, and hide inefficiencies and poor quality; if no inventories are held any inefficiency becomes obvious and any poor quality work requiring rework is highlighted because under a JIT system such rework would hold up the processing further down the line. So defective items are detected much sooner than if large batches are produced involving possibly many defective items not detected until subsequent processing.

*7/Variable Costing and JIT Costing*

Consequently the number of defective items produced declines dramatically, and any problems can be fixed before even a small batch has been completed, leading to higher quality.

## JIT COSTING

Thus, when a firm employs JIT systems (of purchasing and production), ideally there are no inventories. Consequently, all the manufacturing expenses incurred during a period become the cost of goods sold for that period. One consequence of this is that the variable costing versus absorption costing debate is irrelevant as far as profit reporting is concerned. More importantly, there should be no need to have ledger accounts for raw material inventory or work-in-process inventory or finished goods inventory (as foreshadowed in Chapter 3). In practice, however, it is unlikely that a zero-inventory position will be realised. Nevertheless it is possible to change the accounting system to match the characteristics of the JIT production approach, and simplify the recording of cost flows in the ledger.

The following features of JIT costing systems reflect such simplified recording processes:

1. There is usually no distinction in the general ledger between raw materials and work in process. A single account labelled Raw and In-Process (RIP) Inventory is used to record both.
2. Because inventory holdings are viewed as an aberration, finished goods inventories may be recorded at their material cost only.
3. Unlike traditional costing systems, costs are not recorded sequentially, but at discrete points in time. There is no single discrete point common to all systems. The events which signal a record in the general ledger are called **trigger points**. The selection of trigger points will affect the way costs are treated as part of inventory value. Two possible sets of trigger points will be illustrated:

    (i) purchase of raw materials, and completion of finished goods
    (ii) purchase of raw materials, and sale of finished goods

### Illustrative Example 7-2

*Trendy Company produces a single product, and uses a standard cost system. On 1 July Trendy switched to a JIT costing system. At this time there were no inventories of raw materials, work in process or finished goods. Standard costs of production are:*

| | |
|---|---:|
| *Direct material per unit* | *$20.00* |
| *Conversion cost per unit* | *40.00* |
| *Total cost per unit* | *$60.00* |

*Details of direct material purchases and production in July:*

*Direct materials sufficient for 3000 units of product were purchased at the standard price.*
*2950 units were started.*
*2800 units of product were completed, with the remaining 150 units estimated to have had all material added but to be 50% complete as to conversion.*
*2500 units of product were sold.*

*Other transactions for July:*

*Production-line employees earned wages of $30 000*
*Other indirect labour costs were $10 000*
*Depreciation on factory and building and equipment $50 000*
*Other overhead expenses $30 000*

| | | | |
|---|---|---|---|
| *Method 1:* | *Using purchase of raw materials as the first trigger point and completion of finished goods as the second trigger point* | | |
| 1 | *Record direct materials purchased* | | |
| | RIP Inventory (3000 x $20) | $60 000 | |
| |     Accounts Payable | | $60 000 |
| 2 | *Record conversion costs incurred* | | |
| | Conversion Costs | $120 000 | |
| |     Accrued Payroll | | $40 000 |
| |     Accumulated Depreciation | | 50 000 |
| |     Sundries | | 30 000 |
| 3 | *Record cost of finished goods completed* | | |
| | Finished Goods (2800 x $60) | $168 000 | |
| |     RIP Inventory (@ $20) | | $56 000 |
| |     Conversion Costs Allocated (@ $40) | | 112 000 |
| 4 | *Record cost of goods sold* | | |
| | Cost of Goods Sold (2500 x $60) | $150 000 | |
| |     Finished Goods | | $150 000 |
| 5 | *Dispose of under-/over-allocated conversion costs to Cost of Goods Sold* | | |
| | Conversion Costs Allocated | $112 000 | |
| | Cost of Goods Sold | 8 000 | |
| |     Conversion Costs | | $120 000 |
| *Ending Inventories appearing in the ledger are:* | | | |
| | RIP Inventory (200 x $20) | $4 000 | |
| | Finished Goods (300 x $60) | $18 000 | |

You will note that under Method 1 work in process (if any) is recorded at only the raw material costs. The RIP Inventory balance represents material costs of the 150 units in closing work in process plus the closing balance of unused material sufficient for 50 units still to be started. Conversion costs will have been charged to finished goods and any under-/over-allocated conversion costs written off to Cost of Goods Sold. The effect of this method is not to reward managers for building up work-in-process inventories. No current period conversion costs can be deferred in work-in-process inventory.

## 7/Variable Costing and JIT Costing

---

*Method 2:*     Using purchase of raw materials as the first trigger point and sale of finished goods as the second trigger point

1     *Record direct materials purchased*

| | | |
|---|---|---|
| RIP Inventory (3000 x $20) | $60 000 | |
|      Accounts Payable | | $60 000 |

2     *Record conversion costs incurred*

| | | |
|---|---|---|
| Conversion Costs | $120 000 | |
|      Accrued Payroll | | $40 000 |
|      Accumulated Depreciation | | 50 000 |
|      Sundries | | 30 000 |

3     *Record cost of goods sold*

| | | |
|---|---|---|
| Cost of Goods Sold (2500 x $60) | $150 000 | |
|      RIP Inventory (@ $20) | | 50 000 |
|      Conversion Costs Allocated (@ $40) | | $100 000 |

4     *Dispose of under-/over-allocated conversion costs to Cost of Goods Sold*

| | | |
|---|---|---|
| Conversion Costs Allocated | $100 000 | |
| Cost of Goods Sold | 20 000 | |
|      Conversion Costs | | $120 000 |

---

*Ending Inventories appearing in the ledger are:*
RIP Inventory (500 x $20)                                   $10 000

---

You will note that under Method 2 the RIP Inventory Account is used for direct material inventory and direct material content of work in process and finished goods. Thus work in process and finished goods are recorded at only their raw material costs. The RIP Inventory balance represents material costs of the 300 units of unsold finished goods, of the 150 units in closing work in process, and the closing balance of unused material sufficient for 50 units still to be started. Conversion costs will have been allocated to cost of goods sold at the time of sale or as any under-/over-allocated conversion costs at the end of the period. The effect of this method is not to reward managers for building up work-in-process or finished goods inventories. No current period conversion costs can be deferred in work-in-process or finished-goods inventory.

### *External Reporting*

Of course, these approaches to recording inventories do not conform to generally accepted accounting principles in respect of external reporting. There is an interesting conflict between what may be required for **compliance** purposes (that is, attaching conversion costs to inventories) and for **control** purposes (that is, discouraging the building up of inventories). Nevertheless, the compliance purpose can be satisfied by computing the costs of closing inventory outside the general ledger records, as follows:

| | |
|---|---|
| Finished Goods (300 units x $60) | $18 000 |
| RIP Inventory | |
|      Raw material (50 x $20) | 1 000 |
|      Work in process | |
|          Material (150 x $20) | 3 000 |
|          Conversion (150 x 0.5 x $40) | 3 000 |
| Total Inventory | $25 000 |

Under Method 1, finished goods are recorded at full cost ($18 000) but raw and in-process inventories are recorded at only $4000 (i.e. their raw material cost: $1000 + $3000). To attach the conversion costs to the in-process inventories the following entry can be made:

| | | |
|---|---|---|
| RIP Inventory (150 x 0.5 x $40) | $3000 | |
| Cost of Goods Sold | | $3000 |

This has the effect of **backflushing** the conversion costs of work in process, treated as an expense in the management accounts, from cost of goods sold into inventory value in the financial accounts.

Under Method 2 finished goods and raw and in-process inventories are recorded at only $10 000 (i.e. their raw material cost - $6000 + $1000 + $3000 respectively). To attach the conversion costs to the finished goods and in-process inventories the following entry can be made:

| | | |
|---|---|---|
| RIP Inventory (for finished goods, 300 x $40) | $12 000 | |
| RIP Inventory (for work in process, 150 x 0.5 x $40) | $3 000 | |
| Cost of Goods Sold | | $15 000 |

This has the effect of **backflushing** the conversion costs of finished goods and work in process, treated as an expense in the management accounts, from cost of goods sold into inventory value in the financial accounts.

This need to backflush conversion costs to obtain full inventory values gave rise to the term **backflush costing** which is another expression used for JIT costing. One of the attractions of JIT costing is its simplicity, but the absence of an audit trail has been voiced as a criticism.

## SUMMARY

Variable (or direct) costing was first developed as an alternative profit concept to better explain the relationship between sales and profit. The major distinguishing feature of variable costing is that it excludes fixed overhead from the cost of products, and writes it off as a period expense.

From a management accounting viewpoint, the separation of costs into fixed and variable categories facilitates cost control and a number of management decision techniques. Thus management accountants have favoured variable costing, although with the advent of modern manufacturing technology and associated large fixed overhead costs, the usefulness of variable costing has probably declined, especially for product-related decisions.

From a financial accounting/external reporting viewpoint variable costing is not favoured because it is claimed that the cost of inventories is understated. Various theoretical arguments have been advanced to support this view.

Both Australian Accounting Standard AAS 2 and the Australian Taxation Office insist on the use of absorption costing for determining the cost of inventories of manufactured goods.

In traditional manufacturing many activities, such as inspection time, move time, queue time and storage time do not add value to a product, and are called non-value-added activities. Moves to JIT production systems have tried to address this problem by focusing on the elimination of such non-value-added activities. The goals of total quality control and zero inventories are means by which non-value-added activities are greatly reduced or eliminated.

Product costing systems are partly determined by the production technology employed. Moves to simplify production processes, such as JIT, provide the opportunity to simplify the costing system, as typified in JIT and backflush costing.

## REFERENCES

J.N. Harris, "What Did We Earn Last Month?", *N.A.C.A. Bulletin*, Section I, Jan 15, 1936.

J.M. Fremgen, "The Direct Costing Controversy - An Identification of Issues", *The Accounting Review*, January 1964, 43-51.

R.D. McIlhattan, "How Cost Management Systems Can Support the JIT Philosophy", *Management Accounting*, Sep., 1987, 21-26.

## QUESTIONS AND PROBLEMS

**7-1** Explain the difference between variable costing and absorption costing in terms of the timing of the release of fixed overhead as an expense.

**7-2** Contrive a two-period numerical example to demonstrate how, under absorption costing, profit could fall in the second period while sales increase.

**7-3** Why is **variable** costing a more appropriate term than **direct** costing?

**7-4** What is meant by the term **non-value-added** costs? Provide examples.

**7-5** Define the five ways that products spend time in the manufacturing process. Which of these may be categorised as non-value-added activities?

**7-6** Describe how JIT costing works, indicating how it differs from conventional costing.

**7-7** Under what conditions will JIT costing and the conventional product costing recording processes lead to the same end of period ledger account balances?

**7-8** **Variable versus absorption costing: fixed overhead differences**
The standard cost specification for a product was:

| | |
|---|---|
| Direct materials (4 kg) | $12 |
| Direct labour (1 hour) | 5 |
| Variable overhead | 4 |
| Fixed overhead | 2 |
| Standard cost per unit | $23 |

During a period the following results were recorded:

| | |
|---|---|
| Actual overhead: Fixed | $5000 |
| Variable | $7000 |
| Units produced | 2000 |

There was no opening or closing work in process.

*Required:*
(a) If standard variable costing is used, what is the under-allocated or over-allocated overhead for the period?
(b) If standard absorption costing is used, what is the under-allocated or over-allocated overhead for the period?

**7-9** **Statements of financial performance under absorption and variable costing**
The Choo Choo Company manufactures a single product which sells for $2.50 per unit. The following data relate to the first two years of the company's operations:

| | Year 1 | Year 2 |
|---|---|---|
| Production (units) | 1500 | 1000 |
| Sales (units) | 1000 | 1300 |
| Factory costs: | | |
|   Variable | $1500 | $1000 |
|   Fixed | $750 | $750 |
| Selling costs – variable | $200 | $260 |
| Administrative costs – fixed | $400 | $400 |

Any cost variances for the year are to be written off to Cost of Goods Sold for that year. For product costing under an absorption cost system, fixed factory overhead is allocated using a predetermined rate based on budgeted fixed factory costs of $750 per annum and practical capacity of 1500 units.

*Required:*
(a) Prepare statements of financial performance for each year based on absorption costing.
(b) Prepare statements of financial performance for each year based on variable costing.
(c) Prepare a reconciliation or explanation of the differences in net profit for each year resulting from the use of these two costing methods.

**7-10 Standard absorption costing: profit compared with standard variable costing**

ABC Company operates a standard absorption costing system. The following data are available:

| | |
|---|---|
| Denominator activity level | 60 000 DLH |
| Sales price per unit | $8.00 |
| Sales in 20X5 | 540 000 units |
| Opening inventory in 20X5 | 30 000 units |
| Closing inventory in 20X5 | 140 000 units |
| Variable manufacturing cost | $5.00 per unit |
| Standard production rate | 10 units/hour |
| Fixed factory overhead rate | $10.00 per DLH |
| Variable selling & administrative costs | $1.00 per unit |
| Fixed selling and administrative costs | $120 000 |

Assume that there were no variances, except for overhead volume variance and that any under-allocated or over-allocated overhead is written off to Cost of Goods Sold.

*Required:*
(a) The standard manufacturing cost per unit was:
  (A) $5.00  (B) $15.00  (C) $6.00  (D) $7.00  (E) $16.00
(b) Under a standard absorption costing system the (under) of (over) allocated fixed overhead was:
  (A) $50 000 under  (B) $50 000 over  (C) $500 000 under
  (D) $500 000 over  (E) None of these.
(c) The operating profit under absorption costing was:
  (A) $1 130 000  (B) $1 030 000  (C) $370 000  (D) $470 000  (E) None of these.
(d) If the company were to use a variable costing system the operating profit would be:
  (A) $260 000  (B) $720 000  (C) $480 000  (D) $360 000  (E) $580 000

**7-11 Standard absorption costing versus standard variable costing: profit reconciliation**

The Endel Manufacturing Company produces a single product and employs a standard absorption cost accounting system. The board of directors is considering conversion to a standard variable cost accounting system and has instructed the cost accountant to prepare profit and loss statements for the year just ended under both systems.

The following data are considered relevant:
*Standard Product Costs*

| | |
|---|---|
| Direct material | $4.00 |
| Direct labour | 12.00 |
| Variable overhead | 4.00 |

*Production Statistics*

| | |
|---|---|
| Normal capacity | 100 000 units |
| Actual production for year | 80 000 units |

| | |
|---|---|
| *Sales* during year @ $50 each | 90 000 units |

*Cost Data*

| | |
|---|---|
| Budgeted fixed overhead | $500 000 |
| Actual fixed overhead | $500 000 |
| Fixed selling & administration expenses | $250 000 |
| Manufacturing standard cost variances (excess incurrence of variable costs) | $10 000 |
| Variable selling & administration expenses | $1.00/unit |

*Required:*
(a) Prepare profit and loss statements for the year on the absorption costing and variable costing bases.
(b) Reconcile and explain any difference in net profit disclosed by the two statements.

**7-12 Variable and absorption costing (moderately difficult)**
The following information is available from the records of XYZ Ltd for the month of September, 20X0:

| | |
|---|---|
| Opening inventory | 10 000 units |
| Production for month | 80 000 units |
| Closing inventory | 20 000 units |
| Variable Costs: | |
| Manufacturing | $5.00 per unit produced |
| Selling | $1.00 per unit sold |
| Administrative | $2.00 per unit sold |
| Fixed Costs: | |
| Manufacturing | $200 000 per month |
| Selling | $40 000 per month |
| Administrative | $60 000 per month |

*Required:*
(a) If there was a net loss of $142 500 under variable costing, what was the unit selling price?
(b) Assume that XYZ Ltd uses an absorption costing system, with fixed manufacturing overhead being budgeted at $200 000 per month and being allocated to production on the basis of a normal level of activity of 100 000 units per month. Any under-allocated or over-allocated overhead is written off each month to cost of goods sold. If the net loss under absorption costing was $60 000, what was the unit selling price?
(c) If the selling price was $16.83 per unit, what was the difference in net profit under absorption costing compared with variable costing?

**7-13 Understanding overhead treatment and its effects on variable and absorption costing**
The following information is available from Scotty Ltd for the month of May, 20X3:

| | |
|---|---|
| Stock of finished goods on hand, 1 May | 400 units |
| Production of finished units during May | 3000 units |
| Stock of finished goods on hand, 31 May | 500 units |
| Variable manufacturing costs | $3.00 per unit |
| Variable selling costs | $2.00 per unit |
| Fixed manufacturing costs | $6000 per month |
| Fixed selling costs | $2000 per month |

The predetermined overhead rate is based on a normal capacity of 3000 units per month. Any overhead variance is written off to Cost of Goods Sold monthly.

*Required:*
(a) If net profit under direct costing were $2150 for May, what must the selling price per unit have been?
(b) If the selling price for May were $10.00 per unit, what was net profit under absorption costing?
(c) When compared with net profit under absorption costing, how much higher or lower was net profit under direct costing for May?
(d) Suppose that normal capacity was 4000 units per month (instead of 3000), and the selling price was $10 per unit. Determine the net profit under absorption costing.

7/*Variable Costing and JIT Costing*

**7-14 Comparative profit statements over 5 years: absorption v. variable costing**

Jim James runs a distillery producing Scotch Whisky. Each year James distils 10 000 barrels of whisky and stores the barrels for four years. Each year he sells 10 000 barrels of four-year old whisky to a retail chain which bottles the whisky and puts its own label on the bottles. Last year's statement of financial performance was as follows:

| James's Distillery<br>Statement of Financial Performance for Year Ended 30 December, 20X5 | | |
|---|---|---|
| Sales (10 000 barrels @ $200) | | $2 000 000 |
| Cost of Goods Sold: | | |
|    Variable costs (10 000 barrels @ $50) | $500 000 | |
|    Depreciation equipment | 100 000 | |
|    Storage costs of ageing whisky - | | |
|    $20 per barrel/year, 40 000 barrels | 800 000 | (1 400 000) |
| General and Administrative Expenses | | (200 000) |
| Net Profit before Taxes | | $400 000 |

During 20X5 the retailer suggested to James that the distillery be doubled in capacity and that he would contract to buy as much as James wanted to produce.

James decided to do so, and starting in 20X6 he distilled 20 000 barrels each year to be aged. All costs shown on statement of financial performance for 10 000 barrels doubled except for general and administrative expenses which increased by $100 000 per year. By 20Y0 the first batch of extra whisky was fully aged and starting in 20Y0 James sold 20 000 barrels of four-year old whisky to the retail chain.

*Required:*
Assuming that prices and costs are stable for the period,
(a) Prepare statements of financial performance for each of the years 20X6 to 20Y0 inclusive on an absorption costing basis.
(b) Prepare statements of financial performance for each of the years 20X6 to 20Y0 inclusive on a variable costing basis.
(c) Which of the costing methods appears to give a more realistic picture of the results of James's Distillery for the years 20X6-20Y0? Why? Under what circumstances does this apply?

**7-15 Switch from absorption costing to variable costing: effect on profits**

XL Co. Ltd is considering the installation of a variable costing system in place of its present absorption costing system. To assist the management in coming to a decision the staff have provided the following estimates in respect of the current year's operations:

| | |
|---|---|
| Normal capacity: units of product | 150 000 |
|                  direct labour hours | 300 000 |
| | |
| Variable manufacturing cost per unit of product: | |
|    Direct materials | $4 |
|    Direct labour, 2 hr @ $3 per hr | 6 |
|    Variable overhead, 2 hr @ $2 per hr | 4 |
|    Total variable manufacturing cost | $14 |

| | |
|---|---|
| Fixed manufacturing overhead | $300 000 p.a. |
| Fixed selling and administration expenses | $180 000 p.a. |
| Variable selling and administration expenses | $2.80 per unit |
| Unit selling price | $25 |

Sales and production data for the year:

| | | |
|---|---|---|
| Sales | | 160 000 units |
| Production | | 140 000 units |
| Opening inventory (valued at standard cost based on absorption costing) | | 25 000 units |
| Variances: | materials | $8 800 favourable |
| | labour | $13 500 unfavourable |
| | overhead (excluding volume variance) | $9 200 unfavourable |

All variances are regarded as period costs and are written off against standard cost of goods sold. The overhead volume variance is still to be calculated.

*Required:*
(a) Prepare statements of financial performance under
  (i) absorption costing, and
  (ii) variable costing
(b) Reconcile the difference in net profit as disclosed by the two statements.
(c) Calculate the effect on the accumulated profits of the company if the management decides to adopt variable costing as from the beginning of the year.

**7-16 Understanding profit differences under absorption and variable costing**

Statements of financial performance of Whitecliff Company for the last three years are as follows:

| | 20X3<br>$ | 20X2<br>$ | 20X1<br>$ |
|---|---|---|---|
| Sales | 1 050 000 | 900 000 | 1 050 000 |
| Cost of Goods Sold: | | | |
|   Inventory Fin Gds, 1 Jan | 260 000 | 0 | 0 |
|   Cost of Goods Manufactured | 780 000 | 1 040 000 | 910 000 |
| | 1 040 000 | 1 040 000 | 910 000 |
|   Less Inventory FG, 31 Dec | 130 000 | 260 000 | 0 |
| Cost of Goods Sold (normal) | 910 000 | 780 000 | 910 000 |
| Add Under-Applied Fixed Overhd | 60 000 | 0 | 30 000 |
| Adjusted Cost of Goods Sold | 970 000 | 780 000 | 940 000 |
| Gross Profit | 80 000 | 120 000 | 110 000 |
| Less Selling & Admin. Expenses | 39 000 | 37 000 | 39 000 |
| Net Profit before Taxes | 41 000 | 83 000 | 71 000 |
| Income Taxes (40%) | 16 400 | 33 200 | 28 400 |
| Net Profit after Taxes | 24 600 | 49 800 | 42 600 |

Sales and production data were as follows:

|  | 20X3 | 20X2 | 20X1 |
|---|---|---|---|
| Number of units produced | 60 000 | 80 000 | 70 000 |
| Number of units sold | 70 000 | 60 000 | 70 000 |

Fixed manufacturing overhead of $3 per unit is included in the cost of goods manufactured, and the total fixed manufacturing overhead was $240 000 for each of the three years. Variable selling and administrative expenses were 20 cents for each unit sold, and these expenses are included in the total selling and administrative expenses. The variable costs per unit were the same in all three years.

*Required:*
(a) If 70 000 units were sold in 20X1 and in 20X3, why was the net profit before taxes lower in 20X3 than in 20X1?
(b) How could the company earn more in 20X2 than in 20X1 with lower sales volume?
(c) Redraft the statements of financial performance for the three years using an alternative cost accounting method which will show changes in profit that correspond with changes in the volume of sales.


**7-17  Just in Time production**
Excell Canning Company produces canned peach halves and sliced peaches. The production process consists of the following steps:

1  Peaches are received at the cannery door in large bins. These bins are carried by forklift to the peeling and seeding room.
2  The bins are lifted and peaches poured into the chute leading into a steaming machine to remove their skins.
3  Workers place the skinned peaches in a hand cart and push the cart to a seeding machine.
4  The skinned peaches are fed by hand into the seeding machine which slices the peaches in half, removes the seed and drops the two halves into a small wire basket.
5  The wire baskets are carried into the next room and poured onto a conveyor belt.
6  Workers at the conveyor belt remove unblemished peach halves and place them in wire baskets.
7  In the spotting process, other workers further along the conveyor belt use knives to cut out faults from blemished peach halves and replace the remaining sound parts on the conveyor belt. At the end of the belt they are dropped into wire baskets.
8  The unblemished peach halves in wire baskets are carried directly to the canning machine in a third room. The spotted halves are carried to a cutting machine, poured into a chute, drop out as sliced peaches into wire baskets and are carried to the canning machine.
9  Canning tin sheet, stored on pallets, is forklifted to the canning machine. An operator places the sheet into the feeding mechanism.
10  Halves and slices are canned with sugar and water in separate batches, as the machine is free. As they come out of the canning process workers place them into large wire baskets.
11  The large wire baskets are lifted by crane and suspended in a cooker. After cooking, the baskets are lifted out and placed on pallets which are forklifted to another room for labelling and boxing. Here, after cooling, they are fed by hand into a machine which labels the cans and boxes them in cardboard boxes containing two dozen cans.
12  Finished boxes are place on pallets and forklifted to a finished goods store, ready for shipment.

*Required:*
(a) Identify the steps that fall into each of the following categories: process time, inspection time, move time, queue time and storage time.
(b) List the steps in the production process that represent non-value-added activities.
(c) Describe how the process might be redesigned to conform to the JIT production philosophy.

**7-18 Conventional versus JIT costing: general journal entries**
Albury Company Ltd held no inventories of raw materials, work in process or finished goods as at 1 June, 20X4. The following events occurred during June 20X4.

1. Raw material costing $200 000 was purchased on credit.
2. Direct labour costs of $80 000 and overhead costs of $160 000 were incurred.
3. $190 000 of direct material was issued to production, and overhead of $150 000 was allocated to production.
4. Goods costing $390 000 were completed (M: $180 000, L: $75 000, O: $135 000).
5. Goods costing $340 000 were sold (M: $160 000, L: $60 000, O: $120 000).

*Required:*
(a) Show general journal entries to record these events under a conventional product costing system.

(b) Show general journal entries to record these events under a JIT costing system assuming:
   (i) purchase of raw materials and completion of finished goods as trigger points;
   (ii) purchase of raw materials and sale of finished goods as trigger points;

**7-19 JIT costing: journal entries for 2 different trigger points; backflush entry**
Wagga Company produces a single product, and uses a standard cost system. On 1 January the company switched to a JIT costing system. At this time there were no inventories of raw materials, work in process or finished goods. Standard costs of production are:

| Direct material per unit | $30.00 |
| Conversion cost per unit | 50.00 |
| Total cost per unit | $80.00 |

Details of direct material purchases and production in January:

> Direct materials sufficient for 5000 units of product were purchased at the standard price.
> 4900 units were started.
> 4700 units of product were completed, with the remaining 200 units estimated to have had all material added but to be 60% complete as to conversion.
> 4600 units of product were sold.

Other transactions for January:

> Production-line employees earned wages of $60 000
> Other indirect labour costs were $40 000
> Depreciation on factory and building and equipment $80 000
> Other overhead expenses $65 000

*Required:*
Prepare general journal entries to record the above transactions in the general ledger assuming:
(a) A JIT costing system using:
   (i) purchase of raw materials and completion of finished goods as trigger points;
   (ii) purchase of raw materials and sale of finished goods as trigger points;
(b) For (a)(i) and (a)(ii) show the journal entry that would be required to backflush costs presently shown as part of cost of goods sold.

## 7-20 JIT costing: multiple choice

On 1 July, 20X5 Bathurst Ltd switched to a JIT costing system. At that time there were no inventories of raw materials, work in process or finished goods. The standard costs of its only product are:

| Direct material | $40.00 |
|---|---|
| Conversion costs | $65.00 |
| Total cost/unit | $105.00 |

Details of direct material purchases and production for July:

Direct materials for 9800 units were purchased at the standard price.
8000 units were completed.
6000 units were sold.
1800 units were held as work in process.

Conversion costs incurred during July were $600 000.

The 1800 units of closing work in process are 50% complete as to conversion costs.

*Required:*

(a) Assume that (1) Bathurst Ltd chooses to use the purchase of raw material input as the first trigger point and the completion of finished units of product as the second trigger point, and (2) no conversion costs are apportioned to work-in-process inventories.

What will be the total cost of work-in-process inventories and finished goods recorded at the end of July?

A  $144 000
B  $282 000
C  $340 500
D  $399 000
E  None of the above

(b) Assume that (1) Bathurst Ltd chooses to use the purchase of raw material input as the first trigger point and the sale of finished units of product as the second trigger point, and (2) for internal reporting purposes no conversion costs are apportioned to work-in-process inventories.

If the company decides to apportion conversion costs to closing inventory for financial reporting purposes, what is the appropriate journal entry to effect this?

A  No journal entry is required

B  Finished Goods                     $130 000
    Cost of Goods Sold                            $130 000

C  Finished Goods                     $130 000
    RIP Inventory                        58 500
        Cost of Goods Sold                        $188 500

D  RIP Inventory                      $247 000
    Cost of Goods Sold                            $247 000

E  None of the above is correct

# PART 2

# ACCOUNTING CONTROL SYSTEMS

# Chapter 8

# Budgeting and Feedforward Control

## THE CONCEPT OF CONTROL

In everyday language the term **control** has various meanings. The Shorter Oxford Dictionary defines the verb control as follows:

1. *To check or verify, and hence to regulate.*
2. *To call to account, reprove (a person), to reprehend.*
3. *To exercise restraint or direction, to dominate, to command.*

From a systems viewpoint, control refers to the process by which a system adapts itself to its environment. A controlled system may be viewed as a process of converting a stream of inputs into a stream of outputs. The process being controlled may be any system, such as an air conditioning system controlled by a thermostat, a biological system such as a plant or animal, or a human organisation such as a manufacturing company.

Otley and Berry (1980) identify four conditions that must be satisfied in order to be able to control a process:

1. There must be objectives which give purpose to activities and which enable more specific targets to be set, against which progress can be monitored.

2. The output of the process must be measurable in terms of the objectives set so that achievements can be assessed.

3. A predictive model of the process is required to determine causes of failure to attain objectives and to evaluate proposed actions designed to correct such failure.

4. Action to reduce deviations from objectives must be possible. If such action is not possible (because of environmental changes) there may be a need to alter the process objectives.

Organisational control refers to the process by which organisations regulate their activities in order to continue to achieve their objectives. These processes consist basically of developing plans to achieve objectives, measuring outputs and comparing them with plans and objectives, and implementing control actions to reduce any deviations.

A comparison between outputs and plans, revealing any deviations between the two, may be performed **ex-ante** or **ex-post**. Ex-post comparisons comprise the measurement of reported **actual** results arising from chosen actions and a comparison of these actual results with desired results which are specified in operational budgets. Any deviation causes a control action to be implemented in order to reduce or eliminate the error by bringing future performance back on target. This is referred to as **feedback control**. More timely feedback control involves monitoring process activities to detect deviations as they occur, rather than waiting for measures of output to be reported.

One objection to the use of feedback control is that errors or deviations are allowed to occur. Further, if there is a time lag between the occurrence of the error and the implementation of corrective action, feedback control is even less appropriate. It is preferable to use anticipatory or **feedforward control**. Instead of waiting for actual output results, predictions are made as to **expected** outputs. If these expectations deviate from desired results, control action is implemented to minimise these deviations. To illustrate, accountants prepare budgets, which are quantitative expressions of management plans, to predict likely outcomes. A cash budget is usually prepared to predict the inflows and outflows of cash during a period, and such a budget may reveal a predicted, undesirable cash deficit. Forewarned of this problem, certain adjustments may be made to overall plans (say delaying a new capital expenditure) and a reworking of the cash budget shows that the problem is overcome. Thus control is achieved ex-ante, before any deviation from objective actually occurs.

The activity of planning is an example of feedforward control; the production of plans is an iterative process in which expected outcomes are compared with aspirations, and if the outcomes fall short, alternative actions are considered until a satisfactory set of outcomes is predicted.

## BUDGETING AND FINANCIAL CONTROL

The annual budget provides a planning framework within which alternatives are evaluated, decisions made and action taken. As well as this feedforward control role, the budget provides a basis for the subsequent evaluation of the implementation of those plans and of those actions taken - this is feedback control discussed in later chapters. This chapter is essentially concerned with the planning or feedforward control role of budgets.

Annual budgets are a form of (feedforward) financial control exercised by managers of organisations to ensure that resources are available when needed by the various activity centres of the organisation. For example, the production department will require particular material, labour and service inputs at various times according to its production schedule. In turn, production schedules depend upon the demands of the sales or marketing departments which require specific quantities of different finished goods and services at various times to meet its sales predictions and commitments. Imposed on these activities is the need to ensure that cash resources are available to meet commitments to employees, suppliers of goods and services, government authorities and so on. This means that cash inflows and outflows throughout the period need to be balanced (or controlled) to ensure continuing smooth functioning of the organisation and to avoid possible liquidity crises.

Although the problem of resource co-ordination and financial control can be handled in an **ad hoc** manner, it is preferable that organisations engage in some formal planning involving the **ex-ante** consideration of resource requirements, flows and their interrelationships. This applies to all businesses including not-for-profit organisations.

Planning can assist management in achieving the appropriate balance, identifying problem areas and providing means for solving these problems. For example, a predicted cash shortage in a given month alerts management to the need to consider some alternatives, such as the review of credit granting and collection policies and practices, the arrangement of short-term or bridging finance, the rescheduling of production, or the delaying of purchase of planned plant and equipment. The formal planning process is usually referred to as the **budgeting process**. Management accounting provides a technology known as the **budgeting system** which is designed to assist management's formal planning and financial control.

## BUDGETING AS A TECHNICAL PROCESS

From a technical viewpoint the budgeting process is one of preparing a set of documents which will provide a detailed explanation of how the organisation is expected to move from a current or anticipated commencing position to some desired future state. Using a **bottom up** approach the management accountant must first develop budget schedules which detail the financial consequences of predictions made by operating managers of their expected performance and their resource requirements. Then the management accountant integrates these various schedules into a provisional,

*8/Budgeting and Feedforward Control*

cohesive organisational plan and prepares budget summaries for consideration and approval by top management.

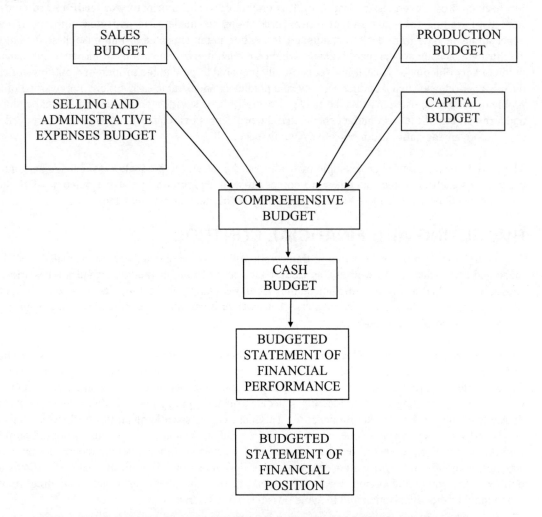

**Figure 8-1: Comprehensive Budget Schedules and Financial Reports**

The top management review of the projected financial consequences may result in acceptance of the budget as is, or more probably, a recommendation for revision. If revision is required the management accountant will assist top management in identifying areas of potential improvement and then liaise with the appropriate operating managers in revising budget expectations. Such a cycle may be repeated many times before a final budget is accepted and promulgated. In a reverse, **top down** process, the final operating budgets will be communicated to individual managers and the implications of the revisions discussed with them to ensure their acceptance. Such acceptance is especially important in motivating managers to achieve the budgets, since these budget figures will be used subsequently as part of the process of evaluating managers' performance.

In some organisations the Comprehensive Budget is called the **Master Budget** and includes **all** the budgets illustrated in Figure 8-1. In practice, organisations may also distinguish between two main components of the Comprehensive or Master Budget. These two components are the **Operating Budget** and the **Financial Budget**.

The **Operating Budget** usually includes the Sales, Production and various Expenses Budgets, as well as the Purchases Budget (which is not illustrated in Figure 8-1. In a merchandising organisation the Purchases Budget is derived from projections made in the Sales Budget, usually in both units and dollars, of the quantity of goods which will need to be purchased from manufacturers and wholesalers in order to meet customer demand. In a manufacturing organisation the Purchases Budget, again usually expressed in both units and dollars, includes the quantity of raw materials, components or sub-assemblies which will need to be purchased from suppliers to meet the requirements previously set in the Production Budget. Collectively then, the Operating Budget comprises that group of budgets which feed into the Budgeted Statement of Financial Performance (formerly Profit and Loss Statement), including Sales, Production, Purchases and Expense budgets.

The other major component of the Comprehensive or Master Budget, the **Financial Budget**, includes details of those budgets which are not directly concerned with operations, but with the sources and uses of finances and other resources in the organisation. The Financial Budget thus includes the Cash Budget, Capital Budget and Budgeted Statement of Financial Position (formerly Balance Sheet), all of which summarise the organisation's plans for acquiring and using cash and other resources. Budgets for Accounts Receivable and Accounts Payable, illustrated later in this chapter, also form part of the Financial Budget, enabling the organisation to make projections of cash inflows from credit customers and cash outflow representing payments to suppliers. These Receivables and Payables budgets assist in the preparation of the Cash Budget and provide the projected balances of Receivables and Payables needed for incorporation in the Budgeted Statement of Financial Position.

## *Steps in Budget Preparation*

Typically, the **comprehensive** budget consists of a number of budget schedules which are integrated to produce budgeted financial reports (e.g. budgeted statement of financial performance, budgeted statement of financial position, budgeted cash flow statement) that will closely resemble the periodic financial reports; usually the only visible difference is that the titles indicate expectations rather than realisations.

Diagrammatically, the basic process may be viewed as one of integrating budget schedules, as shown in Figure 8-1. The Sales Budget is usually the cornerstone of the budget system and may be developed from a variety of sources: sales managers may estimate sales volumes; forecasting and estimation models may be used to predict sales volumes, which are sometimes calculated by estimating the total industry market and the organisation's expected market share; market analysis may assist in estimating sales prices. Eventually what must be prepared are estimates of dollar and unit sales for each product.

The Selling Expense Budget is developed with regard to the sales budget and requirements in respect of number of salespeople, their salaries and commissions, and transport costs for salespeople and for distribution of products. The Administration Budget is concerned with estimates of general and administration costs associated with the sales and production levels proposed: general office expenses, debtors and creditors control, settlements to suppliers and receipts from customers, general management and accounting functions, and so on.

The Production Budget must be synchronised with the sales budget in terms of the number of units of each product required. For the given sales volumes and desired inventories, it is necessary to estimate production costs: direct materials required and their purchase cost, direct labour expense and overhead costs.

A Capital Budget focuses on the costs of acquiring new capital assets such as plant and machinery.

All of the preceding budgets have implications for the inflow and outflow of cash. Such implications are summarised in the Cash Budget which is concerned not only with the size of such flows, but very importantly, with their timing and the consequences for liquidity and solvency.

After all budget schedules are integrated in the Comprehensive Budget, the financial consequences are summarised in the budgeted financial statements, as depicted in Figure 8-1.

## *Illustrative Example 8-1*

*Chullora Chair Company manufactures a standard line of chairs which it sells for $20 per chair. The company employs a standard variable costing system.*

*There are a number of manufacturers competing in this market whose total size is estimated to be 500 000 chairs in 20X1. Chullora's share of the market is estimated to be 10% in 20X1.*

*8/Budgeting and Feedforward Control*

Each chair is assembled from one frame sub-assembly, one shell sub-assembly and four plastic tips. The standard assembly time is 6 minutes (0.1 hour). Each frame is made by Chullora using a standard 5 metres of steel tubing, requiring a standard 0.1 hour of labour. The standard tubing cost is $1.00 per metre. The shells are purchased from another manufacturer for $7.20, and plastic tips cost $5.00 per hundred. Standard labour rates are $8 per hour. Variable overhead (mainly power) is charged to products at the rate of $5 per standard direct labour hour. The standard cost of one chair is thus $15:

| | | |
|---|---|---|
| Shell | 1 @ $7.20 | $7.20 |
| Tubing | 5m @ $1 | 5.00 |
| Tips | 4 @ $0.05 | 0.20 |
| Frame labour | 0.1 hr @ $8 | 0.80 |
| Assembly labour | 0.1 hr @ $8 | 0.80 |
| Variable Overhead | 0.2 hr @ $5 | 1.00 |
| | | $15.00 |

Other expenses anticipated for 20X1 are:

| | | |
|---|---|---|
| Fixed Overhead: | Rent | $15 000 |
| | Insurance | $4 000 |
| | Salaries | $40 000 |
| Selling Expenses: 5% of gross sales revenue | | |
| Administration Expenses: | | $50 000 |

Inventory policy is to maintain a finished goods inventory level of 5% of the budget year's demand and a raw materials inventory level of 2% of annual consumption for all raw materials.

Customers are given 1 month's supply on credit, and one month's credit is received on raw material purchases. All other expenses are paid in cash in the year in which they are incurred.

The company's statement of financial position at 31 December, 20X0 is as follows:

| | | | |
|---|---|---|---|
| **Shareholders' Equity** | | | |
| Paid-up Capital | | | $150 000 |
| Retained Profits | | | 68 000 |
| | | | $218 000 |
| *Represented by:* | | | |
| **Current Assets** | | | |
| Bank | | $100 000 | |
| Accounts Receivable | | 80 600 | |
| Inventories: | | | |
| Raw Materials: | Shells | 7 200 | |
| | Tubing | 5 000 | |
| | Tips | 200 | |
| Finished Goods | | 30 000 | 223 000 |
| **Less Current Liabilities** | | | |
| Accounts Payable | | 40 000 | |
| Provision for Dividend | | 20 000 | |
| Provision for Taxation | | 25 000 | 85 000 |
| **Working Capital** | | | 138 000 |
| **Add Noncurrent Assets** | | | |
| Land and Building | | 200 000 | |
| **Less Noncurrent Liability** | | | |
| 15% Loan | | 120 000 | 80 000 |
| | | | $218 000 |

The company tax rate is 39% of taxable income and is payable in the year following the year of income. Company policy is to pay 50% of net profit after tax as dividends in the year after the profit is earned. As well as interest on the loan calculated at the annual rate of 15% on the opening balance, a repayment instalment of $20 000 is to be made on the last day of the year.

*Required:*
*Prepare operating budget schedules to produce a budgeted statement of financial performance for the year 20X1 and a budgeted statement of financial position as at the end of 20X1.*

The following steps are taken to prepare the budgets:

1. **Sales Budget**. It is usual to begin the budgeting exercise with the limiting factor which is usually sales. Once sales have been determined, every other budget relates to this level of operations.

    | SALES BUDGET | | |
    |---|---|---|
    | Total market (units) | | 500 000 |
    | Market share (units) | 10% | 50 000 |
    | Selling price | | $20 |
    | Sales ($) | | $1 000 000 |

    The $1 000 000 is the budgeted sales figure to go in the statement of financial performance. Sometimes production is the limiting factor. For example, insufficient productive capacity, limited raw materials (say of produce in activities like tuna or other canning processes), shortages of labour etc. may limit production to less than could be sold. In such cases the limiting factor, e.g. production capacity, should be the starting point for budgeting.

2. **Production Budget** Once sales units have been determined the production budget in units can be completed. Units produced = budgeted sales + any increase in inventories (sales + desired closing inventory - expected opening inventory):

    | PRODUCTION BUDGET | | |
    |---|---|---|
    | Sales (units) | | 50 000 |
    | Desired Closing Inventory FG | (5%) | 2 500 |
    | Total requirements | | 52 500 |
    | Less Opening inventory FG | | 2 000 |
    | Budgeted production (units) | | 50 500 |

    The 2000 units of Opening Inventory of Finished Goods is determined by dividing the $30 000 for finished goods in the statement of financial position by the unit cost of $15 per chair.

3. **Purchases Budget** Once the production level has been determined the required quantities of raw materials can be calculated. Given the inventory policy with respect to raw materials, the quantities to be purchased can be determined (production requirements + desired closing inventory raw materials - expected opening inventory raw materials). In this example, the physical quantities of opening inventory of raw materials are determined by dividing the statement of financial position (31/12/X0) figures by the unit costs. For example, Shells = $7200/$7.20 = 1000 units. Multiplying purchase quantities by price produces purchases in dollars:

| PURCHASES BUDGET | | SHELLS | TUBING | TIPS |
|---|---|---|---|---|
| Production units (chairs) | | 50 500 | 50 500 | 50 500 |
| Materials per unit (#,m,#) | | 1 | 5 | 4 |
| Production requirements | | 50 500 | 252 500 | 202 000 |
| Add Desired C/Inventory RM (2%) | | 1 010 | 5 050 | 4 040 |
| | | 51 510 | 257 550 | 206 040 |
| Less O/Inventory RM | | 1 000 | 5 000 | 4 000 |
| Purchases RM (units) | | 50 510 | 252 550 | 202 040 |
| Unit cost | | $7.20 | $1.00 | $0.05 |
| Purchases ($) | $626 324 | $363 672 | $252 550 | $10 102 |

4. **Closing Inventory Budget** The dollar values of closing inventories of raw materials and finished goods are required for the statement of financial performance and statement of financial position. The physical units (from the Production Budget and the Purchases Budget) are multiplied by their unit costs:

| BUDGETED CLOSING INVENTORY COSTS | | | | |
|---|---|---|---|---|
| | CHAIRS | SHELLS | TUBING | TIPS |
| Budgeted C/Inventories (units) | 2 500 | 1 010 | 5 050 | 4 040 |
| Unit cost | $15.00 | $7.20 | $1.00 | $0.05 |
| Budgeted C/Inventories ($) | $37 500 | $7 272 | $5 050 | $202 |

5. **Budgeted Production Costs** These figures are required to determine the cost of goods manufactured, and then cost of goods sold. Of course, with a standard cost system, the budget detail could be substantially reduced. If an actual or normal cost system is in place using, say, the FIFO assumption, it is necessary to take care in calculating the direct material section of the production costs (O/Inventory + Purchases - Closing Inventory), otherwise incorrect costs may be calculated and the statement of financial position will probably not balance.

| BUDGETED PRODUCTION COSTS | | | | |
|---|---|---|---|---|
| Number of Chairs Produced: | | | 50 500 | |
| MATERIALS | U.C. | # | | |
| Shells | $7.20 | 1 | $363 600 | |
| Tubing | $1.00 | 5 | 252 500 | |
| Tips | $0.05 | 4 | 10 100 | $626 200 |
| LABOUR | | | | |
| Frame | $8.00 | 0.1 | 40 400 | |
| Assembly | $8.00 | 0.1 | 40 400 | 80 800 |
| VARIABLE OVERHEAD | | | | |
| Frame | $5.00 | 0.1 | 25 250 | |
| Assembly | $5.00 | 0.1 | 25 250 | 50 500 |
| | | | | $757 500 |

6. **Budgeted Cost of Goods Sold** This is straightforward once the production budget has been prepared, and the closing inventory values determined. Actually, the previous budget and the cost of goods sold budget could be combined if desired. The opening inventory of Finished Goods ($30 000) comes from the 31/12/X0 Statement of Financial Position; the Variable Cost of Goods Manufactured from the production costs budget (step 5) and the Closing Inventory of Finished Goods ($37 500) from step 4.

| BUDGETED COST OF GOODS SOLD | |
|---|---|
| Opening Inventory Finished Goods | $30 000 |
| Variable Cost of Goods Manufactured | 757 500 |
| Goods Available for Sale | 787 500 |
| Less Closing Inventory Finished Goods | 37 500 |
| Cost of Goods Sold | $750 000 |

7. **Budgeted Statement of Financial Performance** Once the previous budgets have been prepared the information for the statement of financial performance is available. The degree of detail in the statement of financial performance depends upon the number of supporting budgets. The number of supporting budgets can be reduced and more detail provided in the statement of financial performance, or vice-versa. In some cases the cash budget and the budgeted statement of financial performance are inter-dependent, especially with regard to interest which, as well as being a cash outflow in itself, is also an expense in the statement of financial performance and may affect tax payments.

| BUDGETED STATEMENT OF FINANCIAL PERFORMANCE | | |
|---|---|---|
| Sales | | $1 000 000 |
| Less Variable Cost of Goods Sold | | 750 000 |
| | | 250 000 |
| Less Variable Selling Expenses | | 50 000 |
| Variable Profit (Contribution Margin) | | 200 000 |
| Fixed Expenses: | | |
| Rent | $15 000 | |
| Insurance | 4 000 | |
| Salaries | 40 000 | |
| Administration | 50 000 | 109 000 |
| Net Operating Profit | | 91 000 |
| Interest on Loan | | 18 000 |
| Net Profit before Tax | | 73 000 |
| Provision for Taxation | | 28 470 |
| Net Profit after Tax | | 44 530 |
| Add O/Balance Retained Profits | | 68 000 |
| | | 112 530 |
| Less Provision for Dividend | | 22 265 |
| C/Balance Retained Profits | | $90 265 |

8. **Budgeted Accounts Receivable and Payable.** To facilitate preparation of the cash budget and the statement of financial position it is desirable to prepare statements to calculate cash movements and closing balances in respect of these accounts. The opening balances come from the 31/12/X0 statement of financial position. The closing balances are 1/12 of the annual sales and purchases respectively (1 month's credit is provided and received, (as per data)).

| BUDGETED ACCOUNTS RECEIVABLE | |
|---|---|
| O/Balance | $80 600 |
| Sales this year | 1 000 000 |
| | 1 080 600 |
| Less C/Balance (1/12 of sales) | 83 333 |
| Cash from Debtors | $997 267 |

*8/Budgeting and Feedforward Control*

| BUDGETED ACCOUNTS PAYABLE | |
|---|---:|
| O/Balance | $40 000 |
| Purchases this year | 626 324 |
| | 666 324 |
| Less C/Balance (1/12 of purchases) | 52 194 |
| Cash to Creditors | $614 130 |

9. **Cash Budget.** We now have sufficient information to prepare the cash budget. This will indicate any likely problems with liquidity and provide the closing balance for the budgeted statement of financial position.

| CASH BUDGET | | |
|---|---:|---:|
| Receipts from Debtors | | $997 267 |
| Less Payments: | | |
| Creditors | $614 130 | |
| Labour | 80 800 | |
| Variable Overhead | 50 500 | |
| Variable Selling Expenses | 50 000 | |
| Fixed Expenses | 109 000 | |
| Interest on Loan | 18 000 | |
| Repayment on Loan | 20 000 | |
| Tax[1] | 25 000 | |
| Dividends[1] | 20 000 | 987 430 |
| Net Cash Flow | | 9 836 |
| Add O/Balance Cash | | 100 000 |
| C/Balance Cash | | $109 836 |

1. These are lagged one year and come from last year's Statement of Financial Position.

10. **Budgeted Statement of Financial Position.** The previous budgets now allow preparation of the budgeted statement of financial position. Not only will this provide a summary of budgeted financial position, but it will also provide a technical check on the accountant's double entry recording. Clearly a non-balancing statement of financial position indicates an error or omission somewhere in the budget schedules.

| BUDGETED STATEMENT OF FINANCIAL POSITION | | |
|---|---|---|
| SHAREHOLDERS' EQUITY | | |
| Paid-up Capital | | $150 000 |
| Retained Profits | | 90 265 |
| | | 240 265 |
| Represented by: | | |
| CURRENT ASSETS | | |
| Bank | $109 836 | |
| Accounts Receivable | 83 333 | |
| Inventories: | | |
|   Shells | 7 272 | |
|   Tubing | 5 050 | |
|   Tips | 202 | |
|   Finished Goods | 37 500 | 243 194 |
| Less CURRENT LIABILITIES | | |
| Accounts Payable | 52 194 | |
| Provision for Dividend | 22 265 | |
| Provision for Tax | 28 470 | 102 929 |
| WORKING CAPITAL | | 140 265 |
| Add NONCURRENT ASSETS | | |
| Land and Building | 200 000 | |
| Less NONCURRENT LIABILITY | | |
| 15% Loan | 100 000 | 100 000 |
| NET ASSETS | | $240 265 |
| Check | | 0.00000000 |

Note the existence of a check figure to calculate any difference, should the statement of financial position fail to balance. This solution was prepared using a spreadsheet, and this standard check allows the computer to calculate any difference to facilitate tracking of errors.

## Illustrative Example 8-2

*Malvina Company's sales in November and December 20X0 were $40 000 and $55 000 respectively. Budgeted sales for the March quarter, 20X1 are:*

| | |
|---|---|
| *January* | *$55 000* |
| *February* | *$40 000* |
| *March* | *$60 000* |

*In any month, 40% of sales are cash sales. Of the credit sales, 20% are collected in the month of sale, 50% in the month following the month of sale, and 30% in the second month after the month of sale.*

*Cash payments average 60% of sales dollars, except that in January, 20X1 $100 000 will be outlaid for purchase of fixed assets.*

*The expected opening balance of cash on 1 January, 20X1 is $50 000. An overdraft has been arranged at the bank, the conditions being that interest is payable at the end of each month, at the rate of 15% per annum on the higher of the month's opening overdraft balance and closing overdraft balance before interest.*

*Required: Prepare a cash budget on a monthly basis for the March quarter, 20X1.*

*8/Budgeting and Feedforward Control*

|  | Nov | Dec | Jan | Feb | Mar | Mar Qr |
|---|---|---|---|---|---|---|
| **MALVINA COMPANY** |||||||
| **CASH BUDGET FOR MARCH QUARTER** |||||||
| Sales | $40 000 | $55 000 | $55 000 | $40 000 | $60 000 | $155 000 |
| Receipts: |  |  |  |  |  |  |
| Cash sales (40%) |  |  | $22 000 | $16 000 | $24 000 | $62 000 |
| Credit sales (60%): |  |  |  |  |  |  |
| Month of sale 20% (of 60%) |  |  | 6 600 | 4 800 | 7 200 | 18 600 |
| Month after sale (50%) |  |  | 16 500 | 16 500 | 12 000 | 45 000 |
| 2nd month after sale (30%) |  |  | 7 200 | 9 900 | 9 900 | 27 000 |
| Total receipts |  |  | 52 300 | 47 200 | 53 100 | 152 600 |
| Less payments |  |  | 133 000 | 24 000 | 36 000 | 193 000 |
| Net operating cash flow |  |  | (80 700) | 23 200 | 17 100 | (40 400) |
| Add Opening Balance |  |  | 50 000 | (31 084) | (8 272) | 50 000 |
| Closing Balance before interest |  |  | (30 700) | (7 884) | 8 828 | 9 600 |
| Interest (1.25% per month) |  |  | 384 | 389 | 103 | 876 |
| Closing Balance |  |  | ($31 084) | ($8 272) | $8 724 | $8 724 |

## *Computer-based Models and 'What If' Analysis*

No matter how carefully managers try to predict future events, the fundamental problem of uncertainty cannot be eliminated. After a preliminary budget plan is formulated many questions arise which in general terms are concerned with the effect on the results **if** an error has been made in forecasting a particular input value. These are often referred to as **what if** questions.

The results of interest include the output variables:

| | |
|---|---|
| Total dollar sales | Cash balance |
| Net profit | Inventory level |
| Net profit ratio | Level of outstanding debt |
| Rate of return on shareholders' funds | Level of additional capital required |
| Dividend payments pursuant to a particular dividend policy | Additional long-term borrowings required |
| | Working capital ratio |
| Income tax payments | Debt-equity ratio |

Input variables about which some uncertainty will exist, and a change in which could affect some or all of the results, could include:

| | |
|---|---|
| Sales volume in units | Levels of inventory to be carried having regard to reliability of raw materials supplies |
| Unit selling prices | |
| Labour rates | |
| Changed award working hours | Transport costs |
| Raw materials costs | Changed import regulations or tariffs |
| Interest rates | |
| Tax rates | Rate of inflation |

Combinations of the two classes of variables give rise to a limitless number of potential **what if** questions, many of which could affect decisions of the managers responsible for adoption of the budgetary plans. For example:

> What would net profit be if sales volume in physical units increased only at 6% (or 7% or 5%) per annum instead of the predicted 8% on which the budget was based? What would the cash balance be? How would the rate of return on shareholders' funds be affected? What if labour rates should be 4% lower than estimated? What if raw materials costs should be 18% higher than predicted?

As well as the **what if** questions arising from uncertainty about estimates and assumptions upon which the budget is based, a further group of **what if** questions arise in the manager's mind. These relate to the optimum level of expenditure to be budgeted in respect of the controllable costs, often referred to as discretionary costs. These include such things as expenditure on staff welfare, advertising, public relations and research and development.

Fortunately the answer to any of these questions can be worked out in a routine manner if a computerised financial model has been built, by simply carrying out the series of calculations to recast the budgets. The speed and accuracy of the computer in processing data can be used to generate answers to **what if** questions quickly. This allows managers to consider more variations to budgetary plans before the final budget is settled and adopted.

The overall objective of corporate or financial modelling is to develop a computer-based model that will assist managers to prepare effective plans for the future operations of the organisation modelled. This applies to the cyclical activity of preparing annual budgets, and forecasts covering several years of operation. Such a model should also provide assistance when the advent of unexpected major changes in the business environment results in the need, immediately, to produce modified plans to adapt to the new conditions. Such a model, then, needs to embody the significant features of the organisation itself, but unnecessary complexity should be avoided. For most business activities a considerable amount of detail will be required in the model.

Grinyer and Wooller (1978) listed the following benefits that might be expected from the use of a computer-based model:

- Greater accuracy and speed of forecasting company performance.

- A means of quickly checking on the internal consistency of planning assumptions.

- Reduction of clerical effort involved in evaluating alternative proposals and in preparing long-term financial plans.

- As a result, freedom to explore a wide range of alternatives, as opposed to the few possible with manual calculations.

- Release of management time, by reduction of routine calculations, for thinking about strategic problems and their solution.

- Fuller allowance for links with other aspects of the business when evaluating a proposal.

- Fuller understanding of the internal complexities of the company by decision makers.

- Deeper insight into the risks inherent in proposed projects.

- A means of highlighting the key aspects of both existing business and new projects.

- A tool for showing managers the extent to which reported performances will be affected by errors in estimates.

The foregoing benefits apply not only to the cyclical or routine preparation of budgets and long-term plans, but also in the control phase of operations. From time to time an unforeseen change in the environment may occur requiring a firm to adapt quickly to the new conditions. Such things as a change in exchange rates, shortage of raw material, or actions of competitors may occur without warning and necessitate modification of existing plans.

Once a model has been built using any type of financial modelling package it is very easy to modify it to examine the likely effects of changes in assumptions. All one has to do is alter the appropriate variable value and the package will provide the new calculations and their effect throughout the model in seconds. Spreadsheet data tables can help in exploring a range of variations in input variables in one go. It is this ability to answer *what if* questions so easily which makes financial modelling packages such powerful and useful tools of financial analysis.

When building reasonably complex models it is an advantage to place key data and assumptions, which are likely to be varied in simulation runs, at the beginning of the model. As the model is built growth rates and percentage relationships are modelled by reference to the cell location in the key assumptions area of the model. When an assumption is to be varied all the user has to do is alter the figure in the key assumption area, rather than search for the location(s) of such figure in the body of the model.

Readers should by now have developed some expertise in the use of spreadsheets. Many of the problems at the end of this chapter are designed to be solved by building spreadsheet models.

## BUDGETING AS A CHOICE PROCESS

The budgeting process as outlined so far has been examined from a technical point of view. Focus on the technical process emphasises an outcome of carefully prepared and co-ordinated budget documents. While technical expertise is required to facilitate the complex preparation task, concentration on technical matters does not help us understand or explain why the particular pattern of resource allocation resulted. It is not usually a matter of chance, but the result of deliberate choice processes. Resources are scarce, and organisational participants compete for shares of such scarce resources. Rather than adopt a technical focus, some writers find it much more interesting to explore and explain how resources are allocated; they view the budget process as a choice process in which competing demands are assessed and choices made as to how resources are to be shared.

### *Perspectives on Choice*

The usual textbook treatment of the budgeting process is from what is known as a **rational perspective**. Management is assumed to have well-defined goals, and considers alternative ways of achieving them. They systematically examine a large range of alternatives and select those which are optimal and incorporate them into the budget. Some well-known techniques have been developed as a rational approach to budgeting: e.g., the use of linear programming, and zero-base budgeting (ZBB).

The use of ZBB may be seen as an effort to impose greater rationality on the budget process and to counter the common characteristic of assuming that the previous period's level of activity or expenditure is appropriate to the budget this period. Under ZBB each manager (or proponent of a program) must justify proposed activities for the budget period as if they were being launched for the first time. The key features of this technique are the specific identification of objectives, the listing of alternatives along with their costs and expected outcomes, and the arrangement of a set of 'decision packages' from which the selections are to be made.

Some of the limitations of taking a rational view are acknowledged in the **satisficing perspective**. Instead of a comprehensive search for alternative courses of action (as implied in the rational perspective) only a limited number of alternatives are considered. The first plan that looks good enough will be selected. For example, rather than trying to develop a budget which will maximise profits, one which provides a satisfactory return (say 10% on invested capital) will be acceptable.

Another approach is that known as the **standard operating procedures (SOPS) perspective**. Because the budgeting process is performed regularly there exist standard operating procedures (however they may have been developed). The use of a budget manual and standardised data collection procedures are examples of SOPS. Such formalisation of procedures may largely determine what the budget outcomes are.

Budgeting is often seen as a **political process** in which power is exercised by individuals who have the ability to exert influence over others. Power can be achieved through such means as formal delegation of authority, the control of resources desired by others, or possession of a particular expertise in demand by others. To the extent that power is important in the budgeting process, the final pattern of resource allocation can reflect the way in which power is distributed in the organisation. Those with the most power get the biggest share of resources. Pfeffer (1977) identifies a number of ways in which power may be exercised in the budgeting process, usually in a covert manner, through seemingly legitimate, democratic procedures such as the use of committees - no-one is seen to be individually responsible for decisions; through the selective use of decision criteria; through control over information and the use of special knowledge.

Part of the political process involves attempts to persuade or cajole others to accept plans and proposals. Such attempts are called **budget ploys**. Some examples are:

❑ arranging reciprocal support for proposals

❑ padding claims for resources in the knowledge that they will be cut back

❑ trying to second guess management's desires when formulating plans and proposals

❑ submitting simple, easily understood proposals to gain acceptance, or conversely, submitting highly technical proposals to preclude rejection

Often goals within an organisation are vague so that budgeting takes on an **incrementalism** perspective. Only small, marginal changes are made to budgets from year to year rather than comprehensive ones. Under this approach last year's budget is the starting point for this year's. Last year's budget allocations are increased by a given percentage to cover inflation and small changes are made where necessary in response to problems encountered. Often the approach is remedial; problems identified with the previous year's performance are corrected rather than focusing on and moving towards predetermined objectives. Objectives are seen to emerge from the choices made as an explanation for, and rationalisation of them.

By taking a broader perspective of budgeting and considering it as a choice process it is possible to gain a better understanding of some budget outcomes as represented in the formal budget documents. It is important to recognise that in practice the budgeting process may not be as rational as accounting budget models may imply. An understanding of the nature of the budgeting process may aid accountants in their attempts to design effective budgeting systems.

### REFERENCES

P.H. Grinyer and J. Wooller, *Corporate Models Today*, 2nd ed., Institute of Chartered Accountants, London, 1978.

D.T. Otley and A.J. Berry, "Control, Organization and Accounting," *Accounting, Organizations and Society*, 5, 2, 1980, 231-246.

J. Pfeffer, "Power and Resource Allocation in Organizations", in B.M. Staw and G. R. Salancik, eds, *New Directions in Organizational Behaviour*, St Clair Press, 1977.

*8/Budgeting and Feedforward Control*

## QUESTIONS AND PROBLEMS

**8-1** What are the four conditions that must be satisfied in order to be able to control a process?

**8-2** Explain the difference between **feedforward** and **feedback** control. What is the advantage of feedforward control? How is budgeting related to feedforward control?

**8-3** What major benefits are expected from using computer-based financial models?

**8-4** What is meant by **what if** type questions in the context of the budgetary process? What is the purpose of asking this type of question? How are financial models used to answer them?

**8-5** Contrast the **rational** and **political** perspectives of the budgetary process.

### USE A SPREADSHEET FOR PROBLEMS 8-6 TO 8-9

**8-6** **Simple budgeted profit and loss**
From the following data develop a financial model for producing forecast statements of financial performance for the next three years:

> Sales - Year 1 $2000, Year 2 $2500, Year 3 $3000.
> Cost of Goods Sold - 55% of Sales Revenue.
> Variable Operating Expenses - 18% of Sales Revenue.
> Fixed Operating Expenses - $600 per year.

**8-7** **Budgeted Statements of Financial Performance for 4 years: growth factors**
Sales in 20X1 were $4000. They are expected to increase by $600 per year to a maximum of $6000. Cost of goods sold is expected to be 52% of sales revenue. Other expenses are expected to be 15% of the sales revenue estimated for the following year (e.g. other expenses in 20X2 will be 15% of estimated 20X3 sales revenue).

Develop a financial model for producing forecast statements of financial performance for the four years 20X2 to 20X5.

**8-8** **Budgeted net profit after tax: 3 year forecasts**
Given the following information prepare forecasts of net profit after tax for the next 3 years after 20X1:

Sales for 20X1 were $1000. Sales for subsequent years = 20X1 Sales growing at 10% per annum (compound).

> Raw Materials = 20% of Sales
> Direct Labour = 10% of Sales
> Manufacturing Expenses = $100 + 5% of Sales
> Other Expenses = $200 + 15% of Sales
> Tax Rate = 49% of Net Profit

**8-9** **Cash budget for 3 years**
Opening cash balance for 20X2 was $800. Receipts for the next three years are estimated at $2000, $2600 and $3100. Estimated payments for the three years are $2400, $3200 and $2600.

Develop a financial model to prepare cash forecasts for the three years in the following format:

Row 1 Opening Balance Cash
Row 2 Receipts (underlined)
Row 3 Cash Available
Row 4 Payments (underlined)
Row 5 Closing Balance Cash (double underline)

**PROBLEMS 8-10 TO 8-17 MAY BE DONE BY HAND, OR USING A SPREADSHEET**

**8-10 Sales budgets**

Breakfast Delight is a company producing two major products, corn flakes and natural muesli. Both products are packaged in 300 gm packets. Corn flakes sell for $3.00 per packet and natural muesli for $5 per packet. Estimated sales (in packets) for March quarter are as follows:

|  | Corn Flakes | Natural Muesli |
|---|---|---|
| January | 50 000 | 60 000 |
| February | 60 000 | 70 000 |
| March | 65 000 | 75 000 |

*Required:*
Prepare a sales budget for each month and the quarter in total, by product.

**8-11 Production budgets**

Doggie Dog Company produces a 250 gm can of deluxe dog food. Projected sales for July to October are shown below:

|  | Forecast Sales (cans) |
|---|---|
| July | 110 000 |
| August | 120 000 |
| September | 125 000 |
| October | 115 000 |

It is company policy to hold closing inventories at the end of each month sufficient to cover 15% of the following month's sales. Assume that this policy was adhered to in June.

*Required:*
Prepare a production budget for September quarter, by month as well as for the quarter as a whole.

**8-12 Raw materials purchases budgets**

Delicious Ice Cream Company produces 2-litre tubs of various flavours of ice cream. Each tub requires various materials including 1.9 litres of cream, costing $1.10 per litre. Budgeted production of ice cream for the next 4 months is as follows:

|  | Production (tubs) |
|---|---|
| October | 200 000 |
| November | 350 000 |
| December | 400 000 |
| January | 500 000 |

Company policy is to hold closing raw material inventories sufficient to satisfy 10% of the following month's production requirements. Inventory of cream at the beginning of October meets this policy requirement.

*Required:*
Prepare a raw material purchases budget for cream for December quarter showing purchases in litres and dollars for each month and for the quarter as a whole.

8/*Budgeting and Feedforward Control*

**8-13 Production and purchases budgets**
Littleton Co. Ltd has prepared the following sales schedule (in units) for the next six quarters:

Q1: 2000   Q2: 5000   Q3: 4000   Q4: 1000   Q5: 2500   Q6: 6000

Production policy requires production to meet the current quarter's sales plus 25% of the following quarter's sales. The process requires one raw material input at the rate of 2 kg per unit of product. The current cost of the raw material is $3/kg but this is expected to increase by 5% at the beginning of the second quarter. Raw materials inventory policy requires that purchases cover current needs and provide for 10% of the next quarter's production needs.

At the beginning of the first quarter both finished goods and raw materials inventory balances are expected to be at the required policy levels.

*Required:*
(a) Prepare the production budget and raw materials purchases budget (units and dollars) on a quarterly basis for the first four quarters.
(b) Because of problems in purchasing varying order sizes, management is considering the implementation of a policy whereby 25% of the total annual needs (rounded to the nearest hundred kg) are purchased at the beginning of each quarter. Recast the raw materials purchases budget accordingly, and comment on management's proposal.

**8-14 Cash collections from cash and credit sales**
AFM Pty Ltd estimates that sales for the first 3 months of 20X4 will be:

|  |  |
|---|---|
| January | $10 000 |
| February | $12 000 |
| March | $15 000 |

From past experience, about one-third of total sales have been cash sales. Bad debts consist of 7% of credit sales. The balance of credit sales is collected in the month after sale. Debtors on 31 December were $8000.

*Required:*
Prepare a statement of cash collections, on a monthly basis for the March quarter, 20X4.

**8-15 Cash budget: service industry**
Dr Healer is the manager of a medical clinic and is concerned about the cash flow shortages which arose somewhat unexpectedly recently in the practice. At 30 June the bank account showed an overdraft of $50 000. Dr Healer believes that the cash flow problems stem from lack of attention to outstanding patient accounts and the purchase of expensive medical supplies in large quantities at irregular intervals.

The good doctor has asked you to help design a spreadsheet to investigate the cash flow problems. You discover the following data:

**Revenue:**
| | |
|---|---|
| May | $120 000 (actual) |
| June | $145 000 (actual) |
| July | $50 000 (budget) |
| August | $150 000 (budget) |
| September | $140 000 (budget) |

Past experience shows that 40% of the consultation revenue is collected in the month of the visit, 30% in the following month, 20% in the second month and 10% was never collected. From July new credit policies are expected to result in a collection pattern of 60%, 20%, 10% and 10% respectively.

*8/Budgeting and Feedforward Control*

The cost of medical supplies was $40 000 in June and is budgeted for $60 000 in August. Half of the suppliers' accounts are paid in the month incurred and half in the following month. Salaries of $40 000 per month and other costs of $25 000 per month are paid in the month incurred.

*Required:*
Prepare a cash budget for the 3 months, July to September to examine the cash flows.

**8-16  Cash budget: minimum cash balance required, line of credit**
On 1 April 20X0 Exotica Ltd commenced business with a cash balance of $30 000. Sales for the next six months are expected to be:

|       |          |           |           |
|-------|----------|-----------|-----------|
| April | $40 000  | July      | $200 000  |
| May   | $60 000  | August    | $250 000  |
| June  | $120 000 | September | $100 000  |

The gross margin on sales is expected to be 60%. The company plans to carry a finished goods inventory equal to expected sales for the next two months. Purchases are paid in the month following purchase.

Variable selling expenses are expected to equal 20% of sales. Fixed selling and administrative expenses are expected to be $30 000 per month, including $1000 depreciation. Eighty percent of the expenses will be paid in the month incurred, the balance in the month following.

Sixty percent of sales are expected to be cash sales. Twenty-five percent of credit sales are collected in the month of sale and 75% in the month following sale.

*Required:*
(a) Prepare a cash budget for the months of April, May and June. Comment on the results.
(b) In the light of your findings in (a) the accountant is told that the company has made an arrangement to borrow funds whenever necessary in order to maintain a minimum cash balance of $10 000. A line of credit has been arranged with the bank requiring interest of 1% per month on borrowed cash. Interest will be paid at the time the loan is repaid. The loan will be repaid as soon as there is sufficient cash to do so.
Using this information, revise the cash budget.

**8-17  Cash budget: comprehensive**
Cedar Company is starting operations on 1 January, 20X0 with no opening inventories. Manufacturing costs of its single product have been budgeted as follows:

| Direct materials | $2.00 per unit |
|---|---|
| Direct labour | $1.00 per unit |
| Factory overhead: | |
| Variable | $0.20 per unit |
| Fixed (including $1000 depreciation) | $5000 per month |

Selling and administrative expenses, including depreciation of $300 per month, are all fixed and total $3000 per month.

Other information is as follows:

The selling price of the product has been set at $5 per unit. Collections are scheduled as follows: 80% in month of sale, 18% in month following sale, and 2% uncollectable.

The inventory of direct materials will be maintained at one-half of the next month's production requirements. Three-quarters of each month's purchases will be paid for in the month of purchase, and the remainder in the following month. A cash discount of 2% will be taken on all purchases.

*8/Budgeting and Feedforward Control*

The direct labour payroll, factory overhead and selling and administrative expenses will be paid for in the month incurred.

Sales and production for the first three month's of the year have been scheduled as follows:

|          | Units Sold | Units Produced |
|----------|------------|----------------|
| January  | 6000       | 10 000         |
| February | 6000       | 10 000         |
| March    | 9000       | 12 000         |

*Required:*
Prepare a budget showing the cash receipts and cash payments for the months of January and February with supporting calculations.

### PROBLEM 8-18 SHOULD BE DONE USING A SPREADSHEET

**8-18**  **Financial model to forecast Statements of Financial Performance for 5 years**
From the following information prepare a financial model that would produce budgeted statements of financial performance for the 5 years 20X2 to 20X6 for Unique Traders Ltd. All necessary calculations should be performed by the computer.

Unique trades in one product only. In 20X1 sales were 30 000 units and volume is expected to increase by 8% each year (compound) to a maximum of 40 000 units per year.

Unit selling price in the years 20X2, 20X3, 20X4 is expected to equal the unit cost of purchases made in the year, marked up by 30% whilst in 20X5 and 20X6 the mark-up is expected to be 35% on purchase cost.

Unit purchase costs for the 5 years are estimated at 20X2 $5.10, 20X3 $5.36, 20X4 $5.68, 20X5 $6.02, 20X6 $6.50.

Closing inventory is to be 15% of estimated sales units for the following year. Closing inventory for 20X1, however, was only 3600 units valued at $17 640. Assume a FIFO cost flow.

General and administrative expenses are expected to equal 14% of sales revenue in each year.

The tax rate is expected to remain unchanged at 40%.
Dividends equal to 65% of after tax profit are to be provided for.
Retained earnings at the end of 20X1 amounted to $3500.

### PROBLEMS 8-19 TO 8-24 MAY BE DONE BY HAND

**8-19**  **Comprehensive budget; absorption and variable costing**
The Snoopy Thomasina Cat Food Company produces one type of cat food which is sold in 25 kg boxes. You are about to prepare budgets for the third quarter of the 20X5 calendar year. The following data are available:

Monthly budgeted sales are expected to be stable at 24 000 boxes per month.

The budgeted selling price is $25 per 25 kg box and this is expected to remain unchanged throughout the third quarter.

The cat food is produced from fish and vegetable residue, and packaged in boxes. Each 25 kg box requires 5 kg of fish residue and 15 kg of vegetable residue. The balance of the weight is moisture content.

Budgeted inventory levels are:

|  | 1 July | 30 September |
|---|---|---|
| Finished boxes of cat food | 19 200 | 14 400 |
| Kilograms of fish residue | 52 000 | 42 000 |
| Kilograms of vegetable residue | 92 000 | 76 000 |
| Boxes (empty) | 48 000 | 32 000 |

Budgeted purchase prices are $1.90/kg for fish residue, $0.32/kg for vegetable residue and $1.18 each for empty boxes.

The direct labour rate (including labour oncosts) is $12 per hour, and 8 minutes are required to produce and fill one box of cat food.
Other cost data available indicate the following:

| | |
|---|---|
| Fixed costs per month: | |
| Manufacturing overhead expenses | $32 000 |
| Selling and administrative expenses | $18 000 |
| Variable costs: | |
| Manufacturing overhead expenses per direct labour hour | $5.40 |
| Selling and administrative expenses | 5% of sales $. |

*Required:*
(a) Prepare a production budget for the third quarter of the 20X5 calendar year.
(b) Prepare a purchases budget for each of the raw materials.
(c) Calculate the budgeted variable manufacturing cost per 25 kg box of cat food.
(d) Prepare a budgeted statement of financial performance using **variable costing** for the third quarter, assuming inventories of raw materials and finished goods at 1 July will be carried at the budgeted cost for the third quarter.
(e) Assume that the budgeted statement of financial performance is prepared using **absorption costing**. Would the budgeted profit be the same as, higher than or lower than the budgeted profit calculated in part (d)? Explain why.

8-20 **Budgeted cash receipts and payments: not for profit organisation**
On attending its first meeting in 20X9 you have been appointed honorary treasurer of the East Coogee Pre-School Kindergarten. The previous treasurer was a bank officer's wife, who has now moved interstate and thus can give you no assistance. Your first task is to prepare an annual budget for 20X9, and set the fees to be charged.

On going through the treasurer's cardboard box containing cheque books, bank deposit books, raffle tickets, fees book, invoices, monthly bank reconciliation statements, postage stamps, etc., you discover a statement of cash receipts and payments for the previous year (shown on next page). After making various inquiries of the teacher, parents on the 20X8 school committee and others, you arrive at the following conclusions:

(i) Salaries and wages are expected to increase by an average of 5% for 20X9.
(ii) You decide to allow 10% for general cost increases in 20X9 on recurrent expenditures other than salaries and wages and repairs and maintenance (to the building).
(iii) Repairs and maintenance should be about $500.
(iv) The fete and other fund raising activities are unknowns and last year's results are your best guess for this year.

## 8/Budgeting and Feedforward Control

(v) Staff have been asked to purchase their own coffee and biscuits.
(vi) Government subsidies are likely to be reduced by $4000 on last year's subsidies.
(vii) Purchases of assets to the sum of $4000 are contemplated by the teacher, if the money is available.
(viii) A cash balance of at least $4000 as at 31 December, 20X9 is necessary to cover salaries in January 20Y0 over the Christmas vacation.
(ix) No debtors' or creditors' balances exist at 1 January 20X9.
(x) The school can accept 75 children, 25 in each of three groups per week:
Group A: 3 mornings per week (9-12) Mon., Tue., Wed.
Group B: 2 mornings per week (9-12) Thu., Fri.
Group C: 4 afternoons per week (1.00-3.30) M,T,W,T.
It is expected that, because of heavy demand, each group will be filled to capacity. Friday afternoon is free for the teacher to carry out administrative duties.

|  |  |  |
|---|---|---|
| East Coogee Pre-School Kindergarten Statement of Cash Receipts and Payments for Year Ended 31 December, 20X8 |||
| **Cash Balances, 1 January 20X8** | | |
| Cheque account[1] | 5 950 | |
| Petty cash | 50 | 6 000 |
| **Add Receipts** | | |
| Fees | 15 586 | |
| Government subsidies | 12 000 | |
| Annual fete (net receipts) | 20 000 | |
| Raffles | 2 000 | |
| Street stalls | 1 400 | |
| Miscellaneous fund raising | 1 614 | 52 600 |
| **Less Payments** | | |
| Teacher's salary | 30 000 | |
| Helper's wages | 12 000 | |
| Purchase of stereo | 1 200 | |
| Piano tune[2] | 400 | |
| Purchase school requisites | 4 800 | |
| Electricity | 900 | |
| Water rates | 1 000 | |
| Telephone | 400 | |
| Lawn mowing[3] | 400 | |
| Purchase drinks etc.[4] | 1 500 | |
| Repairs and maintenance | 400 | |
| Photocopying paper and envelopes | 1 200 | 54 200 |
| **Cash Balances, 31 December 20X8** | | 4 400 |
| These cash balances consist of: | | |
|    Cheque account | | 4 300 |
|    Petty cash | | 100 |
| | | $4 400 |

1. There are no bank or government charges levied on this account.
2. Past experience indicates that the piano needs tuning once every three years.
3. During the last 20 weeks of the year the lawns were mowed on 10 occasions at $40 per time. Previously parents had taken turns to mow the lawns but it had become increasingly difficult to get volunteers so that the mowing was contracted out.
4. Orange cordial and fresh fruit for children mid-morning and mid-afternoon, and includes $100 for coffee and biscuits for staff and visitors.

*Required:*
(a) Prepare a cash budget for the kindergarten to determine the total fees revenue required in 20X9.
(b) Calculate the annual fees required per child from each group, where the different groups are charged on the basis of their fair share of the total teaching time available.

**8-21 Comprehensive cash budget with short-term borrowing**

The controller of the Jo and Flo Peanut Packing Company prepares a cash budget by quarters each year as part of the company's overall planning program.

The company's operations consist of processing and canning the annual peanut crop, a highly seasonal commodity. All manufacturing operations take place in the quarter October-December, although sales are made throughout the year. The company's financial year runs from 1 July to 30 June.

The sales manager has forecast that sales for the coming year ending 30 June 20X2 will be $1 950 000. He expects that the pattern of sales will be:

| | |
|---|---|
| First quarter (July-September, 20X1) | 20% |
| Second quarter (October-December, 20X1) | 40% |
| Third quarter (January-March, 20X2) | 20% |
| Fourth quarter (April-June, 20X2) | 20% |

All sales are on credit. The opening balance of receivables as at 1 July, 20X1 is expected to be collected in the first quarter. Subsequently collections are expected to be two-thirds in the quarter in which sales take place and one-third in the quarter following.

Purchases of materials are scheduled as $120 000 in the first quarter, $360 000 in the second quarter and none in the third and fourth quarters. Payment is made in the same quarter as the purchases.

Direct labour of $350 000 is incurred and paid in the second quarter.

Overhead cost is expected to be $480 000 in the second quarter and $150 000 in each of the other three quarters. These sums include depreciation which is $200 000 for the year charged equally to each month. All other overhead costs are paid in cash during the month in which they are incurred.

Selling and administration expenses are expected to be $25 000 per quarter plus 5% of sales revenue. All these expenses are paid in cash during the quarter in which they are incurred.

The company has a line of short-term credit with the State Trading Bank for financing its seasonal working capital needs. The company plans to maintain a minimum cash balance of $8000. It borrows only in multiples of $5000 and repays as soon as it is able without impairing the minimum cash balance. Repayments may be made in multiples of $5000 only. Interest is at 15% per annum. For planning and budgeting purposes it is assumed that all borrowing is made at the beginning of a quarter and the repayments are made at the end of a quarter. Under the terms of the credit arrangements, interest for each quarter is to be paid on the last day of that quarter.

The company plans to spend the following sums on the purchase and installation of noncurrent assets: $100 000 first quarter, $150 000 third quarter and $50 000 fourth quarter.

Account balances as at 1 July, 20X1 are expected to be:
| | |
|---|---|
| Cash | $8 000 |
| Accounts receivable | $125 000 |

*8/Budgeting and Feedforward Control*

No outstanding borrowings from the bank are expected at 1 July, 20X1.

*Required:*
(a) Prepare the cash budget for the year ending 30 June, 20X2.
(b) What is the maximum sum which the Jo and Flo Peanut Packing Company will have to borrow from the State Trading Bank during the year ending 30 June, 20X2?
(c) Comment briefly on the usefulness of the cash budget, which you have prepared, for planning the company's financing requirements.

**8-22  Cash budget by selected dates during the month**

Ajax Company, which manufactures aluminium containers, has recently incurred a run down in cash because of some essential, large capital expenditures, and anticipates a short-term liquidity problem, especially during the month of May. The following information is available:

(i) Sales were budgeted at 60 000 units per month in April, June and July, and 45 000 units in May. The selling price is $2 per unit. All sales are on credit and are billed on the 15th and the last day of each month, 2% cash discount if paid within 10 days, 30 days net. Sales occur evenly throughout the month and 50% of customers pay within the discount period. The remainder pay at the end of 30 days except for the uncollectables which average 0.5% of gross sales.

(ii) The inventory of finished goods on 1 April was 12 000 units. Company policy is to start each month with a finished goods inventory of 20% of anticipated sales for that month. There is no work in process.

(iii) The inventory of raw materials on 1 April was 11 400 kg. At the beginning of each month raw materials inventory is to be not less than 40% of production requirements for the month. Materials are purchased in a fixed order size of 10 000 kg per order. Raw materials purchases each month are paid on the 15th day of the month following purchase.

(iv) All labour costs are paid on the 15th and last day of the month in which incurred.

(v) All manufacturing overhead and selling and administrative expenses are paid on the 10th of the month following the month in which incurred. Selling expenses are 10% of gross sales. Administrative expenses, including depreciation of $500 per month on office furniture and fixtures, total $16 500 per month.

(vi) The monthly manufacturing budget, based on production of 50 000 units per month, is as follows:

| | |
|---|---|
| Direct materials (25 000 kg @ $1) | $25 000 |
| Direct labour (variable expense) | 20 000 |
| Variable overhead | 10 000 |
| Fixed overhead (including $2000 depreciation) | 5 000 |
| Total manufacturing expenses | $60 000 |

(vii) The cash balance on 1 May is expected to be $5000.

*Required:*
(a) Prepare schedules to calculate:
  (i) Receipts from debtors during May, itemised by significant dates;
  (ii) Raw materials purchases to be paid for in May.
(b) Prepare a cash budget for the month of May. Set out the budget in such a way that you can determine the maximum size of the expected cash deficit during the month, given the available data.

(c) Assuming that management requires a margin of safety of a minimum cash balance of $5000, calculate the size of the loan required.

**8-23** **Purchases, cash receipts and payments**

Dynamo Company is a wholesaler of machine parts and operates from its office and warehouse at Parramatta. The company's busy season is July to September. In June 20X8 the Chief Accountant was gathering information for the preparation of a cash budget to determine whether she would have to use the company's credit facility at a local bank.

The sales forecast for 20X8 included the following data:

| | |
|---|---|
| June | $217 500 |
| July | 325 600 |
| August | 337 200 |
| September | 296 400 |
| October | 243 100 |
| November | 211 300 |

In addition, the Chief Accountant had gathered the following information:

(1) Cost of sales averages 60 percent of sales.

(2) Operating expenses are $37 400 per month plus 10% of sales, all paid during the month incurred except for $2800 in depreciation.

(3) The company keeps an inventory level equal to the budgeted sales requirements for the next two months and pays for its purchases in the month following the month of purchase.

(4) Typically, its customers pay for their purchases in the second month following purchase.

(5) The Chief Accountant would like to keep a cash balance of at least $30 000 and was therefore not happy at the projected balance of $28 750 at the end of June (see below). The arrangement with the local bank is such that, if required, the company could borrow and repay only in multiples of $10 000. Further, since the bank considered Dynamo to be a valued customer, no interest would be charged in such circumstances.

(6) Statement of financial position data as at 30 June include:

| | |
|---|---|
| Cash | $28 750 |
| Accounts Receivable | 416 300 ($198 800 from May, $217 500 from June) |
| Inventory | 367 200 |
| Accounts Payable | 198 240 (anticipated from expected purchases in June) |

*Required:*

The Chief Accountant has asked you to prepare the following budget schedules for each of the months of July, August and September and for the quarter ended 30 September in total:

(i) Purchases budget
(ii) Cash payments budget
(iii) Cash receipts budget
(iv) Cash budget showing whether the company will need to use its credit facility. Where necessary indicate the sum to be borrowed or repaid.

**8-24** **Cash budget for quarter: minimum cash balance required**

You are the management accountant for Umbrellas Unlimited, a distributor of a compact umbrella to various retail outlets. One of your major responsibilities is to produce comprehensive cash and profit budgets for each quarter, the next being April to June, 20X9.

A prime objective in using these budgets is to manage the company's bank loan facility. Your aim is always to have a cash balance of $50 000 at the start of each month. It is necessary to draw on the loan facility at the end of the previous month to have the necessary cash available. Your policy is to repay as much of the loan as feasible at the end of each month while still maintaining the required minimum cash balance. Interest of 5% per month on the loan balance is paid at the end of each month.

The sales (units) forecast for the next six months of 20X9 is:

| April | 65 000 umbrellas |
|---|---|
| May | 100 000 |
| June | 50 000 |
| July | 30 000 |
| August | 28 000 |
| September | 25 000 |

The sales pattern reflects expected increased sales for both Mother's Day and the onset of the rainy winter period, with sales tapering off into spring.

The current selling price of the umbrellas is $10 each. All sales are on credit due within 60 days with no discount for early payment. Usually about 30% are collected in the month of sale, the remainder in the following month. Bad debts are negligible. The umbrellas are purchased from the manufacturer for $4 each. Purchases are usually paid in full in the month following purchase. It is current company policy to have sufficient inventory on hand at the end of each month to supply 40% of the next month's sales.

Monthly operating expenses are:

| Sales commissions | 4% of sales $ |
|---|---|
| Advertising | $200 000 |
| Rent | 18 000 |
| Salaries | 106 000 |
| Electricity | 7 000 |
| Prepaid Insurance expensed* | 3 000 |
| Depreciation | 14 000 |

\* Insurance is paid annually in November each year.

Unless otherwise indicated, the above expenses are paid in cash in the month in which they are incurred. Umbrellas Unlimited also plans cash purchases of new equipment for $200 000 in May and for $150 000 in June.

An abbreviated company statement of financial position at the end of March shows:

| Statement of Financial Position as at 31 March, 20X9 |||||
|---|---|---|---|---|
| Cash | 100 000 | Accounts Payable** | | 100 000 |
| Accounts Receivable* | 320 000 | Dividends Payable*** | | 16 000 |
| Inventory (26,000 units) | 104 000 | Capital | | 800 000 |
| Prepaid Insurance | 22 000 | Retained Profits | | 580 000 |
| Equipment (net) | 950 000 | | | |
| Total assets | $1 496 000 | Total equities | | $1 496 000 |

\*   From March sales
\*\*  From March purchases
\*\*\* To be paid in May

*Required:*
(a) Prepare a schedule of expected cash collections from sales for each month and in total for the June quarter.
(b) Prepare a schedule of inventory purchases in units and dollars for each month and in total for the June quarter.
(c) Prepare a cash budget for each month and in total for the June quarter.

## PROBLEMS 8-25 TO 8-30 REQUIRE SPREADSHEET SOLUTIONS

**8-25** The budget department of the Easy-Way Manufacturing Company has prepared the following estimates for the five years 20X5-20X9:

**Sales** 100 000 units in 20X5, increasing by 5% p.a.
**Selling Price** $10 per unit in 20X5, increasing by 3% p.a.
**Production Costs**
Raw materials: 2 units of material for each unit of finished goods - cost $1.50 each in 20X5, increasing by 2% p.a.
Direct labour: $2 per unit of finished product in 20X5, increasing by 4% p.a.
Factory Overhead:   Variable: 50% of direct labour cost
                    Fixed: $51 000 in 20X5, increasing by 1% p.a.
An actual cost system is used.
**Selling and Administration Expenses** $50 000 fixed per year plus 5% of dollar sales.
**Inventories**
Raw Materials: 5000 units at 1/1/X5 valued at $6250. Desired year-end inventories (units) 5% of following year's production units.
Finished Goods: 10 000 units at 1/1/X5 valued at $60 000. Desired year-end inventories (units) 10% of following year's sales units.
**Income Tax Rate** 40%

**Note** All percentage increases are compound increases.

*Required*
(a) A production budget for each of the five years indicating units to be produced.
(b) A purchases budget for each year indicating unit purchases and their cost.
(c) A budgeted statement of financial performance for each of the five years (showing details of cost of goods manufactured). Assume a FIFO cost flow. There are no opening or closing work-in-process inventories.
(d) Assume that all manufacturing cost increases have been underestimated by 1% (e.g. raw materials increase 3% instead of 2%). Modify your model to produce new purchases budgets and statement of financial performances for each of the five years.

**8-26** Electra Ltd manufactures a product which sold in December Quarter, 20X5 for $60 per unit. The price is expected to decrease by 1.5% per quarter as the market becomes more competitive. Quarterly cost data for December Quarter, 20X5 were as follows, with projected quarterly increases in parentheses:

**Variable**

| | |
|---|---|
| Selling & Administrative Expenses | $5/unit sold (0.5%) |
| Direct Materials | $8/unit manufactured (0.25%) |
| Direct Labour | $10/unit manufactured (0.75%) |
| Variable Overhead | $4/unit manufactured (0.1%) |

**Fixed**

| | |
|---|---|
| Selling & Administrative Expenses | $20 000/quarter (0.5%) |
| Manufacturing (including $10 000 depreciation) | $30 000/quarter (no increase) |

(All percentage increases are compound)

Electra pays all bills in the month in which the expenses are incurred.

All expenses are cash unless otherwise noted.

All sales are on credit. Half of each *month's* sales are collected during the month of sale and the remaining half the month after sale.

The company wishes to maintain a finished goods inventory equal to 20% of the following *month's* sales and a raw materials inventory sufficient for 10% of the following *month's*

*8/Budgeting and Feedforward Control*

production. Projected *monthly* sales for 20X6 and 20X7 are uniform within each quarter (i.e. each month's sales volume is one-third of the quarterly total). Sales increase from 6000 units per *quarter* for March Quarter 20X6 by 10% (compound) per quarter.

All units of sales, production and inventories should be rounded (normal rounding) to whole units and all costs and prices rounded *up* to the nearest whole cent.

A FIFO cost flow assumption is used in valuing all inventories. Fixed manufacturing overhead is allocated to units of production on the basis of expected annual production over the calendar year. (Hint: do *not* round the overhead allocation rate.) No variances are written off quarterly.

Estimated tax liability on profits is recorded quarterly at a rate of 49%, but only paid in March Quarter each year in respect of profits of the previous year ended 30 June. Annual dividends are also paid in March Quarter, having been provided for the previous October. A 5% dividend will again be proposed and provided for in October 20X6, profits permitting.

The company's Statement of Financial Position as at 31 December, 20X5 was as follows:

|  | $ |  | $ |
|---|---|---|---|
| **Shareholders' Equity** |  | **Noncurrent Assets** |  |
| 100 000 $1 Ord Shares | 100 000 | Buildings & Equipment | 600 000 |
| Retained Profits | 283 800 | Less Accumulated Depn | 100 000 |
|  | 383 800 |  | 500 000 |
| **Current Liabilities** |  | **Current Assets** |  |
| Provision for Tax* | 175 000 | Cash at bank | 1 500 |
| Provision for Dividends | 5 000 | A/cs Receivable | 49 500 |
|  | 180 000 | Inventories: |  |
|  |  | Fin Gds(400 units) | 11 200 |
|  |  | Dir Mats(200 units) | 1 600 |
|  |  |  | 63 800 |
|  | 563 800 |  | 563 800 |

* $100 000 in respect of Y/E 30/6/X5

*Required:*
Build a financial model to produce for the calendar year 20X6 the following reports by quarter and for the year as a whole. Do not build separate models - all reports must be in the one model.

(a) Production budgets (units)
(b) Purchases budgets (units and dollars)
(c) Cost of Goods Sold budgets
(d) Budgeted Statement of financial performances
(e) Cash budgets
(f) Budgeted Statement of financial positions at end of each quarter.

Note that your model should be sufficiently general to handle changes to the data or assumptions.

(g) Suppose that the marketing department advises that sales volume (units) are more likely to *decrease* by 10% per quarter from the 6000 units estimated for March Quarter, 20X6. Make the necessary change to your model and produce revised reports to reflect this change.

8-27  The Big Y Company is a new company formed with a capital of 600 000 ordinary shares of $1 each fully paid. Big Y has no other assets, but has arranged to lease property and equipment.

Big Y will commence manufacturing a new non-carbonated drink called Y-Not in July 20X5. Projected sales are 200 000 cases per month. Y-Not will wholesale for $20 per case. Due to heavy promotion, July Selling and Distribution costs will be $1 per case, falling to $0.50 per case in subsequent months.

Manufacturing costs comprise:

> Bottles @ $4.00 per case
> Mix @ $5.00 per litre (each case requires 2 litres of mix)
> Labour and overhead - fixed at $215 000/month (cash)

An actual cost system is in use, with a FIFO cost flow assumption. Big Y has no opening inventories, of course. Effective from 31 July, management desires to have closing inventories of raw materials equal to 10% of the following month's anticipated use (to nearest unit) and closing inventories of finished goods equal to 15% of the following month's sales (to nearest case).

General and administrative expenses are $20 000 per month (all cash).

It is anticipated that all sales will be on credit, and that one-half of the credit sales revenue will be collected during the month of sale and one-half will be collected during the month after sale. One-half of the collections during the month of sale will receive a 2% discount for prompt payment.

It is intended that all debts be paid immediately. Big Y has arranged overdraft facilities with its bank, ABC Bank, to cover cash deficits. Interest on overdraft is 1.5% per month on the overdraft balance at the end of each month, payable in the following month.

*Required*

Prepare for each month of September Quarter, 20X5:
(a) A production budget (in cases).
(b) Appropriate cost calculations for (i) bottles, (ii) mix and (iii) labour and overhead.
(c) A purchases budget (units and dollars)
(d) Dollar values of closing inventories
(e) A budgeted statement of financial performance.
(f) A cash budget.
(g) A budgeted statement of financial position at the end of each of the three months.

8-28  Bright Paint Co. Ltd manufactures white plastic paint in 4-litre cans. The company has only recently entered this competitive market.

**Market and Sales Potential**

The total market for this product has been assessed at two million 4-litre cans in 20X1. This market is expected to increase by 3% per annum.

Bright's share of the market in 20X2 is estimated to be 10%, but it expects to obtain a further 2% of the market each year up to a maximum of 16%.

Bright's wholesale selling price in 20X1 was $8 per 4-litre can. To allow for expected cost increases the selling price will be increased by 8% per year (compound).

## 8/Budgeting and Feedforward Control

### The Production Process

The company buys the two secret ingredients, called Material X and Material Y, and mixes them for 1 hour in the ratio X:Y = 3:1. During processing there is a volume loss of 4%. After mixing, the finished product is poured into cans which are sealed and labelled.

### Manufacturing Costs

Raw materials are purchased in 200-litre drums, X costing $120 per drum and Y costing $140 per drum. Cans cost $0.50 each. The mixing process costs $96 per batch, each batch consisting of a total input of 400 litres. The canning process costs $0.50 per can.

All costs are averages for 20X1. Raw materials are expected to increase by 4% per annum, cans at 6% per annum and processing and canning costs at 10% per annum (all compound).

### Production Quantities and Inventories

The company wishes to maintain the following year-end inventories:

|  | Inventories Desired | 20X1 Closing Inventory |
|---|---|---|
| Completed Cans | 10% Sales Next Year | 20 000 |
| Work in Process | Nil | Nil |
| Raw Materials (Drums): X | 12 | 9 |
| Y | 4 | 3 |
| Cans | 500 | 300 |

In calculating production quantities fractional batches should be rounded *up*, thus increasing closing inventory of completed cans where appropriate. Similarly, raw materials X and Y must be purchased in whole drums, so that closing inventories may exceed those desired.

The company uses the FIFO assumption for costing sales and inventories.

### Other Expenses and Payments

Selling expenses are 1% of sales revenue. Administration costs were $15 000 in 20X1 and are expected to inflate at 7% per annum.

Ignore Depreciation of Plant and Equipment.

The bank overdraft is incurring interest at 16% per annum, calculated on the average of the overdraft balances at the beginning and end of each year. Interest is debited to the Bank account on the first day of the following year.

Corporate tax is 40% of taxable profit, payable in the following year (on a calendar year basis).

Company policy is to pay 50% of net profit after tax as dividends in the year after the profit is earned.

Customers are given 1.5 months' supply on credit. One month's credit is received on purchases.

All other expenses are paid in cash in the year in which they are incurred.

Bright Paint's statement of financial position as at the end of 20X1 is as follows:

| Statement of Financial Position of Bright Paint Co. Ltd as at 31 December, 20X1 |||||
|---|---|---|---|---|
| **Shareholders' Equity** | | | **Noncurrent Assets** | |
| Paid-up Capital | 20 000 | | Plant & Equipment | 50 000 |
| Retained Profits | 1 650 | | | |
| | 121 650 | | **Current Assets** | |
| | | | Accounts Receivable | 10 000 |
| **Current Liabilities** | | | Inventories: | |
| Bank Overdraft | 13 000 | | Finished Goods | 90 000 |
| Interest on Overdraft | 400 | | Raw Materials: X | 1 080 |
| Accounts Payable | 7 600 | | Y | 420 |
| Provision for Dividend | 5 000 | | Empty Cans | 150 |
| Provision for Tax | 4 000 | | | 101 650 |
| | 30 000 | | | |
| | $151 650 | | | $151 650 |

*Required*

Build a financial model to prepare for the five years 20X2 to 20X6 the following:
(a) Sales budget in units and dollars.
(b) Budgets (units) for production, inventories and purchases.
(c) Production costs and $ values for purchases and inventories
(d) Budgeted statements of financial performance.
(e) Cash budgets.
(f) Budgeted statements of financial position at year end.

8-29 Nezter Enterprises is a family business which is prepared to enter any kind of operation which is thought to be profitable and within the scope of their resources. At 1 January, 20X0 the business financial position is as shown in the statement of financial position below:

| Nezter Enterprises Pty Ltd Statement of Financial Position as at 31 December, 20W9 |||
|---|---|---|
| **Shareholders' Equity** | | |
| Paid-up Capital | | $80 100 |
| Retained Profits | | 13 983 |
| | | 94 083 |
| *Represented by:* | | |
| **Current Assets** | | |
| Cash | $80 375 | |
| Inventory * | 14 | 80 389 |
| **Less Current Liabilities** | | |
| Accounts Payable | 56 | |
| Provision for Tax | 3 000 | |
| Provision for Dividend | 2 250 | 5 306 |
| **Working Capital** | | 75 083 |
| **Noncurrent Assets** | | |
| Plant and Equipment at cost | 20 000 | |
| Less Accumulated Depreciation | 6 000 | |
| | 14 000 | |
| Shed | 5 000 | 19 000 |
| | | $94 083 |

* Fertiliser valued at cost of ingredients only.

Nezter is planning the following operations over the next five years:

To continue to produce and sell garden fertiliser. They buy the raw ingredients, nitrogen, phosphorus, potash and an inert material and mix them together in a mixing machine in the proportions 5% nitrogen, 10% phosphorus, 5% potash and 80% inert material. When thoroughly mixed they pour the fertiliser into plastic bags holding 5 kg, seal the bags and store them in a storage shed.

The raw ingredients are bought in 100 kg bags, the costs of which, in 20W9, were

| | |
|---|---|
| Nitrogen | $10 per bag |
| Phosphorus | $12 per bag |
| Potash | $6 per bag |
| Inert material | $1 per bag |

These costs are expected to increase at 5% (compound) per annum.

No inventories of raw materials are held. Nezter buys sufficient ingredients to mix batches of 2000 kg of fertiliser. As soon as each purchase order arrives the ingredients are mixed, bagged and stored. Purchases are on credit and there is usually one lot of ingredients unpaid for at the end of each year.

Nezter does not plan to hold any specific levels of inventory of mixed and bagged fertiliser, but operates on the principle of purchasing and producing the standard batch size whenever there are only one hundred 5 kg bags left in the storage shed. At 1 January, 20X0 there are 100 bags on hand.

Ten thousand 5 kg bags were sold for 75 cents per bag in 20W9. The unit sales are expected to increase by 2% per year (compound) and the selling price will be adjusted upwards by 10% at the beginning of each year to allow for cost increases. All sales are for cash.

Apart from the raw ingredients, explicit production costs consist of depreciation on mixing and pouring equipment, electric power and plastic bags. The family, which does all the work, does not draw wages but accepts a share of the profits in the form of dividends on their shares.

The annual depreciation charge on the equipment is calculated as 10% on cost. Electric power in 20W9 came to $5 per batch and is expected to increase by 7% per annum (compound). Plastic bags cost $2 per hundred (paid for in cash) and increases of about 4% per annum (compound) are anticipated. No inventories of bags are held. Power and bags used and depreciation charges are written off as period expenses.

The fertiliser is sold from the shed to buyers who arrange their own delivery.

Nezter has been approached by a potential borrower, H. Leverage, wishing to finance an investment. Nezter decides to lend her $75 000 as from 1 January 20X0. The conditions of the loan are:
- The period of the loan is 8 years.
- Interest is to be charged at 10% per annum on the balance outstanding at the beginning of each year.
- Repayments are to be made in equal annual instalments over the eight years. Such repayments will be made once per year on 31 December. Each equal instalment will comprise partly interest and partly a repayment of principal. The interest payment for the period is subtracted from the total instalment and the remainder becomes the principal repayment.

Tax is levied at 50 cents in the dollar on profit and is payable in the year following its derivation. Three-quarters of the after-tax profits are distributed as dividends in the year following the profit earnings.

*Required:*

Build a financial model so that Nezter Enterprises can examine their planned activities over the next five years, 20X0-20X4. Your model should be capable of producing the following reports:
(a) Budgeted statement of financial performance for each year
(b) Cash budget for each year
(c) Budgeted statement of financial position at end of each year
(d) A report showing the status of the loan each year for the whole of the 8 years. The report should show for each year principal payment, interest payment, balance of principal outstanding, interest to date.

**8-30** School Rulers Pty Ltd manufactures wooden school rulers. The company has only recently entered this competitive market.

### Market and Sales Potential
A number of manufacturers compete in this market whose total size was assessed at 3 333 000 rulers in 20X8. Because of declining school enrolments this market is expected to decrease by two percent per annum (compound).

This company's share of the market in 20X9 is estimated to be 30%, and it expects to obtain a further one percent of the total market each year. Due to limitations in factory capacity there is a ceiling on total annual sales of 1 million rulers.

Selling prices in 20X8 were 25c per ruler. To allow for expected cost inflation School Rulers will increase the price by 8% (compound) each year from 20X8.

### The Production Process
The company buys timber in standard cut lengths with the dimensions 8000 mm x 120 mm x 30 mm. These lengths are first passed through a cutting machine which slices each length of timber into 8000 mm batons, 3 mm thick and 30 mm wide. The batons are subsequently fed into a printing machine which simultaneously prints a 30 cm rule and cuts the baton into ruler lengths with 1 cm spare at each end (i.e. each ruler is actually 32 cm long). Assume there is no wastage or spoilage.

### Manufacturing Costs
The timber is purchased for $5 per lineal metre.

Direct labour rates are $9.60 per hour and each ruler involves one minute of direct labour time. Manufacturing overheads consist of $20 000 per annum fixed costs and variable costs of $0.60 per direct labour hour. Overhead is allocated to production on the basis of expected annual production.

All manufacturing costs are averages for 20X8. Timber is expected to increase at 10% per annum (compound), direct labour at 6% per annum (compound) and variable manufacturing overhead at 4% per annum (compound). Fixed overhead is not expected to vary except for the depreciation component (see below).

### Production Quantities and Inventories
The company wishes to maintain the following inventories:

|  | Inventory Desired as % of Following Year's Requirements | 20X8 C/Inv Qty |
|---|---|---|
| Finished rulers | 10% (of Sales) | 100 000 |
| Work in Process | Nil | Nil |
| Raw materials-timber lengths | 25% (of Production) | 200 |

No work in process is carried. Once the company has to start cutting a new length of timber the whole length is converted to finished rulers before the factory closes for the day. Hence the desired production and closing inventory of finished rulers will usually not be realised, but will be exceeded because cutting of a new length of timber will begin and must be completely processed. Similarly, the desired closing inventory of timber must be in whole lengths and partial lengths should be rounded up to the next whole length.

The company uses the FIFO assumption for determining the cost of goods sold and cost of inventories.

**Other Costs and Payments**
Selling expenses are one percent of sales revenue. Administration costs were $10 000 in 20X8 and other fixed costs were $5000; both of these are expected to inflate at 9% per annum (compound).

Corporate tax is 40% of taxable profit and is payable in the following year. Tax is calculated on a calendar year basis.

Company policy is to pay 75% of net profit after tax as dividends in the year after the profit is earned.

Customers are given 1.5 months' supply on credit. One month's credit is received on timber purchases. Assume that all other expenses are paid in cash in the year in which they are incurred.

The fixed overhead expenses include Depreciation on Machinery of 18% on a diminishing value basis.

**Statement of Financial Position of School Rulers Pty Ltd as at 31 December 20X8**

| | | | |
|---|---|---|---|
| **Shareholders' Equity** | | | |
| Paid-up Capital | | | $160 000 |
| Retained Profits | | | 1 700 |
| | | | 161 700 |
| *Represented by:* | | | |
| **Current Assets** | | | |
| Cash | | 50 000 | |
| Accounts Receivable | | 25 000 | |
| Inventories - Finished Rulers | | 23 000 | |
|     - Raw Material (timber) | | 8 000 | 106 000 |
| **Less Current Liabilities** | | | |
| Accounts Payable | | 3 400 | |
| Provision for Dividend | | 11 600 | |
| Estimated Tax Liability | | 10 300 | 25 300 |
| **Working Capital** | | | 80 700 |
| **Noncurrent Assets** | | | |
| Land and Buildings | | 100 000 | |
| Machinery at cost | 50 000 | | |
| Less Accumulated Depreciation | 9 000 | 41 000 | 141 000 |
| | | | 221 700 |
| **Less Noncurrent Liability** | | | |
| 10 percent loan | | | 60 000 |
| | | | 161 700 |

**Note:** No repayments are expected to be made on the loan.

*Required:*

Build a financial model to prepare forward estimates for the five years 20X9 to 20Y3 to indicate operating plans and derive budgeted statements of financial performance and cash flow statements for each year and statements of financial position at the end of each year. Your model should follow this sequence:
1. Sales budgets in units and dollars
2. Production and Purchases budgets (units)
3. Unit production costs for materials, labour and overhead and for finished rulers.
4. Purchases and closing inventories in dollars.
5. Statements of financial performance.
6. Closing balances of Accounts Receivable and Payable and the cash flows in respect of these accounts.
7. Cash budgets.
8. Statements of financial position (in vertical form).
9. Add lines to your model to show:
   (a) Net profit after tax as % of Shareholders' Funds
   (b) Proposed dividend as % of paid-up capital
10. At the beginning of 20Y1 an investment of $30 000 in additional machinery would provide capacity for production of an extra one million rulers per year. Evaluate this as a possible course of action for the company. Depreciation for the new machinery would be on the same basis as for the existing machinery.
11. Assume that the course of action suggested in (10) were adopted. Evaluate the effect of an annual advertising expenditure of $20 000 from 20Y1 onwards, on the assumption that this would result in market share increasing by 3% per year from 20Y1 (instead of 1%).
12. Disregarding changes referred to in (10) and (11) evaluate the effects on the company if price per ruler were increased by 12% (compound) each year instead of 8%, resulting in the company's market share remaining at 30% throughout the 5 year period.
13. Disregarding changes referred to in (10), (11) and (12) evaluate the effects on the company if, due to market pressures and in order to achieve the proposed growth in market share, it became necessary to reduce the selling price to 22c in 20X9, increasing thereafter at 8% (compound) each year. Suggest some possible courses of action that the company might consider if this situation eventuated.

# Chapter 9

# Feedback Control: Flexible Budgets and Standard Cost Variances

## THE CONTROL PROCESS

In Chapter 8 we examined the role of budgets as a form of planning exercised by managers in order to achieve organisational objectives. Such planning is part of the control system cycle; as plans are implemented performance is monitored, by comparing outputs with plans, to detect any deviations. If deviations are detected corrective action is taken to eliminate such deviations by bringing future performance back on target, or by revising plans if changed circumstances so warrant. Such corrective action may be taken ex-ante, in anticipation of unfavourable deviations (feedforward control), or ex-post, after actual results are realised (feedback control).

The planning process involves the setting of operational targets or sub-goals as a means of achieving the overall objectives of the organisation. For example, an overall objective may be to earn a return of 20% on capital. Such an objective is not operational as expressed, because it does not specify how such a return on investment is to be achieved. There may be a number of ways in which such a return could be earned. The objective has to be operationalised in the form of specific product (or service) sales targets, and production (or activity) targets. Resources must be available when needed by the various activity centres. Cash flows have to be anticipated and planned to ensure adequate liquidity to meet commitments. These plans are co-ordinated in budgets.

Once plans have been established and co-ordinated in the comprehensive budget, the next step in the control cycle is to implement them. Implementation involves motivation of employees and managers to perform, and ensuring that subsequent performance is satisfactory. The control process may involve varying degrees of intervention by management, depending on the traits of particular individuals, and on group attitudes.

### Personal Control and Motivation

To some extent, individuals may be self-motivated to perform because they derive self-satisfaction and feelings of competency from a job well done. Such willingness to apply oneself to a particular task is sometimes referred to as **personal** (or **self** or **individual**) control. With such individuals no formal control mechanisms are usually necessary - they are 'self starters'.

Although some individuals are self-motivated and exercise personal control, others need to be motivated by means of such management interventions as the provision of organisational rewards for successful budget achievement, and maybe sanctions for non-achievement. Successful management intervention requires an understanding of how employees can be motivated.

When an individual accepts organisational goals and strives to achieve them s/he engages in what is called **functional behaviour**. What is it that motivates individuals to engage in functional behaviour, to attempt to achieve budget targets? In a general sense, the degree to which an individual is motivated depends on the rewards expected and the values placed on those rewards. Because of individual differences and preferences, however, individuals vary in their valuation of rewards. One person may be motivated by money while another by a personal sense of achievement. Rewards may be **intrinsic** or **extrinsic**.

Intrinsic rewards are those that come from within oneself, such as personal satisfaction and feelings of competency from performing a task well, or from achieving a goal, and feelings of self-esteem. Extrinsic rewards are delivered by others: money, bonuses, promotion, fringe benefits, and praise from a superior. Clearly the reward system has to take account of people's needs and what motivates them. Psychologists have developed several theories of individual motivation, broadly classified as **content** theories of motivation and **process** theories of motivation.

## Content Theories of Motivation

Content theories of motivation are concerned with **what** things motivate people. Typically researchers have tried to identify particular needs or desires which drive people. They believed that individuals could be motivated by providing them with the opportunity to satisfy unfulfilled needs - by matching rewards and needs. Two well-known content theories are those of Maslow and Herzberg.

Maslow (1954) constructed a hierarchy of common human needs, ranging from the most basic needs (food, shelter, clothing) to higher needs including belongingness and love, esteem, and self-actualisation. Maslow claimed that higher needs will not be gratified until the lower ones are satisfied. Once a particular level of needs is largely satisfied those needs no longer motivate as individuals lift their sights to higher, unfulfilled needs. If you're starving you could be motivated to do something by a promise of food, but once you've had enough to eat the offer of more food is unlikely to motivate you.

Following this theory, in order to motivate people to work it is necessary to know which of their needs are unsatisfied. Some critics have also said that Maslow's pyramid of needs is not universal or descriptive of all cultures, and hence is not general enough.

Herzberg (1966) believed that today's society reasonably guaranteed the satisfaction of our lowest and basic needs, and focused on factors related to a job and the workplace. He suggested a two-factor 'motivation-hygiene' theory which discriminated between those factors relating to **job content** and those relating to **job context**. Factors which relate to the job itself he called **motivation factors**: challenging work, increased responsibility, and recognition for achievements. Factors that dealt with the 'environmental' aspects (context) he called **hygiene factors**: office comfort, supervision conditions, interpersonal relations, money, and security.

The hygiene factors, it was claimed, will not create job satisfaction, although their absence would lead to dissatisfaction. Thus hygiene factors are not positive motivators: a poor salary is a significant cause of job dissatisfaction, but a high salary does not necessarily lead to job satisfaction. There has been some criticism of the classification of money as a hygiene factor, because monetary-based incentive schemes and bonus schemes are widely used.

Following Herzberg, the way to motivate people is to provide motivational factors: a stimulating job is more motivating than luxurious surroundings.

## Process Theories of Motivation

Process theories of motivation are concerned, not with **what** motivates, but with **how** people are motivated. Researchers have tried to explain the **process** by which management intervention can facilitate the satisfaction of people's needs, and hence motivate high performance. The two most popular theories are **expectancy theory** and **goal setting theory**.

### *Expectancy Theory*

Expectancy theory (e.g., Vroom 1964, Lawler 1973, Ronen and Livingstone 1975) holds that motivation is influenced by valued outcomes (intrinsic and extrinsic rewards) expected to flow from particular levels of individual performance, and the likelihood that those outcomes (rewards) will be realised. This likelihood is a function of two separate beliefs:

(1) the likelihood that a given level of effort by the individual will produce a certain level of performance - this likelihood is called **expectancy** and is referred to as the effort-performance (E→P) linkage; and

(2) the likelihood that this level of performance will lead to particular outcomes - this likelihood is called **instrumentality** and is referred to as the performance-outcome (P→O) linkage.

This is a subjective, expected utility model in which an individual considers a number of possible effort levels together with the probabilities that such effort levels will lead to outcomes that have utility for him; he selects that level of effort which maximises his expected utility. Thus, motivation is higher with higher levels of expected utility, but with increasing goal difficulty, expected utility (and hence motivation) will eventually decline because expectancy falls as it is realised that the required level of effort is too demanding or unattainable.

## *Goal Setting Theory*

Goal setting theory (for example see Locke 1968; Locke et al 1981) asserts that assigned, difficult, specific goals (if accepted) lead to higher performance than easy, or vague, or 'do your best' goals. There is abundant evidence that the harder the goal the higher the performance. This positive relationship is explained by at least two factors: (1) specific goals direct attention to relevant (productive) activities and hence minimise resources expended on unproductive activities; (2) difficult, personal goals cause an increase in effort levels during task performance.

It may appear that goal setting theory and expectancy theory are conflicting. Goal setting theory suggests that performance is directly proportional to goal difficulty, and that the higher the goal the higher the performance. In contrast, expectancy theory suggests that individuals will lose motivation and give up after a certain threshold level of goal difficulty, because the probability that effort will produce the required performance (i.e. expectancy) falls when goals become difficult. However, goal setting theory is based on the premise of an accepted goal. In fact, the theories are complementary: expectancy theory can explain how individuals select particular goals and why an assigned goal will often be chosen as a personal goal. Once a goal is chosen, goal setting theory suggests that higher levels of chosen goal difficulty will lead to higher performance.

## Relevance of Theories of Motivation

Given the diversity of human nature it is not easy to generalise from these theories of motivation. If management tries to motivate individual performance by focusing on unfulfilled needs, it is difficult to envisage a single set of needs common to all organisational participants. It would be an insurmountable task to try and identify individual needs and implement separate reward systems for each individual. It is desirable, however, to assign goals to individuals in order to promote performance. This is exactly what happens in the budgeting process. The trick is to establish the appropriate level of goal difficulty in order to motivate and not demotivate individuals. The accepted wisdom is reflected by Stedry (1960) who conducted an experiment to determine the optimum level of difficulty for budget standards and concluded that standards should be perceived to be tight but attainable. It is generally thought that a 'tight' budget is one which has less than 50% chance of being achieved. An alternative scenario is reflected in a real-world setting. Merchant and Manzoni (1989) in a field study involving 54 profit centres in 12 corporations found that budget targets were not extremely difficult but were set to be achievable about 8 years in 10. This suggested that although the targets were perceived ex-ante as being difficult, ex-post they had an 80% chance of being realised, and were thus highly achievable.

## Budgetary Participation

It has been suggested that if managers participate in the budgetary (goal setting) process they are more likely to internalise the budget goals and accept them as their own standards of performance. Having accepted them they should then perform to those standards. Consequently, we would expect to find that increased participation leads to increased performance. The results of management accounting research, however, are ambiguous. Only weak support has been found for such a direct relationship. Rather, several studies have found relationships between participation and other variables such as morale and attitude, or that a link between participation and performance was dependent on factors such as the personality of the manager (Brownell, 1981) and the emphasis placed on the budget by a supervisor in evaluating a subordinate (Brownell, 1982).

A more recent study by Libby (1999) focused on the idea that although subordinate managers may "have a voice" (participate) in setting the budget, in the end their advice may be apparently ignored. Thus they may regard their participation as only pseudo-participation, and hence become demotivated.

Libby discovered that such demotivation may be avoided by a superior providing the subordinate with an explanation for the subordinate's apparent lack of influence over the final budget.

There is always the danger that some managers may take advantage of their participation by deliberately biasing the budget targets in order to make them easier to achieve. Lowe and Shaw (1968) identified three major motivational causes for managers to submit biased budget estimates:

(1) The **reward system** (e.g. bonuses, promotion for achieving budget) motivate submission of low estimates to make the budget easier to attain.
(2) **Company norms** (e.g. in respect of past growth rates) is likely to promote acceptance of the norm even when managers think otherwise.
(3) **Managerial insecurity** (e.g. because of recent poor performances) may motivate a manager to promise higher performance in the future even though such performance is unlikely to be achieved.

Lowe and Shaw also found that top management was not very good at detecting the existence of bias, nor at adjusting forecasts when bias was detected.

## *Social Control*

In addition to the individual motivational factors that cause individuals to act in certain ways, it is important to recognise that there are social influences on people's behaviour resulting from group interactions. Such social forces may reinforce functional behaviour, or as is often the case, they may promote **dysfunctional behaviour** (behaviour in which an individual pursues personal goals which are not in the interests of the organisation). These social influences have been labelled **social controls** (Hopwood, 1974) and "emerge from the shared values and the mutual commitments of members of a group to one another". Of particular relevance is the enforcement of **group norms**.

Group norms are the unofficial rules and standards which govern the social interactions of organisational participants. These rules may be explicitly promoted, or they may be unspoken but implicitly accepted by group members. Group norms in the workplace usually focus on appropriate work practices and performance levels (for example, produce ten units per hour). Group norms may be positive and induce behaviour which is consistent with organisational objectives, but they may be more likely to lead to enforcement of restricted output levels. The establishment of positive group norms in respect of achieving budget plans would greatly assist in achieving organisational objectives.

## *Administrative Controls*

In addition to the need for motivating employees and managers to perform, the implementation of budget plans is further reinforced by what have been called **administrative controls** (Hopwood, 1974). Administrative controls are "formal rules and standard procedures used to regulate the behaviour of subordinate managers and employees", and include the following. Organisation manuals delineate responsibilities, patterns of relationships and authority for decisions. Channels of communication control the flow of information which is available to participants, and reinforce the hierarchical structure. Job descriptions and standard operating procedures are developed to specify how tasks should be performed. Recruitment policies specify educational experience, aptitude qualities and professional experience in order that personnel are carefully selected. Training programs ensure that employees understand procedures and rules, and also help shape their values to the underlying organisational philosophy.

A particularly important administrative control is the performance evaluation system used to motivate managers and employees to achieve budget targets, and to determine whether managers have been successful in doing so. It may also be integrated with a formal reward system to reinforce desirable behaviours and successful performance. Performance evaluation systems are designed to assess actual performance by comparing it with planned performance, and to facilitate conclusions from the comparison. The success of a performance evaluation system in motivating and securing desired performance depends upon the nature and characteristics of the performance measures used and their appropriateness, as well as the ability to discriminate between performance which has been affected by environmental rather than behavioural factors. The appropriateness of performance measures will be discussed in Chapter 11. For the moment our concern is to ensure that the performance evaluation system, as part of the feedback control cycle, takes account of environmental uncertainty by adjusting, if circumstances have changed, the planning budget figures against which actual performance is compared. Such an adjustment is effected by using what is called a **flexible budget**.

## FEEDBACK CONTROL

Feedback control involves comparisons of actual results with budget plans, and considers actions which might correct future deviations between the two. Corrective actions might involve modifying performance to better meet plans in the future, or maybe reviewing and altering plans (and budgets) in the light of changed circumstances.

The first step in feedback control consists of comparing actual operating results with budget plans, and highlighting variances which might be favourable or unfavourable. If these variances are significant (or material), further investigations may take place to determine their cause(s) so that appropriate corrective action may be implemented. Consider the data in illustrative example 9-1.

---

*Illustrative Example 9-1*

ABC Company produces a single product. The budget for the year ended 30/6/X1 was based on a planned output of 10 000 units. Budgeted costs for the production department were as follows:

**ABC Company Production Department**
**Budgeted Costs for Year Ended 30/6/X1**

| | |
|---|---:|
| Production units | 10 000 |
| Direct Materials | $200 000 |
| Direct Labour | 40 000 |
| Variable Overhead | 60 000 |
| Fixed Overhead | 100 000 |
| | $400 000 |

Actual production was 10 200 units. Actual production costs were $213 150 for direct materials, $42 630 for direct labour, $61 000 for variable overhead and $99 000 for fixed overhead.

Required: Prepare a performance report comparing actual costs with budget, showing any variances.

---

The report might look like this:

**ABC Company Production Department**
**Cost Performance Report for Year Ended 30/6/X1**

| | Actual | Budget | Variance | |
|---|---:|---:|---:|---|
| Production units | 10 200 | 10 000 | 200 | Fav. |
| Direct Materials | $213 150 | $200 000 | $13 150 | Unfav. |
| Direct Labour | 42 630 | 40 000 | 2 630 | Unfav. |
| Variable Overhead | 61 000 | 60 000 | 1 000 | Unfav. |
| Fixed Overhead | 99 000 | 100 000 | 1 000 | Fav. |
| | $415 780 | $400 000 | $15 780 | Unfav. |

As you can see, the planned production costs of $400 000 have been exceeded by $15 780. Relying on these figures the production department manager may well receive an unfavourable performance evaluation. But would such an evaluation be fair to the manager?

Actual costs have been compared with those in the original comprehensive or planning budget. This original budget was based on a target activity level of 10 000 units of product. Such a budget is sometimes called a **static budget**, because it has been geared to a single volume of activity. It can be observed however, that the actual volume produced exceeded the target of 10 000 units, by 200 units. In this sense, the manager could be said to have been **effective** because he achieved the target set. We can question, however, whether such a performance report is informative in reporting the manager's **efficiency** when it compares the costs incurred at one volume level (10 200 units) with budgeted costs at a different, lower volume level (10 000 units). A subordinate manager may perceive the use of a static budget by a superior in evaluating his performance as quite unfair - and rightly so!

The solution to this problem is to prepare a **flexible budget**. A flexible budget is a budget which has been adjusted to reflect the change in volume of activity from that assumed in the original comprehensive budget. As a matter of course, after the budget period has expired, the original budget should be 'flexed' (adjusted) to indicate what costs should have been, in the light of the actual volume achieved. Then actual costs should be compared with the flexible budget allowances.

## Steps in Preparing a Flexible Budget

1   *Classify costs as fixed or variable.*
    In order to prepare a flexible budget it is necessary to know about the cost behaviour of the various budget items in the original comprehensive budget. In particular, it is necessary to determine whether each cost item is a fixed or a variable cost. Clearly, only the variable costs would change in a flexible budget, because the fixed costs should be the same at differing volume levels.

    For our example, except for fixed overhead, all other costs would be treated as variable:

    | Cost Item | Cost | F or V |
    |---|---|---|
    | Direct Materials | $200 000 | V |
    | Direct Labour | $40 000 | V |
    | Variable Overhead | $60 000 | V |
    | Fixed Overhead | $100 000 | F |

2   *Convert variable costs to a 'per unit' basis.*
    Each of the cost items in the original comprehensive budget which is identified as a variable cost should be divided by the output volume planned (10 000 units in our example).

    | Cost Item | |
    |---|---|
    | Direct Materials | $200 000/10 000 = $20 per unit |
    | Direct Labour | $40 000/10 000 = $4 per unit |
    | Variable Overhead | $60 000/10 000 = $6 per unit |
    | Total | = $30 per unit |

3   *Prepare the flexible budget for the actual output volume.*
    In our example the actual output volume is 10 200 units. In preparing the flexible budget each variable cost item is calculated by multiplying the per unit cost calculated in step 2 by the actual volume of 10 200 units. The fixed cost item will not change from that shown in the original comprehensive budget. Then actual costs can be compared with the flexible budget allowances:

    **ABC Company Production Department**
    **Improved Cost Performance Report for Year Ended 30/6/X1**

    | | p.u. | Actual | Flexible Budget | Variance | |
    |---|---|---|---|---|---|
    | Production units | | 10 200 | 10 200 | | |
    | Direct Materials | $20 | $213 150 | $204 000 | $9 150 | Unfav. |
    | Direct Labour | $4 | 42 630 | 40 800 | 1 830 | Unfav. |
    | Variable Overhead | $6 | 61 000 | 61 200 | 200 | Fav. |
    | Fixed Overhead | | 99 000 | 100 000 | 1 000 | Fav. |
    | | | $415 780 | $406 000 | $9 780 | Unfav. |

A somewhat different picture now emerges. The overall variance, while still unfavourable, is now seen to be about 60% of the original variance ($9 780 v. $15 780). The variable overhead variance has switched from $1000 unfavourable to $200 favourable. Direct materials and direct labour still show unfavourable variances, albeit smaller than previously. The fixed overhead variance, naturally, has not changed.

## Flexible Budget Formula

Apart from the tabular form of Cost Performance Report presented in Step 3 above, the flexible budget can also be expressed in the form of a flexible budget formula. This enables us to present a range of flexible budgets at various activity levels.

For ABC Company the flexible budget formula is

$$\$100\,000 + \$30 \text{ per unit.}$$

This formula summarises both the fixed and variable cost components for the Production Department, illustrating that $100 000 is the budgeted fixed cost and $30 per unit is the budgeted variable cost of production. Given that actual production was 10 200 units, and substituting into the flexible budget formula, the total flexible budget would be

$$\$100\,000 + \$30(10\,200) = \$406\,000.$$

Thus the overall variance of $9780 Unfavourable can also be derived. While the flexible budget formula does not demonstrate which individual items contributed to the overall variance, the formula can nevertheless be used as a convenient tool for quickly and simply calculating the overall variance during a period.

We can also present detailed flexible budgets at various activity levels if we use the formula concept for each item in the budget. For ABC Company each cost item was simply a variable or a fixed cost. Some of them could have been mixed costs consisting of a fixed and a variable component; this can also be easily handled. Recall that we established the following formula for each item:

| Cost Item | |
|---|---|
| Direct Materials | $200 000/10 000 = $20 per unit |
| Direct Labour | $40 000/10 000 = $4 per unit |
| Variable Overhead | $60 000/10 000 = $6 per unit |
| Fixed Overhead | $100 000 per year |

Using this information we could construct a number of flexible budgets for ABC Company For the year ended 30/6/X1 – say at 9 600, 9 800, 10 000, 10 200 and 10 400 units:

**ABC Company Flexible Budget for 20X1**

| Units | p.u. | 9,600 | 9,800 | 10,000 | 10,200 | 10,400 |
|---|---|---|---|---|---|---|
| Direct materials | $20 | $192,000 | $196,000 | $200,000 | $204,000 | $208,000 |
| Direct labour | $4 | 38,400 | 39,200 | 40,000 | 40,800 | 41,600 |
| Variable overhead | $6 | 57,600 | 58,800 | 60,000 | 61,200 | 62,400 |
| Fixed overhead | | 100,000 | 100,000 | 100,000 | 100,000 | 100,000 |
| Total | | $388,000 | $394,000 | $400,000 | $406,000 | $412,000 |

## *Flexible Budgets and Standard Cost Variances*

An extension to the role of flexible budgets allows us to isolate and calculate efficiency variances. For example, in the Improved Cost Performance Report shown above the variances represent a possible combination of price and efficiency variances. If two flexible budgets are prepared, one in respect of actual inputs consumed (for the output produced) as demonstrated above, and the second in respect of standard inputs allowed (for the output produced), any differences between the figures in the two flexible budgets are measures of efficiency or inefficiency in the consumption of inputs. If the inputs in both flexible budgets are valued at standard cost, we have a measure of standard cost efficiency (or usage) variances. Also, the differences between actual costs (of actual inputs) and the flexible budget in respect of actual inputs are measures of standard cost price variances.

### Illustrative Example 9-2

This is an extension of example 9-1. Suppose that ABC Company's product has the following standard cost specification:

| | | |
|---|---|---|
| Direct Materials | 2 kg @ $10 | $20 |
| Direct Labour | 0.2 DLH @ $20/hr | 4 |
| Variable Overhead | $30/DLH | 6 |
| Fixed Overhead | $40/MH (0.25 MH/unit) | 10 |
| Standard cost per unit | | $40 |

Note that DLH = direct labour hours and MH = machine hours.

The previously illustrated static budget was prepared at standard cost based on a volume of 10 000 units, determined as follows:

| | | |
|---|---|---|
| Direct Materials | 10 000 x 2 kg x $10 | $200 000 |
| Direct Labour | 10 000 x 0.2 DLH x $20 | 40 000 |
| Variable Overhead | 10 000 x 0.2 DLH x $30 | 60 000 |
| Fixed Overhead | 10 000 x 0.25 MH x $40 | 100 000 |
| | | $400 000 |

The overhead allocation rates were derived from two overhead cost pools:

| | | |
|---|---|---|
| Variable Overhead: | $60 000 | Base: 2000 DLH |
| Fixed Overhead: | $100 000 | Base: 2500 MH |

Thus the overhead allocation rates could be calculated:

Variable Overhead rate = $60 000/2000 DLH = $30/DLH
Fixed Overhead rate = $100 000/2500 MH = $40/MH

Material purchase price was $10.50 per kg. Actual direct material issued to production was 20 300 kg, and 2030 direct labour hours were worked for an average $21 per hour.

Required: Calculate material, labour and overhead variances.

## Material Variances

Let us assume that the quantity of direct material purchased was equal to the quantity used, 20 300 kg. For the 10 200 units of product the standard direct material quantity allowed is 10 200 x 2 kg = 20 400 kg.

[The reader should note that the assumption that the quantity of direct material purchased was equal to the quantity used simplifies the calculation of material price and efficiency variances. The spreadsheet example in the appendix to this chapter illustrates the more normal situation where there is a divergence between quantity purchased and quantity used.]

We can analyse the direct material flexible budget variance as follows:

## 9/Flexible Budgets and Standard Cost Variances

|  | MATERIALS VARIANCES |  |
|---|---|---|
| **Actual Cost** | **Flexible Budget** | **Flexible Budget** |
| Actual Inputs x Actual Price | Actual Inputs x Standard Price | Standard Inputs x Standard Price |
| AQ  20 300<br>AP  $10.50<br>$213 150 | AQ  20 300<br>SP  $10.00<br>$203 000 | SQ  20 400<br>SP  $10.00<br>$204 000 |
|  | MPV<br>$10 150 UF | MEV<br>($1000) F |
|  | TOTAL FLEXIBLE BUDGET VARIANCE<br>$9150 UF |  |

The observant reader will note that the above analysis is exactly the same as in Chapter 6 although the term flexible budget was not used. Also, we have used the term material **efficiency** variance (MEV) instead of the term used in Chapter 6, material **usage** variance (MUV). Either term is acceptable but we have adopted the word efficiency here to be consistent with the other efficiency variances.

Being able to break up the variance in this way shows us that, despite the unfavourable flexible budget variance of $9150, the production department manager was actually very efficient in material usage ($1000 favourable) because 100 kg less than the standard quantity allowed were used. On the other hand, the purchasing department have paid $0.50 per kg more than the standard price, and it is this price which is responsible for the net unfavourable variance. It is possible that the purchasing department bought higher grade material than specified in the standard, and this resulted in less wastage than usual, leading to the favourable efficiency variance. Thus we see that the price and efficiency variances may be inter-related, and establishing the causes of the variances may not be as straight forward as it may seem.

## Labour Variances

Similarly the direct labour flexible budget variance of $1830 UF may be analysed. The standard direct labour hours allowed for the production of 10 200 units = 0.2 x 10 200 = 2040:

|  | LABOUR VARIANCES |  |
|---|---|---|
| **Actual Cost** | **Flexible Budget** | **Flexible Budget** |
| Actual Inputs x Actual Price | Actual Inputs x Standard Price | Standard Inputs x Standard Price |
| AH  2 030<br>AP  $21.00<br>$42 630 | AH  2 030<br>SP  $20.00<br>$40 600 | SH  2 040<br>SP  $20.00<br>$40 800 |
|  | LRV<br>$2030 UF | LEV<br>($200) F |
|  | TOTAL FLEXIBLE BUDGET VARIANCE<br>$1830 UF |  |

Again we see that although the total flexible budget variance is unfavourable the production department manager was actually efficient in the use of direct labour, using 10 hours less than standard, leading to a favourable labour efficiency variance (LEV) of 10 hours x $20 = $200. Of course, it may be that if the material were of a higher grade than standard, less time was required to process it.

The major cause of the flexible budget direct labour variance is now seen to be an unfavourable labour rate variance (LRV) of $2030. Clearly the actual rates of pay exceeded standard. This may have been the result of recent increases in award wages, or perhaps higher skilled workers than normal may have been used. The latter could be an alternative or contributing explanation for the favourable labour efficiency variance.

## Variable Overhead Variances

The analysis of the flexible budget variable overhead variance is similar to the analysis of direct labour variances. However, variable overhead costs may consist of a variety of costs such as supplies, energy costs, and repairs. Ideally, multiple cost drivers would be identified to more accurately allocate overhead to products. In this example, since there is only one product, the issue is not critical, and the example uses direct labour hours as an allocation base, simplifying the analysis. If there were multiple products, it would be not uncommon to use multiple drivers and thus the following type of analysis would have to be repeated for different cost pools requiring different allocation bases.

A second difference from direct labour variances is that the term **spending variance** is used instead of price or rate variance. With direct material or labour the variance refers to the price of the single item. For variable overhead the variance may refer to spending on a variety (or basket) of variable overhead items. Furthermore, the spending variance can incorporate changes in the quantity of variable overhead items used per unit of the allocation base (DLH here) as well as changes in prices. Actual variable overhead costs can vary from the flexible budget allowance because (1) different prices (from standard) were paid for resources, or (2) different quantities (from standard usage) of those resources were consumed, or both.

Finally, it should be noted that the flexible budget allowance based on standard inputs allowed is equal to the overhead allocated to Work in Process account.

| VARIABLE OVERHEAD VARIANCES ||||
|---|---|---|
| **Actual Cost** | **Flexible Budget**  Actual Inputs x Standard Price | **Flexible Budget**  Standard Inputs x Standard Price  (Allocated Variable OH) |
|  | AH 2 030  SP $30.00 | SH 2 040  SP $30.00 |
| $61 000 | $60 900 | $61 200 |
|  | VOHSV  $100 U | VOHEV  ($300) F |
| UNDER(OVER) ALLOCATED VARIABLE OVERHEAD  ($200) F ||||

The total flexible budget variance is equal to the under- or over-allocated variable overhead. In this case, it is $200 favourable (over-allocated), and may be broken into the two components, variable overhead spending variance (VOHSV) and variable overhead efficiency variance (VOHEV). The spending variance was $100 unfavourable, indicating that variable overhead spent was $100 more than (flexible) budget allowance. The variable overhead efficiency variance was $300 favourable. The total variable overhead variance is the algebraic sum of the two, $100 UF + $300 F = $200 F. Care is required in interpreting the efficiency variance. It does not mean that the workers were frugal or efficient in the use of variable overhead items such as electricity or indirect materials. It arose because there was less consumption of the underlying cost driver, direct labour hours, than the standard allowed: actual DLH 2030 as against standard of 2040, i.e. 10 DLH favourable x $30 per hour = $300

*9/Flexible Budgets and Standard Cost Variances*

favourable. In other words, they were efficient in the use of the cost driver, which of course should lead to lower overhead cost.

## Fixed Overhead Variances

As we have seen, only the variable costs in a budget can be flexed. When preparing flexible budgets for different volumes, the fixed costs would be the same. Thus there is no point in preparing two flexible budgets for fixed overhead (one for actual inputs and one for standard inputs allowed) because the budgeted fixed overhead would be the same at each level. In contrast to variable overhead, there is no such thing as an efficiency variance for fixed overhead. The difference between actual fixed overhead and budgeted fixed overhead (the flexible budget variance) is the fixed overhead spending variance (FOHSV).

The other fixed overhead variance is equal to the difference between budgeted fixed overhead and the fixed overhead allocated to Work in Process. When predetermined overhead rates are used, if the actual volume is not equal to the denominator volume used to determine the allocation rate, there will be a fixed overhead variance, which is called a **volume variance**, or **production volume variance** or **denominator variance** or **capacity variance**. In example 9-2, the budgeted fixed overhead was $100 000, and was to be allocated to product using standard machine hours as an allocation base. Each unit of product requires 0.25 standard machine hour, and thus the budgeted 10 000 units called for 10 000 x 0.25 = 2500 machine hours. Hence the fixed overhead rate (FOHR) was set at $40 per standard machine hour ($100 000/2500). Now if actual production does not equal budgeted production the fixed overhead allocated will not equal budgeted fixed overhead, leading to a volume variance. If the volume of production is less than budget the volume variance will be unfavourable (under-allocated), and if actual volume exceeds budget the volume variance will be favourable (over-allocated). Since in this example actual production exceeded budgeted production by 200 units we would expect a favourable volume variance equal to 200 units x 0.25 standard hours x $40 FOHR = $2000 favourable. Note that the standard machine hours allowed for 10 200 units @ 0.25 MH/unit = 2550, as shown below:

| FIXED OVERHEAD VARIANCES |||
|---|---|---|
| **Actual Cost** | **Flexible Budget** | **Allocated Fixed O/H** |
|  | Budgeted Fixed Overhead | Standard MHours x FOH Rate |
|  |  | SH  2 550 |
|  |  | FOHR  $40.00 |
| $99 000 | $100 000 | $102 000 |
|  | FOHSV ($1000) F | VOLUME VARIANCE ($2000) F |
| UNDER(OVER) ALLOCATED FIXED OVERHEAD ($3000) F |||

We see that the actual fixed overhead (recorded in the Overhead Control account) was $99 000 while the fixed overhead allocated via the Overhead Allocated account was $102 000. The difference of $3000 (over-allocated) resulted jointly from a favourable spending variance of $1000 (spent less than budget) and a favourable volume variance of $2000 (standard machine hour volume for the output produced exceeded budgeted denominator machine hour volume).

## Accounting Entries for Overhead Variances

The following entries illustrate the closing of the allocated overhead account(s) and overhead control accounts and isolation of the variances, typically at year end. It is assumed that separate overhead accounts are used for variable and fixed overhead.

| | | |
|---|---|---|
| Variable Overhead Allocated | $61 200 | |
| Variable Overhead Spending Variance | $100 | |
|     Variable Overhead Efficiency Variance | | $300 |
|     Variable Overhead Control | | $61 000 |

| | | |
|---|---|---|
| Fixed Overhead Allocated | $102 000 | |
|     Fixed Overhead Spending Variance | | $1 000 |
|     Fixed Overhead Volume Variance | | $2 000 |
|     Fixed Overhead Control | | $99 000 |

If separate variable and fixed overhead accounts are not used the entries would be combined as follows:

| | | |
|---|---|---|
| Overhead Allocated | $163 200 | |
| Variable Overhead Spending Variance | 100 | |
|     Variable Overhead Efficiency Variance | | $300 |
|     Fixed Overhead Spending Variance | | $1 000 |
|     Fixed Overhead Volume Variance | | $2 000 |
|     Overhead Control | | $160 000 |

### *Variance Investigation*

Once standard cost variances have been calculated and highlighted, the next step in feedback control is to decide whether each variance is of sufficient magnitude and significance to investigate its cause. Basically, variances result from either random or non-random occurrences. Standard costs are average costs that should be achieved. People's performance varies from day to day, and hour to hour, so that a certain degree of random variation should be expected. The problem is to identify the limits of what is considered random variation, so that if a variance exceeds these acceptable limits it should be investigated. A second consideration is its materiality. It costs money to investigate variances (an investigator's time, the department manager or foreman's time, down time etc.) and thus some kind of cost/benefit test should be used as well in determining whether to investigate a variance.

## SUMMARY

Planning, part of the control process, involves setting operational targets as a means of achieving overall organisational objectives. The control process also involves the motivation of managers and employees to perform at a sufficiently high level to achieve budget goals, the monitoring of performance to detect deviations from plans, and the implementation of rewards and sanctions for performance outcomes.

Motivation is a complex process. Some individuals have personal control: they are self-motivated by the satisfaction and feelings of competency from a job well done. Others have to be actively motivated by whatever means possible.

Various theories of motivation have been advanced. Content theories of motivation emphasise that individuals are motivated by the expectation of fulfilling various personal needs, and focus on what these needs are. Process theories focus on the way in which needs are satisfied and individuals motivated. Expectancy theory and goal setting theory are two popular process theories.

Having managers participate in setting budgetary goals has been promoted as an administrative means of motivating them to achieve those goals. Although participative budgeting is generally accepted as desirable and sensible, its success has not been unambiguously proven. Indeed, there is some evidence that participation results in the formation of budgetary slack through managers deliberately biasing budget targets downwards to ensure easy achievement.

The social group in which workers participate can influence behaviour through the imposition of unofficial rules and standards, known as group norms, which often restrict performance below levels that otherwise might be achieved.

Organisations usually have a set of formal rules and procedures, known as administrative controls, by which employee behaviour is regulated. An important administrative control is the performance evaluation system which is used to motivate and reward employees and managers. The performance evaluation system is an essential part of the feedback control cycle.

Feedback control involves comparisons of actual results with budget, a consideration of variances between the two, and appropriate corrective action.

Operating results should be compared with flexible budget allowances for the actual output achieved. The use of flexible budgets permits the isolation of standard cost efficiency variances for direct materials, direct labour and variable overhead.

The calculation of standard cost variances focuses attention on undesirable results. It may prompt an investigation to find the causes of the variances in an endeavour to bring future performance back on track, or result in alteration to future plans and the budget if circumstances have changed since the budget was first formulated.

## REFERENCES

P. Brownell, "Participation in Budgeting, Locus of Control and Organizational Effectiveness", *The Accounting Review*, October 1981, 844-860.

P. Brownell, "The Role of Accounting Data in Performance Evaluation, Budgetary Participation and Organizational Effectiveness", *Journal of Accounting Research,* 20, 1, Spring 1982, 12-27.

F. Herzberg, *Work and the Nature of Man*, Staples, 1966.

A. Hopwood, *Accounting and Human Behaviour*, Prentice-Hall, 1974.

E.E. Lawler III, *Motivation in Work Organizations*, Wadsworth, 1973.

T. Libby, "The Influence of Voice and Explanation on Performance in a Participative Budgeting Setting", *Accounting, Organizations and Society*, 24, 2, 1999, 125-137.

E.A. Locke, "Towards a Theory of Task Motivation and Incentives", *Organizational Behavior and Human Performance*, 3, 1968, 157-189.

E.A. Locke, K.N. Shaw, L.M. Saari and G.P. Latham, "Goal Setting and Task Performance: 1969-1980", *Psychological Bulletin*, 90 (1), 1981, 125-152.

E.A. Lowe and R.W. Shaw, "An Analysis of Managerial Biasing: Evidence from a Company's Budgeting Process", *Journal of Management Studies*, 5, 1968, 304-315.

A. Maslow, *Motivation and Personality*, Harper, 1954.

K.A. Merchant and J.F. Manzoni, "The Achievability of Profit Center Budget Targets: A Field Study", *The Accounting Review*, LXIV, 539-558.

J. Ronen and J.L. Livingstone, "An Expectancy Theory Approach to the Motivational Impacts of Budgets", *The Accounting Review*, October 1975, 671-685.

R.C. Stedry, *Budget Control and Cost Behaviour*, Prentice-Hall, 1960.

V.H. Vroom, *Work and Motivation*, Wiley, 1964.

## APPENDIX

### Using a Spreadsheet to Calculate Standard Cost Variances

In Chapter 6 you may have built a spreadsheet model for calculating standard cost variances. Here is another version to show the variances for the illustrative example in this chapter. Assume that the quantity of direct materials purchased was 25 000 kg, that is 4700 kg more than the quantity used. Then the centre flexible budget column (actual inputs x standard price) for direct materials must be broken into two columns, the left for purchases and the right for usage:

### STANDARD COST VARIANCE ANALYSIS

**DATA**

| MATERIALS | |
|---|---|
| AQp | 25,000 |
| AP | $10.50 |
| SP | $10.00 |
| AQu | 20,300 |
| SQ/unit | 2.00 |
| Output | 10,200 |

| LABOUR | |
|---|---|
| AH | 2,030 |
| AR | $21.00 |
| SR | $20.00 |
| SH/unit | 0.20 |
| Output | 10,200 |

| VARIABLE OVERHEAD | |
|---|---|
| Actual | $61,000 |
| OH Rate/hr | $30.00 |
| AH | 2,030 |
| SH/unit | 0.20 |
| Output | 10,200 |

| FIXED OVERHEAD | |
|---|---|
| Actual | $99,000 |
| Budget | $100,000 |
| OH Rate/hr | $40.00 |
| SH/unit | 0.25 |
| Output | 10,200 |

**MODEL**

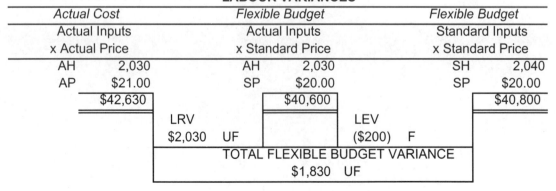

## VARIABLE OVERHEAD VARIANCES

| Actual Cost | Flexible Budget | Flexible Budget |
|---|---|---|
| | Actual Inputs | Standard Inputs |
| | x Standard Price | x Standard Price |
| | | (Allocated Variable OH) |
| | AH   2,030 | SH   2,040 |
| | SP   $30.00 | SP   $30.00 |
| $61,000 | $60,900 | $61,200 |
| | VOHSV | VOHEV |
| | $100 UF | ($300) F |
| | UNDER(OVER) ALLOCATED VARIABLE OVERHEAD | |
| | ($200) F | |

## FIXED OVERHEAD VARIANCES

| Actual Cost | Flexible Budget | Allocated Fixed O/H |
|---|---|---|
| | Budgeted | Standard Hours |
| | Fixed Overhead | x FOH Rate |
| | | SH   2,550 |
| | | FOHR   $40 |
| $99,000 | $100,000 | $102,000 |
| | FOHSV | VOLUME VARIANCE |
| | ($1,000) F | ($2,000) F |
| | UNDER(OVER) ALLOCATED FIXED OVERHEAD | |
| | ($3,000) F | |

Try developing a generalised model to replicate these calculations. The model should be generalised so that it will work for any problem: that is, the calculations should be automated so that once the data are entered the rest is automatic. You can then use this to check your calculations for any problem.

*9/Flexible Budgets and Standard Cost Variances*

## QUESTIONS AND PROBLEMS

9-1  What is meant by the term **personal control**? What is its relevance?

9-2  Explain the difference between **content** and **process** theories of motivation.

9-3  Using (1) expectancy theory, and (2) goal setting theory, predict the likely effects on motivation of assigning a difficult budget target to a manager.

9-4  A group of teachers was assembled to mark student essay answers to an external school examination. The markers were divided into five groups, one group for each of the five questions set. After an initial training session the markers were told that they should mark 16 essays per hour. At lunch on the second day, after 3 hours of marking, the markers discussed their task, agreeing that the target 16 per hour was too difficult, and that they should all aim to mark 13 per hour. All markers adjusted their rate to 13 per hour.

Discuss the control issues which emerge from this example.

9-5  What have flexible budgets to do with feedback control?

9-6  What is the advantage of using a flexible budget rather than a static budget for performance evaluation?

9-7  Can flexible budgets be useful at the beginning of an accounting period as well as at the end? Explain.

9-8  Explain how a variable overhead spending variance differs from a price variance for direct materials or direct labour.

9-9  **Simple flexible budget**
Fremantle Company manufactures fibreglass masts for 12 metre yachts. Last year the company produced 100 masts for total production costs of $5 000 000. Of these costs, $3 000 000 were fixed costs.

Assuming the same cost structure, what is the expected cost of producing 120 masts this year?

9-10  **Flexible overhead budget**
The accountant for Payne Manor, a local private hospital, has been studying the cost of electricity. The hospital uses 20 kilowatt hours of electricity per patient-day at a cost of $0.15 per kilowatt hour. There is also a fixed service availability charge of $0.50 per day.

*Required:*
(a) Construct a flexible budget formula for the daily costs of electricity at the hospital.
(b) If the hospital has an average patient load of 30 patients per day, what would be the average daily cost of electricity?
(c) Prepare a columnar flexible budget for electricity costs for a quarter (assume 90 days) for 2500, 2700 and 2900 patient days. List variable and fixed electricity costs separately.

9-11  **Flexible budget and performance report**
Rolfe Company Pty Ltd prepares a comprehensive budget for planning purposes and uses a flexible budget to help control operating costs.

At the end of 20X2 management received the following condensed statement of financial performance for the year:

## 9/Flexible Budgets and Standard Cost Variances

| Statement of Financial Performance - 20X2 | | | |
|---|---:|---:|---:|
| Sales | | | $10,000,000 |
| Less Cost of Goods Sold: | | | |
| Direct materials | | $2,000,000 | |
| Direct labour | | 1,500,000 | |
| Variable factory overhead | | 600,000 | |
| Fixed factory overhead | | 1,000,000 | 5,100,000 |
| Gross Profit | | | 4,900,000 |
| Less Operating Expenses: | | | |
| Selling and Distribution: | | | |
|   Variable | $600,000 | | |
|   Fixed | 900,000 | 1,500,000 | |
| Administrative: | | | |
|   Variable | 800,000 | | |
|   Fixed | 1,200,000 | 2,000,000 | 3,500,000 |
| Net Operating Profit | | | $1,400,000 |

The budget committee decided on the following changes for the coming year, 20X3:
- A 20% sales volume increase with no price changes
- Fixed administrative expenses to increase by $100 000

At the end of 20X3 the actual results were as follows:

| | |
|---|---:|
| Sales | $11 500 000 |
| Direct materials | 2 350 000 |
| Direct labour | 1 750 000 |
| Variable factory overhead | 675 000 |
| Fixed factory overhead | 1 025 000 |
| Variable sell & distn expenses | 690 000 |
| Fixed sell & distn expenses | 910 000 |
| Variable administrative expenses | 950 000 |
| Fixed administrative expenses | 1 350 000 |

*Required:*
(a) Present the comprehensive planning budget for 20X3.
(b) Prepare a budget report comparing actual and budgeted costs for 20X3.

**9-12 Static and flexible budgets**

Department A, a production cost centre of Vacuum Enterprises, experiences the following factory overhead expenses:

| | |
|---|---|
| Indirect labour: | $4 per hour. For each hour of direct labour there is ½ hour of indirect labour required. |
| Light and power: | 5 cents per kilowatt hour. The usage is almost directly variable with machine hours at 100 kilowatt hours per machine hour. |
| Depreciation Machinery: | Straight-line, $10 000 per annum. |
| Maintenance: | $10 000 per year plus $2 per machine hour. |

At the beginning of 20X7 it was anticipated that the department would work at normal capacity producing 10 000 units of output during the year. Standards of performance have been set, one unit of product requiring 1 direct labour hour and ½ machine hour in Department A.

*Required:*
(a) Prepare a factory overhead budget for Department A at the anticipated output level of 10 000 units.
(b) Select a single allocation base and develop fixed and variable predetermined overhead allocation rates for Department A. Briefly justify your choice of allocation base.
(c) During 20X7 the following results were noted:

| | |
|---|---|
| Production | 9900 units |
| Direct labour hours | 9800 |
| Machine hours | 4980 |
| Factory overhead | |
| - Fixed | $19 000 |
| - Variable | $52 000 |

Calculate appropriate overhead variances explaining which ones are controllable at the departmental level.

(d) In the light of your answers to parts (a) and (b) comment on the validity of the variances calculated in part (c).

**9-13 Overhead ledger accounts, flexible budget, overhead variances**

Operations in the Base Metal Stamping Company are relatively simple. A job order cost system is employed. There is no work in process at the end of the day. A single plant-wide rate is used for allocating factory overhead costs. The rate is computed each quarter using anticipated production levels for the next quarter. Estimated factory overhead costs at various production levels have been prepared as follows:

| Production Level | Estimated Factory Overhead Cost |
|---|---|
| 600 000 units | $840 000 |
| 900 000 units | $1 035 000 |
| 1 200 000 units | $1 230 000 |
| 1 500 000 units | $1 425 000 |
| 1 800 000 units | $1 620 000 |

It is anticipated that production for March Quarter 20X9 would be 900 000 units. Actually 870 000 units were produced and factory overhead costs incurred were $990 000. At the end of the quarter 120 000 units remained in the Finished Goods inventory, which is valued on a FIFO basis.

*Required:*
(a) Show the relevant overhead ledger accounts as they would appear at the end of March Quarter before closing off any variances, and calculate the total overhead variance for the quarter.
(b) Calculate the estimated factory overhead cost that would have been expected for the production level of 870 000 units.
(c) Assuming that variances are closed off to Profit and Loss at the end of each quarter, calculate
(i) the amount of factory overhead allocated in arriving at Net Profit for the quarter;
(ii) the amount of factory overhead carried on the Balance Sheet at the end of the quarter;
(iii) any overhead variances that you can, and explain which ones that you cannot calculate and why.

## 9-14 Calculating overhead variances

Standard Company, which produces a single product, has developed budgeted overhead rates for 20X0, based on a denominator capacity level of 180 000 standard direct labour hours, as follows:

Cost per unit:
- Variable  2 hours @ $3 = $6
- Fixed     2 hours @ $5 = $10
- Total                    $16

The following data relate to 20X0:

80 000 units were produced during the year.
165 000 direct labour hours were worked for a cost of $644 000.

Actual overhead was $1 378 000, $518 000 variable and $860 000 fixed.

*Required:*

Calculate for 20X0 the
(a) variable overhead spending variance;
(b) variable overhead efficiency variance;
(c) fixed overhead spending variance;
(d) fixed overhead production volume variance.

## 9-15 Standard costs, flexible budget, overhead volume variance (absorption and variable costing)

Alpha Beta Company produces widgets. Based on a denominator level of activity of 100 000 direct labour hours, a standard prime cost of $800 000 and a standard conversion cost of $1 600 000 should be incurred per annum.

Each widget requires 1 kg of a secret ingredient, requires a standard direct labour time of 30 minutes at the standard rate of $4 per direct labour hour, and is charged $2 for fixed overhead.

This year 230 000 widgets were produced requiring 100 000 direct labour hours. Costs incurred in the manufacturing process were:

| Direct materials | $483 000 |
| Direct labour | 450 000 |
| Fixed overhead | 395 000 |
| Variable overhead | 810 000 |

*Required:*
(a) What is the standard material, labour and overhead cost per widget? What is the total standard cost per unit?
(b) Draft a flexible budget for the year, and compare actual costs with budget, calculating and labelling variances (F or UF). Group all fixed costs together, and all variable costs, separately subtotalled.
(c) Calculate the production volume variance. What type of product costing system gives rise to a production volume variance? What characteristics of this system cause such a variance?
(d) Determine the amount of under- or over-allocated overhead for the year under:
   (i) standard absorption costing, and
   (ii) standard variable (direct) costing.
   Explain the reason for the difference under the two systems.
(e) Management had recently engaged a firm of management consultants to determine the current standard costs because they believed that the old standards were incorrect and required revision. The basis for this belief was that actual costs had never coincided with standard costs. Discuss the validity of management's belief.

## 9/Flexible Budgets and Standard Cost Variances

**9-16** **Standard process costing, variances and journal entries (comprehensive)**

The Confused Manufacturing Company manufactures one standard product, Thingamebobs in one manufacturing process. A standard cost system is employed and all inventories are carried at standard cost values.

The standard cost sheet for one Thingamebob includes the following data:

---
*Direct Material*
  2 kg of X        @ $0.40 per kg
  3 kg of Y        @ $1.40 per kg

*Direct Labour*
  2 hours          @ $3.50 per hour

*Factory Overhead*
  Is allocated at a standard rate per direct labour hour, the rate being determined annually on the basis of the factory overhead budget at the normal level of capacity, which is 40 000 direct labour hours per month.

---

The factory overhead budget has been determined at three levels of activity as follows:

| **Monthly Factory Overhead Budget 20X5/20X6** | | | |
|---|---|---|---|
| Direct labour hours | 30,000 | 40,000 | 50,000 |
| Indirect labour | $37,500 | $50,000 | $62,500 |
| Power | 4,000 | 5,000 | 6,000 |
| Supplies | 3,000 | 4,000 | 5,000 |
| Repairs and Maintenance | 5,000 | 6,000 | 7,000 |
| Factory rent | 5,000 | 5,000 | 5,000 |
| Depreciation – Plant and Equipment | 10,000 | 10,000 | 10,000 |
| Supervision | 24,000 | 24,000 | 24,000 |
| | $88,500 | $104,000 | $119,500 |

Production details for the month of May, 20X6 were as follows:
  Finished units        20 750

At the beginning of the month 4000 units were in process, 100% complete as to both materials and 50% complete as to conversion.

At the end of the month 10 000 units were in process, 100% complete as to material X, 50% complete as to material Y and 25% complete as to conversion.

Details of costs, purchases and usages for May were:

| Materials | Purchases | 50 000 kg of X @ $0.38 |
|---|---|---|
| | | 70 000 kg of Y @ $1.45 |
| | Usage | 54 000 kg of X |
| | | 64 500 kg of Y |
| Direct Labour | | 47 500 hours for $161 250 |
| Overhead incurred | Fixed | $39 000 |
| | Variable | 71 500 |
| | | $110 500 |

*Required:*
(a) What is the standard cost of one Thingamebob?
(b) Calculate and prepare journal entries for all standard cost variances for the month of May, assuming that the overhead accounts are closed off at the end of the month.

**9-17 Standard cost variances for materials, labour and overhead**

Degreaso Ltd manufactures a commercial solvent that is used for industrial maintenance. The solvent is sold by the drum, and the standard cost per drum is as follows:

| | | |
|---|---|---|
| **Materials** | | |
| 20 litres of raw material | | $20 |
| 1 empty drum | | 1 |
| Total materials | | $21 |
| **Direct Labour** | | |
| 1 hour | | 7 |
| *Standard Prime Cost* | | $28 |
| **Factory Overhead** | | |
| Allocated at $10 per DLH | | 10 |
| *Total standard cost per drum* | | $38 |

The annual budget for factory overhead expenses had been set at two levels of operations: normal capacity of 144 000 drums per annum and 25% of normal capacity, 36 000 drums. Details are as follows:

| Annual Factory Overhead Budget | | |
|---|---|---|
| Output | 144 000 drums | 36 000 drums |
| *Expenses:* | | |
| Depreciation of factory building & machinery | $510 000 | $510 000 |
| Supervision and indirect labour | 786 000 | 246 000 |
| Other factory overhead | 144 000 | 36 000 |
| Total | $1 440 000 | $792 000 |

Various cost studies have revealed that all cost functions are linear over the range indicated in the flexible budget and that budgeted fixed costs do not vary from month to month.

During June, 20X0 the company produced and sold 6000 drums, which is 50% of monthly normal capacity. Costs incurred during June were:

| | | |
|---|---|---|
| Raw materials: | | |
| 120 000 litres were purchased for $115 000 | | |
| 140 000 litres were used. | | |
| 8500 drums were purchased for $8500 | | |
| 6000 drums were used. | | |
| Direct labour: | | |
| 6500 hours were worked at a cost of $47 000 | | |
| Factory overhead: | | |
| Depreciation of building and machinery | | $43 000 |
| Supervision and indirect labour - fixed | | 4 000 |
|                                             - variable | | 32 000 |
| Other factory overhead | | 7 650 |
| Total factory overhead | | $86 650 |

*Required:*

(a) Compute the following variances for the month of June, 20X0, indicating whether each is favourable or unfavourable:
    (i) Materials price variance (at purchase)
    (ii) Materials usage variance
    (iii) Labour rate variance
    (iv) Labour efficiency variance
    (v) Factory overhead variances showing fixed and variable components (only for total overhead, not each item separately).

(b) Briefly explain why the volume (denominator) variance is of such magnitude.

9-18 **Standard process costing and standard cost variances**

Chikka Pharmaceuticals Ltd processes a single-compound product known as Nolux and uses a standard process costing accounting system. The production process requires preparation and blending of two materials in large batches, with a variation from the standard mixture sometimes necessary to maintain quality. Chikka's cost accountant became ill at the end of May and you were engaged to determine standard costs of May production and to explain any differences between actual and standard costs for the month. The following information is available for the blending department:

(i) The standard cost sheet for a 250 kg batch shows the following standard costs:

|  | Quantity | Rate | Cost |  |
|---|---|---|---|---|
| *Materials:* |  |  |  |  |
| Mucilloid | 125 kg | $0.28 | $35 |  |
| Dextrose | 125 kg | 0.20 | 25 | $60 |
|  | 250 kg |  |  |  |
| *Labour:* |  |  |  |  |
| Preparation and blending | 5 hr | 6.00 |  | 30 |
| *Overhead:* |  |  |  |  |
| Variable | 5 hr | 2.00 | 10 |  |
| Fixed | 5 hr | 0.60 | 3 | 13 |
| Total standard cost per 250 kg batch |  |  |  | $103 |

(ii) During May 410 batches of 250 kilograms each of the finished compound were transferred to the packaging department.

(iii) All materials and conversion costs are added uniformly throughout the production process in the blending department. Opening work in process at 1 May consisted of 16 batches 75% complete, while closing work in process at 31 May consisted of 36 batches estimated to be 50% complete. Work-in-process inventories are carried in the accounts at standard cost.

(iv) During the month of May the following materials were purchased and put into production:

|  | kg | Price/kg | Total Cost |
|---|---|---|---|
| Mucilloid | 57 200 | $0.34 | $19 448 |
| Dextrose | 52 800 | 0.22 | 11 616 |
|  | 110 000 |  | $31 064 |

(v) Wages paid for 2106 hours of direct labour at $6.50 per hour totalled $13 689.

(vi) Actual overhead costs for the month, $5519.

(vii) The standards were established for a normal production volume of 100 000 kilograms (400 batches) of Nolux per month. At this level of production, fixed factory overhead was budgeted at $1200 per month and variable factory overhead was budgeted at the rate of $2 per direct labour hour.

*Required:*
(a) Prepare a schedule presenting the computation for the blending department of:
 (1) May production in both batches and kilograms
 (2) The standard cost of May production itemised by components of materials, labour and overhead.
(b) Prepare schedules computing the differences between actual and standard costs and analysing the differences as:
 (1) Material price and usage variances
 (2) Labour rate and efficiency variances
 (3) Overhead spending, efficiency and volume variances

## 9/Flexible Budgets and Standard Cost Variances

**9-19 Standard process costing and calculation of variances**

Kingsford Company manufactures a single product, Bonzo. The standard cost specification sheet shows the following standards for one unit of Bonzo:

| | |
|---|---|
| 5 kg of material X @ $8/kg | $40 |
| 2 hr direct labour @ $12/hr | 24 |
| Overhead: Fixed $4/DLH | 8 |
| Variable $2/DLH | 4 |
| Standard cost for 1 unit Bonzo | $76 |

Material X is added at the commencement of the manufacturing process, while conversion costs are incurred uniformly throughout the process.

The fixed overhead allocation rate is based on normal capacity of 240 000 direct labour hours per annum. Fixed overhead and production are expected to be spread evenly throughout the year.

Work in process on 1 June, 20X2 consisted of 900 units of Bonzo, two-thirds complete. During June 9900 units were completed. Work in process at 30 June comprised 1000 units 80% complete. There was no spoilage.

Actual costs incurred in June were:

| |
|---|
| 60 000 kg of material X were purchased @ $8.20 per kg. |
| 51 000 kg of material X were used. |
| 19 800 direct labour hours were worked at an average wage rate of $12.40 per hour. |
| Actual overhead incurred: Fixed $84 000 |
| Variable $38 000. |

*Required:*
(a) Calculate the equivalent units of Bonzo produced in June.
(b) Using your calculations in (a) and the data provided, calculate any variances which might be useful to management, indicating whether they are favourable or unfavourable.

**9-20 Accounting performance reports: flexible budgets, variances, journal entries**

Ms Hopwood, CPA, is the Managing Director of Greenhorn Limited. She places a high reliance on accounting measures in performance evaluation. Consequently she was concerned that the annual financial reports would show that the Kensington Division was not 'living within its budget'. Ms Hopwood's fears were momentarily allayed when Bruce, the divisional manager of Kensington, marched triumphantly into her office to report that division costs were lower than the original budget of $32 400. Experience, however, told Ms Hopwood that something was amiss in Bruce's analysis, so she went to gather further information from Sheila, Greenhorn's Financial Controller.

Sheila revealed the following information about the budgetary process in Kensington Division in 20X3:

(i) At present Kensington Division uses standard absorption costing and flexible budgeting.
(ii) The budget was drafted for an output of 600 units given a denominator activity level of 1800 standard direct labour hours.
(iii) Each unit of product requires a standard quantity of 3 kg of raw material at a standard cost of $2 per kg.
(iv) Direct labour was budgeted at $4 per hour.
(v) Indirect labour charges amounted to a standard $7.50 per unit (all indirect labour varies with direct labour hours worked).
(vi) Heat and lighting were budgeted at $800 per annum and factory administration costs at $8400 per annum, both independent of activity level.
(vii) Although she had unfortunately lost some of the pages from her budget document, she knew that the total budgeted variable costs summed to $18 000 and the total budgeted fixed costs came to $14 400. The only figures she could not find were those for depreciation (classified as a fixed factory overhead expense) and factory supplies (classified as a variable overhead expense).

Sheila had not yet received the final draft of the reports for Kensington Division but she did have the following information for 20X3:

(i)   500 units were produced requiring 1600 direct labour hours.
(ii)  There was no inventory of direct materials on hand at the beginning of 20X3. All purchases of direct materials in 20X3 were made at $1.80 per kg and the standard quantity of direct materials was issued from the stores.
(iii) Indirect labour charges averaged $2.50 per direct labour hour.
(iv)  Direct labour was paid $4.25 per hour.
(v)   Factory supplies cost $2500.
(vi)  Heat and lighting exceeded the original budget by 6.25%.
(vii) There was no depreciation budget variance.
(viii) Factory administration costs amounted to $8500.

*Required:*

As Ms Hopwood's assistant you are required to:
(a) draft the original budget for 600 units. Include sub-totals for total variable costs and total fixed costs.
(b) draft a performance report showing flexible budget (at standard) for the volume level of 20X3, actual results and variances. Show subtotals for variable costs and fixed costs. What is the total budget variance?
(c) Calculate the following variances under standard absorption costing:
   (i) materials price variance (calculated on issue);
   (ii) labour efficiency variance;
   (iii) variable overhead efficiency variance; and
   (iv) fixed overhead volume variance.
(d) Prepare journal entries to allocate overhead costs on the basis of direct labour hours under:
   (i) standard absorption costing, and
   (ii) standard variable costing.
(e) Determine the amount of under- or over-allocated overhead using:
   (i) normal absorption costing;
   (ii) standard absorption costing; and
   (iii) standard variable costing.
(f) Comment on the financial performance of Kensington Division in the light of Bruce's statement and the above analysis.

**9-21  Accounting performance evaluation**

Union Manufacturing Company produces two sizes of frypans, large and small, in its Press Department. The small frypan can be pressed on either Machine A or Machine B. It takes 3 standard machine minutes to press the small frypan on either machine. The large frypan can only be pressed on Machine B, taking 3 standard machine minutes. Only frypans are pressed on these two machines.

Once pressed, frypans are transferred to the Packaging Department where the handles are attached and the frypans packed for delivery to customers.

The following monthly budget information is available for Machine A and Machine B. Machine costs are assumed to vary directly with machine hours worked, even though maintenance costs are semi-variable.

| Budgeted Conversion Costs | | |
|---|---|---|
| | Machine A | Machine B |
| Number of Frypans | | |
| - small | 2000 | |
| - large | | 2000 |
| Standard Machine Hours | 100 | 100 |
| | $ | $ |
| Labour (100 hours @ $16/hr) | 1600 | 1600 |
| Electricity | 200 | 300 |
| Maintenance | 300 | 400 |
| Oil | 100 | 200 |
| Other | 200 | 300 |
| Total | $2400 | $2800 |
| Average Conversion Cost per Standard Machine Hour | $24.00 | $28.00 |

The labour rate of $16 per hour is based on payments to fully qualified machine operators. Frequently apprentices are used to operate these machines.

The standard product costs of frypans are as follows:

| Standard Cost per Frypan | | |
|---|---|---|
| | Small Frypans | Large Frypans |
| Material | $1.00 | $1.60 |
| Conversion Cost | 1.20 | 1.40 |
| Total | 2.20 | 3.00 |

During the month of April, 2000 small frypans and 2200 large frypans were produced. Owing to a machine breakdown, however, only 1000 small frypans were produced on Machine A, the balance being produced on Machine B. The press operator on Machine A was transferred to another department as soon as the Maintenance Supervisor had inspected Machine A and determined that it would require two to three weeks to be repaired. The costs incurred and machine hours worked were as follows:

| | Machine A | Machine B |
|---|---|---|
| | $ | $ |
| Labour | 800 | 2300 |
| Electricity | 120 | 450 |
| Maintenance | 750 | 600 |
| Oil | 60 | 300 |
| Other | 130 | 450 |
| Actual Machine Hours | 55 | 155 |

Materials were issued to the Press Department at a standard cost for small frypans of $2000 and for large frypans of $4000. Some of the material issued for the large frypans was found to be defective.

There was no opening or closing work in process.

Frypans are transferred to the Packaging Department at the standard product cost rates of $2.20 for small frypans and $3.00 for large frypans.

## 9/Flexible Budgets and Standard Cost Variances

*Required:*
(a) Calculate the material usage variance incurred in April for each product.
(b) Labour time sheets showed a total of 210 hours worked, 55 on Machine A and 155 on Machine B. Calculate the labour rate variances, by machine, for April.
(c) Calculate the cost of frypans transferred to the Packaging Department.
(d) Prepare a report to evaluate the performance of operating the two machines in the Press Department for April. The report should contain a comparison of actual costs with flexible budget costs, for each machine. Base flexible budget costs on the actual machine hours worked. For each machine include a column showing the variances for the month.
(e) Calculate the standard machine hours allowed and the machine efficiency variances for each machine during April.
(f) Calculate the difference in budgeted costs of producing the 1000 small frypans on Machine B rather than on Machine A.
(g) As the Accountant of Union Manufacturing Company analyse the performance of the Press Department for April and summarise your conclusions in a report to the Production Plant Manager. This report should include a discussion of material usage variances, labour and maintenance costs, the efficiency of operating the two machines and the impact of machine breakdowns.

**9-22 Accounting performance reports and flexible budgets**

Bolton Pty Ltd is a medium-sized manufacturing company involved in the production and distribution of motor vehicle accessories. In order to take advantage of modern data processing techniques management has set up a computing department (EDP Services) to provide both accounting and other information services to the operating divisions.

Although activity is fairly constant throughout the year there are occasional peaks of activity owing to either problems within the department (for example, software or hardware problems) or 'special' assignments submitted to the operating divisions.

The manager of EDP Services is responsible for the efficient running of his department and his performance is gauged on a monthly basis by comparing actual results against the monthly budget. While not responsible for capital expenditure decisions, the manager is usually consulted on such matters by top management.

The budget for EDP Services is prepared on the basis of 250 (8 hour) working days per annum. The computer is normally run for 8 hours each working day. The main costs of the department are related to labour. The department has the following staff:

| | |
|---|---|
| 3 Assistants | $25 000 p.a. each |
| 1 Programmer | $35 000 p.a. |
| 1 Manager | $50 000 p.a. |

These annual costs include the base salary plus labour on-costs such as workers' compensation insurance premiums and employer superannuation contributions.

The static budget for September, 20X8 is shown below:

## 9/Flexible Budgets and Standard Cost Variances

| EDP Services - Operating Budget for September, 20X8 |||
|---|---:|---:|
| Activity level budgeted - 22 days, 176 operating hours |||
| *Labour costs:* | | |
| Assistants | $6600 | |
| Programmer | 3080 | |
| Manager | 4400 | $14 080 |
| *Operating costs:* | | |
| Power ($4/hour of operation) | 704 | |
| Computer Stationery ($10/hour of operation) | 1760 | |
| Maintenance ($2000/month) | 2000 | |
| Depreciation ($8000/month) | 8000 | |
| Administration costs* | 1000 | 13 464 |
| | | $27 544 |

\* The Head Office allocates administration costs to divisions and service departments. The budgeted allocation to EDP Services for the year is 5% of the budgeted Head Office costs of $240 000, and is apportioned equally to each month.

Results for September 20X8 were as follows:

1. During the period some data files were lost and had to be recreated. To clear the backlog it was necessary for the 3 assistants to work a total of 24 hours overtime and run the computer for an extra 8-hour shift. The assistants were paid time and one-half for these overtime hours.
2. In addition to her normal hours, the programmer worked on two Saturdays (8 hours each day) to complete a special, urgent project for the Corporate Planning Office (the project was submitted during the month). The programmer was paid double time for Saturday work. This extra work did not involve the operation of the computer facilities.
3. Labour rates have not changed from budget during the month.
4. Other costs incurred or charged during September 20X8 were:

|  |  |
|---|---|
| Power | $700 |
| Stationery | $2470 |
| Maintenance | $2800 |
| Depreciation | $8000 |
| Administration (5% of actual Head Office costs) | $1400 |

A performance report for the manager has been prepared according to company policy. The manager's superiors have expressed some concern at what appear to be poor results for the period.

*Required:*
(a) Prepare the performance report for EDP Services for September 20X8 on the basis currently being used by Bolton Pty Ltd.
(b) Comment on the weaknesses of this report as a basis for evaluating the performance of the manager of EDP Services.
(c) In the light of your comments in (b) prepare a performance report based on a comparison of the actual results against the flexible budget for September 20X8. Explain any assumptions you make and the basis for your cost classifications.
(d) As a member of the Head Office accounting staff you have been requested to analyse the performance of the manager of EDP Services. Management also is considering making the EDP Services Department a profit centre whereby the department will charge users for work done, and the manager will be evaluated in terms of net profits. Management believes this will result in greater efficiency. They wish you to evaluate this proposal as well. Summarise your conclusions and recommendations in a brief report to management.

## 9/Flexible Budgets and Standard Cost Variances

**9-23 Comprehensive review problem: activity based costing, budgeting, variances**

Modern Manufacturing Company Ltd produces and sells two products, $P_1$ and $P_2$, which sell for $30 and $35 respectively. Last year's profit and loss statement was as follows:

| Profit and Loss Statement for Y/E 31 December, 20X3 | | | |
|---|---|---|---|
| | $P_1$ | $P_2$ | Total |
| Sales (100 000, 20 000) | 3 000 000 | 700 000 | 3 700 000 |
| Less Standard Cost of Goods Sold | 1 700 000 | 440 000 | 2 140 000 |
| Gross Margin | 1 300 000 | 260 000 | 1 560 000 |
| Less Selling and Administration Expenses: | | | |
|     Fixed | | | 100 000 |
|     Variable (5% of Sales) | | | 185 000 |
| Net Profit | | | 1 275 000 |

Modern operates a standard cost system. The standard cost of each product, based on the normal volume of 100 000 units of $P_1$ and 20 000 units of $P_2$, was determined as follows:

| Standard cost of products | $P_1$ | $P_2$ |
|---|---|---|
| | $ | $ |
| Direct materials | 10.00 | 8.00 |
| Direct labour (@$20/DLH) | 5.00 | 10.00 |
| Overhead (@ $8/DLH)* | 2.00 | 4.00 |
| Total cost per unit | 17.00 | 22.00 |

\* The predetermined overhead rate of $8 per direct labour hour was calculated at the standard level of activity of 35 000 direct labour hours for the normal production volume, based on the following budgeted overhead costs:

| | |
|---|---|
| Materials handling | $25 000 |
| Setup labour | 80 000 |
| Depreciation Plant (Fixed) | 90 000 |
| Electricity (Variable) | 35 000 |
| Supervision (Fixed) | 50 000 |
| Total | $280 000 |

Modern has introduced a just-in-time purchasing system for raw materials components, and has run down finished goods inventories at 31 December, 20X3, to zero. From 1 January 20X4 Modern plans to introduce an activity based costing system for regular product costing. Of the overhead costs, Depreciation, Electricity and Supervision are believed to be basically volume-related and will, for the present, continue to be allocated on the basis of standard direct labour hours. The other two items are activity-related. Materials handling is believed to be driven by the number of receipts of material components; a new shipment of each component for each product is received at the commencement of each production run. Setup labour is driven by the number of production setups; each product requires the same resources for each setup. The following data are relevant:

| | $P_1$ | $P_2$ |
|---|---|---|
| Annual production | 100 000 units in 5 runs | 20 000 units in 10 runs |
| Number of material components | 4 per unit | 10 per unit |

Modern requires a budget for the year ended 31 December, 20X4. Sales (units and dollars) are expected to be the same as for the previous year. Production is expected to be at the standard normal volume. All costs will be unchanged except for Materials Handling $30 000 and Setup Labour $90 000 (both increases).

*Required:*

For the year ended 31 December, 20X4, answer the following, showing all calculations:
(a) (i) In respect of the volume-related overheads, calculate the predetermined overhead recovery rate, and then the budgeted volume-related overhead per unit for each product.
(ii) Calculate the budgeted activity-related overhead charge per unit for each product.
(iii) Calculate the total standard cost per unit for each product.
(b) Assuming that the sales of both product will be evenly distributed throughout the year, prepare a production budget (in units) for each product, by quarters. Assume also, that:
(i) there are no inventories of either product at 1/1/X4.
(ii) a new production run is only begun for either product when it is necessary to satisfy sales demand.
(iii) any production runs begun during a quarter are finished in the same quarter.
(iv) the intention is to finish each quarter with no, or minimum finished goods inventories. Because of assumptions (ii) and (iii) there will necessarily be some inventories when production run sizes do not match sales demand.
(c) Prepare a budgeted profit and loss statement for the year, with a supporting schedule showing the budgeted cost of goods manufactured by product for each quarter. The supporting schedule should also show the budgeted cost of goods sold by product for each quarter.
(d) If direct (variable) costing were used, what would you expect the budgeted annual net profit to be? Explain your answer.
(e) Suppose that at 31 December, 20X4 it was observed that actual production was equal to budget, but that the number of direct labour hours worked were 36 000, and that the actual volume-related overhead costs were as follows:

| | |
|---|---|
| Depreciation Plant | $90 000 |
| Electricity | 35 500 |
| Supervision | 52 000 |

Calculate overhead spending, efficiency and production volume variances, giving possible explanations for each.

# Chapter 10

# Responsibility Accounting and Accounting Controls

In Chapters 8 and 9 we discussed the idea that organisational plans are co-ordinated in the comprehensive budget in which operational targets are set as a means of achieving the overall objectives of the organisation. It was noted that feedback control involves comparisons of actual financial results with budget plans, to highlight variances. These comparisons require the use of flexible budgets to adjust budget plans when the actual level of operations varies from that originally planned. In this chapter we are concerned with the focus of such comparisons - the managers in charge of responsibility centres - and what should be shown in the performance reports.

## ORGANISATION STRUCTURE

To attain the operational goals and targets expressed in the budget, an organisation must co-ordinate the activities of all the employees, from the top executive down to the lowest supervised worker. This co-ordination is achieved by managers who have been appointed to control the various activities in centres (or departments) within the organisation. These managers are assigned the authority and responsibility for making the decisions necessary to co-ordinate the human, physical and financial resources under their control, in order to achieve budget targets. The sphere of activity assigned to a manager is known as a **responsibility centre**. Budget targets (operational sub-goals) are set for each responsibility centre, and each manager is held accountable for controlling resources and achieving budget targets.

The term **organisation structure** is used to describe the arrangement of lines of responsibility and to depict the decision making hierarchy within an organisation. Different organisation structures reflect different responsibility linkages and different ways of carving up the management function. Some firms may organise primarily by business function: Production, Marketing, Personnel, Accounting, etc. Others may organise by product lines, Product A, Product B, Product C, etc., in which case the manager of an individual division (eg., Product A) would have decision making authority with regard to all the functions within that division - production, marketing, and so forth.

## RESPONSIBILITY ACCOUNTING

No matter how the organisation is structured, the basic principle is that top managers subdivide activities under their control into smaller areas of responsibility, and appoint managers to control these responsibility centres. For example, a production manager might subdivide production activities into Production Planning, Inspection, Workshop, Storekeeper and Purchasing. In turn, the activities of each of these responsibility centres may be further subdivided. For example, the Workshop activities might be subdivided into Machining, Welding and Assembly with appropriate managers. The organisation structure that results from these subdivisions tends to form a pyramid. At the base are subordinate workers, supervised by lower level managers. These lower level managers report to superiors (middle level managers) who in turn report to their superiors (top management).

Each manager of a responsibility centre is held accountable for controlling the activities within his centre. Higher level managers have broader responsibilities than lower level managers, and at the top, the managing director is ultimately responsible for the overall performance of the organisation. Managerial performance in each responsibility centre may be measured by comparing the dollar results of actions with financial plans expressed in the budget. This system of performance evaluation is called a **responsibility accounting system** which is a form of administrative control.

## Responsibility Centres

The type of financial performance measures used to evaluate responsibility centre managers depends upon the type of responsibility centre. A common classification of responsibility centre types is concerned with the factors which are controllable by the manager:

**Cost centre** in which the manager is said to be able to control costs, and is held responsible for costs only (eg. a production centre).

**Revenue centre** in which the manager is said to be able to control revenues, and is held responsible for revenues only (eg. a sales centre).

**Profit centre** in which the manager is said to be able to control costs and revenues and thus profits, and is held responsible for profits earned.

**Investment centre** in which the manager is said to be able to control investments in capital assets as well as profits, and is held responsible for both.

## Controllable Performance

In a responsibility accounting system the over-riding principle is that managers should be held responsible for the revenues which they generate and the cost of resources whose consumption they can control. As Ferrara (1964) writes in respect of costs:

> Implicit in the concepts of responsibility accounting and cost control is the idea that it is appropriate to charge to an area of responsibility only those costs which are subject to the control of the person in charge of each area of responsibility. The costs which are not controllable by one individual or group are always controllable by another individual or group. There is no place in the framework of responsibility accounting for the idea of a noncontrollable cost. All costs are controllable at some point in time by some person or group.

To be controllable, a cost should be primarily subject to the influence of a particular manager of a responsibility centre over a given time span. Despite Ferrara's claims, in practice controllability may be difficult to isolate because of:

(1) **Divided Responsibility**: There may be divided responsibility for the incurrence of some costs. For example, the costs incurred by a repairs and maintenance centre depend on decisions by the manager of that centre as well as the amount of service demanded by other responsibility centre managers (eg., a production supervisor). In general, there tend to be interdependencies between organisational units, and this makes it somewhat difficult to isolate an individual manager's performance.

(2) **Time Span**: Performance reports typically focus on short periods of a year or less, but a current manager may have inherited longer term cost contracts entered into by a predecessor. Thus the current manager really has limited control over those previously contracted costs, even though they are identified as falling within the control of that centre's manager.

Despite the inherent problems, a responsibility accounting system requires assignment of controllable costs and revenues to centres. A solution in practice is that a performance report for a responsibility centre should distinguish between the centre and the manager. Managers should be evaluated in terms of the financial results that they can control or substantially influence. Some costs and revenues may be traced to the centre, but are not controllable by the manager. Thus the performance report should distinguish between controllable (by the manager) results and the results of the centre itself. By maintaining this distinction, the economic viability of the centre can be evaluated as a separate issue from the manager's performance (even good managers may fail to succeed with weak centres).

## Illustrative Example 10-1

*Waratah Company manufactures anaesthesia machines. Its organisation structure is shown in Figure 10-1.*

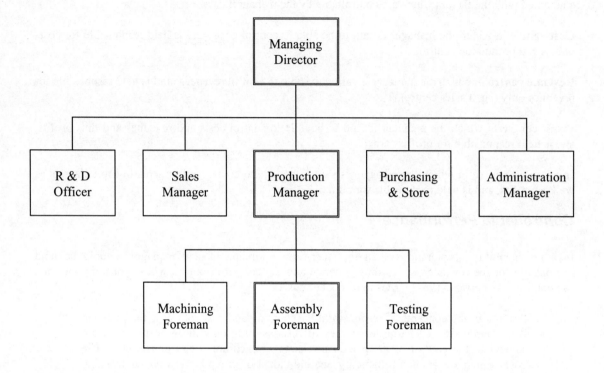

**Figure 10-1: Organisation Chart**

*There are three production departments, Machining, Assembly and Testing, and the foreman of each of these departments is responsible to a Production Manager. The Production Manager, along with other managers at his own level, is responsible to the Managing Director. These relationships are indicated by the double-edge boxes.*

Commencing with reports at the foreman's level, the following three reports (see Figures 10-2, 10-3 and 10-4) illustrate the pyramid structure of responsibility reporting.

## Assembly Foreman's Report

Figure 10-2 shows a monthly performance report for the Assembly Department. This report does not show actual costs, although they often are shown. However, actual costs can be determined easily by adding the budget figures and the variances. The emphasis here is on the variances rather than the actual figures, emphasising exceptions.

| WARATAH COMPANY - ASSEMBLY DEPARTMENT ||||||
| --- |
| Monthly Performance Report ||||||
| Item | Budget || Variance ||
|  | This Month | Year to Date | This Month | Year to Date |
| Direct Material (see Fig. 10-3) | $400,000 | $2,000,000 | ($3,000) | $ 1,000 |
| Direct Labour (see Fig. 10-3) | 300,000 | 1,300,000 | 5,000 | 14,000 |
| Controllable Overhead |  |  |  |  |
| Supervision | 6,000 | 16,000 | - | - |
| Provn for Leave Entitlements | 50,000 | 210,000 | 1,000 | 1,500 |
| Supplies | 1,000 | 3,000 | 50 | 100 |
| Materials Handling | 5,000 | 18,000 | 100 | - |
| Total (see Fig. 10-3) | 62,000 | 247,000 | 1,150 | 1,600 |
| Total Controllable Costs | 762,000 | 3,547,000 | 3,150 | 16,600 |
| Non-Controllable Overhead |  |  |  |  |
| Rent | 1,000 | 4,000 | 100 | 300 |
| Allocated costs: |  |  |  |  |
| Research & Development | 6,000 | 20,000 | - | 700 |
| Stores | 1,000 | 3,500 | (50) | - |
| Total Non-Controllable Costs | 8,000 | 27,500 | 50 | 1,000 |
| TOTAL | $770,000 | $3,574,500 | $3,200 | $17,600 |

**Figure 10-2**

Monthly reports similar to this would also be prepared for the foremen of the Machining and Testing departments. Copies of these reports would also go to the Production Manager to whom these foremen are responsible.

## *Production Manager*

The Production Manager would be given a report summarising those sent to the departmental foremen, as shown in Figure 10-3. The Production Manager's report is largely a summary of the reports of the three foremen, with the controllable overhead of his own department added because these costs are controllable by him. A copy of this report would also go to the Managing Director to whom the Production Manager is responsible.

Similar reports would be prepared for each of the other managers at this level: Research and Development, Sales, Purchasing and Store, Administration. Copies of each of these would go to the Managing Director as well.

| WARATAH COMPANY - PRODUCTION DEPARTMENT ||||
|---|---|---|---|
| **Production Manager's Monthly Performance Report** ||||
| Item | Budget || Variance ||
| | This Month | Year to Date | This Month | Year to Date |
| Direct Material | | | | |
|   Machining | $200,000 | $800,000 | $2,000 | $5,000 |
|   Assembly (see Fig. 10-2) | 400,000 | 2,000,000 | (3,000) | 1,000 |
| Total (see Fig. 10-4) | 600,000 | 2,800,000 | (1,000) | 6,000 |
| Direct Labour | | | | |
|   Machining | 30,000 | 100,000 | (1,000) | (3,000) |
|   Assembly (see Fig. 10-2) | 300,000 | 1,300,000 | 5,000 | 14,000 |
|   Testing | 70,000 | 300,000 | 2,000 | 5,000 |
| Total (see Fig. 10-4) | 400,000 | 1,700,000 | 6,000 | 16,000 |
| Controllable Overhead | | | | |
|   Production Manager's Office | 12,000 | 53,000 | 1,750 | 3,400 |
|   Machining | 40,000 | 150,000 | 500 | 1,500 |
|   Assembly (see Fig. 10-2) | 62,000 | 247,000 | 1,150 | 1,600 |
|   Testing | 10,000 | 35,000 | 100 | 300 |
| Total (see Fig. 10-4 | 124,000 | 485,000 | 3,500 | 6,800 |
| TOTAL | $1,124,000 | $4,985,000 | $8,500 | $28,800 |

Figure 10-3

| WARATAH COMPANY ||||
|---|---|---|---|
| **Managing Director's Monthly Performance Report** ||||
| Item | Budget || Variance ||
| | This Month | Year to Date | This Month | Year to Date |
| Sales | $1,500,000 | $7,500,000 | $100,000 | $450,000 |
| Less Controllable Costs: | | | | |
| Direct Material (see Fig. 10-3) | 600,000 | 2,800,000 | (1,000) | 6,000 |
| Direct Labour (see Fig. 10-3) | 400,000 | 1,700,000 | 6,000 | 16,000 |
| Controllable Overhead | | | | |
|   Managing Director's Office | 20,000 | 80,000 | 100 | 400 |
|   Research & Development | 10,000 | 38,000 | - | 2,000 |
|   Sales | 18,000 | 74,000 | 1,500 | 5,000 |
|   Production (see Fig. 10-3) | 124,000 | 485,000 | 3,500 | 6,800 |
|   Purchasing & Store | 5,000 | 21,000 | (50) | 100 |
|   Administration | 3,500 | 15,000 | 200 | 1,500 |
| Total Controllable Costs | 1,180,500 | 5,213,000 | 10,250 | 37,800 |
| Net Operating Profit | $319,500 | $2,287,000 | $89,750 | $412,200 |

Figure 10-4

The Managing Director's performance report (Figure 10-4) covers all phases of the organisation and includes all costs, including those of his own department. As the reports move upwards in the organisation they become broader in scope, but show less detail in respect of each item. As they move downwards they become narrower in scope but more detailed. Thus, if detailed information is required in respect of any item it is necessary to go down the line.

The responsibility accounting system is a form of administrative control producing measures of the **financial** outcomes of managers' actions. As mentioned earlier, the type of financial performance measures used depends on the type of responsibility centre, whether it is a cost, revenue, profit or investment centre. In example 10-1 the Assembly Department was treated as a cost centre, and so the Foreman's performance was evaluated on the basis of a comparison of actual (controllable) costs with budgeted costs (which could also be standard costs). The Managing Director's performance could be evaluated in terms of the profit earned by the company; or the profit could be expressed as a percentage of the capital invested in, or total assets of the company - known as **return on investment**. Such a measure is common in decentralised organisations.

## DECENTRALISED ORGANISATIONS

When we hear the term **decentralisation** used, particularly by government spokespersons, we often think in terms of geographical dispersion. For example, there have been well-publicised attempts at "decentralisation" in New South Wales as a means of relieving population pressure on the city of Sydney, by promoting the expansion of certain country towns. To achieve this, some government departments have been moved - eg., the Central Mapping Authority, which has gone through several name changes and is now known as Land and Property Information, was moved to Bathurst. Actually, such actions have not been very successful overall, because government employees have largely resisted attempts to coerce them into moving house to the country.

As the term is used in this book, however, **decentralisation** refers to the **delegation of authority for decision making**. Decentralisation becomes attractive and necessary as organisations grow and there is a need to manage diverse and complex activities. There are many ways to divide the decision making tasks of an organisation for the purposes of delegating responsibility and authority. The term **differentiation** is used to describe how an organisation structures itself, ie. the way it chooses to decompose the tasks that must be accomplished in order to implement its strategy. The mode of differentiation into subunits determines the potential scope or range of activities that each subunit can undertake. There are three common modes of differentiation: (1) **functional**, (2) **divisional**, and (3) **matrix**.

### *Functional Structure*

An organisation can differentiate along functional lines, that is according to the functions that are performed, such as Production, Marketing, Finance, Personnel, and Research and Development. Figure 10-5 illustrates a functional structure.

**Figure 10-5: Functional Organisation Structure**

The activities within each function are performed repetitively, so that specialisation and technical competence are emphasised. This is usually an appropriate structure when the organisation has a limited number of products and economies of scale are more important than rapid market response, eg. when product life cycles tend to be long.

## Divisional Structure

Organisations may be differentiated along products or product lines. These are called divisionalised organisations. Figure 10-6 illustrates this form of decentralisation.

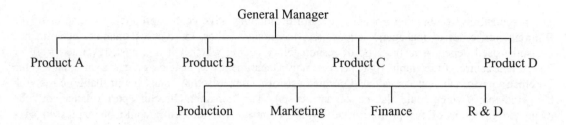

**Figure 10-6: Divisional Organisation Structure**

Each division duplicates the functions of all the other divisions. For example, each of the Product Divisions has a Production Department, each has its own Marketing Department, and so on. This structure generally provides a good training ground for managers because each division is, in a sense, a mini-company.

## Matrix Structure

The matrix structure combines features of the functional and divisional structures. In this form of differentiation functional areas are overlaid by projects or products. This type of organisation is built around sub-managers who are responsible simultaneously to both project (or product) managers and functional managers, see Figure 10-7.

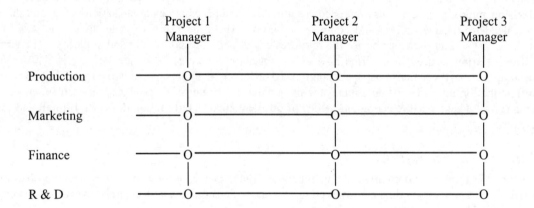

**Figure 10-7: Matrix Organisation Structure**

The matrix structure tends to be most effective in organisations which undertake relatively short, unusual projects requiring high creativity. Functional specialists may be part of a project group and a functional group. They are usually highly qualified and professional employees.

While differentiation determines the potential scope or range of **activities** that each subunit can undertake, decentralisation determines what **decisions** each unit is accountable for. The degree of decentralisation depends upon many factors, but the most important generally is organisational size.

## Benefits of Decentralisation

From an administrative viewpoint decentralisation has a number of benefits:

1. It frees top management from day-to-day involvement in operations so that they can concentrate on strategic planning.
2. Decisions can be made with local information, more quickly, because referral to superiors is not necessary.

3. It avoids the problem of cognitive and information overload which would be present if there were only a few decision makers.
4. It provides a training ground for junior managers. If decision making were centralised there would be no training of the next generation of managers.
5. The autonomy provided to subunit managers motivates them to perform. If "managers" just followed instructions they would lose interest - they need to be allowed to make decisions.

## *Disadvantage of Decentralisation*

The major disadvantage of decentralisation is the loss of control suffered by top management. Authority for decisions is vested in subunit managers who have to be motivated to pursue organisational objectives. All managers should be focusing on the same goals and objectives - this is sometimes called **goal congruence**. Such motivation requires what are called **integrating mechanisms** to get the organisation to function as a cohesive whole. Common integrating mechanisms include direct supervision, co-ordination by prior planning, the use of rules and committees, and appropriate performance measures.

A common integrating mechanism for decentralised organisations is the use of accounting performance measures. The types of measures used depend on the level of responsibility, ie. the type of responsibility centre. Earlier, four types of responsibility centre were identified: cost centre, revenue centre, profit centre and investment centre. Here we specifically consider performance measures for profit and investment centres, since decentralised subunits usually take one of these two forms.

## *Profit Centres*

The use of accounting profit as a measure of performance is widespread, especially in profit centres, suggesting that it has certain fundamental strengths. Profit summarises the results of a number of heterogeneous activities in a single measure, money. It allows managers to focus on a single criterion which they understand and which can be used to compare a range of profit-making activities.

Profit, based on historical cost accounting, does have its limitations. Profit is equal to revenues minus costs. Costs, in particular, are likely to be measured in a mixture of dollars of differing purchasing power, especially when they comprise allocations (such as depreciation) of long-lived assets purchased in different time periods. In addition, the allocations of joint and common costs, and of depreciation, are arbitrary, so that profit may be sensitive to the choice of allocation methods.

Another problem with the use of profit as a single performance measure is that it is usually based on a single year's activity. Thus managers may pursue short-run profits at the expense of the long run, in order to look good. Emphasis on short-run profit may, for example, induce a manager to "economise" by ignoring regular service and maintenance of machinery and equipment, or to delay the replacement of older equipment in order to minimise depreciation charges against revenues. Such tactics may work in the short run, and the manager hopes that (s)he will be promoted to another centre before the effects of such misguided actions are felt - ie., it will be someone else's problem.

Despite these criticisms, however, profit is still used as a performance measure in profit centres. As a means of overcoming these problems some organisations try to implement multiple performance measures, financial and non-financial. Non-financial measures may include: inventory turnover, labour efficiency, percentage of on-time deliveries, schedule attainment, units per hour, and throughput time. Non-financial performance measures are dealt with in Chapter 11.

## *Investment Centres*

One of the problems in comparing the performance of different centres and their managers on the basis of profit is that such comparisons ignore the size of the investments that have been made in the different centres. It is not unreasonable to expect centres with large investment bases to earn higher profits than those with smaller investment bases. So when a manager is responsible for (ie. can control) the level of investment in a centre, a more appropriate measure of performance is one which relates the profit earned to the investment base. Three such measures are **Return on Investment** (ROI), **Residual Income** (RI) and **Economic Value Added** (EVA).

## Return on Investment

ROI is simply income (or profit) divided by investment; that is, it is an accounting rate of return:

$$\text{Return on Investment} = \frac{\text{Income}}{\text{Investment}}$$

ROI measures how productively a manager uses the assets entrusted to him/her. It provides a single, comprehensive, financial measure of performance. Also, because it is expressed as a ratio, ROI is often considered to be an excellent way of comparing operations of different sizes and types.

There are variations in how organisations calculate both the numerator and denominator of ROI. The denominator particularly, can be measured in a variety of ways. Solomons (1968) raised a number of questions, for example:

1. Should investment mean **all** assets, **net** assets, or **fixed** assets **plus net current** assets?

2. How should fixed assets be valued - at **cost**, **net book value**, or **market value**?

3. How should shared assets, or assets controlled centrally, be computed in ROI?

4. When should the investment base be measured - at the **beginning** or **end** of the period, or as the **average** over the period?

A consideration of these questions indicates the possibilities for a variety of numbers which could emerge from the ROI calculation.

Sometimes the ROI calculation is broken down into two parts; this is known as the Du Pont method in recognition of the pioneering use of this method by the Du Pont chemical company:

$$\text{ROI} = \frac{\text{Income}}{\text{Investment}} = \frac{\text{Income}}{\text{Sales}} \times \frac{\text{Sales}}{\text{Investment}}$$

The first term, Income/Sales, measures the percentage margin on sales, while the second term, Sales/Investment, measures investment turnover. This form of the calculation illustrates that ROI can be increased by:

1. increasing sales revenue,
2. decreasing costs, or
3. decreasing investment

while holding the other two constant.

> ### Illustrative Example 10-2
> *Bathurst Company has two divisions, A and B. Figure 10-8 summarises financial data for the company for the year 20X2. The company does not allocate to each division the long-term debt of the company.*

We can see that on the basis of operating profit figures, Division B is outperforming Division A, $105 000 for Division B versus $75 000 for Division A.

Let us focus on Division A to begin with.

|  | Division A | Division B | Total |
|---|---|---|---|
| Sales | $1,000,000 | $1,500,000 | $2,500,000 |
| Less: |  |  |  |
|   Cost of Goods Sold | 600,000 | 1,000,000 | 1,600,000 |
|   Other Expenses | 325,000 | 395,000 | 720,000 |
|  | 925,000 | 1,395,000 | 2,320,000 |
| Operating Profit | $75,000 | $105,000 | 180,000 |
| Interest on long-term debt (10%) |  |  | 70,000 |
| Net Profit before Tax |  |  | 110,000 |
| Income Tax (40%) |  |  | 44,000 |
| Net Profit |  |  | $66,000 |
| *Average Book Values for 20X2:* |  |  |  |
|   Current Assets | $200,000 | $250,000 | $450,000 |
|   Non-current Assets | 300,000 | 500,000 | 800,000 |
|   Total Assets | $500,000 | $750,000 | $1,250,000 |
| Current Liabilities | $15,000 | $35,000 | $50,000 |
| Long-term Debt |  |  | 700,000 |
| Shareholders' Equity |  |  | 500,000 |
|  |  |  | $1,250,000 |

**Figure 10-8: Financial Data for Bathurst Company for 20X2**

It can be seen that this division is earning 15% on investment:

$$\text{ROI} = \frac{\text{Income}}{\text{Investment}} = \frac{\$75,000}{\$500,000} = 0.15$$

where **Income** is Division A's *Operating Profit* and **Investment** is *Total Assets* employed by Division A.

This return of 15% is the joint result of a return of 7.5% on sales and an investment turnover of 2:

$$\text{ROI} = \frac{\text{Income}}{\text{Sales}} \times \frac{\text{Sales}}{\text{Investment}}$$
$$= \frac{\$75,000}{\$1,000,000} \times \frac{\$1,000,000}{\$500,000}$$
$$= 0.075 \times 2 = 0.15$$

Division A can increase this return to 20% in a number of ways.

(a) Reduce investment to $375 000:

$$\text{ROI} = \frac{\text{Income}}{\text{Sales}} \times \frac{\text{Sales}}{\text{Investment}}$$
$$= \frac{\$75,000}{\$1,000,000} \times \frac{\$1,000,000}{\$375,000}$$
$$= 0.075 \times 2.67 = 0.2$$

(b) Reduce expenses by $25 000 (increasing income to $100 000):

$$\text{ROI} = \frac{\text{Income}}{\text{Sales}} \times \frac{\text{Sales}}{\text{Investment}}$$
$$= \frac{\$100,000}{\$1,000,000} \times \frac{\$1,000,000}{\$500,000}$$
$$= 0.1 \times 2 = 0.2$$

(c) Increase sales to $1 333 333 while maintaining the current percentage margin on sales:

$$\text{ROI} = \frac{\text{Income}}{\text{Sales}} \times \frac{\text{Sales}}{\text{Investment}}$$
$$= \frac{\$100,000}{\$1,333,333} \times \frac{\$1,333,333}{\$500,000}$$
$$= 0.075 \times 2.67 = 0.2$$

There are, however, problems with using ROI. One common problem is that a division may be reluctant to take advantage of an investment which is profitable for both the division and the company as a whole, because by doing so the division's overall performance falls. This is illustrated in Example 10-3.

### Illustrative Example 10-3

*This is an extension of Example 10-2. Suppose that the cost of capital is 10%. Division A, you recall, was earning 15% on investment ($75 000/$500 000). There is now an opportunity requiring additional investment of $100 000 to earn a further $12 000 per annum.*

The ROI on this new investment opportunity is 12%:

$$\text{ROI} = \frac{\text{Income}}{\text{Investment}} = \frac{\$12,000}{\$100,000} = 0.12$$

Thus this is a profitable opportunity because the return exceeds the cost of capital of 10%. However, the new ROI on total investment would be 14.5%:

```
ROI  =  Income/Investment
     =  ($75,000 + $12,000) / ($500,000 + $100,000)
     =  $87,000 / $600,000
     =  0.145
```

This would represent a decrease, below the previous rate of return of 15%, and thus the division's performance would appear to have worsened. Therefore a manager may be tempted to refuse this profitable investment opportunity because it would lower the total divisional ROI.

A second problem with ROI is that comparisons between divisions may be misleading. Consider Example 10-4.

### Illustrative Example 10-4

*Continuing with Example 10-2, from Figure 10-8 we see that Division B earns $105 000 on assets of $750 000. Compare the performance of Divisions A and B.*

Division B's ROI is 14% ($105,000/$750,000) and, although division B has a higher absolute operating profit, when we take into account the investment involved, it appears to be less profitable than Division A which has an ROI of 15%. As we shall see in example 10-6, this conclusion is not quite correct.

## Residual Income

Many companies have adopted an alternative measure of divisional performance, called **residual income** or RI. RI was developed to eliminate problems found with using the ratio ROI. The RI technique was popularised by General Electric.

Residual Income is the net income remaining after deducting a charge for the use of invested capital. The appropriate charge may be based on the minimum required rate of return that new investments should earn, or the actual cost of capital, or an imputed interest charge. The technique is illustrated in Example 10-5.

### *Illustrative Example 10-5*

*Referring to Example 10-3, assume the cost of capital is 10%. Using residual income as a performance measure, compare the performance of Division A before and after the proposed new opportunity.*

|  | Before | After |
|---|---|---|
| Investment | $500,000 | $600,000 |
| Income | 75,000 | 87,000 |
| Capital charge 10% | 50,000 | 60,000 |
| **Residual Income** | **25,000** | **27,000** |

Contrary to the result using ROI as a measure of performance, the use of RI demonstrates that it is profitable for Division A to accept the new investment since Division A's RI increases by $2000 - from $25 000 to $27 000. RI will always increase when a division adds investments which earn a rate of return in excess of the cost of capital. And of course, top management would always prefer a division to have a higher RI.

### *Illustrative Example 10-6*

*Referring to Example 10-4, compare the performance of Divisions A and B using RI as a performance measure.*

|  | Division A | Division B |
|---|---|---|
| Investment | $500,000 | $750,000 |
| Income | 75,000 | 105,000 |
| Capital charge 10% | 50,000 | 75,000 |
| **Residual Income** | **25,000** | **30,000** |

Recall that using ROI Division A (15%) appeared to be more profitable than Division B (14%). Using RI, however, Division B's performance is seen to be superior because, after both have covered the cost of capital, Division B returns the higher profit.

Residual Income is not without its problems also. Because it is an absolute number, RI is not a function of divisional size. It is easier for a larger division to earn a given RI than it is for a smaller division. For example, suppose Division A has an investment base of $500 000 while Division B has $1 000 000 investment. Given a cost of capital of 10%, it is easier for Division B to earn an RI of $50 000 than it is for Division A. Division A would need an income of $100 000 - deduct capital charge of 10% of $500 000 leaves a residual income of $50 000. Division B, which is twice as large, needs only one and a half times A's income, $150 000 - deduct capital charge of 10% of $1 000 000 leaves a residual income of $50 000.

Thus it is more difficult to compare divisions of different sizes using RI. Although RI is a more useful formula than ROI for making decisions about asset acquisitions, it does have the potential dysfunctional characteristic of tempting divisions to reduce assets so as to reduce capital charges. Consequently we have seen a gradual realisation that any single performance measure, such as ROI or RI, tends to be too narrow. Multiple performance measures, some of a non-financial nature, are preferable to any single measure of performance.

## Economic Value Added (EVA®)

One of the most contemporary measures of investment centre performance is economic value added (EVA®) (Stewart, 1994). EVA was developed from the residual income concept. It differs from residual income in three respects:

1. It adjusts divisional operating income to an after-tax basis
2. The investment base excludes current liabilities, i.e. total assets less current liabilities
3. The capital charge is taken to be the weighted average cost of debt and equity capital

EVA is defined as follows:

**EVA = After-tax Operating Profit – [WACC x (Total Assets – Current Liabilities)]**

where WACC = weighted average cost of capital

Economic value added is a dollar measure of the amount of shareholder wealth that is created. It is closely related to Shareholder Value Analysis (SVA), another technique for measuring the creation of shareholder wealth.

Just as we expect an investment centre to produce a positive RI, we should also expect a positive EVA.

### Illustrative Example 10-7
*Referring to the Bathurst Company (see Figure 10-8), compare the performance of Divisions A and B using EVA as a performance measure.*

We need to calculate the three components, after-tax operating profit, WACC, and total assets less current liabilities:

**After-tax operating profit** - Multiply pre-tax operating profit by (1 – tax rate):

|  | Division A | Division B |
|---|---|---|
| Pre-tax operating profit | $75 000 | $105 000 |
| Multiply by (1-40%) | 0.6 | 0.6 |
| After-tax operating profit | $45 000 | $63 000 |

**Weighted average cost of capital (WACC):**
The weighted average cost of capital is the after-tax average cost of all long-term funds used by Bathurst Company. There are two sources of long-term funds, long-term debt and shareholders' funds (equity capital). The WACC is based on market values. Assume that the market value of Bathurst Company's long-term debt is equal to the book value, $700 000 while the equity capital's book value of $500 000 has a market value of $700 000:[1]

|  | Capital | Proportion |
|---|---|---|
| Market value of long-term debt | $700 000 | $700 000/$1 400 000 = 0.5 |
| Market value of equity capital | $700 000 | $700 000/$1 400 000 = 0.5 |
| Total long-term capital | $1 400 000 | = 1.0 |

The interest rate on long-term debt is 10% and the company's tax rate is 40%. Therefore the after-tax cost of long-term debt is (1-0.4) x 0.1 = 0.06 or 6%. The cost of equity capital is the opportunity cost to investors of not investing their capital in an investment of similar risk – say 9%.

Therefore the WACC = 0.5(6%) + 0.5(9%) = 3% + 4.5% = 7.5%

Alternatively, it can be calculated as $\dfrac{(0.06 \times \$700\,000) + (0.09 \times \$700\,000)}{\$700\,000 + \$700\,000} = 0.075\ (7.5\%)$

---

[1] The market value exceeds the historical book value which does not reflect the current values of the company's assets and various intangible assets such as the company's brand name.

**Total Assets less Current Liabilities**
This is the measure of investment used in the EVA calculation. Another way of expressing it is working capital plus non-current (long-term) assets. For Bathurst Company divisions the calculations are:

|  | Division A | Division B |
|---|---|---|
| Total Assets | $500 000 | $750 000 |
| Current Liabilities | 15 000 | 35 000 |
| **TA – CL =** | **$485 000** | **$715 000** |

**EVA**
Putting this altogether we get

|  | Division A | Division B |
|---|---|---|
| Total assets – current liabilities | $485,000 | $715,000 |
| After-tax operating profit | 45,000 | 63,000 |
| WACC: 0.075(TA-CL) | 36,375 | 53,625 |
| **Economic Value Added** | **8,625** | **9,375** |

So we see again that Division B is seen to be outperforming Division A. After covering the costs of capital both divisions are creating additional shareholder wealth.

## CRITICISMS OF RESPONSIBILITY ACCOUNTING

Fundamental to responsibility accounting is the concept of control: responsibility centre managers should be held responsible for costs, revenues and invested capital over which they have control. There have been criticisms, however, of this notion of accounting control systems. McNally (1980) suggests that accounting control systems fail to differentiate properly between controllable and noncontrollable outcomes, because:

- accounting systems may rely on the formal organisation design for assigning responsibility for costs, revenues and invested capital. But the organisation chart fails to depict the control exerted via the informal organisation - systems of social and personal controls.

- the responsibility accounting system may not match the contemporary, formal pattern of responsibility because of lengthy time lags between the change in authority of a manager and consequential adjustment to the responsibility accounting system.

- responsibility accounting systems assign costs to individuals when perhaps control is more a group phenomenon. The narrow focusing of responsibility for costs may lead to tunnel vision as subordinate managers focus on their narrow areas of concern. This may contribute to interdepartmental conflicts and deferring or passing over desirable choices as subordinate managers argue over the allocation of costs.

Hirst (1983) also questions the claims that responsibility accounting systems are the ideal type of control system. He claims that a manager will have control over measured outcomes if the manager has sufficient **power** to influence these outcomes. Hirst maintains that there will be such controllability of financial outcomes, and hence responsibility accounting is appropriate, in instances of low task uncertainty. Low task uncertainty occurs when there is a highly repetitive task in a sub-unit which does not have to confront a large degree of outside influence. Conversely, the manager of a responsibility centre which is subject to many outside (exogenous) factors, such as material supply interruptions or uncertain demand for a product, and which performs novel, non-routine tasks, will have little power to control all the financial outcomes. In this case less reliance can be placed on financial outcomes from the responsibility accounting system in judging managerial performance, and additional non-financial performance measures need to be introduced.

More recently, McNair (1990) has challenged traditional responsibility accounting on the ground that it ignores the interdependencies which exist within organisations. He questions the assumption underlying responsibility accounting that maximising individual performance will lead to maximum organisational success. This assumption, he says, is incompatible with the realities of today's manufacturing environment; activities in organisations are linked and integrated across functional and departmental lines, so that the focus should be on the relationship between activities rather than on individual responsibility centre performance. Successful companies focus on total throughput time for a product or set of activities rather than on individual efficiencies. Only team results are measurable, he claims.

The need for co-operation suggests that the exercise of individual and social controls may be more relevant than the imposition of administrative controls in securing effective organisational performance. Traditional responsibility accounting systems trace costs to individual managers, whereas the group or team has more impact on performance and should be the focus of responsibility accounting measures. This has become more pertinent as many organisations have moved away from hierarchical structures to flatter structures, stripping organisations of multiple layers of authority and responsibility. In such organisations the lines of authority are often not as clear. Many of these organisations use team approaches and so a team, rather than a single manager may instead be responsible and accountable for operations and control of a sphere of operations.

Under traditional responsibility accounting systems, meeting the standard rather than improving on it is the goal. An alternative is a yardstick based on past performance which should be bettered and in turn become the yardstick for the next period. The latter approach focuses on becoming better consistently and continuously, and supports the goal of continuous improvement which is pursued by many modern organisations. It is not clear, however, that merely improving on the past is sufficient. Rather than use past (possibly poor) performance as a yardstick, benchmarking may be used as a means of setting externally based, industry best yardsticks. These external yardsticks may support superior performance initiatives more effectively than a rolling average of actual historical performance. Benchmarking is further discussed in Chapter 11.

## SUMMARY

Feedback control involves ex-post comparisons of actual performance with budget and identification and implementation of appropriate actions to correct significant deviations.

An important performance evaluation system is the responsibility accounting system. A responsibility accounting system is a form of administrative control based on the organisation structure which reflects managerial responsibilities.

The responsibility accounting system produces measures of the financial outcomes of managers' actions. The type of financial performance measures used to evaluate managers depends on the type of responsibility centre; eg., cost centre, profit centre, investment centre. Performance reports should distinguish between controllable and noncontrollable outcomes.

Profit and investments centres are typically associated with decentralised organisations. Decentralisation refers to the delegation of authority to make decisions in an organisation. The way in which decisions are delegated is termed differentiation - how the organisation is structured. Three common modes of differentiation are functional, divisional and matrix structures.

Although decentralisation has a number of benefits it does reflect a loss of control by top management. To overcome this, management employs integrating mechanisms to motivate functional decision making. One common integrating mechanism is the use of accounting performance measures such as ROI, RI and EVA. Unfortunately, any single financial measure of performance tends to have dysfunctional consequences. Multiple measures of performance are needed to overcome dysfunctional effects.

The responsibility accounting system relies on the notion of controllability of outcomes. It has been argued that accounting control systems may fail to differentiate between controllable and noncontrollable items. If managers have little power to control financial outcomes, additional non-financial performance measures must be introduced. Further, because of interdependencies among centres as well as the emergence of flatter organisation structures, perhaps the responsibility accounting system should focus on group or team performance across the whole production process, or at least across the sphere of operations for which the team is accountable.

## REFERENCES

W.L. Ferrara, "Responsibility Accounting - A Basic Control Concept", *N.A.A. Bulletin*, September 1964, p. 11.

M.K. Hirst, "The Controllability of Financial Outcomes", *Abacus*, 19, 1, 1983, pp. 29-38.

C.J. McNair, "Interdependence and Control: Traditional vs. Activity-based Responsibility Accounting", *Journal of Cost Management*, 4, 2, Summer 1990, pp. 15-24.

G. McNally, "Responsibility Accounting and Organisational Control: Some Perspectives and Prospects", *Journal of Business Finance and Accounting*, 7, 2, 1980, pp. 165-181.

D. Solomons, *Divisional Performance: Measurement and Control*, Irwin, 1968.

G.B. Stewart III, "EVA®: Fact and Fantasy", *Journal of Applied Corporate Finance*, Summer 1994.

# QUESTIONS AND PROBLEMS

**10-1** What is the relationship between **responsibility accounting** and **organisation structure**?

**10-2** How are responsibility centres classified? Explain the relevance of such classification?

**10-3** What is meant by decentralisation? Why do firms decentralise?

**10-4** Describe three modes of differentiation in organisation structure. When is each appropriate?

**10-5** How is each of the performance measures **return on investment, residual income** and **economic value added** calculated? What are the advantages and disadvantages of each?

**10-6** **Identifying responsibility for costs**
Suppose that no payroll tax is payable if a firm's annual payroll is less than $170 000. If the annual payroll is $170 000 or more, payroll tax is phased in, calculated as

$$0.05 \times [\text{Payroll} - (170\,000 - 2/3(\text{Payroll} - 170\,000))]$$

up to the point where all payroll is subject to payroll tax.

Suppose that the budgeted level of operations for the coming year involves a total payroll of $150 000. Subsequently, Manager A has an additional proposal approved involving additional payroll of $40 000 per annum, and at the same time Manager B secures approval for an additional proposal requiring additional payroll of $50 000 per annum.

*Required:*
(a) What is the expected payroll tax payable for the year, given that these two proposals have been accepted?
(b) Under a responsibility accounting system, who is responsible for this cost? Explain.

**10-7** **Responsibility for costs**
After receiving her first cost report since becoming department head in the ladies' ready-to-wear, Ann Round is shocked to find an item called *Holiday Pay*. "Why should I be responsible for that?" she exclaims. "They aren't working for me while they are on holidays. The accountants have goofed this time."

Did the accountants goof? Explain your answer.

**10-8** **Static versus flexible budgets**
Retep Pty Ltd is a medium sized manufacturing company with several production plants throughout the Sydney metropolitan area. The performance of individual plant managers is evaluated on the basis of a monthly comparison of actual costs against the budget. Plant managers are not responsible for selling activities or major capital investment decisions. For some time now the plant general manager had been concerned with fluctuating monthly results. He had identified the cause as the use of a static budget technique. The monthly production level was budgeted as one-twelfth of expected annual sales, and costs were budgeted accordingly. However, monthly sales levels, and hence production levels, tended to fluctuate during the year as products have a relatively short shelf life. In response to the perceived problem, the cost accountant in each plant was recently instructed to prepare monthly reports using flexible budgets.

In setting up the new system careful analysis of cost behaviour patterns and production volume levels in recent months was undertaken, and flexible budget schedules were prepared. For example, the overhead budget schedule for the relevant range of production for the Lidcombe plant is as follows:

## 10/Responsibility Accounting and Accounting Controls

|  | Per Direct Labour Hour | Direct labour Hours |  |  |
|---|---|---|---|---|
|  |  | 150,000 | 200,000 | 250,000 |
| **Overhead Costs** |  |  |  |  |
| *Variable Costs:* |  |  |  |  |
| Indirect Labour | $0.80 | $120,000 | $160,000 | $200,000 |
| Supplies | 0.13 | 19,500 | 26,000 | 32,500 |
| Power | 0.07 | 10,500 | 14,000 | 17,500 |
| *Total Variable Costs* | $1.00 | $150,000 | $200,000 | $250,000 |
| *Fixed Costs* |  |  |  |  |
| Supervisory Labour |  | $64,000 | $64,000 | $64,000 |
| Heat and Light |  | 15,000 | 15,000 | 15,000 |
| Property Taxes |  | 5,000 | 5,000 | 5,000 |
| *Total Fixed Costs* |  | $84,000 | $84,000 | $84,000 |
| *Total Overhead Costs* |  | $234,000 | $284,000 | $334,000 |

The plant is expected to work 200 000 production hours in a typical month, which at standard would result in 50 000 units of output.

The manufacturing cost reports were prepared for the first three months after the flexible budget program was approved, and the results were pleasing to the Lidcombe plant manager. In particular, variations from budget for overhead costs have been minimal, as reflected in the report prepared for November, presented below. During November 50 500 units were manufactured. Despite these results, **profitability** of the plant was low, in keeping with the previous 15 months. The plant general manager is concerned that this is because of poor cost control and wonders whether the introduction of flexible budgets had been a good idea after all.

**Retep Pty Ltd - Lidcombe Plant**
**Manufacturing Expense Report**
**November 20X7**

220,000 actual direct labour production hours

|  | Actual Cost | Budgeted Cost | Variance over(under) |
|---|---|---|---|
| **Overhead Costs** |  |  |  |
| *Variable Costs:* |  |  |  |
| Indirect Labour | $177,000 | $176,000 | $1,000 |
| Supplies | 27,400 | 28,600 | ($1,200) |
| Power | 16,000 | 15,400 | $600 |
| Total Variable Costs | $220,400 | $220,000 | $400 |
| *Fixed Costs* |  |  |  |
| Supervisory Labour | $65,000 | $64,000 | $1,000 |
| Heat and Light | 15,500 | 15,000 | $500 |
| Property Taxes | 5,000 | 5,000 | $0 |
| Total Fixed Costs | $85,500 | $84,000 | $1,500 |
| Total Overhead Costs | $305,900 | $304,000 | $1,900 |

*Required:*
(a) Calculate the variances for November if the static budget technique were still being used. Prepare a report explaining why the flexible budgeting approach is an improvement over the static budgeting approach in terms of:
 (i) cost control;
 (ii) evaluation of the plant manger's performance;
 (iii) motivation of the plant manager.
(b) The plant general manager has asked you, as the head office accountant, to review procedures in the light of his concern with the new system. You are required to briefly discuss any problems with the way in which the report is being currently prepared. Prepare a new manufacturing expense report for November which overcomes these problems.
(c) In terms of your report in (b), for each cost category analyse the total variance due to:
 (i) spending; and
 (ii) efficiency.
Explain what steps the plant manager might take to reduce these variances.

**10-9 Performance report and analysis of results**

The Students Union of a large metropolitan university operates a cafeteria on campus to provide nourishing meals to students and staff. Each month a financial report is prepared to assess operations and evaluate the performance of the cafeteria manager. The cafeteria manager is responsible for hiring, training and supervising cafeteria staff, ordering stock and providing a quality service at a reasonable price. He is also responsible for arranging overtime or temporary staff if demand is high.

The Students Union conducts a number of activities (such as a newsagency and a coffee shop) as well as the cafeteria. Premises for these activities are rented from the university. Cleaning of the premises is done by cleaning contractors under a fixed, annual contract with the Students Union. Capital expenditure decisions relating to the various activities are made by the Board of the Students Union.

The reporting system of the Students Union operates in the following way. A budget is prepared for each activity, being essentially the operating plan for the month. At the end of each month actual results are compared with a flexible budget. Variances are calculated and used as the basis for investigation and evaluation. At the end of the financial year, each manager is paid a bonus based on the net profit of his or her activity.

The monthly budget for the cafeteria is developed using the following information. The cafeteria operates for 250 days each year. During session time records show an average of 400 customers per day, while a quarter of this number use the cafeteria during recess periods. Past records indicate the following:

| | |
|---|---|
| Average expenditure per customer: | $9.00 |
| | |
| Average cost per customer: | |
| Food and drink | 3.00 |
| Disposables (plastic utensils, serviettes) | 0.60 |
| | |
| Daily labour costs: | |
| During session - 10 staff @ $75.00 | 750.00 |
| During recess - 5 staff @ $75.00 | 375.00 |

Other costs per day*:
| | | |
|---|---|---|
| Manager's salary | 150.00 | |
| Rent | 60.00 | |
| Cleaning | | 150.00 |
| Depreciation of Equipment | 75.00 | |
| Allocated Students Union Head Office Costs (based on expected sales) | 120.00 | |

* Calculated as 1/250 of total budgeted costs.

During August 20X7 the cafeteria was open for 21 days of which 5 were during the mid-session break. Records showed that 7050 customers purchased meals and the following revenue was earned and costs incurred.

| | |
|---|---|
| Receipts | $67 500 |
| Costs: | |
| Food and drink | 26 250 |
| Disposables | 3 750 |
| Labour | 16 125 |

All other costs were as budgeted except for cleaning costs which were $3450. Oil from the deep fryer leaked on the floor and required special services from the cleaning contractor.

*Required:*
(a) Prepare a report to evaluate the performance of the cafeteria manager for August 20X7. The report should compare actual revenue and costs with a flexible budget based on 7050 customers. Include a column showing the variances for the month.
Outline the reasons for the cost classifications that you used in the report.
(b) Labour time sheets show that a total of 200 person-days were worked during August. Calculate the labour rate and the labour efficiency variances for August 20X7.
(c) As the accountant for the Students Union you have been requested to analyse the performance of the cafeteria manager for August 20X7. In discussion with the manager you have been informed that there was a one-day conference held on campus during the recess week resulting in unusual demand. This required the hiring of some temporary staff for the day. Summarise your conclusions and recommendations in a short report to the Board of the Students Union.

**10-10 Analysing an accounting control system**

Cackus Ltd has two product lines, knitted goods and artificial leather, which are produced and sold by independent divisions. The oldest division, Hesta, produces knitted fabrics and converts these into clothes. Over 95% of the production in this division comprises standard items such as pyjamas and underwear. The Bonda division produces artificial leather which is used in the manufacture of children's toys and a variety of adult products. The leather, which is cut to various sizes by skilled cutters, is sold directly to the manufacturers of the final products.

Figure 1 shows the organisation chart of Cackus Ltd.

The general manager spends several days each month visiting divisional offices and counselling the managers on their various problems. He spends more time at Bonda because of the frequent problems which arise in the division because of the uncertain supply of raw materials, their variable quality, and the uncertain demand for leather from the manufacturers of the adult products.

Even though the demand for some of Hesta's products is seasonal, variations are quite predictable and the operations have been trouble-free for some years. Recently, however, members of the relatively strong Production Workers Union have been making representations to the manager of Hesta about the pay and conditions of the production personnel.

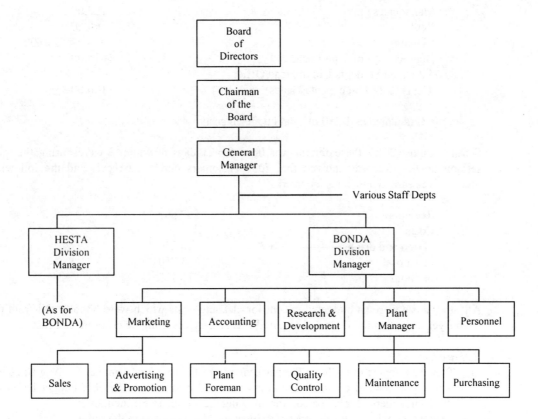

**Figure 1**

### The Control System

The company is highly structured with an attempt in each division to clearly define areas of responsibility, establish specific (vertical) communication channels and document many aspects of each division's operations (eg., establishment of job procedures manuals, plans and performance reports). An important means of structuring the company's operations is the accounting control system. The company is divided into a number of responsibility centres.

At the division level, each manager is responsible to the general manager for the profitability of his/her division. In addition, each manager's remuneration is tied to performance. The managers receive a fixed salary and a substantial bonus for exceeding their profit budgets. Typically, the general manager takes a hard line if the managers do not meet their profit budgets. Within each division department heads are responsible for the financial outcomes associated with their departments, and their remuneration is, in part, tied to their budget performance. At the plant level in each division the company uses a standard cost system to control material and labour, and a flexible budget to control manufacturing overhead. In addition, standard operating procedures and job descriptions exist for all production tasks.

### Some Concerns

The general manager is unhappy with the profit budget performance reports. First, he is uncertain as to the rate of return in each division. Second, the budgets for Bonda consistently show large variances (often favourable) yet his contact with the divisional manager (the fourth manager in two years) indicates that she has the knowledge, ability and the capacity to run the division effectively. Third, the general manager typically knows what is likely to be in the performance reports before they arrive. Fourth, although the divisional manager for Hesta usually meets budget, market share has been falling. Finally, the general manager is concerned about the disagreements which frequently occur at Bonda. To illustrate, the sales manager recently accepted a rush order from one of the manufacturers of adult products. To meet this order it was necessary for the purchasing section to place a rush order for raw materials with a new supplier. The materials were expensive and of poor quality. The poor quality resulted in an increase in the labour efficiency variance, particularly in the cutting section. As a consequence, the production manager came into conflict with the sales manager. The production manager felt that the unfavourable cost variances associated with her department were caused by the sales manager's actions and, as a consequence, she was loath to accept rush orders in the future. The sales manager felt that this was a ridiculous attitude to take because, overall, the special order was profitable for the division.

*Required:*
(a) Outline some reasons why the manager of the Bonda Division might find the existing accounting control system to be unacceptable.
(b) What effects might the accounting control system have on the motivation and behaviour of the manager of the Bonda Division?
(c) In the light of the difficulties experienced by managers of the Bonda Division, and the general manager's concern, outline an approach to the redesign of the company's control system for the Bonda Division.
(d) Would you argue for or against the redesign of the company's control system for Bonda being extended to the Hesta Division?

**10-11 Performance report: improving the budget report**
The Gold Coast District Hospital is located in a well-known summer resort area. The population of the district doubles during the summer holiday season (November to February) and hospital activity more than doubles during these months. The hospital is organised into several departments. Although it is a relatively small hospital its pleasant surroundings have attracted a well-trained and competent medical staff.

An administrator was hired in July 20X2 to improve the efficiency of the hospital. Among the new ideas he has introduced is responsibility accounting and the provision of regular quarterly cost reports to department managers. Previously cost data were presented to department managers infrequently. Excerpts from the administrator's announcement of new procedures are as follows:

The hospital has adopted a *responsibility accounting system*. From now on you will receive quarterly reports comparing the costs of operating your department with budgeted costs. The reports will highlight the differences (variances) so that you can zero in on the departure from budget costs; this is called *management by exception*. Responsibility accounting means that you are accountable for keeping the costs in your department within the budget. The variations from the budget will help you identify what costs are out of line and the size of the variations will indicate which ones are most important. Your first such report accompanies this announcement.

The annual budget for 20X3 was constructed by the new administrator. Quarterly budgets were computed as one quarter of the annual budget. The administrator compiled the budget from an analysis of the prior three years' costs. This analysis showed that all costs increased each year, with more rapid increases between the second and third years. He considered establishing the budget at an average of the prior three years' costs, hoping that the installation of the system would reduce costs to this level. However, in view of the rapidly increasing prices he finally chose 20X2 costs less 3% for the 20X3 budget.

The report received by the laundry department manager is shown below. The budgeted activity level measured by patient days and kilograms of laundry processed was set at 20X2 volume, which was approximately equal to the volume of each of the past three years.

*10/Responsibility Accounting and Accounting Controls*

| Gold Coast District Hospital<br>Performance Report - Laundry Department<br>for Quarter Ending 31 March, 20X3 ||||||
| --- | --- | --- | --- | --- |
|  | BUDGET | ACTUAL | (OVER)<br>UNDER<br>BUDGET | PERCENT<br>(OVER)<br>UNDER<br>BUDGET |
| Patient days | 9,500 | 11,900 | (2,400) | (25) |
| Kg laundry processed | 125,000 | 162,500 | (37,500) | (30) |
| Costs: |  |  |  |  |
| Laundry Labour | $27,000 | $37,500 | ($10,500) | (39) |
| Supplies | 3,300 | 5,625 | (2,325) | (70) |
| Water, Water Heating and Softening | 5,100 | 7,500 | (2,400) | (47) |
| Maintenance | 4,200 | 6,600 | (2,400) | (57) |
| Supervisor's Salary | 9,450 | 11,250 | (1,800) | (19) |
| Allocated Administrative Costs | 12,000 | 15,000 | (3,000) | (25) |
| Depreciation Equipment | 3,600 | 3,750 | (150) | (4) |
|  | $64,650 | $87,225 | ($22,575) | (35) |

Administrator's comments: Costs are significantly above budget for the quarter. Particular attention needs to be paid to labour, supplies and maintenance.

*Required:*
(a) Critically evaluate the way in which the quarterly budget has been prepared, and the variations from budget reported, for the Laundry Department.
(b) Recast the Laundry Department performance report in order to overcome the problems identified in part (a). You will need to make a number of assumptions in doing so. State clearly what these assumptions are and your rationale for making them.
(c) In light of the performance report constructed in part (b), comment on the performance of the Laundry Department supervisor for the March quarter.
(d) Discuss the possible effects on the laundry department supervisor of the budgetary system being used, with reference to expectancy theory and/or goal setting theory where appropriate.

**10-12 Responsibility accounting: allocating costs to cost centres**
Excell Canning Company, producer of canned fruit and vegetables, concentrates on canning peach halves and sliced peaches during March quarter each year, and has budgeted the following expenses for Quarter ending 31 March, 20X7:

| **Budgeted Expenses**: |  |
| --- | --- |
| Peaches - 495 000 kg @ $0.30 | $148 500 |
| Sugar | 10 000 |
| Cans | 30 000 |
| Labels and Boxes | 2 000 |
| Salaries and Wages | 156 000 |
| Depreciation Machinery | 10 000 |
| Indirect Materials | 2 000 |
| Water | 1 000 |
| Power | 2 000 |
| Delivery Expenses | 15 000 |
|  | $376 500 |

*10/Responsibility Accounting and Accounting Controls*

You have been approached, as an expert in management accounting, to help install a responsibility accounting system and to allocate these budgeted costs to various cost centres for cost control and for product costing purposes.

On conducting further enquiries you discover the following information about the company's peach canning operations:

(a) Peaches are purchased in season and processed immediately. In the first process, peeling, the peaches are machine steamed to remove their skins.
(b) In the second process, seeding, another machine slices the peaches in half and removes the seed.
(c) The peaches are then sent on a conveyor belt for canning. On the way workers pick out peaches with faults, cut out the faulty spots with a knife, and replace the remaining sound parts on the conveyor. This process is called spotting.
(d) In the final operating section, canning, the peaches are placed in cans with sugar syrup, cooked, labelled and boxed. Unblemished peach halves are canned as is, while the remaining peaches are sliced and canned as sliced peaches. One-third of the peaches are canned as halves.
(e) The weight loss in the fruit is almost exactly compensated for by the added sugar syrup.
(f) The peaches are canned as 825 gm tins and sell for $1.20 for halves and $1.00 for sliced peaches.
(g) The Salaries and Wages shown in the present quarterly budget are made up as follows:

|  |  |  |  |
|---|---|---|---|
| Salary of Factory Manager |  |  | $15 000 |
| Wages of Sections: | *Foremen* | *Operatives* |  |
| Peeling | $10 000 | $8 000 |  |
| Seeding | 10 000 | 8 000 |  |
| Spotting | 10 000 | 40 000 |  |
| Canning | 10 000 | 20 000 |  |
| Repairs & Maintenance | 10 000 | 15 000 |  |
|  | $50 000 | $91 000 | 141 000 |
| Total Salaries and Wages |  |  | $156 000 |

(h) Depreciation Machinery, Indirect Materials and Power costs are incurred approximately equally by all five sections. Water is used approximately 70% by Canning, the remaining 30% being shared equally by the other three production centres.
(i) The factory manager's salary is allocated equally to all five departments.
(j) Repairs and Maintenance costs are assumed to be shared equally by the four operating sections.

*Required:*
(i) What is the budgeted net profit for Excell for the quarter?
(ii) Prepare an expense budget for the company for the quarter to:
 (a) allocate costs to each cost centre for cost control purposes;
 (b) distinguish controllable from noncontrollable costs;
 (c) re-allocate costs where necessary on an absorption costing basis for product costing.

**10-13 Responsibility accounting: performance report**

"Just look at these figures. I am surrounded by incompetents. Do I have to go down and show the production people how to run a factory?" The Managing Director looked as if he were about to have a coronary as he pushed a short report across the desk at you. You had joined the company earlier that week as personal assistant to the Managing Director who felt that his lack of formal training in accounting put him at a disadvantage.

The significant contents of the report are shown below.

## 10/Responsibility Accounting and Accounting Controls

**Production Performance Report for Quarter Ending 30 June, 20X9**

| Item | Actual | Budget | Variance |
|---|---|---|---|
| Output (units) | 1 210 | 1 100 | 110 Fav |
| Labour Costs: | | | |
|   Direct | $10 000 | $9 500 | $ 500 Unfav |
|   Indirect | 8 000 | 7 800 | 200 Unfav |
| Material Costs: | | | |
|   Direct | 12 200 | 11 000 | 1 200 Unfav |
|   Indirect | 4 000 | 3 900 | 100 Unfav |
| Other Manuf. O/head | 13 000 | 8 000* | 5 000 Unfav |
| | $47 200 | $40 200 | $7 000 Unfav |

\* 1/4 total annual budget of $32 000. Fixed manufacturing overhead expenses are not incurred uniformly throughout the year.

"I know that we have pushed the factory to produce 1210 units instead of the planned 1100, but that does not excuse a 17% increase in costs," the Managing Director said as he glanced down the figures.

Although you were not able to obtain an analysis of the "other manufacturing overhead" costs for the current quarter or for the previous eight quarterly reporting periods in time for your analysis, your investigation brought the following facts to light for the previous two operating years:

| | For 20X7 | For 20X8 |
|---|---|---|
| Actual Output | 4 000 units | 4 800 units |
| Indirect Labour | $30 400 | $32 000 |
| Indirect Material | $14 400 | $16 800 |
| Other Manufacturing Overhead | $31 500 | $32 500 |

*Required:*
(a) Discuss any limitations of the above performance report for the quarter as a basis for control and indicate how the report might be improved.
(b) Prepare for the Managing Director an alternative report concerning the production department performance. Mention any assumptions that you make.

**10-14 Improving a performance report**

Murrumbidgee Manufacturing Company employs departmental budgets and performance reports in planning and controlling its process costing operations. Department A's budget for January was for the production of 1000 units of equivalent production, the normal volume for a month. The following performance report was prepared for January by the company's accountant:

| Variable Costs | Budget | Actual | Variance |
|---|---|---|---|
| Direct Material | $20 000 | $23 100 | $3 100 Unfavourable |
| Direct Labour | 10 000 | 10 500 | 500 Unfavourable |
| Indirect Labour | 1 650 | 1 790 | 140 Unfavourable |
| Power | 210 | 220 | 10 Unfavourable |
| Supplies | 320 | 330 | 10 Unfavourable |
|   Total Variable Costs | $32 180 | $35 940 | $3 760 Unfavourable |
| **Fixed Costs** | | | |
| Rent | $ 400 | $ 400 | |
| Supervision | 1 000 | 1 000 | |
| Depreciation | 500 | 500 | |
| Other | 100 | 100 | |
|   Total Fixed Costs | $2 000 | $2 000 | |
| **Total Costs** | $34 180 | $37 940 | $3 760 |

Direct material is introduced at various stages of the process. All conversion costs are incurred uniformly throughout the process. With the exception of fixed overhead which is allocated at the rate of $2 per equivalent unit of conversion, all actual production costs are entered in the Work-in-Process account.

There are no opening inventories at 1 January. Of the 1100 new units started in January, 900 were completed and shipped. There is no finished goods inventory. The units in process at 31 January were estimated to be 75% complete as to direct materials and 80% complete as to conversion costs. There is no shrinkage, spoilage or waste of materials.

*Required:*
(a) Calculate the amount of under- or over-allocated overhead during January.
(b) Examine the performance report carefully and comment on any deficiencies in its construction.
(c) Construct a performance report which overcomes the deficiencies outlined by you in part (b), and indicate how it overcomes these deficiencies.

**10-15** **Evaluating and improving a performance report**
J.R. Ewing graduated from a leading university with an Arts degree. Despite his lack of a business background, his uncle took him into his established business, the Containo Container Company. When his uncle retired, J.R. succeeded him as Managing Director. The company is a leading manufacturer of beer bottles. In addition to the bottles, it also makes the cartons in which the bottles are transported to the customers' factories. It buys precut cardboard cartons direct from another manufacturer and only has to shape, staple and glue them.

One day in April the supervisor of the package department came into J.R.'s office and asked for a pay rise. He argued his point with figures from the first-quarter performance report as shown below. He argued that he was operating below his budget in six of nine categories and was right on budget in another, and that he had saved the company $2200 overall in only three months. During the quarter ended 31 March, 20X8 the supervisor had been paid $5000.

J.R. did not like the idea of handing out a pay rise, but at the same time he wanted to be fair to his supervisor. Since he did not have a business degree the figures meant little to him, so he told the supervisor that he would discuss it with the company's accountant.

As the accountant, you are asked to examine the costs of production in the Package Department and tell J.R. just what the figures mean. J.R. has indicated that he thinks the supervisor may be claiming credit for cost savings on items not within his span of control.

The direct material consists mainly of the precut cardboard. Indirect labour includes the supervisor's salary and the cost of getting the material to the workers. Indirect material consists mainly of wire and small motors for the stapling machines and glue for the gluing machines. General factory overhead is applied equally to each department.

The production records reveal that during the three months ended 31 March, 20X8 the package department produced 148 200 cartons, even though the production schedule for that period had called for 150 000 cartons. The standard output rate in this department is 30 cartons per direct labour hour. A carton is completed when it has been shaped, stapled and glued.

## THE CONTAINO CONTAINER COMPANY
### Performance Report, Package Department
### for Three Months Ended 31 March, 20X8

|  | Budgeted Fixed | Budgeted Variable (5000 DLH*) | Budget Total | Actual | Over (Under) Budget |
|---|---|---|---|---|---|
| Direct material |  | $8,000 | $8,000 | $8,000 |  |
| Direct labour |  | 40,000 | 40,000 | 39,500 | ($500) |
| Indirect labour | $5,000** | 15,000 | 20,000 | 19,000 | (1,000) |
| Indirect material |  | 4,000 | 4,000 | 5,600 | 1,600 |
| Power |  | 15,000 | 15,000 | 17,000 | 2,000 |
| Maintenance # | 1,000 | 12,000 | 13,000 | 12,000 | (1,000) |
| Depreciation | 12,000 |  | 12,000 | 10,000 | (2,000) |
| General factory overhead | 16,000 |  | 16,000 | 15,000 | (1,000) |
| Scrap & wastage |  | 3,000 | 3,000 | 2,700 | (300) |
|  | $34,000 | $97,000 | $131,000 | $128,800 | ($2,200) |

* Direct Labour Hours   ** The supervisor's salary

# Maintenance:

|  |  |  |  |  |  |
|---|---|---|---|---|---|
| Material |  | $9,000 | $9,000 | $4,000 | ($5,000) |
| Labour | 1,000 | 3,000 | 4,000 | 8,000*** | 4,000 |
|  | $1,000 | $12,000 | $13,000 | $12,000 | ($1,000) |

*** Includes $1000 as a share of the fixed cost of maintenance labour supervision.

*Required:*
(a) Examine the performance report carefully and comment on any deficiencies in its construction.
(b) Construct a performance report which overcomes the deficiencies in the present performance report and indicate how it overcomes these deficiencies.
(c) Write a brief recommendation to Mr J.R. Ewing as to whether the supervisor should be granted a pay rise based on your analysis.

**10-16 Simple calculation of ROI and RI**
The following data relate to Dubbo Division of Sturt Company for 20X4.

| Income | $200 000 |
|---|---|
| Sales | $2 500 000 |
| Investment | $1 000 000 |

*Required:*
(a) Calculate ROI using the Du Pont method.
(b) Show three ways by which the manager of the Dubbo Division could lift the division's ROI to 25 %.
(c) If Sturt Company's minimum desired rate of return on invested capital is 10%, calculate the 20X4 residual income of the Dubbo Division.

## 10-17 Evaluating additional investments

Division A of ABC Company has the following results for 20X0.

| | |
|---|---|
| Income | $15 000 |
| Sales | $200 000 |
| Investment | $100 000 |

*Required:*
(a) Calculate ROI and RI for the year, given that cost of capital is 10%.
(b) The manager of Division A is considering an additional investment of $20 000 which it is estimated would produce additional income of $2400 per annum.
   (i) Calculate whether this is a profitable investment, given that the cost of capital is 10%.
   (ii) What would be the new return on investment for the Division if it undertook this new additional investment.
   (iii) Do you think that the manager would undertake this new investment? Why?
   (iv) If Sturt Company used residual income to measure the performance of divisional managers, would this make any difference to your conclusions in (iii)?

## 10-18 Using ROI and RI to compare divisional results

XY Company has two divisions, X and Y, whose results for 20X2 were as follows:

| | X | Y |
|---|---|---|
| Income | $225 000 | $160 000 |
| Investment | $1 500 000 | $1 000 000 |

*Required:*
(a) Using ROI as a divisional performance measure, which Division's manager was the more successful?
(b) If the cost of capital is 10%, using RI as a divisional performance measure, which Division's manager was the more successful?
(c) Which manager do you believe was the more successful? Why?

## 10-19 ROI, RI and EVA

The following information is available for Wagga Company:

| | Division 1 | Division 2 |
|---|---|---|
| Pre-tax Operating Profit | $400 000 | $1 500 000 |
| Total Assets | 2 000 000 | 10 000 000 |
| Current Liabilities | 500 000 | 3 000 000 |

*Required:*
(a) Using ROI as a divisional performance measure, which Division's manager was the more successful?
(b) If the cost of capital is 12%, using RI as a divisional performance measure, which Division's manager was the more successful?
(c) Wagga Company has long-term debt with a market value of $3 000 000 and an interest rate of 10% and equity capital with a market value of $3 000 000 at a cost of equity of 14%. The tax rate is 40%. Calculate the EVA for each division.

## 10-20 ROI, RI and EVA

The following information is available for Albury Company:

| | Division A | Division B |
|---|---|---|
| Pre-tax Operating Profit | $225 000 | $480 000 |
| Total Assets | 1 950 000 | 2 850 000 |
| Current Liabilities | 360 000 | 600 000 |

*10/Responsibility Accounting and Accounting Controls*

*Required:*
(a) Using ROI as a divisional performance measure, which Division's manager was the more successful?
(b) If the cost of capital is 12%, using RI as a divisional performance measure, which Division's manager was the more successful?
(c) Albury Company has long-term debt with a market value of $2 700 000 and an interest rate of 10% and equity capital with a market value of $1 800 000 at a cost of equity of 15%. The tax rate is 40%. Calculate the EVA for each division.
(d) What would you conclude about the performance of each division?

**10-21  Divisional performance, transfer pricing**

White Products Ltd operates through two state branches, and each state manager enjoys a high degree of autonomy. The two managers are ambitious and considerable rivalry exists concerning results achieved.

The following comparative summary of results for the year ended 31 December, 20X8 has been prepared in the head office of the company and made available by the General Manager, to both state managers for comment.

|  | NSW | VICTORIA | TOTAL |
|---|---|---|---|
|  | $000's | $000's | $000's |
| Sales | 12 000 | 10 000 | 22 000 |
| Cost of Goods Manufactured and Sold | 7 200 | 7 000 | 14 200 |
| Gross Margin | 4 800 | 3 000 | 7 800 |
| Selling & Administrative Expenses | 1 200 | 1 200 | 2 400 |
| Branch Profit | 3 600 | 1 800 | 5 400 |
|  | $000's | $000's | $000's |
| Net book value of assets | 11 250 | 5 000 | 16 250 |

Among the comments received by the General Manager are the following:

**From the NSW Manager**
It is unfair to me to compare results in this way, because my assets are all company owned whereas in Victoria they have the following leased assets:

|  | Value | Annual Lease Rental |
|---|---|---|
|  | $000's | $000's |
| Factory Land | 1 000 |  |
| Factory Buildings | 3 000 |  |
| Total | 4 000 | 600 |
| Factory Plant & Equipment | 2 000 | 500 |

**From the Victorian Manager**
The profit figures are not comparable because we were required to take product components in the form of electric motors from the NSW branch at a cost of $1.5 million when we could have bought them from an outside supplier for $1 million, and in any event the variable cost of production of the motors in NSW branch was only $0.75 million.

*Required:*
(a) Disregarding the comments of the State Managers, calculate for each branch:
  (i) Branch profit as a percentage of sales
  (ii) Turnover of assets
  (iii) Rate of return on net assets
  (iv) Residual income for each branch after charging 30% imputed interest on the value of net assets
(b) Assume that the NSW Manager's comments are correct, and for comparison purposes, recalculate the rate of return on net assets for Victoria after making a notional increase to the net assets figure and adjusting the profit to take account of notional depreciation on

buildings at 2½% and plant and equipment at 10% per annum. Comment briefly on this comparison.

(c) If the Victorian Manager's comments are correct and if the Victorian Branch had been allowed to purchase electric motors from the outside supplier for $1 million, calculate the effect on the 20X8 profit result for:
(i) the NSW Branch
(ii) the Victorian Branch
(iii) the company as a whole.

(d) Which manager do you consider recorded the better performance for 20X8? Explain.

**10-22** **Transfer pricing and divisional performance in multinational company**
An Australian company ABC Ltd carries on operations in two other countries X and Y. The three regional General Managers each report to the Managing Director.

Country X has a company tax rate significantly lower than that in Australia.

Country Y, because of balance of payments problems, has strict exchange control regulations which make it difficult to repatriate profits to Australia.

A newly appointed Accounting Controller is concerned about the following summary report prepared in a standard format, in Australian currency, for presentation to the Managing Director.

| Report on Regional Operations for Year Ended 30 June, 20X9 | | | | |
|---|---|---|---|---|
| | Aust. | X | Y | Total |
| *Australian Currency* | *$000* | *$000* | *$000* | *$000* |
| Average Investment 20X8/X9 | 4 375 | 1 500 | 2 500 | 8 375 |
| Sales | 10 000 | 4 050 | 4 000 | 18 050 |
| Cost of Goods Sold | 6 200 | 2 800 | 2 500 | 11 500 |
| Gross Margin | 3 800 | 1 250 | 1 500 | 6 550 |
| Expenses | 2 818 | 844 | 1 068 | 4 730 |
| Profit before Tax | 982 | 406 | 432 | 1 820 |
| Rate of Return on Investment | 22.45% | 27.07% | 17.28% | 21.73% |

The controller knows that the Managing Director uses the report to compare the performance of his General Managers.

The controller has obtained further information about the activities for the year, as follows:

(i) Due to favourable labour costs, and to achieve economies of scale, all of the Company's requirements for component 3679 are manufactured in Country X. Fifty thousand units of 3679 were sold to the Australian operation at $10 per unit. Of these, 30 000 were used by the Australian operation, and the other 20 000 were marked up by 20% to $12 and resold by the Australian operation to the operation in Country Y. The only justification for the 20% mark-up by the Australian operation was to comply with a Head Office request aimed at restricting apparent profit in Country Y.

(ii) Component 7423 for reasons of secrecy was made only by the Australian operation using a special process. Thirty thousand units of 7423 were sold within the company at $20 per unit, 10 000 of these going to Country X and 20 000 to Country Y. Variable costs of manufacture amounted to $12 per unit. Fixed overheads at the secret plant where 7423 was made were charged at $5 per unit on the basis that the plant would operate at only 60% capacity for the year.

*Required:*
(a) Assume that at the beginning and end of the year no units of either 3679 or 7423 were held in inventories.
(i) It was determined that component 3679 could have been obtained from an outside source and that the price would have been $8 per unit. Adjust the profit before tax for each of the three regions to show the results as they would have been had a transfer price

of $8 per unit been used and the transfer from X to Y made directly and not through Australia.

(ii) Make a further adjustment to the profit before tax for each region to show what profit figures would have been if the transfer price for 7423 had been calculated on the basis of full absorption costing at normal capacity of 75% with a mark-up of 10% on that cost.

(b) On the basis of the profit figures calculated for the three regions in part (a)(ii), calculate for each region:
(i) Profit before tax to sales ratio as a percentage,
(ii) Rate of return on investment, and
(iii) Residual income after allowing for a desired return on funds of 16% before tax.

**10-23 Transfer pricing and divisional performance**

Household Appliances Ltd is a divisionalised company in which each of the two divisions operates as an independent investment centre. For the coming financial year the pre-tax target rate of return for the divisions and for the company as a whole is 15%.

Division A produces electric motors and plans to sell 60% of its output to Division B for use in the production of tumble clothes dryers, while the remainder are to be sold to an outside user who has contracted to buy 2000 motors. No further outside sales appear possible. Division A is planning to produce 5000 motors (normal capacity) in the coming year.

Variable cost per motor is $30 while fixed production costs of $50 000 are expected in Division A. Division A allocates fixed costs on the basis of normal capacity, regardless of actual production.

The sales price for external sales is $55 per motor. For the purposes of internal pricing the manager of Division A sets a profit mark-up of 50% on full absorption cost in order to earn a satisfactory return on divisional assets employed, $500 000.

Division B has in the past purchased all its motors from Division A. Division B's costs consist of the transfer-in cost, additional variable production costs of $48 per dryer and $60 000 fixed production costs are allocated to dryers on an expected annual production basis. Division B plans to produce 3000 dryers in the coming year.

Division B sells the finished dryers to retailers for $180 each. Assets employed in Division B total $1 140 000.

An external supplier has offered to provide two-thirds of Division B's electric motor requirements for the coming year at a price of $45 each.

*Required:*
(a) Calculate the expected profit and rate of return on investment for each division and for the company as a whole, in the coming year, if Division B purchases its motors from Division A, and sells its entire output to retailers.
(b) Prepare divisional and corporate profit and loss statements on an absorption costing basis on the assumption that Division B accepts the offer from the external supplier and Division A adjusts its planned output accordingly. Calculate the company and divisional rates of return. On the basis of these calculations state whether it would be in the best interests of the company for Division B to accept or reject the offer.

**10-24 Comparing performance of two divisions**

The following figures for 20X1 relate to two divisions of a very large corporation having many other divisions. Results for these two divisions are compared because of similarity of operations and markets served.

|  | Division | |
|---|---|---|
|  | A | B |
|  | *$000* | *$000* |
| Sales | 3200 | 2000 |
| Profit before Tax | 800 | 600 |
| Investment | 3100 | 2700 |
| Depreciation charged before arriving at profit | 400 | 700 |

Top management evaluates performance of divisions and divisional managers on a pre-tax basis and will not approve investment proposals unless they have an expected pre-tax return on investment of at least 22%.

*Required:*

(a) On the basis of the above information make all calculations you consider relevant to a comparison of the performances of the two divisions and comment on the results achieved by each.

(b) The General Manager of Division B in his management report, made the following comments in relation to the performance of his division:

"Because of the size of the corporation as a whole, and because the assets of the company are widely dispersed geographically throughout the operations of numerous divisions, it is corporate policy that many of the assets are not insured, the company preferring to bear the risk itself of some insurable losses.

During 20X1, as you are aware, this division suffered an uninsured loss of $170 000 which, though not really material in the overall corporate result, did have serious impact on our performance. Our net income of $600 000 was after allowing for that loss.

In addition, it was a corporate level policy decision to provide ample capacity in our recently built plant to cater for long-term potential growth of the market. In consequence, our profit suffers from the impact of a very high depreciation charge of $700 000 calculated at the rates set down in company standard practice instructions. Our plant is only 60% utilised, and it is necessary to bear in mind that the depreciation of $700 000 charged before arriving at profit before tax envisages full utilisation of plant. Of course a more realistic view of our profit performance would be obtained if the depreciation charge were notionally reduced to, say $420 000.

Our present sales volume, which is considered very satisfactory having regard to the current overall size of the market, could have been adequately serviced on an investment of $2 100 000.

I draw your attention to these matters because I know that comparisons are made between results of similar operating divisions, and I consider that in any such comparison, due regard should be had to the effects of corporate policy decisions on the results of a particular division."

Re-calculate any of the performance measures that you calculated for Division B in part (a) that you think are affected by the General Manager's remarks, making any comments you feel are necessary, and again compare the results of the two divisions.

(c) The figures (except for the depreciation charge) given for Division A in part (a) for 20X1 are repeated below with comparative figures for 20X0.

|  | Division A | |
|---|---|---|
|  | **20X0** | **20X1** |
|  | *$000* | *$000* |
| Sales | 2300 | 3200 |
| Profit before Tax | 740 | 800 |
| Investment | 2700 | 3100 |

Using appropriate performance measures, compare the results for the two years. If you feel that an unsatisfactory trend could be developing, suggest what further analysis, using more detailed records of the division, might help to pinpoint the cause of the decline in performance.

# Chapter 11

# Performance Measurement: Multiple Measures

In Chapter 10 we looked at responsibility accounting and its reliance on accounting performance measures. The responsibility accounting system is a form of administrative control producing measures of the **financial** outcomes of managers' actions. We saw that the type of financial performance measures used depends on the type of responsibility centre, whether it is a cost, revenue, profit or investment centre. In each case, however, performance is evaluated, and control exercised, on the basis of accounting performance measures. In the case of a cost centre the manager's performance is evaluated from a comparison of actual (controllable) costs with budgeted (or standard) costs for a number of important cost items. Sometimes performance evaluation is based on a single, summary measure of performance, such as profit, or return on investment, or residual income. One of the problems with using only accounting measures of performance is that they may fail to capture all of the important dimensions of responsible performance.

Another problem with accounting performance measures, especially summary measures of performance, is that such measures may produce unintended consequences because of the way in which subordinate managers react to them. In designing the performance evaluation system one objective should be to induce subordinates to engage in functional behaviour, that is behaviour directed towards the achievement of organisational goals. Incomplete performance evaluation systems may instead induce dysfunctional behaviour whereby managers endeavour to look good on the measures used, but in doing so take actions against the organisation's interests. A typical example would be an attempt by a manager to increase reported profit by delaying expenditure on essential maintenance, or by delaying the purchase of new equipment (thus keeping depreciation expense down). In the following section we look more carefully at some important features of performance measurement.

## IMPORTANT ASPECTS OF PERFORMANCE MEASUREMENT

### *Characteristics of Performance Measures*

Three important and desirable characteristics of performance measures can be identified: **completeness**, **objectivity** and **controllability** (Lawler and Rhode, 1976).

### Completeness

Completeness refers to the extent to which a system produces performance measures which capture all the important features of a task. Naturally it is desirable to have a set of performance measures which is complete. Typically, the use of a single measure of performance tends to reflect an incomplete system. It is quite difficult to capture all the important features of a manager's responsibilities within a single, summary measure. Subordinates will tend to focus their attention and effort towards looking good on that measure, or those measures by which their performance is evaluated. They will tend to refrain from actions which would lower their performance score in the short term. Also, they will tend to ignore other features of their responsibility which may be important to the organisation but which are not captured by the measures used. For example, a divisional manager who is evaluated in terms of return on investment, may defer equipment replacement, or resist new investments because of the short term reduction in ROI which would arise from the large increase in investment. Or a purchasing officer may order large quantities to obtain a quantity discount and so achieve a favourable price variance (the performance measure) while ignoring the extra costs the organisation will incur by having to hold excessive quantities for long periods. In these cases the performance measure is incomplete and should be supplemented by other measures.

## Objectivity

An objective performance measure is one which does not require personal judgment by the superior but can be scored independently by different judges who would concur. In contrast, a subjective performance measure requires personal judgment, and there might be as many different scores as there are evaluators. For example, an objective measure for a production manager might be the number of defective units produced, whereas a subjective measure might be the level of employee morale on the production line. Objective measures are more likely to motivate desirable behaviour because subordinate managers can see the connection between their behaviour and the objective measure. Where subjective measures are used, subordinate managers may not understand the relationship between their behaviour and the subjective evaluation of their performance, and they may doubt that their performance is measured fairly.

## Controllability

Controllability refers to the extent to which the performance measure can be influenced or controlled by subordinate managers. It is desirable that managers should be able to influence (or control) the performance measure so that successful managerial effort is rewarded by an improved performance score. Some performance measures are influenced jointly by actions taken by several managers; for example, the quality of material purchased may affect production quality and cost. Other performance measures may be influenced by factors external to the organisation; for example, profit is influenced not only by actions taken by a manager but also by activities of competitors and by general market and economic conditions. In these cases it is difficult to determine each manager's responsibility for overall performance.

### *Source of Discrimination*

The accuracy and fairness of performance evaluation is perceived to depend on who actually measures subordinate performance and makes comparisons - ie, acts as the discriminator. It is desirable that the discriminator be a trusted person. Extrinsic rewards frequently are based on budget performance, and so a subordinate needs to regard the performance report as credible, otherwise there is little incentive to perform.

### *Communication*

While it is possible for a performance report to be communicated to a variety of people in the organisation, it is particularly important that a report is communicated to the person being evaluated in order to provide feedback for personal control and motivation. It is also important that the report is communicated to the superior who has the power to reward good performance or punish poor performance.

The frequency and rapidity with which performance measures are reported have an important impact on the use made of that information. From a motivational viewpoint, the results of performance evaluation should be communicated as soon as possible, and with a frequency consistent with the cycle time of the activity being undertaken.

### *Dysfunctional Behaviour*

When performance evaluation systems lead subordinates to engage in behaviour which is directed towards their own personal goals rather than to the achievement of organisational goals, we say that they are engaging in **dysfunctional behaviour**. Such dysfunctional behaviour flows directly from the measures used to evaluate their performance. Four main types of dysfunctional behaviour have been identified by Lawler and Rhode (1976): **rigid bureaucratic behaviour**, **strategic behaviour**, **invalid data reporting** and **resistance**.

### Rigid Bureaucratic Behaviour

Rigid bureaucratic behaviour (RBB) occurs when subordinates focus their attention on activities that are measured, and engage in behaviour with a view to looking good in terms of the performance measures used. If the performance measures are incomplete RBB may ensue, in which attention is paid to measured activities but not to other activities which are not measured. For example, suppose an employment agency conducts a number of tasks including interviewing clients, helping them fill out application forms, counselling them, referring them to jobs, and so on. Suppose that the agency evaluates personnel performance on the basis of the number of interviews conducted. The likely effect is that personnel will concentrate on conducting as many interviews as possible with scant regard to the successful placement of people in employment or to other activities regarded as essential by the agency and its clients.

## Strategic Behaviour

As well as the long-term RBB described above, subordinates may engage in strategic behaviour which is a short-term behaviour change in order to look good or acceptable for a period of time. Two examples are 'storming' and end of period budget spendups. Storming involves a short burst of activity following a period of slack performance in order to meet the budget by the end of the period. For example, Lawler and Rhode report that in the Moscow Pump and Compressor Plant in December 1940, 3.4% of the month's output was produced in the first 10 days, 27.5% in the second 10 days, and 69.1% in the third 10 days.

Examples abound of end of period budget spendups because failure to spend all the budget allocation would result in loss of the unspent portion as well as a possibly reduced allocation in subsequent periods. The *Sydney Morning Herald* of 29 April, 1985 reported:

> The NSW Parliamentary Public Accounts Committee has launched a major inquiry into the habit of some State Government departments and authorities 'spending up' towards the end of the financial year.
>
> This follows the disclosure that a number of departments are spending more than 70 per cent of their total budgets in some areas in the last two months of the financial year.

## Invalid Data Reporting

Invalid data reporting (IDR) can occur when individuals are motivated to manipulate data. It can relate to the future and the past. It can be pursued in budget forecasts in order to generate slack so that the probability of achieving budget is increased. IDR can also be pursued to cover up poor performance by, for example, misreporting actual production and charging costs to other departments. IDR is generally associated with important and non-routine tasks. If a task is not perceived to be important there is little motivation to falsify data. If a task is routine the outcome is relatively predictable and consequently IDR would be easily detected.

## Resistance

Resistance can arise in response to a change in the performance evaluation system. Resistance refers to the refusal of subordinates to accept the measures produced by the new system and to endeavours to thwart its operation and to make it look bad. Resistance may arise when people feel threatened by:
- replacement by an automated system or by new experts.
- more accurate and complete measurement of their performance.
- changes in work patterns and social relationships.
- a reduction in their autonomy and opportunities for fully utilising their skills.

## *Use of Accounting Controls in Performance Evaluation*

Managers are concerned with making judgments about the performance of their subordinate, responsibility centre managers. In their evaluations they may use performance measures produced by the responsibility accounting system. We have seen that certain **features** of these performance measures (eg., incompleteness, uninfluenceability, subjectivity) may lead to dysfunctional behaviours. In addition, concern has been expressed with the **way in which** accounting performance measures are used by managers.

Hopwood (1972) was concerned with the way in which managers used budget reports in evaluating subordinate managers, and the consequent psychological, social and organisational effects. He studied cost centre managers in a large U.S. manufacturing company, and identified three styles of evaluation used by managers:

- **Budget constrained style** in which the superior stresses the need to continually meet the budget on a short-term basis. Such a style is said to involve a **high reliance on accounting performance measures** (HRAPM).
- **Profit conscious style** which is a less myopic and more flexible approach to performance evaluation. A manager would accept a short-term budget overrun if it would be offset by greater long-term benefits to the organisation - eg., a temporary loss on disposal when switching to a more efficient, lower cost machine. The profit conscious style is characterised as a **medium reliance on accounting performance measures** (MRAPM).
- **Non-accounting style** which is a residual and undeveloped category in the analysis. The non-accounting style places very little or no emphasis on accounting data in performance evaluation. For example, in a research and development laboratory scientists may not place any importance on financial results but on researcher reputation and so on. This style involves a **low reliance on accounting performance measures** (LRAPM).

In the research site, consisting of highly interdependent cost centres, Hopwood observed various undesirable consequences associated with the relatively rigid budget-constrained style of evaluation: a high level of job related tension, poor relations with colleagues and superiors, and manipulation of accounting information (i.e. invalid data reporting). The use of the more flexible profit conscious style, however, avoided many of these harmful side effects. Hopwood also noted a contagion effect in which managers tended to use the same evaluation style as adopted by their own superiors. Thus there was a tendency to pass an evaluation style down the line.

In a subsequent study by Otley (1978) in a setting of independent profit centres, virtually all managers used budgetary and accounting information in performance evaluation. In contrast to Hopwood's findings, there was little impact of the rigid budgetary style of evaluation on job related tension or data manipulation, This style did lead, however, to an emphasis on short-term results.

Hirst (1981) noted that this apparent conflict between the findings of Hopwood and Otley can be explained by the nature of the task being performed. He argued that tasks may vary from relatively routine, where there is low task uncertainty, to relatively novel and non-routine, where there is high task uncertainty. Hirst proposed that a medium to high reliance on the use of accounting performance measures was more appropriate, and would minimise the incidence of dysfunctional behaviour, in situations of low task uncertainty. Conversely, in situations of high task uncertainty, a medium to low reliance on accounting performance measures would minimise the incidence of dysfunctional behaviour. In a subsequent empirical test Hirst (1983) confirmed this basic proposition.

This research should be borne in mind when designing and implementing accounting control systems. Responsibility accounting emphasises budget variances as important feedback in the control process. These variances can be further analysed (as in Chapter 9) to isolate different contributory factors to the overall variances. The concern is that emphasis placed on budget reports and summary accounting performance measures may lead to dysfunctional behaviour and undesirable outcomes in some situations. Sole reliance on financial measures of performance, often single measures, is almost certain to be inadequate. Also, in a competitive environment, such considerations as customer satisfaction and the need for continuous improvement are not reflected in such performance measures.

## Role of Standard Costs

As was stated earlier, the type of financial performance measures used to evaluate managers depends upon the type of responsibility centre. Typically a production plant is treated as a cost centre, and the managers are responsible for controlling costs. Performance evaluation consists of comparing actual costs incurred with budgeted costs, and to record any variances. These variances are supposed to indicate whether a manager has been successful in controlling costs and has turned in acceptable performance. The use of a standard cost system, in conjunction with budgeted costs, improves this accounting control system by providing measures of efficiency by which to appraise actual cost levels. As we saw in Chapters 6 and 9, a standard cost variance may be subdivided into, for example, price and efficiency variances, in order to more accurately pinpoint the source(s) of the variance.

In recent years there has been some criticism of the appropriateness of standard costs and variance analysis in modern operating environments. One criticism relates to the relative infrequency with which such variances are reported and acted upon. Monthly reports would be typical. but there is a need for more timely appraisal, perhaps daily, or hourly, or per batch.

A second criticism is that conventional cost variance analysis may tend to restrict management's focus to a small set of overall performance indicators, with undesirable dysfunctional consequences. For example, an emphasis on labour efficiency variances may encourage rather than penalise a build-up of inventory as managers seek to keep workers and machines busy. Similarly, output may be increased to absorb overhead so as to eliminate any overhead volume variance. Or purchasing officers may either buy lower quality materials from suppliers, or buy normal quality but in large batches in order to secure quantity discounts (at the expense of increased carrying costs), both designed to achieve a favourable price variance.

Third, direct labour has been decreasing as a proportion of total product cost. Consequently, labour price and efficiency variances are of less significance than formerly. Also, many conversion costs are fixed in the current operating period, with the result that any changes in output levels has less effect on operating costs. Hence labour and overhead efficiency variances are not very useful in managing operations.

Finally, because many firms have adopted just-in-time systems, long term contractual arrangements are entered into in respect of materials and component supplies. These arrangements may emphasise high quality materials with frequent and reliable deliveries at the contracted price, so that material price variances are not an issue.

Nevertheless, performance evaluation is important and requires a comparison of actual performance with some baseline figure. This target could be a forecast, an estimate, an engineered standard, or budget. Any differences between actual and target represent signals for either rewards or corrective actions. Unfortunately, the notion of a standard cost as a target to be achieved is at odds with the philosophy of seeking continuous improvement through product and process development. Of course, it is possible to constantly update standard costs, although this may be quite expensive and troublesome to do. It may, in fact, be more practical to use nonfinancial performance measures and cost trends. What organisations seek is a broader appraisal of manufacturing or service effectiveness, with more complete performance measures, and a focus on meeting world-class competition.

## CONTEMPORARY MANAGEMENT PRACTICES

Organisations engaged in world-class manufacturing or service organisations trying to match world-class standards face the challenges of:

- a product market consisting of diverse and discerning customers who require well-priced, high-quality, innovative products and services to be supplied as and when demanded; and
- intense and skilled competition in obtaining factors of production from resource markets and in securing viable shares of product/service markets.

To be successful, organisations have to review and continually improve all aspects of their processes: product design, procurement, layout of facilities, the use of technology, production scheduling, distribution and delivery, and customer service. This also requires attention to organisational systems, philosophy and culture.

World-class organisations have responded to these challenges by adopting contemporary management interventions which include **business process re-engineering**, **total quality management**, **continuous improvement, benchmarking** and **strategic performance measurement**.

### *Business Process Re-engineering*

There are two ways in which organisations can approach the task of improving business processes: either by way on ongoing **incremental** improvements, or by **radical** change and innovation. Business process re-engineering (BPR) is concerned with radical changes to business processes in order to achieve large improvements in performance. The primary focus of BPR is on the outcomes required to achieve customer satisfaction. These outcomes are achieved by redesigning business processes. Rather than try to fix problems incrementally, the focus is on major revision of the way in which work is done in order to reap large gains to the organisation by way of greater customer satisfaction, more efficient operations and lower costs. Advocates of BPR argue that the greatest gains are to be achieved in the areas of product development, customer service, and product and service delivery.

Hammer (1990) describes the application of BPR by Mutual Benefit Life, an insurance company, to the process of writing new insurance policies. The stimulus for applying BPR was dissatisfaction with the then current procedures. The process used to involve 30 discrete steps spanning 5 departments and involving 19 people to process applications. Typically the time to process an application varied between 5 and 25 days, with most of the time spent shuffling documents and information between departments. The president, intent on improving customer service, demanded a 60% improvement in productivity.

The BPR team developed a new process, creating the position of *case manager*. Each case manager had total responsibility for processing an application from its receipt through to the issue of a policy. The task was supported by access to shared computer databases which provided all required information, and by expert systems to assist employees with limited experience to make sound decisions.

This empowerment of individuals and re-engineering of the processes reduced typical turnaround to 2 to 5 days, and reduced staff numbers, while the case managers could handle more than twice the number of applications previously processed prior to re-engineering.

Management accountants contribute to BPR as members of multi-disciplinary teams; BPR relies on a team approach to problems.

## *Total Quality Management*

There are many vague definitions of TQM. Hand (1992), however, provides a useful one (p.26):

> *Total quality management (TQM) is a strategic approach to producing the best products and services through a process of continuous improvement of every aspect of a company's operation.*

This definition emphasises that TQM is concerned with **all aspects** of an organisation's performance, not just manufacturing. It goes beyond simply meeting technical specifications. An important part of TQM is statistical quality control, but this is only a **part of it**. Statistical quality control (SQC) is concerned with the variability of processing and outputs, and with meeting technical specifications to ensure compliance with Australian or international quality standards. The following example illustrates the SQC approach.

---

### *Illustrative Example 11-1*

*The Electronic Company produces integrated circuits in an advanced production process. Output is sampled by randomly measuring the number of integrated circuits produced in an hour with the intention of identifying any faults in the process and to improving the process over time. On the basis of past sampling the average hourly production ($\bar{x}$) is 30 units and the standard deviation of the hourly average ($\sigma_{\bar{x}}$) is 3 units.*

*The most recent random hourly observation showed an output of 26 units. Does this result indicate an in-control production process, or does it suggest that there has been a shift in the process mean (lower production)?*

---

A useful way of monitoring production using such sample data and to answer questions of the type asked is to use a statistical control chart. Such charts show the process mean, the control limits for an in-control process, and a plot of the process sample means obtained over time. In this particular example we are concerned with the mean hourly production rate. If the sample observation of 26 units falls within the control limits the process is assumed to be in control (IC) and any variation from the mean is assumed to be the results of random fluctuation due to chance causes. If, however, the sample observation falls outside the control limits it is assumed that the process is out of control (OOC), meaning that the mean has shifted and that corrective action is called for.

The control limits are determined on the basis of statistical considerations. If the limits are too narrow (too close to the mean) there is an increase in the risk of committing a Type I error - concluding that the process is OOC when it is really operating within normal limits. If the control limits are too wide (too far from the mean) there is an increase in the risk of committing a Type II error - concluding that the process is IC when, in fact, the process mean has shifted.

There are different approaches for setting the control limits. One approach is to control the risk of committing a Type I error by specifying the significance level, $\alpha$. Another approach is to set control limits at either two or three standard deviations from the mean - $2\sigma$ or $3\sigma$ limits. This procedure is equivalent to specifying $\alpha$ levels of 0.045 and 0.003 respectively for $2\sigma$ and $3\sigma$ limits (using the standard normal distribution and 2-tail tests of significance).

We will set $2\sigma$ control limits, meaning that the control limits will be located 2 standard deviations above and below the mean. Thus the control chart has a mean of 30 units, an upper control limit (UCL) of 36 units [30 + 2(3)], and a lower control limit (LCL) of 24 units [30 - 2(3)]. The sample observation of 26 units indicates that the process is IC because 26 falls inside the control limits, as shown on the control chart in Figure 11-1.

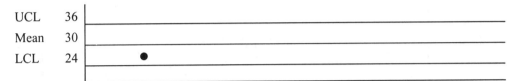

**Figure 11-1: Electronic Company Statistical
Control Chart - Average Hourly Output**

The interpretation of control charts is actually more complex because attention is also focused on runs of observations towards the control limits and lack of conformity to the assumptions of the normal distribution, eg., two-thirds of the sample observations should fall within 1 standard deviation of the mean, in our example, between 27 and 33 units per hour.

Control charts can also be used for financial management. For example, Firm A monitors accounts receivable performance using SQC techniques. They use a control chart to monitor the average collection period of debtors, as illustrated in Figure 11-2. In 1990 the mean collection time was just over 24 days. Upper and lower control points were established at points 3 standard deviations above and below the mean respectively. The UCL was a little over 28 days and the LCL just under 20 days. Monthly average collection periods were plotted on the control chart. The process is usually regarded as being in control if these monthly averages fall within the UCL and LCL.

Although the control chart might indicate that the process is in control it does not mean that it is being performed as well as it might be. In other words, there may be room for process improvement by either lowering the mean collection period or by reducing the variability around the mean (compressing the distance between the UCL and LCL). The control chart in Figure 11-2 shows both such improvements at the end of 1992 when the mean was reduced to 22 days and the control limits tightened. The reduction in the mean indicates greater efficiency while the tighter control limits show more consistent quality of performance.

SQC is only a small part of TQM, as already mentioned. TQM embraces all organisational functions such as purchasing (eg., selection of suppliers, acquisition of resources), distribution (eg., delivery to customers), marketing (eg., advertising), service (eg., after-sales service), finance (eg., invoicing customers), and of course, production.

The basic tenet of TQM is the satisfaction of customers. Everyone in an organisation has a customer, be it internal or external. The next person on an assembly line is an internal customer. The recipient of a management report is an internal customer. If external customers are not satisfied they will probably move their business to another firm. If an internal customer does not receive quality service there will be pressure on the provider to rectify the problem, or else the customer will have to fix the problem. Either way the organisation incurs additional costs.

11/*Performance Measurement: Multiple Measures*

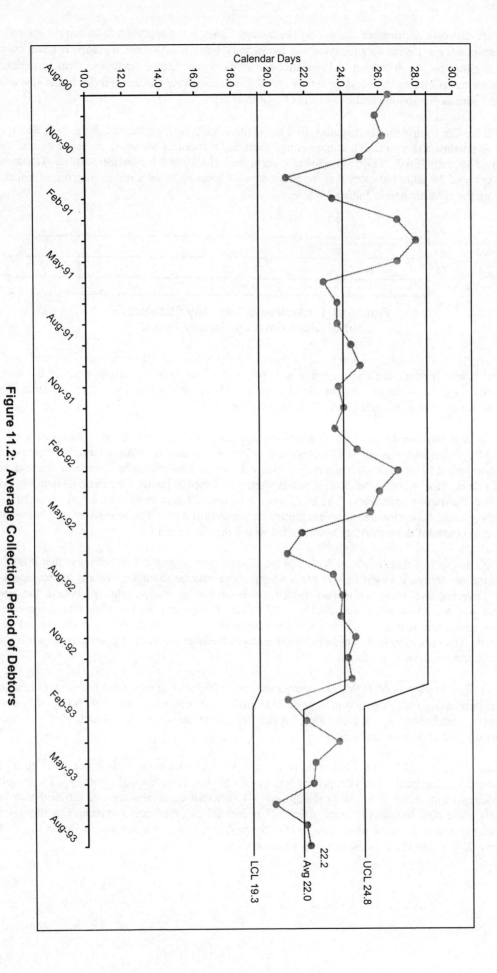

**Figure 11.2: Average Collection Period of Debtors**

Under TQM everyone in the organisation is responsible for and has a commitment to quality. This means getting things right the first time, every time. Manufacturers should not have to recall products to correct problems. It is aggravating to deliver a quality product on time but have the customer's invoice contain an error. Underpayment of wages by the paymaster upsets employees who themselves are committed to quality work. It is better to prevent problems rather than fix them after irritating the customer (internal or external).

Many companies regard quality as a competitive weapon. Toyota Australia emphasised its high quality standards for components in the then new 1993 Camry model. In 1991 the NRMA rated the Subaru Liberty the best quality car on the Australian market; following this Subaru successfully exploited quality as a competitive weapon. While the motor vehicle industry in general was suffering from the recession, Subaru could scarcely supply enough vehicles to satisfy demand.

It is not always sufficient to produce a product which meets specifications and generates no warranty claims or complaints. Customers have to be delighted, not just satisfied. Scherkenbach (1986, p. 30) says:
> ... there is a big difference between getting no complaints and having people brag about using your products and services!

Scherkenbach goes on to argue that to have people brag about your products and services requires anticipating customer needs and expectations and consistently meeting them through continuous improvement. TQM, then, is not only concerned with the satisfaction of current customer needs but also seeks to continuously improve the efficiency and effectiveness of products and services.

## *Continuous Improvement*

Perhaps one of the most vital ingredients of TQM is the drive for continuous improvement. Continuous improvement is driven by the objective of delivering enhanced value to customers and owners over the long term. It is sought in the activities associated with each product and service in a firm's strategic portfolio. Thus better quality, lower cycle time, higher productivity, flexibility and innovation are moving targets in each and every activity and process in an organisation. In this way daily practice can have strategic effects within the guiding philosophy of continuous improvement. Strategy development is driven by a search for sustainable competitive advantages which can be transformed into shareholder or owner value.

The adoption and implementation of strategies is guided by an understanding of comparative advantages and disadvantages. Some competitors may be seen to be superior in satisfying key strategic performance indicators that are indicative of customer preferences - eg. by better meeting customer time or quality requirements. This suggests that their activity structures or processes are superior. However, based on other indicators, our firm may be seen as having a relative advantage. Continuous improvement initiatives may thus be directed towards redressing disadvantages and capitalising on and sustaining advantages. Of course, the competitors will not be standing still but also improving, so that great effort is required to overtake competitors who already lead in certain areas.

## *Benchmarking*

Benchmarking is frequently used as a formal approach to the pursuit of continuous improvement. Benchmarking is the process of identifying the best performer in respect of a product, service, function, process or activity, and using its performance level as a target or **benchmark** against which to judge one's own performance. The objective is to improve one's own performance to equal or exceed the identified benchmark as part of an ongoing improvement process.

The benchmark may be established **internally**, for example when the same activity is performed in different locations, divisions or departments within the organisation. For example, Kodak (Australasia) use as benchmarks the performance of the best overseas division in what is a multinational organisation. When they observe a gap between their own performance and higher performance of the benchmark, they endeavour to close half the gap in one year, because they know that the benchmark target will not stand still. If they do not get close to the current benchmark quickly it will keep moving ahead of their own performance. Of course, a limitation of this approach is that it may not provide the best benchmarks. Other companies outside the group may be better performers.

Alternatively, an **external** benchmark may be provided by a direct and superior competitor. In many cases, however, it may be difficult to gain access to competitors' data. Furthermore, the business practices of these competitors may not represent **best in class** performance. In this situation it may be possible to establish benchmarks by identifying organisations which are not direct competitors but which nevertheless have similar functions or processes and perform similar activities which they perform better than any direct industry competitor. This approach to benchmarking focuses on best work processes rather than on the business practices of a particular organisation or industry.

No matter how it is identified, the **ideal** sets a **benchmark** for achievement and becomes a goal for continuous improvement. The ultimate value in benchmarking lies in the linking of activities to strategic performance indicators. This linkage gives coherence to continuous improvement processes and provides direction which is focused on the firm's strategies.

## *Strategic Performance Measurement*

The continuous improvement process needs to be supported by a system of performance measurement; progress can be judged by the use of appropriate performance indicators. As we have seen conventional performance evaluation using accounting controls and financial performance measures may lead to dysfunctional behaviour. Such measures tend to restrict management's focus to a relatively small subset of overall performance indicators. What is required is a broader appraisal of managerial performance using more complete performance measures. Common indicators for world-class performance include **quality, time, productivity, flexibility** and **innovation**.

## *Quality*

Continuous improvement efforts should commence by identifying the **quality drivers** in product related processes - i.e. those factors which drive the level of product quality. For example, activities such as product design, testing or inspection at various stages of a process are concerned with assuring or improving quality. Associated quality drivers might be the number of tests or inspections made throughout the process. Another activity associated with quality is rework. The relevant drivers might be identified as material specifications, employee training and equipment calibration.

The issue of quality may be approached using both financial and nonfinancial performance measures. Nonfinancial measures may address three major areas: supplier performance, plant performance and customer acceptance.

### Supplier Performance

The organisation's performance will be enhanced if its suppliers deliver quality goods, in the right quantities, on time and without the need for incoming inspection. Supplier performance can be measured by:
- Frequency and percentage of defects.
- On-time delivery performance.
- Fairness of price and settlement terms.
- Co-operation in solving problems.

### Plant Performance

The organisation's performance will be enhanced by safe, high yield, high quality production activities. Plant performance can be measured by:
- Parts per million (PPM) defect rate.
- Percentage yields: zero defects = 100% yield.
- Percentage of first-pass yields (ie., percentage of items completed without any rework).
- Number of plant days between accidents.
- Percentage of on-time deliveries.
- Number of engineering change orders per period.

## Customer Performance

Well-satisfied customers are essential. Performance measures include:
- Number of customer complaints.
- Number of failures at customer locations.
- Number of returns.
- Number of warranty claims (and their cost).
- Percentage of repeat orders.
- Percentage on-time deliveries.
- Mean delivery delay.
- Customer ratings of products.
- Elapsed time from receipt of order until delivery to customer.

### Cost of Quality

The financial measure of quality may be called the **cost of quality** which attempts to provide a single measure of all the costs of ensuring a product meets specifications as well as the costs incurred because of the failure of the product to meet specifications. These costs can be classified into four categories, *prevention, appraisal, internal failure* and *external failure* (Morse and Roth, 1987):

## Prevention Costs

These costs are incurred in order to prevent the production of non-conforming products. They include:
- Costs of designing and administering a quality assurance program.
- Costs of development of improved production processes.
- Costs of equipment to produce higher quality products.
- Costs of ensuring supply of quality raw materials and component parts.
- Costs of tooling, calibration and preventative maintenance programs.

## Appraisal Costs

These costs are incurred to identify those products which do not meet specification. They include:
- Cost of inspecting and testing programs for purchases, work in process and finished goods.
- Cost of quality audits and statistical quality control programs.
- Cost of field testing.

## Internal Failure Costs

These are the costs incurred when defects are detected within the organisation before the product is delivered to customers. These costs include:
- Cost of scrap, repair and rework.
- Cost of downtime associated with trouble-shooting a process.
- Cost of discounts on sale of seconds.

## External Failure Costs

These are the costs incurred when defective products reach the customer. They include:
- Cost of handling customer complaints and claims.
- Warranty and replacement costs.
- Product liability costs.
- Loss of customer goodwill.

Most of these costs of quality will be recorded somewhere in the cost system, but their identification as quality costs may be difficult because at the time of recording they are not flagged as such. Some costs, such as the costs associated with loss of customer goodwill, like all opportunity costs, will not be recorded at all.

The allocation of quality costs among the four categories is a somewhat subjective exercise requiring reasonable and supportable judgements. Management may be surprised to learn how much is spent on quality-related costs. There may be high payoffs from shifting quality costs from the last three categories to the Prevention category.

In a study of four small Sydney manufacturing enterprises (Birkett et al., 1992) the authors observed that the issue of quality appeared to be given a high priority. Of these firms, two exporting firms had achieved AS 3902 accreditation. A third firm saw quality as the key to its ability to price at a premium. All four were aware of the complex relationships between cost and quality and had some interest in probing this further. For example, while both firms with accreditation used extensive testing procedures, they were aware that this might not be a cost-effective way of delivering quality.

## *Time*

For many firms time is a critical variable in creating value for customers and in sustaining competitive advantage. Improved time management is important for the following reasons. First, short product lead time, that is, being able to bring a new product to market in a short time, can give a firm a competitive advantage, particularly when the product is of a type which has a short life cycle. Japanese manufacturers have been able to bring out new products faster than their U.S. counterparts. Stalk (1988) reported that Japanese manufacturers were able to develop a new television in one-third of the time required by U.S. producers, and automobiles in one-half the time of U.S. or German manufacturers. In 1981 Honda and Yamaha were engaged in a battle for supremacy in the motor cycle market after Yamaha announced the opening of a new factory with the aim of being the world's largest motor cycle manufacturer. At this time both Honda and Yamaha had 60 models. Not to be outdone, during the following 18 months Honda introduced or replaced 113 models while Yamaha only managed 37 changes to its product line. Yamaha was swamped by Honda's model changes, at one time holding 12 months' inventory in dealer showrooms. Eventually Yamaha surrendered its attempts to be number one, having been beaten by Honda's time management in product development.

Second, on-time delivery can be a critical source of customer value, especially when prompt product/service delivery is highly valued by customers. Third, rapid response in meeting customer requests for service can increase immediate revenues as well as promote future business through a reputation for service. Fourth, reduced product throughput times can increase a firm's capacity for additional work, can lower the holding of working capital and can increase the productivity of labour and fixed assets. Faster throughput time is an implicit ingredient of just-in-time production practices.

In the Birkett et al. (1992) study the authors observed that the issue of time management was of concern to two of the four firms. A firm in the computer supplies industry realised that their significant competitive advantage lay in their ability to supply large electronic companies with cable requirements to satisfy their customers' JIT inventory policies. Success depended vitally on orders being completed and despatched on time. Their ability to meet these schedules without relying on large inventory build-ups (which they could not afford) required careful time management. Similarly, a rubber products manufacturer perceived that its key to success was its ability to satisfy customer orders on time.

## *Productivity*

Typically productivity is measured in physical terms. However, improvements measured in physical terms do not necessarily translate into long-term profitability improvements. For example, yields may rise through the use of more expensive inputs whose costs more than offset the benefits of improved yields. Also, productivity can be improved but at the expense of product quality, so that customer value decreases and in the long term shareholder value declines. For example, Day and Fahey (1990) describe the experience of Schlitz Brewing in the U.S.A. In the early 1970s Schlitz reduced brewery labour per barrel, switched to low-cost hops, and shortened the brewing cycle by 50%. Profits soared, as did the share price. Consumers were slow to react, but by 1976 there were continual complaints and market share was slipping. In 1978 Schlitz tried to restore quality but they could not overcome consumer disenchantment. Market position fell from number 2 in 1974 to number 7 in 1981, while share price slumped from $69 to $5.

Continuous productivity improvement requires the identification of physical productivity drivers and how they affect profitability. Physical productivity drivers include technology, work methods, plant layout, employee skills and motivation, experience and learning, management skills, employer-employee relationships, and time. Key outputs of activities and processes can be defined and related to the critical resource inputs to give productivity measures. Then these measures can be compared against suitable benchmarks to identify the need or opportunity for continuous improvement initiatives. Some productivity measures are:

- Ratio of process time to available time for bottle-neck equipment.
- Occupancy rates in hotels and motels.
- Direct labour hours per unit or transaction.
- Ratio of actual to standard number of units per period at practical capacity.
- Standard cost efficiency measures.

These measures relate to the productivity of particular resources rather than of the firm as a whole. Where the productivity of equipment or labour is pursued as a goal in its own right rather than as a means of achieving broader corporate goals there is a danger that throughput will be reduced and overall costs increased. Operating each sub-unit as efficiently as possible does not necessarily lead to the firm as a whole operating as effectively as possible.

## *Flexibility*

Flexibility refers to the capacity of a firm to provide customers in a timely fashion with an array of differentiated products and services. Improved competitive advantage may flow from an increased variety of up-to-date products. The provision of such variety, however, may impose strains on manufacturing and servicing processes. One way to meet this goal is to maintain excess capacity to provide time for repeated setups. Another is to hold large inventories of work in process and finished goods. These ways of achieving increased flexibility will probably not be cost effective. Alternative ways of increasing flexibility include:

- Building relationships with flexible and reliable suppliers.
- Simplifying product designs and manufacturing processes.
- Reducing and standardising parts and components used in products.
- Enhancing the manufacturability of products.
- Delaying the point at which differentiation takes place.
- Employing a flexible and multi-skilled workforce.
- Using automated material handling systems, for example computer-controlled equipment that automatically moves materials, parts and products from one production stage to another.
- Using **flexible manufacturing systems** (FMS), for example an integrated system of computer-controlled machines and automated material handling equipment which is capable of producing a variety of technologically similar products. These systems allow a firm to produce short runs of 1 or more of a particular product and switch immediately to another product. Thus the production line consists not of batches of identical products but a variety of models intermixed on the line.

The provision of increased flexibility involves both costs and benefits. Improvements in flexibility are likely to require investment in flexible manufacturing systems, changes in product design, and new training programs. These changes, however, may produce savings in resource consumption by reducing inventories and reducing cycle time, as well as increasing customer value by better responding to their requirements. For example, Porter and Millar (1985) described how Sulzer Brothers adopted information technology and automation which allowed it to increase from five to eight the number of cylinder bore sizes available in their low speed marine diesel engines. This improvement in manufacturing flexibility allowed their shipowner customers to select an engine more precisely suited to their needs and thereby recoup significant fuel savings.

## *Innovation*

Innovation is the capacity of a firm to continually develop and supply products and services that are differentiated from those of its competitors in terms of perceived customer value. Innovation provides the ability to sustain competitive advantage over time. It may yield products with superior performance, or distinctive style, new products, products which open new markets, or products with drastically reduced prices.

Innovation may be pursued through research and development activities within a firm, or by inter-firm arrangements (for example, to share technology). Continuous improvement endeavours should commence by identifying innovation drivers. Typical drivers might be the desire to be best, the need to respond to competitors' actions or market and technological changes, the ability to perceive and promote customer benefits in new product developments, a system of individual and group recognition and reward for creative endeavours, and the presence of a culture that encourages teamwork, fun and excitement, that encourages everyone to do things differently and better - and that acknowledges and rewards people who excel (Taylor, 1990, p. 100).

The effectiveness of the innovation process is difficult to measure. A number of proxy measures can be used:
- Number of new products or services developed per year.
- Percentage of product and service concepts reaching launch.
- Percentage of successful products and services of those launched.
- Time from concept to prototype, from prototype to launch, from concept to launch of products or services.
- Average development cost per new product or service.
- Relative performance on these dimensions compared with major competitors.

## MULTIPLE PERFORMANCE MEASURES

Current trends in performance evaluation are towards multiple performance measures of both a financial and nonfinancial nature. Multiple performance measures should concentrate on key success factors (KSFs). They may be compared with ideal targets, or trends may be targeted. Multiple performance measures are more complete and appropriate than single, or a small set of, performance indicators. The key success factors are those which will allow the firm to survive and thrive in its markets by building and sustaining a competitive advantage. KSFs should focus on quality, time, flexibility, productivity and innovation. Actual performance should be compared with ideal targets (benchmarking), or last period's performance (continuous improvement), rather than with a static and perhaps outdated budget or standard, in order to emphasise long term cost improvement and profit enhancement.

A set of measures and targets based on ideal performance (adapted from Kaplan and Atkinson, 1989) may comprise:

| | |
|---|---|
| **Unit Cost** | Standard manufacturing cell cost per hour divided by the number of units produced per hour under ideal conditions. |
| **Cycle Time** | The theoretical time through a manufacturing cell with no allowance for down time. |
| **On-Time Delivery** | The ideal is 100% of deliveries on time with the required mix of products. |
| **Quality** | The ideal is zero defects. |
| **Linearity of Production** | This is concerned with the proportion of a month's production completed each day. The ideal is 0%, meaning that production was absolutely linear, and that daily production was equal to the monthly production goal divided by the number of working days in the month, on each and every day. 10% would mean that on 10% of the days in the month production departed from linearity. |
| **Inventory Turnover** | The number of days per year divided by the ideal cycle time. |
| **Scrap** | The ideal is zero scrap. |
| **First Pass Yield** | The ideal is 100% of items becoming finished goods without the need for any rework. |

Management accountants need to measure and report on these KSFs, comparing actual performance with the ideal targets. These reports would differ from conventional budget reports by incorporating multiple performance measures of both a financial and nonfinancial nature. Unlike comparisons with past performance or currently attainable standards, the use of ideal targets and benchmarks as bases for comparison emphasises the pursuit of long term cost reduction and profit enhancement and the need for continuous improvement towards these ideals.

## The Balanced Scorecard

Business executives have realised that traditional accounting measures like return on investment and earnings per share do not necessarily give the right signals for continuous improvement and innovation. Research and practice have focused on trying to remedy these inadequacies. One approach focused on making financial measures more relevant. Another approach has been to focus on operational measures, such as cycle time and defect rates, assuming that if the operational measures are right then the financial results will follow.

Kaplan and Norton (1992) observe that senior executives do not rely on only financial, or only operational measures; they want a balanced presentation of both. They devised what they call a **balanced scorecard** which combines financial measures that provide the results of past actions and operational measures that are the "drivers of future financial performance":

> Think of the balanced scorecard as the dials and indicators in an airplane cockpit. For the complex task of navigating and flying an airplane, pilots need detailed information about many aspects of the flight. They need information on fuel, air speed, altitude, bearing, destination, and other indicators that summarize the current and predicted environment. Reliance on one instrument can be fatal. Similarly, the complexity of managing an organization today requires that managers be able to view performance in several areas simultaneously. (p.71)

Kaplan and Norton explain that the balanced scorecard provides answers to four questions:

1. How do customers see us? (customer perspective)
2. What must we excel at? (internal business perspective)
3. Can we continue to improve and create value? (innovation and learning perspective)
4. How do we look to shareholders? (financial perspective)

They suggest that firms should develop a limited number of measures for each perspective - measures that focus on the critical factors for their firm.

Customer concerns tend to centre on **time, quality, performance and service**, and **cost**, and hence performance measures should relate to these. The internal business perspective should look at parameters that the company considers most important for competitive success; factors like **cycle time, quality, employee skills** and **productivity**. Because the targets for success keep changing, a company's ability to **innovate, improve** and **learn** are important; thus measures should focus on new products (**percent of sales from new products**) as well as specific rates of improvement for **on-time delivery, cycle time, defect rate** and **yield**. Financial performance measures indicate whether company strategy is contributing to "bottom-line" improvement, and appropriate measures could include **cash flow, quarterly sales growth and income**, and **increased market share and return on equity**.

Kaplan and Norton claim that the balanced scorecard promotes understanding of interrelationships and transcends functional barriers; it "keeps companies looking - and moving - forward instead of backward".

# SUMMARY

Desirable characteristics of performance measures are completeness, objectivity and controllability. Performance measurement systems may have a number of characteristics which can cause subordinates to engage in dysfunctional behaviour. Four types of dysfunctional behaviours have been identified: rigid bureaucratic behaviour, strategic behaviour, invalid data reporting, and resistance.

The use of accounting controls in performance evaluation can be very rigid and result in dysfunctional performance, as well as having psychological and social effects. Under some circumstances it has been shown that the use of a budget-constrained style of evaluation can lead to job related tension and poor relationships between managers, their colleagues and their superiors.

The reliance on standard cost variance analysis as a performance evaluation technique has been criticised because performance reports are not timely, measures are incomplete, and modern practices have reduced the importance of material and labour variances.

In attempting to match world-class standards, organisations are adopting more contemporary management practices including business process re-engineering, total quality management, continuous improvement, benchmarking and strategic performance measurement.

Strategic performance measures focus on world class performance indicators, such as quality, time, productivity, flexibility and innovation. The current trend is towards multiple performance measures which concentrate on key success factors; these are captured in a "balanced scorecard" which combines financial and operational performance measures.

## REFERENCES

W.P. Birkett, M.R. Barbera, W.F. Chua, V.A. Fatseas, P.F. Luckett and J.S. Macmullen, *Cost Management in Small Manufacturing Enterprises*, Australian Centre for Management Accounting Development, 1992.

G.S. Day and L. Fahey, "Putting Strategy into Shareholder Value Analysis", *Harvard Business Review*, March-April, 1990, 156-162.

M. Hammer, "Reengineering Work: Don't Automate, Obliterate", *Harvard Business Review*, July-August, 1990, 104-112.

M. Hand, "Total Quality Management - One God but Many Prophets", in M. Hand and B. Plowman (eds), *Quality Management Handbook*, Butterworth Heinemann, 1992, pp 26-46.

M.K. Hirst, "Accounting Information and the Evaluation of Subordinate Performance: A Situational Approach", *The Accounting Review*, 56, 1981, 771-784.

M.K. Hirst, "Reliance on Accounting Performance Measures, Task Uncertainty and Dysfunctional Behaviour: Some Extensions", *Journal of Accounting Research*, 1983, 596-605.

A. Hopwood, "An Empirical Study of the Role of Accounting Data in Performance Evaluation", *Empirical Research in Accounting, Supplement to Journal of Accounting Research*, 10, 1972, 156-182.

R.S. Kaplan and A.A. Atkinson, *Advanced Management Accounting*, 2nd edn, Prentice-Hall, 1989.

R.S. Kaplan and D.P. Norton, "The Balanced Scorecard - Measures that Drive Performance", *Harvard Business Review*, January-February 1992, 71-79.

E.E Lawler III and J.G. Rhode, *Information and Control in Organizations*, Goodyear, 1976.

R.D. McIlhattan, "How Cost Management Systems Can Support the JIT Philosophy", *Management Accounting*, Sep., 1987, 21-26.

W. Morse and H.P. Roth, *Quality Costs*, National Association of Accountants, 1987.

M.E. Porter and V.E. Millar, "How Information Gives You Competitive Advantage", *Harvard Business Review*, July-August, 1985, 149-160.

W.W. Scherkenbach, *The Deming Route to Quality and Productivity*, Mercury, 1986.

G. Stalk, "Time - the Next Source of Competitive Advantage", *Harvard Business Review*, July-August, 1990, 41-51.

W. Taylor, "The Business of Innovation: An Interview with Paul Cook", *Harvard Business Review*, March-April 1990, 96-106.

## QUESTIONS AND PROBLEMS

**11-1** List and describe three desirable characteristics of performance measures.

**11-2** What is meant by the term **dysfunctional behaviour**? What causes it? Describe four main types of dysfunctional behaviour.

**11-3** In the following situations explain what dysfunctional consequences the performance measures may induce, and suggest more appropriate alternative measures:

(a) In an employment agency, staff are evaluated on the basis of the number of clients they interview.
(b) In a social work agency case workers have a quota for the number of cases they must investigate each month.
(c) The manager of a job shop is evaluated on the basis of the number of jobs completed each month.
(d) A transport company pays truck drivers on the basis of the number of kilometres driven.
(e) Managers of cost centres are paid a bonus of $1000 each time their monthly performance report reveals that total centre costs are below budget. Each month the budget is set at 95% of the previous month's actual costs.

**11-4** (a) A manager was evaluated by his superior as a poor performer because he overspent on his repairs and maintenance budget, even though it was in preparation for a long production run. What style of evaluation was used by his superior?
(b) The superior decided to accept the manager's explanation and to monitor repairs and maintenance spending over the coming months. What style of evaluation best describes this approach?

**11-5** What is BPR? Briefly describe how it is done.

**11-6** What is TQM? Explain its basic tenet.

**11-7** What is **benchmarking**? Explain its relationship to **continuous improvement**.

**11-8** List three major performance areas which nonfinancial quality measures may address. For each area provide three examples of nonfinancial performance measures.

**11-9** What are the four cost categories which provide financial measures of **cost of quality**?

**11-10** Give three examples of prevention costs.

**11-11** What is the difference between internal failure costs and external failure costs?

**11-12** Classify each of the following costs as a **prevention**, **appraisal**, **internal failure** or **external failure** cost:

(a) Using an ohmmeter to ensure that finished coils of electrical cable have no breaks.
(b) Repair of products sold last year.
(c) Cost of rewelding faulty body joints on a motor vehicle assembly line.
(d) Cost of a 5-day training program for operators learning to use CNC machines with a lower production defect rate.
(e) Cost of servicing dishwashers under warranty.
(f) Sale of seconds at a reduced price.
(g) Paying a premium to a raw materials supplier for a guarantee of zero defects in supplies.
(h) Testing supplies of raw material components to ensure zero defects.

**11-13** Why is time management important for competitive advantage?

**11-14** Identify three nonfinancial measures of productivity.

**11-15** What is the objective of flexibility in manufacturing? List some advantages that accrue from increased flexibility.

**11-16** List four measures of innovation.

**11-17** List four KSF targets based on ideal performance.

**11-18** What are the four organisational perspectives which balanced performance measures should address?

**11-19 Statistical control chart**
Below are 15 weeks' observations of average service time for cleaning motel rooms at the Sleep-In Motel:

| Week | Average Service Time (Minutes) |
| --- | --- |
| 1 | 29 |
| 2 | 30 |
| 3 | 25 |
| 4 | 45 |
| 5 | 28 |
| 6 | 30 |
| 7 | 33 |
| 8 | 27 |
| 9 | 31 |
| 10 | 32 |
| 11 | 35 |
| 12 | 26 |
| 13 | 25 |
| 14 | 28 |
| 15 | 33 |

*Required:*
(a) Use this historical data to calculate the mean and standard deviation of the average cleaning times. You can use Excel to do this, Tools/Data Analysis/Descriptive Statistics.
(b) Prepare a statistical control chart by plotting the weekly average cleaning times over the 15 weeks, and showing the mean and upper and lower control limits of 2 standard deviations. You can use the Excel Chart Wizard to do this, once you have calculated the limits
(c) What does this chart indicate?

**11-20 Quality control chart**
Prepare a quality control chart from the following sequential monthly cycle time data. The desired level of performance is 140, with an upper control limit of 160 and a lower control limit of 120. What does the chart indicate?

| Month | Average Cycle Time (Hours) |
|---|---|
| January | 124 |
| February | 175 |
| March | 147 |
| April | 97 |
| May | 153 |
| June | 132 |
| July | 228 |
| August | 152 |
| September | 172 |
| October | 112 |
| November | 138 |
| December | 141 |

**11-21 Statistical quality control**

A machine washes bottles at the rate of 400 000 per day, half of them before lunch and half of them after lunch. The machine is inspected and adjusted every morning. At lunch time a supervisor receives a report on the level of bottle breakages in the morning session, and decides whether to inspect and adjust the machine prior to the afternoon shift.

Breakages are normally distributed, with a mean half-day breakage rate of 0.5 per cent, and a standard deviation of 0.15 per cent.

The lunch time report today reveals that during the morning 1595 bottles were broken. Should the supervisor inspect and adjust the machine prior to the afternoon shift if he uses a statistical control chart in which the UCL and LCL are set:

*Required:*
(a) based on a significance level of 0.05 (2-tail)?
(b) $2\sigma$ from the mean?

**11-22 Statistical quality control**

The Metal Machining Company bores alloy castings as a first process in manufacturing brake wheel cylinders for cars. When properly adjusted the boring machine has a weekly mean defective rate of 1 percent with a weekly standard deviation of 0.3 per cent (the rate is normally distributed). On average, 11 000 cylinders are produced each week. Last week there was a 1.75% defective rate.

*Required:*
(a) Using a significance level of 0.05 (2-tail), would you conclude that the machine is properly adjusted?
(b) Using a statistical control chart with $3\sigma$ limits,
  (i) what are the upper and lower control limits?
  (ii) would you conclude that the machine is properly adjusted?

## 11/Performance Measurement: Multiple Measures

**11-23 Costs of quality**

The following information is available for KL Company for two years:

|  | Year 1 | Year 2 |
|---|---|---|
| Sales | $2 000 000 | $1 800 000 |
| Costs: |  |  |
| Process inspection | 16 000 | 18 000 |
| Scrap | 18 000 | 19 000 |
| Quality training | 200 000 | 130 000 |
| Warranty repairs | 40 000 | 45 000 |
| Testing equipment | 60 000 | 60 000 |
| Customer complaints | 25 000 | 30 000 |
| Rework | 160 000 | 180 000 |
| Preventive maintenance | 130 000 | 90 000 |
| Materials inspection | 60 000 | 50 000 |
| Field testing | 95 000 | 125 000 |

*Required:*

(a) Classify these items into costs of prevention, appraisal, internal failure or external failure.
(b) Group these costs into each category. For each item, and each group total, calculate the ratio to sales for each year. Also show the total costs of quality for each year.
(c) Can you draw any conclusions from these calculations?

**11-24 Costs of quality**

The following information is available for HK Company for two years:

|  | Year 1 | Year 2 |
|---|---|---|
| Sales | $980 000 | $880 000 |
| Costs: |  |  |
| Process inspection | 6 600 | 7 500 |
| Scrap | 7 400 | 7 700 |
| Quality training | 79 000 | 52 000 |
| Warranty repairs | 17 000 | 19 000 |
| Testing equipment | 28 000 | 28 000 |
| Customer complaints | 11 200 | 13 500 |
| Rework | 68 000 | 74 000 |
| Preventive maintenance | 54 000 | 38 000 |
| Materials inspection | 26 000 | 19 000 |
| Field testing | 37 000 | 50 000 |

*Required:*

(d) Classify these items into costs of prevention, appraisal, internal failure or external failure.
(e) Group these costs into each category. For each item, and each group total, calculate the ratio to sales for each year. Also show the total costs of quality for each year.
(f) Can you draw any conclusions from these calculations?

**11-25 Costs of quality**

At the beginning of 20X4 Wodonga Company started a quality improvement program directed at reducing the number of defective units produced. By the end of 20X4 it was reported that both scrap and rework had decreased over the 20X3 levels. As the management accountant you have been asked for an assessment of the financial impact of the quality improvement program. You have collected the following data:

|  | 20X3 | 20X4 |
|---|---|---|
|  | $ | $ |
| Sales | 20 000 000 | 20 000 000 |
| Scrap | 800 000 | 600 000 |
| Rework | 1 200 000 | 800 000 |
| Product inspection | 200 000 | 250 000 |
| Warranty costs | 1 600 000 | 1 200 000 |
| Quality training | 80 000 | 160 000 |
| Inspection of materials | 120 000 | 80 000 |

*Required:*
(a) Classify the costs as prevention, appraisal, internal failure and external failure costs.
(b) Calculate quality cost as a percentage of sales for each year.
(c) By how much did profit increase because of quality improvements?
(d) Assuming no change in revenue, if quality costs can be reduced to 2% of sales in 20X5, how much additional profit will be earned through quality improvements in 20X5?

## 11-26 Linearity of production

In a processing department there were 20 working days last month. The production goal for the month was 4000 units of a single product. During the month the pattern of actual production was as follows:

| Production Units | Number of Days |
|---|---|
| 250 | 1 |
| 225 | 2 |
| 200 | 7 |
| 175 | 4 |
| 150 | 4 |
| 125 | 2 |
|  | 20 |

*Required:*
Calculate the measure of linearity of production.

## 11-27 Linearity of production

In a processing department there were 22 working days last month. The production goal for the month was 2200 units of a single product. During the month the pattern of actual production was as follows:

| Production Units | Number of Days |
|---|---|
| 150 | 2 |
| 125 | 1 |
| 100 | 10 |
| 75 | 4 |
| 50 | 3 |
| 25 | 2 |
|  | 22 |

*Required:*
Calculate the measure of linearity of production.

*Appendix: Key Answers to Problems*

# APPENDIX

## KEY ANSWERS TO PROBLEMS

**Chapter 2**

2-9     (a)    COGM = $10 000
       (b)    $10

2-10    COGM = $91 378

2-11    (a)    COGM = $2 747 550
        (b)    Profit after Tax = $369 240

2-12    Direct material consumed = $14 000
         COGS = $30 000
         C/Bal FG = $18 000

2-13    (b)    $2.20

2-14    (b)    Net Loss $43 620

**Chapter 3**

3-13    C

3-14    Materials placed in production = $110 000

3-15    Materials purchased = $50 000 + GST

3-16    Indirect materials issued = $15 000

3-18    Salaries and wages paid = $50 000

3-19    B

3-20    (a)    $432
        (b)    $84

3-21    (a)    $176 000
        (b)    $32 000

3-22    Overhead allocated = $32 000

3-23    Cost of completed production = $120 000

3-24    $4500 under-allocated

3-25    $2000 over-allocated

3-26    $352 000

3-27    D

3-28    B

3-29    (a)    $104/DLH
        (b)    Machining: $200/DLH   Finishing: $40/DLH
        (c)    Machining: $80/MH   Finishing: $40/DLH
        (d)    (a)   $6240    (b)   $5600       (c)   $3200
        (f)    (a)   $5200    (b)   $5200
        (h)    (b)   $5600    (c)   $5600

3-30    (a)    $6.50/DLH
        (b)    $55 000 over-allocated

*Appendix: Key Answers to Problems*

| | | |
|---|---|---|
| 3-31 | (a) | $3/DLH |
| | (b) | $1000 |
| | (c) | $13 250 under-allocated |
| | | |
| 3-32 | (a) | B |
| | (b) | D |
| | | |
| 3-33 | (a) | P1: $29 625  P2: $40 375 |
| | (b) | P1: $29 400  P2: $40 600 |
| | (c) | P1: $29 500  P2: $40 500 |
| | | |
| 3-34 | (a) | P1: $57 941  P2: $62 059 |
| | (b) | P1: $58 235  P2: $61 765 |
| | (c) | P1: $57 835  P2: $62 165 |
| | | |
| 3-35 | (a) | Component manufacture: $150 250  Assembly: $131 750 |
| | (b) | Component manufacture: $149 850  Assembly: $132 150 |
| | (c) | Component manufacture: $149 955  Assembly: $132 045 |
| | | |
| 3-36 | (a) | P1: $119 000  P2: $114 000 |
| | (b) | P1: $121 250  P2: $111 750 |
| | (c) | P1: $120 095  P2: $112 905 |
| | | |
| 3-37 | (a) | P1: $119 167  P2: $100 833 |
| | (b) | P1: $116 222  P2: $103 778 |
| | (c) | P1: $117 523  P2: $102 477 |
| | | |
| 3-38 | (a) | P1: $23 750  P2: $51 250 |
| | (b) | P1: $25 600  P2: $49 400 |
| | (c) | P1: $22 925  P2: $52 075 |
| | | |
| 3-39 | | Cost of production completed = $155 000 |
| | | |
| 3-40.1 | | COGS = $175 000 |
| | | |
| 3-41 | | $31 000 |
| | | |
| 3-42 | (a) | Savings a/c: $10.83  Cheque a/c: $2.17 |
| | (b) | Savings a/c: $3.00  Cheque a/c: $10.00 |
| | | |
| 3-43 | (a) | $6.67/DLH |
| | (b) | P1: $85.00  P2: $16.67  P3: $45.00  P4: $28.34 |
| | (c) | P1 |
| | (d) | Drop P3 and P4 |
| | (e) | Do not drop any |
| | | |
| 3-44 | (a) | (i) Machining $5/MH  Setups $100/setup  Receiving $15/receipt  Packing $50/order |
| | | (ii) X: $153 000  Y: $131 000 |
| | (b) | Yes, setups and packing. |
| | | |
| 3-45 | | Type A: $2.39 |
| | | Type B: $3.44 |
| | | |
| 3-46.1 | | A1: $12 |
| | | A2: $8 |
| | | |
| 3-47 | (a) | $77.20 |
| | (b) | $75.07 |
| | | |
| 3-48 | (a) | P1: $89.50    P2: $114.50 |
| | (b) | P1: $67.00    P2: $152.00 |
| | (c) | P1: $67.25    P2: $151.58 |
| | | |
| 3-49 | (a) | Standard: $36m  22.50%  Deluxe: $10.5m  35.00%  Total: $46.5m  24.47% |
| | (b) | Standard: $42.9m  26.81%  Deluxe: $3.6m  12.00%  Total: $46.5m  24.47% |

*Appendix: Key Answers to Problems*

3-50 Part A: (2) $13.48/1000 bars
   Part B: (1) (c) (i) $8.66/1000 bars (ii) $241/setup
      (2) (a) (i) 20 000 bars $269.60 100 000 bars $1348
         (ii) 20 000 bars $414.20 100 000 bars $1107

## Chapter 4

4-3 (a) $3/DLH
  (b) $1000
  (c) $13 250 under-allocated

4-4 (a) $46 000
  (b) $36 000

4-5 (a) $110 000
  (b) $42 500

4-6 Cost of jobs completed = $34 520 C/WIP = $22 900

4-7 Cost of jobs completed = $41 400 C/WIP = $30 000

4-8 (a) $8000
  (b) $6000
  (c) $24 000
  (d) $10 000
  (e) $1000 under-allocated
  (f) $12 000

4-9 $5600

4-10 $53 000

4-11 (b) Net operating profit = $22 000

4-12 (a) $9 per professional hour
   (b) Net operating profit = $895 000

4-13 (a) Jobs completed = $49 150, C/WIP = $33 820

4-14 (a) $44 500
   (b) $45 900
   (c) $350 over-allocated

4-15 $11 800

4-16 (a) $22 000
   (b) $37 500
   (c) $13 000
   (d) $190 500

4-17 (a) C
   (b) D
   (c) A
   (d) D
   (e) A
   (f) B
   (g) E
   (h) D
   (i) A

4-18 (c) (i) $22 690; $23 960
     (ii) 140: $600 141: ($1500) 142: $1450 143: $2490
   (e) $2220 under-allocated

4-19 (a) $147 500

4-20 (b) $8178

*Appendix: Key Answers to Problems*

4-21  (a) Material 13 500, conversion 14 500
      (b) Material 12 900, conversion 14 050

4-22  (a) Material 15 000, conversion 13 500
      (b) Material 10 000, conversion 12 500

4-23  (a) Material 1: 24 000, Material 2: 19 000, Conversion: 20 500
      (b) Material 1: 20 000, Material 2: 15 000, Conversion: 18 900

4-24  (a) $7.50
      (b) $15.50
      (c) $465 000
      (d) $105 000

4-25  (a) C/WIP = $3760.24, Transferred = $133 439.76

4-26  Units transferred: $428 358  C/WIP: $82 642

4-27  (a) $42 000
      (b) $43 482

4-28  (a) $1 537 500
      (b) $1 551 762

4-29  (a) $1 261 500; $43 300
      (b) $1 261 600; $43 200

4-30  (a) $250 000; $48 000
      (b) $247 966; $50 034

4-31  FG: $274 887  P1: C/WIP = $22 218  P2: C/WIP = $14 045

## Chapter 5

5-11  (a) Standard $35.00  Deluxe $42.50
      (b) $6900; $2100

5-12  COGM: 101: $25 000  102: $41 250  103: $29 250  104: $5500
      C/WIP: M: $4725  CC: $2925  TC: $7650

5-13  Loud: $3057.00
      Quiet: $2935.50

5-14  (a) B
      (b) D

5-15  (a) B
      (b) D

5-16  Mixon: $404 485.49
      Dixon: $295 514.51

5-17  A: $672 000, B: $168 000

5-18  Yes, $50 gain

5-19  (a) XA1: ($8400)  XA2: $136 000  Total: $127 600
      (b) XA1: $28 933  XA2: $82 667  Total: $111 600

5-20  (a) 100: $12 622  101: $23 081  102: $40 872
      (b) No. Decrease by $12 000

5-21  (a) $2.50
      (b) Produce C - $105 000 better off.

*Appendix: Key Answers to Problems*

5-22     (a)     (i) A: $25 000  B: $20 000  C: $5000
                      (ii) A: $25 000  B: $15 000  C: $10 000
         (b)     Process (still a loss)

5-23     (a)     XA384: $16 000  XB541: $26 500
         (b)     XA384: $14 000  XB541: $10 500

5-24     (a)     (i) A-grade: $112 500  B-grade: $67 500
                      (ii) A-grade: $108 000  B-grade: $72 000

5-25     (a)     B
         (b)     D

**Chapter 6**

6-7      (a)     $45
         (b)     $11 250

6-8      $830.67

6-9      C

6-10     $10 000 F

6-11     (a)     $100 UF

6-12     MPV = $1500 UF,  MUV = $2000 UF

6-13     MPV = $275 F,  MUV = $750 UF

6-14     (a)     LRV = $9900 UF  LEV = $3000 F

6-15     (a)     LRV = $500 UF  LEV = $2000 F

6-16     (a)     LRV = $84 000 F  LEV = $70 000 UF

6-17     (a)     MPV = $2600 UF,  MUV = $4000 UF
                 LRV = $5000 UF,  LEV = $10 000 UF

6-18     MPV = $12 500 F,  MUV = $3000 UF
        LRV = $3500 UF,  LEV = $1000 UF

6-19     (a)     $18
         (b)     2033, LRV = $406.60 UF

6-20     (a)     MPV = $44 000 UF  MUV = $12 000 UF
         (b)     $19.50

6-21     $20.50

6-22     (a)     $2.925
         (b)     E

6-23     (a)     $1400 F
         (b)     $320 F
         (c)     $662.50 UF
         (d)     $400 F
         (e)     $$180 F

6-24     (a)     X: 10 000 Labour: 10 100 Overhead: 10 100
         (b)     MPV=$12 000 UF  MUV=$8000 UF  LRV=$7920 UF  LEV=$4800 F  OH=$800 UF

6-25     (a)     A: 10 000  B: 10 000  CC: 9600
         (b)     $130 500; $17 000
         (c)     (i) A:$1100 UF B:$1050 F     (ii) A:$2500 UF B:$1000 UF
                (iii) $1680 UF          (iv) $1920 UF  (v) $6400 UF

*Appendix: Key Answers to Problems*

| 6-26 | Mat X: PV | = $6400 UF | UV | = $9000 UF |
|---|---|---|---|---|
| | Mat Y: PV | = $0 | UV | = $9000 UF |
| | LRV | = $26 000 UF | LEV | = $20 000 UF  OHV = $50 000 UF |

6-27 (a) (i) $4894 (ii) $1528

## Chapter 7

7-8   (a)   $1000 over-allocated
      (b)   $0

7-9   (a)   $400; $390
      (b)   $150; $540

7-10  (a)   C
      (b)   B
      (c)   D
      (d)   D

7-11  (a)   Absorption Costing NP = $1 800 000  Variable Costing NP = $1 850 000

7-12  (a)   $10.25
      (b)   $11.14
      (c)   AC > VC by $20 000

7-13  (a)   $8.50
      (b)   $6700
      (c)   DC < AC by $200
      (d)   $6650

7-14  (a)   20X6-20X9 $300 000  19Y0 $900 000
      (b)   20X6-20X9 $200 000  19Y0 $900 000

7-15  (a)   (i) $778 100 (ii) $818 100
      (c)   Reduced by $50 000

7-20  (a)   B
      (b)   C

## Chapter 8

8-6   Net Profit: Year 1 ($60)  Year 2 $75  Year 3 $210

8-7   Net Profit: 20X2 $1428  20X3 $1626  20X4 $1884  20X5 $1980

8-8   NPAT: 20X2 $128  20X3 $156  20X4 $186

8-9   C/Bal Cash 20X4 = $300

8-10  For the quarter $1 025 000

8-11  For the quarter 355 750

8-12  For the quarter $2 048 200

8-13  (a)   Required Production: Q1 2750  Q2 4750  Q3 3250  Q4 1375
          RM Purchases: Q1 $17 700  Q2 $28 980  Q3 $19 294  Q4 $9923
      (b)   Shortfall in Q2

8-14  January $10 773  February $10 200  March $12 440

8-15  Jul ($37 500), Aug ($3500), Sep $20 500

8-16  (a)   C/Bal Cash: April $28 400  May ($45 800)  June ($74 400)
      (b)   C/Bal Cash: April $28 400  May $10 000  June $10 000

8-17  Net Cash Flow: January ($16 750)  February ($12 820)

8-18  NPAT: 20X2 $12 131  20X3 $14 098  20X4 $16 286  20X5 $24 485  20X6 $26 844

*Appendix: Key Answers to Problems*

8-19   (a)   67 200 boxes
     (b)   Fish $619 400  Vege $317 440  Boxes $60 416
     (c)   $17.80
     (d)   NP $278 400

8-20   (a)   $27 000
     (b)   A: $388.80/child  B: $259.20/child  C: $432.00/child

8-21   (a)   C/Bal Cash: Q1 $28 500  Q2 $8688  Q3 $8375  Q4 10 750
     (b)   $555 000

8-22   (c)   $22 900

8-23   (i)   Qr Purchases $480 960
     (ii)   Qr Payments $752 140
     (iii)   Qr Receipts $741 900
     (iv)   Borrow $70 000 in July and $60 000 in August. Repay $110 000 in September.

8-24   (a)   Qr Collections $2 120 000
     (b)   Qr Purchases $804 000
     (c)   C/Bal Cash 30 June $50 000

**Chapter 9**

9-9   $5 400 000

9-10   (a)   $0.50 + $3 x patients
     (b)   $90.50

9-11   (a)   Budgeted net operating profit = $2 300 000
     (b)   Total variance = $175 000 UF

9-12   (a)   Total $75 000
     (b)   Fixed $4/MH  Variable $11/MH
     (c)   VOHSV = $2780 F  VOHEV $330 UF  FOHSV $1000 F  VV = $200 UF

9-13   (a)   OH variance = $10 500 F (over-allocated)
     (b)   $1 015 500
     (c)   (i) $852 000  (ii) $138 000  (iii) Flexible Budget Variance $25 500 F
         Volume Variance $15 000 UF

9-14   (a)   $23 000 UF
     (b)   $15 000 UF
     (c)   $40 000 F
     (d)   $100 000 UF

9-15   (a)   DM $2.00 DL $2.00 OH $6.00 Total $10.00
     (c)   $60 000 F
     (d)   (i) $175 000 over-allocated  (ii) $110 000 over-allocated

9-16   (a)   $17.20
     (b)   X: MPV $1000 F  MUV $200 UF  Y: MPV $3500 UF  MUV $1050 F
         LRV $5000 F  LEV $17 500 UF  VOHSV $2125 F  VOHEV $7750 UF
         FOHSV $3000 F  VV $2625 F

9-17   (a)   (i) $5000 F     (ii)   $20 000 UF
         (i) Drums $0 (ii)     Drums $0
         (iii) $1500 UF     (iv)     $3500 UF
         (v) VOHSV $650 UF  VOHEV $3000 UF  FOHSV $1000 F  VV $24 000 UF

9-18   (a)   (1) Batches 416 EU  Kg 104 000 EU
         (2) DM $24 960  DL $12 480  VOH $4160  FOH $1248  Total $42 848
     (b)   Mucilloid MPV $3432 UF  MEV $1456 UF
         Dextrose MPV $1056 UF  MEV $160 UF
         LRV $1053 UF  LEV $156 UF  OHSV $107 UF  OHEV $52 UF  OHVV $48 F

9-19   (a)   DM 10 000 EU  CC 10 100 EU
     (b)   MPV $12 000 UF  MEV $8000 UF  LRV $7920 UF  LEV $4800 F
         VOHSV $1600 F  VOHEV $800 F  FOHSV $4000 UF  FOHVV $800 F

304

*Appendix: Key Answers to Problems*

9-20   (c)   MPV $300 F  MEV $0  LRV $400 UF  LEV $400 UF
                VOHSV $100 UF  VOHEV $400 UF  FOHSV $150 UF  VV $2400 UF
      (e)   (i) $1850 under-allocated  (ii) $3050 under-allocated  (iii) $500 under-allocated

9-21   (a)   $480 UF
      (b)   A: $80 F  B: $180 F
      (c)   $11 000
      (e)   A: 50 MH  $120 UF  B: 160 MH  $140 F
      (f)   $200

9-23   (a)   (i) $5/DLH  P1: $1.25  P2: $2.50
            (ii) P1: $0.05 (Mats Handling) + $0.30 (Setup Labour)
                   P2: $1.25 (Mats Handling) + $$3.00 (Setup Labour)
            (iii) P1: $16.60  P2: $24.75
      (d)   $1 260 000
      (e)   FOHSV $2000 UF  VOHSV $500 F  VOHEV $1000 UF  VV $0

**Chapter 10**

10-6   (a)   $5833

10-8   (c)   VOHSV $400 UF  VOHEV $18 000 UF  FOHSV $1500 UF

10-9   (b)   LRV $1125 UF  LEV $1125 UF

10-12   (i)   $263 500

10-14   (a)   $120 over-applied

10-16   (a)   20%
       (b)   Reduce investment to $800 000; Reduce expenses by $50 000;
             Increase sales to $3 125 000.
       (c)   $100 000

10-17   (a)   15%; $5000
       (b   (i) Yes  (ii) 14.5%  (iii) No  (iv) Yes

10-18   (a)   Y
       (b)   X

10-19   (a)   ROI: Div 1 = 20%    Div 2 = 15%
       (b)   RI:   Div 1 = $160 000  Div 2 = $300 000
       (c)   EVA: Div 1 = $90 000  Div 2 = $200 000

10-20   (a)   ROI: Div A = 11.54%  Div B = 16.84%
       (d)   RI:   Div A = ($9000)  Div B = $138 000
       (e)   EVA: Div A = ($17 640  Div B = $72 000

10-21   (a)   (i) NSW 30%  VIC 18%  (ii) NSW 1.07  VIC 2
           (iii) NSW 32%  VIC 36%  (iv) NSW $225  VIC $300
       (b)   23.86%
       (c)   (i) $750 decrease  (ii) $500 increase  (iii) $250 decrease

10-22   (a)   (i) AUST $1002  X $306  Y $512  TOTAL $1820 ($000)
           (ii) AUST $930  X $330  Y $560  TOTAL $1820
       (b)   (i) AUST 9.60%  X 8.35%  Y 14.00%  TOTAL 10.32%
           (ii) AUST 21.26%  X 22.00%  Y 22.40%  TOTAL 21.73%
           (iii) AUST $230  X $90  Y $160  TOTAL $480

10-23   (a)   Div A $90 000 18.00%  Div B $156 000 13.68%  Company $246 000 15.00%
       (b)   Div A $30 000 6.00%  Div B $186 000 16.32%  Company $216 000 13.17%
           Reject.

10-24   (a)   A: ROI 25.81% RI $118 000  B: ROI 22.22% RI $6000
       (b)   A: ROI 25.81% RI $118 000  B: ROI 50.00% RI $588 000

*Appendix: Key Answers to Problems*

**Chapter 11**

11-19    (a)    Mean = 30.47 min, SD = 5.027 min

11-21    (a)    Adjust
           (b)    Do not adjust

11-22    (a)    Out of adjustment
           (b)    (i) UCL 209 [or 1.9%] LCL 11 [or 0.1%] (ii) Yes

11-23    (b)    Total cost of quality: Y1: $804 000, 40.20%, Y2: $747 000, 41.50%

11-24    (b)    Total cost of quality: Y1: $334 200, 34.10%, Y2: $308 700, 35.08%

11-25    (b)    20X3 20%   20X4 15.45%
           (c)    $910 000
           (d)    $2 690 000

11-26    65%

11-27    54.5%

# INDEX

Absorption costing, 160-5
  profit, 163
Accounting controls, 244-58
  in performance evaluation, 279-80
Accounting performance measures, 277
Activity based costing, 50-54
Activity based management, 54
Actual costing, 118
Administration budget, 183
Administrative controls, 217
Alternative standard cost systems, 143
Analytic process, 120

Backflush costing, 32, 169
Balanced scorecard, 291
Benchmarking, 3, 285-6
Bills of materials, 79
Budget, 181
  biased estimates, 217
  capital, 183
  cash, 182-3, 188-9
  closing inventory, 186
  comprehensive, 182, 214, 244
  financial, 182-3
  flexible, 219-20
  master, 182
  operating, 182
  participation, 216-7
  ploys, 193
  preparation, 183-9
  production, 185
  purchases, 185
  sales, 182, 185
  schedules, 175, 177
  static, 218
  targets, 216
Budgeted -
  accounting statements, 185-9
  cash flow statement, 188
  statement of financial performance, 187
  statement of financial position, 188
Budgeting, 180-92
  as a choice process, 192-3
  as a political process, 193
  as a technical process, 181-90
  bottom-up approach, 181
  process, 181
  system, 181
Business process re-engineering (BPR), 281-2
Byproducts, 123-4

Capacity -
  concepts, 43-4
  expected annual, 43
  normal, 43
  practical, 43
  theoretical, 43
Capacity variance, 224
Capital budget, 182-3
Cash budget, 182-3, 188-9
Cellular production, 165
Competitive support, 2-3
Completeness (of performance measure), 277-8
Compliance, 2-3
Comprehensive budget, 182, 214, 244
Computer-based models (of budgeting), 190-2
Content theories of motivation, 215
Continuous improvement, 3, 165, 285
Control, 2-3, 164, 180
  process, 214
  system, 4, 214
Controllability (of performance measure), 278
Controllable -
  cost, 245
  performance, 245-9
Conversion, 88
  cost, 18, 32-3, 88-92
Cost, 15
  centre, 44, 236, 240
  direct, 15
  driver, 15, 40, 45-54
  fixed, 15-16
  flows, 18-20
  indirect, 15
  object, 15
  obviation, 164
  of goods manufactured, 18
  of goods sold, 18-9, 32
  of quality, 287-8
  pool, 40, 44-46
  product, 17-8
  unit, 16
  variable, 15-6
Currently attainable standard, 136
Customer -
  service, 3
  value, 3

Decentralisation, 249
  benefits, 250-1
  disadvantages, 251
Decentralised organisation, 249
  divisional structure, 250
  functional structure, 249
  matrix structure, 250
Delivery docket, 33
Denominator -
  level of activity, 44
  variance, 224
Departmental overhead rate, 45
Differentiation, 249
Direct –
  cost, 15
  costing, 160, 164

*Index*

expense, 18
labour, 17, 32, 79, 88
materials, 17, 32, 35, 79, 88
materials issue, 34-5, 81-2
method of overhead allocation, 47
Divisional structure, 250
Dysfunctional behaviour, 217, 278-9
invalid data reporting, 279
resistance, 279
rigid bureaucratic behaviour, 278
strategic behaviour, 279

Economic value added (EVA), 256
Equivalent units, 88-9
Expectancy, 215
theory of motivation, 215-6
Extrinsic rewards, 214-5

Feedback, 87, 180-1
control, 180-1, 214, 218
Feedforward control, 181, 214
FIFO, 35-6, 92-3
Financial modelling, 5
packages, 5-6
Financial control, 181
Fixed overhead, 41
spending variance, 224
variance, 224
volume variance, 224
Finished goods, 84
Flexibility, 289
Flexible budget, 219-20
formula, 220
steps in preparing, 219-20
variance, 220-4
Freight inward, 34
Functional -
behaviour, 214
organisation structure, 249

Goal -
congruence, 251
setting theory, 216
Group norms, 217
GST, 34, 56

Holding gain, 35
Hygiene factor, 215

Ideal standard, 136
Idle capacity costs, 44
Incremental -
cost, 124
revenue, 124
Incrementalism (in budgeting), 193
Indirect –
cost, 15
labour, 17, 37-9

materials, 17, 35, 81-3
Innovation, 3, 289-90
Inspection time, 165
Instrumentality, 216
Integrating mechanism, 251
Intrinsic rewards, 214-5
Inventory -
finished goods, 18-9
raw materials, 18-9
Investment centre, 245, 251

Job, 78-9
card, 79
cost card, 79, 82
cost sheet, 79, 82-3
costing system, 79-87
Job costing, 79-87
Joint -
cost, 119-20
cost allocation, 120-2
net realisable value method, 122
physical measures method, 121
relative sales value method, 121
products, 120
Joint costs and decision making, 123-4
Just-in-time (JIT) -
costing, 166-8
production, 32, 165
system, 32-3

Key success factors, 3, 290

Labour, 36-8
distribution of costs, 37
efficiency variance, 140
oncosts, 36-38
overtime, 38
payment of, 37
rate (price) variance, 139-40
time record, 37, 79
time standard, 136
LIFO, 35-6

Manufacturing -
overhead, 17, 32
statement, 20-2, 78
Material -
price variance, 137-8
quantity standard, 136
usage variance, 138-9
Materials, 33-5
acquisition, 33-4
issue of, 34-5
requisition, 33, 35, 79
storage, 34

Net realisable value (joint cost allocation), 122
Non-value-added –

activity, 165
cost, 165
time, 165
Normal costing, 118-9

Objectivity (of performance measure), 278
Operation costing, 78, 118-9
Operational budgets, 180
Organisation structure, 244
Organisational control, 180
Output cost object, 78
Overhead, 39-49
  allocated, 83-4
  allocation, 40-9
    ABC methods, 50-4
    actual rate, 41
    direct method, 47
    predetermined rate, 41
    reciprocal services method, 49
    step method, 48
  application rate, 79
  capacity concepts, 43
  control account, 42
  control procedures, 40
  cost pool, 44-6
  costs, 40
  departmental rates, 45
  manufacturing, 17, 32
  plantwide rate, 44
  recovery rate, 79
  total variance, 141
  two-stage allocation, 46-49
  variance, 42-3

PAYG tax, 36
Performance evaluation, 217
  budget constrained style, 280
  non-accounting style, 280
  profit conscious style, 2 80
  system, 217
Performance measures, 277-81
  accounting controls, 279-80
  characteristics, 277-8
  communication, 278
  completeness, 277-8
  controllability, 278
  multiple, 290-1
  objectivity, 278
  source of discrimination, 278
Performance measurement, 277-91
  contemporary practices, 281-91
  in investment centres, 251-7
  in profit centres, 251
Performance report, 218-9
Period cost, 18, 160, 164
Periodic system, 33
Plantwide overhead rate, 44
Political process (in budgeting), 193

Prime cost, 18
Process -
  cost sheet, 88
  costing, 78, 88-96
    equivalent units, 88-9
    FIFO method, 92-3
    physical flow, 89
    system, 88-96
    weighted average method, 91-2, 94-5
  theories of motivation, 215-6
  time, 165
Product –
  cost, 17-8, 32, 160, 164-5
  costing, 3, 32, 78
    systems, 3
  quality, 165
Production -
  budget, 185
  cost centre, 40
Productivity, 288-9
Profit centre, 245, 249, 251
  performance measure, 251
Proration (of overhead variance), 43
Purchase -
  order, 33
  requisition, 33
Purchases budget, 185

Quality, 3, 286-7
Queue time, 165

Rational perspective in budgeting, 192
Raw and in-process account, 33, 166
Raw materials stock ledger card, 81-2
Receiving report, 33
Reciprocal services method (of overhead allocation), 49, 59-60
Residual income, 255
Responsibility accounting, 244-58
  criticisms, 257-8
  system, 244-58
Responsibility centre, 245
Return on investment, 252-4
  Du Pont measure, 252
Revenue centre, 245, 249
RI – see Residual income
RIP inventory, 166
ROI - see Return on investment

Sales budget, 182, 185
Satisficing perspective in budgeting, 192
Selling expense budget, 182
Separable cost, 122-3
Service department, 40
Social controls, 217
Spending variance, 223-4
Split-off point, 120-2
Standard cost, 135-43

*Index*

    role in performance measurement, 280-1
    specification sheet, 136
    system, 135-43
    variances, 138-41, 221-5
Standard direct labour cost, 139
Standard inputs, 135-6
Standard price, 137
Standard quantity allowed, 137-40
Static budget, 218
Statistical quality control, 282-4
Step method of overhead allocation, 48
Stock shortage, 35
Storage time, 165
Stores ledger card, 34, 81-2
Strategic performance measurement, 286-90
Subsidiary ledger, 79, 81
Subsidiary records, 81-4
Suppliers invoice, 34
Support service centre, 40
Synthetic process, 120

Throughput time, 165
Time, 3, 288
Total overhead variance, 141
Total quality management, 282-8
Transferred-in cost, 93-4
Trigger point, 166

Unit cost, 16, 32

Value-adding activities, 3, 165
Variable cost, 15-6
Variable costing, 160-5
Variable overhead variance, 223-4
  efficiency variance, 223
  spending variance, 223
Variable profit, 161
Variance, 135
  capacity, 224
Variance investigation, 225
Volume variance, 224

Weighted average cost, 91-2, 94-5
What if analysis, 190-2
What if questions, 5, 190-2

Zero defects, 165, 290
Zero inventories, 165